OUR INQUISITIVE MINDS

Reading and Young Children

READING AND YOUNG CHILDREN

Verna Dieckman Anderson, Ed.D.

The Macmillan Company   Collier-Macmillan Limited, London

Third Printing, 1970

Library of Congress catalog card number: 68–10998

THE MACMILLAN COMPANY
866 THIRD AVENUE, NEW YORK, NEW YORK 10022
Collier-Macmillan Canada, Ltd., Toronto, Ontario

Printed in the United States of America

THE CHALLENGE OF A BOOK

I give you nothing if you cannot understand;
There is much that I would give to you
But which you alone must choose to take.
What you do with what you take
No one can predict.

—VERNA DIECKMAN ANDERSON

Preface

The "special methods" course which looks at the teaching of reading and writing in terms of mental health and leadership to one side, and crayons versus primary pencils on the other, will not help teachers to handle the very profound difficulties children face in relating themselves to written language. The English department's course in Restoration Comedy may be in itself an excellent course, but its potency in preparing excellent teachers is at best dubious.

What future teachers need, and cannot find now, is the course which attempts to explore the profound aspects of the deceptively simple material they are going to teach, which analyzes case by case the types of difficulty that children find in approaching such material, which suggests tools and techniques and methods of presentation that may help children overcome the difficulties. The elementary teacher, for example, needs a solid grounding in linguistics as it relates to the teaching of reading.[1]

Because student teachers have often been heard to voice such an opinion this book is an attempt to meet the needs of beginning

[1] Martin Mayer. "Teacher Training," *The Schools.* New York: Doubleday, 1963, p. 473.

teachers. It is intended for college students preparing to become teachers of children, preschool through the sixth grade. The "what" of teaching is always preceded by the "why" and followed by the "how." Practical suggestions are given for each job that must be done. When many suggestions are needed but would make a chapter too bulky, they have been put in an appendix at the end of the book.

Too many books conceal themselves beneath a cloak of language unfamiliar to a student coming into education after two years in liberal arts. Educational jargon is a language unto itself. This book is an attempt to exercise "the art of plain talk." It is hoped that the book will be easily understood by all who would read it.

The first chapter deals with the concept of "reading": as it is experienced in the home, in various walks of life, and with various purposes, skills, and appreciations. Because definition is the epitome of understanding, it is reserved for the end of the chapter.

Next to be considered is the linguistics of reading—our language with its many peculiarities and inconsistencies that make any one method of teaching reading inadequate in and of itself. Following this chapter are suggestions for term projects that may or may not be used, as an instructor prefers. The questions at the end of each chapter may be used flexibly as time permits.

Recent research shows that the greatest determinant of success in any approach to reading is the *teacher*. Thus a chapter is devoted to the essentials in becoming a good teacher of children learning to read.

The next two chapters unfold the total development of preschool children with emphasis on the many experiences that go into helping children become well-rounded individuals ready for a meaningful approach to reading. The many variables are explained so that the beginning teacher knows and accepts the "who" of her teaching as the most important part of the teaching act. These chapters give parents insight into the finest contributions they can make toward their child's later success in school. They give Head-Start teachers the very basic experiences essential to *all* children and often so lacking in the underprivileged. These two chapters may be omitted in colleges where students have a good background course in child growth and development.

Much consideration is given to the simple beginnings of reading— the importance of which only experienced first-grade teachers can truly appreciate. The word-recognition skills include phonics, but because of the very thorough approach to phonics as a "tool" (not an end in itself) an entire chapter is devoted to it. This is followed by "linguistics" as a general term and as it can be applied to the teaching of reading.

The various approaches to the teaching of reading currently used are presented and explained, followed by a chapter on the skills and competencies children are expected to achieve. The next chapter —on evaluation—places emphasis on diagnosis and follow-through in the best interests of children. A chapter is devoted to consideration of children with reading problems. Organization and materials depend on the children and the job to be done and detailed explanations are given. The last chapter explains research, not too specifically but as it relates to beginning teachers. The chapter reassures, challenges, and inspires the beginning teacher to approach her chosen profession with dignity, courage, and the vitality of youth.

I am grateful to the librarians who served far beyond the call of duty, to those who cooperated so graciously in contributing photographs, to the many professors I have had who exemplified what good teaching should be, to my publisher for his explicit confidence, to my friends for their encouragement, to my associates everywhere for ideas we shared, and finally, to the hundreds of students everywhere who helped to give me the insights and the thrill of teaching reading.

V. D. A.

Contents

Reading and Young Children

The Sunday paper provides family togetherness and affords many purposes, skills, and outcomes of reading.

The Many Meanings
of Reading

Family Reading

In over forty-five million homes throughout the United States on Sunday mornings a bulky newspaper is brought in from the doorstep and sections are distributed to various members of the family: Grandmother may get the News Section; a teen-age son may ask for Sports; Mother may be given the Home Section; a teen-age daughter takes the Society Section; Grandfather wants the crossword puzzle; Father keeps the financial pages and tosses the funnies to two young children on the floor. Soon everyone is absorbed in his or her interests. Later, sections are exchanged and further explorations are made into the great variety of offerings on those printed pages. An exchange of remarks might sound something like this:

"Hey, Pop, see what funny things Blondie did today."

"John, I see that the council voted to put the park proposition on the ballots this spring."

"Mom, take a look at the new spring fashions. It says that pink

1

will be very popular. I wonder if you could make over my old pink linen to look like this."

"My goodness! I see that vandals broke into two more churches. Whatever is the world coming to? When I was that age young folks were kept too busy to get in trouble."

"I see that the stock market took another rise. I can't account for a rise at this time of the year."

"I see that the Smith house is up for sale. I guess Hank got that transfer all right."

"Here's a recipe for blintzes. Everyone in favor of me giving it a try say I!"

"Can anyone help me with a six-letter word meaning 'to do again,' and the second letter is 'e'?"

"Dad, they're having a sale on surf boards at that new sporting goods store. If you'll give me an advance on my allowance for two months I could buy a good one for half price."

"Be sure to read this article on rock gardens in the Home Section and if everyone agrees to help we'll start one down by the weeping willow."

"Dad, will you show me how they figure batting averages?"

"Dad, you said that you'd read the funnies to me as soon as you finished that page. Let's hear it before Mom finishes those blintzes."

What went into that session of family reading? There was a recognition of speech symbols; a transposing of those symbols into words, phrases, and sentences; an interpretation of meanings; a reflective thinking of what was previously known and these thoughts related to what was read; and in many cases there was a projection of thought beyond what was actually read. Some of it resulted in action, some in plans, some in appreciations, some in concern, some in speculations, and some in enjoyment. Reading is all of this and sometimes more.

The little girl was *reading* pictures. She knew what Blondie was doing even though she could not read the words, and she looked forward to having her father read it to her. These children observe adults reading and they know that knowing how to read must be important. Some day they, too, will enter the vast field of adult reading. What will it hold for them? The remainder of this chapter gives an overview of the scope of reading and the succeeding chapters present the nature of reading and the developmental process of becoming efficient and discriminating readers.

There is a family "togetherness" in the sharing of the Sunday paper. Daily newspapers, magazines, and books are often a point of departure for family discussions, sharing of information, and leisure time activity. A child feels near and dear to a parent who will read to him, whether it be factual material he wants to know about or whether it be an adventure into the realm of storyland. Reading provides stimulating recreation for "alone" moments, too, when, for example, the wife sits down with a second cup of coffee and some of her home magazines after the other members of the family have taken off for school and work. Yes, reading is an important part of home and family life in America today.

Between 1940 and 1960 while the United States population increased by 37%, newspaper sales went up 45%, magazine sales increased by 110%, books published and sold went up 445% and newsmagazine circulation went up 250%. In 1940 the average American bought one book a year. In 1960 the average American bought five books a year. Almost a billion books were published and sold in our country in 1960 alone, and every day a million paperbacks are sold. There are newspapers in 86% of the households and 78% of the time they are read by two or more family members. There are over fourteen thousand paperback titles for home libraries at very nominal cost.[1]

These figures were compiled in 1965 and these numbers are increasing by leaps and bounds.

No accounting has been made of newspapers that are passed on to others, clippings that are put to many uses, libraries and places of business that make reading materials available to great numbers of people, microfilm of many newspapers and its uses, plus the reading materials that come from England and other countries.

No analysis is made of the quality of this vast amount of printed material. We do know that the problem of pornography is increasing, and the best way of combating it is to help children develop better interests. We do not know how many people who are the consumers of pornography would be purchasing good literature if they had had the opportunities of developing broad interests and good taste. We do know that people are reading, that there is much material available, and that the home and schools have the responsibility of helping children become able, selective, and appreciative readers.

Reading in and out of the home today is by no means limited to publications. We live in a culture with increasing demands on ability to read. Thousands of items are bottled, packaged, or wrapped with labels bearing instructions, listing ingredients, and explaining

1 *The Reading Explosion,* International Paper Co., New York, 1965.

uses. Outside the home our environment calls upon our ability to read road signs, maps, menus, time payment contracts, real estate contracts, work contracts, drivers' license examinations, programs, and advertisements galore. A shopping excursion calls for the reading of price tags, labels indicating fabric content, washing instructions, and the name of designer or manufacturer. Knitting instructions, pattern book references, food labels, carton contents, and store directories are reading experiences common to any shopper. The reading process—in addition to deciphering symbols of various kinds, reflection on meanings, retrospect and comparison of values—includes decision making in terms of what has been read and interpreted.

Reading in Selected Professions and Careers

Reading has many meanings in various fields of interest and endeavor. A few fields in which reading is of vital importance are presented here to bring about a greater understanding of the many forms that reading takes, the skills it involves, and the lifelong interests and appreciations it can bring about.

LITERATURE

To the poet or one who enjoys reading poetry and prose, reading is the smooth recognition of harmoniously constructed passages conveying mankind's thoughts, feelings, and appreciations. These readers are so mindful of sensitivity and eloquence that little thought is given to processes of word recognition or reading difficulties. Reading skills have become so automatic and refined that the reading process serves the purpose of yielding satisfaction from the composition or rendition of good literature. Not only the thought content but also the fluency and rhythmic quality of well-chosen words and phrases are highly significant in the field of literature.

To spend an evening listening to someone like Mark Van Doren or Charles Laughton read literature and to observe a vast auditorium of people enthralled into deep silence by the superb rendition of well-chosen gems of poetic or prose masterpieces is to realize that, in Van Doren's own words, "A good oral reader enters the heart of the listener." Here the skills of oral reading are mastered and refined to the extent that the oral reading process almost automatically transfers the thoughts, feelings, and substance of an author's printed communication, through an accomplished reader's speech, to a listening and appreciative audience. He sweeps you along with the magnetism of a voice attuned to the beauty, pathos, joys, and mysteries flowing from the passages of well-chosen books. Good literature has no dimensions or limitations, and each reader or listener is free to take from it what he will.

A good book gives you a life you haven't time to live on a clock and it gives you a geography you cannot enter physically, an imaginative landscape. A great book is different from a good book in the size of the landscape and in the dimension of the light it gives you. If you think you can get to be a full human being without having some contact with the experiences that the race has stored, I think you are wrong. It need not be any one list. I am talking about reading not as a matter of accumulating facts, that's a separate and entirely respectable process, but as a process of accumulating experiences.[2]

David Russell once said that a writer only begins a book. It is the reader who completes it. The reader takes what he can from the printed pages, but it is the thoughts and feelings that are stirred up within the reader that carry him beyond the mere print. A book, whether it be written for children or adults, is only as good as the effect it has on the reader.

We react to reading intellectually, emotionally, aesthetically, and with value judgment, with varying degrees of feeling in each case. Recall the times you may have wept as you read parts of *Little Women* or *Uncle Tom's Cabin,* the times you chuckled over *Alice in Wonderland,* the suspense you felt as you entered the cave with Tom Sawyer. Consider the value judgment you exercised as you read *Pinocchio.* Could anyone read a Laura Ingalls Wilder book without sensing the beauty in her well-written descriptive passages?

However, not always do we need to take specific meaning from what we read or from what is read to us.

Some of the greatest poems in the English language defy any effort to state what they mean. Blake's "Tiger, Tiger, Burning Bright" is one of them. You can guess the area in which its meaning vibrates, but I don't think there is anyone in the world who can say what that poem means. Yet all readers of English poetry recognize that it is one of the great lyrics. It's a mysterious kind of experience. If you try to parse out the language there is some you can't account for. Or perhaps one that's even better

2 John Ciardi, "The Well Read Man," in *New Perspectives in Reading Instruction,* Mazurkiewicz, Albert J., ed. New York: Pitman Publishing Corp., 1964, pp. 86–87.

known is Coleridge's "Kubla Khan." What does that mean? Can you get it restated into three good English sentences that make sense? If that's the kind of question you ask, you should go stand in the corner. It destroys the life of the thought. It is like a dream. It charms with meaning, but it won't release it all. It haunts you with the suggestion of meaning. You know that it's meaningful, but exactly what defies you. You get that experience in many poems.[3]

The same is true in some children's literature. The very young child listening to nursery rhymes seldom derives meanings from them. Consider "Little Miss Muffet sat on a tuffet eating her curds and whey," "Sing a song of sixpence, a pocket full of rye," or any of Lear's nonsense poems, and much of Dr. Seuss' stories. A child sits on the lap of an adult enchanted by the rhythm of the nursery rhymes and the sounds of the words as well as by the fact that they are being read "to him." Certainly not all of what we would read to children should be meaningless, but some such well-chosen selections add mirth and the relaxation of the contact with the reader.

Whether the reading is done for oneself or for an audience, the effectiveness depends greatly on how it is read. The mechanics of reading, word and phrase recognition, and rapid comprehension and interpretation must be so well established that the reader can lose himself in the substance of what is being read and let it dictate "how" it is to be read.

There is one thing about good writing (and poetry is foremost in this, but it's true of the novel, too); it has a notation as complete as that of the notation that goes with music. It says this passage must be read slowly. It says this passage must hurry up. It says here you must emphasize as if the drums were going slowly. And here you leap along. There is no confusion. There's a notation that is invisible, but it's there. . . . Reading speed is fine if you're reading pages of facts, or just something you don't have to have a feeling toward. But it's not reading skill if it doesn't know enough to slow down on such a line as, "When Ajax strides some rock's vast weight to throw, the verse too wavers and the line goes slow." Certain passages say, "read me slowly," or "read me emphatically." The notation tells you that: the punctuation, the metrics.[4]

Consider how briskly an elementary school teacher would read "The Song of the Brook" to a class of youngsters, or how slowly and softly a kindergarten teacher would read *Sleepy Forest* if she is to get the intended effect. A teacher comes to know which stories are best for children to read themselves and which are enhanced by

---

3 Ciardi, *op. cit.*, p. 91.
4 Ciardi, *op. cit.*, p. 90.

being read aloud, and she comes to know what goes into good oral reading to accommodate children's listening and appreciation.

Mark Van Doren, from his eminent position in the field of literature, has this to say about reading:

Every book that is worth reading is one that makes us want to read the next page no matter what it is . . . We're always reading in the expectation of what will come next. . . . We have done the thing that reading demands—we have sat down alone and silent to give our minds to another, to surrender ourselves to somebody else who has written this thing. The reader is a surrenderer first and last. . . . I believe studies have been made, psychological tests, of persons reading. It is an active experience. No one reads perfectly relaxed. No one reads as if he were just sort of letting something pass him by. Anyone who is truly reading is grasping, seizing something and working with it. . . . The desire to read is the desire to know. We read because we want to know more. And of course I mean more than the desire for information. It finally means, when it's most exciting and interesting, the desire to know what we already know and yet do not know that we do. . . . I personally believe that every student should be asked at least once a day to read something out loud and make sense of it, real sense. Until he has learned to do that, and I mean something that he never saw before, I believe he is not a reader. The way he can prove to you that he is a reader is when he can read something aloud so that he can understand it and furthermore like it. . . . I think we should reveal that reading is an art and what is read is forms of art because writing is an art. . . . The sentence is the heartbeat of the mind. . . . All there is to reading after all is reading a book one sentence at a time—not one word at a time, but one sentence at a time—not missing any sentence and not missing what is there.[5]

HISTORY

To the historian, reading is the unfolding of man's records of achievements and failures. So intent is he on the content of his reading material, which is so voluminous that one lifetime seems too short to encompass it all, that fleeting moments can scarcely be given to any consideration of the reading process itself. Much of history has been written from various points of view, and events of recent happenings are reported with somewhat conflicting stories. Skimming, critical analysis, comparisons, and reflective and projective thinking are components of the historian's struggle with reading.

Charles Beard, the great historian, was once asked how long it would take him to write the history of the world after his many

5 Mark Van Doren, "In Praise of Reading." *Explorations in Reading,* June, 1962.

years of study. He pondered for a while. At first he thought it might take seven years. Then after further thought he said that it might be done in three years. Suddenly he came to the conclusion that all of history could be summarized in four ancient proverbs: The mills of the gods grind slowly but they grind exceedingly fine; the bee fertilizes the flower whose nectar it robs; whom the gods would destroy they first make mad with power; and night must fall before we can see the light of the stars.[6]

As we read those statements, each of us in our own reflective thinking may make very different historical associations, and perhaps none would have the scope of association that Charles and Mary Beard would have. Yet all of us are impressed that ancient proverbs, stated so succinctly, can call up so many mental associations and relationships. Reading is like that—we take from it only in proportion to what we bring to it.

MATHEMATICS

To the mathematician, reading is precise understanding that he attaches to charts and figures. Shades of meaning have little place in his world of accuracy and accountability. Consider the slide rule, the compass, the sextant, blueprints, and the uses to which they may be put. Exactness and a highly technical background are associated with the reading of those working in fields related to mathematics.

LAW

To the lawyer, reading is browsing through and pondering on recorded cases to determine how justice has been and can be determined. Studious perusal of great bound volumes is part of his daily life. Interpretations and applications determine his success. He is keenly interested in what the law does not say as well as in what it does say. To the lawyer, reading is often a manipulation of phraseology and reinterpretation of what has been read, with varying degrees of significance given to this or that item.

PERFORMING ARTS

To the actor, reading is accepting as one's own, speech and actions from printed scripts. From those symbols must come all the pathos,

---

[6] George S. Counts, in *Charles A. Beard: An Appraisal,* ed. by Howard Beal. Lexington: University of Kentucky Press, 1954, pp. 251–2.

comedy, tragedy, and realism that make for acclaim. For the actor, reading is a process of being, doing, saying what the script calls to mind.

CHEMISTRY

To the pharmacist, reading is the transferring of symbols into germ-killing, life-preserving, and health-restoring compounds. Each day finds new ingredients added to the crowded shelves from which he makes his selections. The incorrect reading of one prescription symbol or bottle label could produce tragedy. Equally important is the accuracy with which he writes the directions for use of the medication and any necessary warnings and precautions. Important, too, is the accuracy with which the consumer reads the label.

LINGUISTICS

To the linguist, reading is an ever-expanding knowledge of language. Linguists have diversified interests. One linguist may spend his time analyzing the dialect of a certain geographical region, while another is busily deciphering the hieroglyphics in ancient tombs. Most linguists are not interested in the actual processes of reading. Only recently have a few attempted to inject a so-called linguistic approach into the teaching of reading to children. A university professor of romance language makes the following comparison:

Reading involves the responding to visual forms with vocal or sub-vocal ones. The "thoughtful" or "meaningful" reactions that accompany or follow this process are responses to the vocalized or sub-vocalized forms and the underlying neurophysiology. Thus, while the reading specialist is inclined to say, "the printed word merely acts as a trigger that releases a meaning we already possess," the linguist believes that the printed word acts as the trigger that releases its oral counterpart, which, in its turn, releases a meaning we already possess.[7]

Only as linguists, psychologists, and educators pool their knowledge will they come to a full realization of how American English can be taught most effectively. It is made up of borrowed words from nearly every known language of the world, plus a great assortment of vocabulary innovations, many of which have no phonemic, phonetic, or structural consistency. To one for whom English is a

[7] James P. Soffietti, "Why Children Fail to Read: A Linguistic Analysis," *Harvard Educational Review*, Spring, 1955.

second language our language is one of the most difficult of all languages. In few other languages are there so many irregularities. These irregularities include both speech sounds and word meanings. Linguists have a vast knowledge of language; psychologists have a vast knowledge of how learning can be achieved and educators have a vast knowledge of the what and how of reading. These knowledges must be brought together.

RESEARCHING

To the researcher, reading is an amalgamated process of gleaning from records nuggets of facts, findings, truths, formulas, and results that he can rapidly combine with his knowledge of possibilities or potentialities, or within visions and dreams of a quest for something better, more effective, more durable, more beautiful. It is this projection of ideas beyond the printed page that makes reading a sort of catalyst in scientific advances.

MARKETING

To the marketing agent, reading is the carefully developed, eye-captivating, sales-appealing, widely-circulated advertisements that prompt children to say, "Mommy, buy this one," teen-agers to feel that they must have one, and parents to be willing to "give it a try." Advertising is a twelve-billion-dollar business, and training courses include a multiplicity of techniques for alluring the unsuspecting public into buying. Federal regulations attempt to eliminate false claims, but broad general appeals to human vanity, thrift, and security are sound psychological approaches to convincing advertising. The intelligent consumer of today needs to read cautiously and compare carefully to get the best for his investments.

LIBRARY SCIENCE

To the librarian, reading is an overwhelming attempt to keep up with old and new publications in many fields of interest. She is in a position of awareness of the range and volume of the publishing business today. She knows that about 18,000 book titles appear on the market in the United States every year. She reads with varying degrees of thoroughness as she critically analyzes materials in terms of the potential readers for whom they are intended.

Summation

There is depth of reading as exemplified by the work of Charles and Mary Beard and their lifetime study of history. There is breadth of reading as exemplified by librarians. There is need for various kinds of reading skills, and always there is the interest in what reading can supply.

Somewhere in the lives of these people, engaged in professions or careers where reading is of major importance, there was inspiration that caused cultivation of a depth and breadth of interest. There was development of skills and grasp of meaning until they became so automatic that other substance could dominate their thinking as they followed their interests.

We know not what effect opportunities for developing the skills of reading and tastes for good reading may have had on those who cannot read or who do not appreciate or enjoy it. We do know to what extent breadth and depth of reading can enrich lives.

We know not how many future public readers, historians, performing artists, chemists, scientists, or professors are in the elementary classrooms of today. But the diversity of skills that children acquire, the ease with which they are helped to comprehend, the various subject areas to which they are exposed, the opportunities they have to nurture interests, and the inspirations that can be generated will determine their destiny. This is a challenge for every teacher.

Reading in Education

The Education Critic

Reading has always been the education critic's target for achieving public attention and support. The complexities of reading and the variables within children and teachers will always create problems and critics thrive on these situations. Seldom do they analyze the causes of problems—their approach is to condemn. If any attempt is ever made at remediation it is usually a simple cure-all that reflects little or no understanding of the peculiarities and inconsistencies of our language, the variables within children and teachers, or the components of an all-inclusive reading program.

THE ELEMENTARY SCHOOL ADMINISTRATORS

Reading is often the most troublesome subject in the school's curriculum. In many instances the administrator feels that his success is based on the reading achievement scores of the children in his school. It seems to be his great responsibility to provide facilities and personnel to raise reading test scores and to prove to the community that everything possible is being done to provide children with the best possible reading instruction. He needs to be well-informed as to what constitutes a good reading program so he can be a bulwark against unfair outside criticism and can support his teachers in their endeavors. He can explain to parents and the public that reading is more than knowledge of phonics, more than exposure to linguistics and more than mere word recognition. The principal, the superintendent, and the schoolboard need to know how reading is being taught in their schools and why it is being taught that way. They should be defenders of justifiable innovation and research as well as of established programs.

THE PRESCHOOL CHILD

If the preschooler is so fortunate as to be born into a home where parents provide worthwhile reading opportunities for him, reading is what Daddy does with the morning paper, what Mother does when she follows the directions on the pudding box before lunch, what the word "Poison" means on the bottle he mustn't touch, what it says on the menu when the family goes out to dinner, or what it says in the song book at church, on the signs along the highway, and in store windows. Twice fortunate is he if someone stands by to answer his question, "What does that say?" And especially, reading is the fun time when he sits on Mother's or Daddy's lap, or when they tuck him into bed and read from the lovely picture books he gets for his birthday, for Christmas, or from the library. Reading time is his chance to have Mother or Daddy all to himself. It is a time when he can slip into the Land of Counterpane, go up in the sky so blue, or dart about with his shadow as the delightful poems of Stevenson's *A Child's Garden of Verses* are read. He may not understand all the happenings but he knows he likes the queer sounding words and the rhythm of the books of Dr. Seuss. He does not care how many times *Peter Rabbit* has been read before, and he knows if you leave

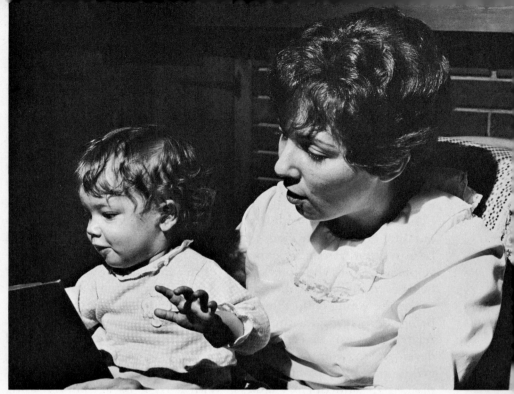

Fortunate is the child who enjoys pictures and stories at home and has an understanding parent to answer such questions as, "Who's that?" "What's that?" and "Why?"

out a single paragraph of *The Three Bears*. He makes friends for life with some of these story-book characters, and he looks upon reading as something wonderful, exciting, and fascinating that he will learn to do when he gets to first grade. Adults, in each case have used the reading process, but this process is taking on meaning to the child. He looks upon it as important, pleasant, and rewarding. Fortunate is the child who at a very young age is allowed to turn the pages of many books and magazines, enjoying the pictures, long before the print is recognizable. But a large percentage of young children have never experienced the joys of childhood that make reading so highly respected or so lofty a goal. These children will come to our schools, too.

Elementary School Children

The reading process ranges from being the school's most thrilling learning experience for many children to an experience of various levels of frustration or utter disregard for others. Through good interpersonal relationships, careful planning, and the use of appealing materials and effective techniques, most children acquire the needed skills and can use reading for many purposes and pleasures. To a great many children, reading is a delightful experience of acquiring skills, gaining interesting information, opening doors to content as broad as the world and life itself, chuckling over the fantasy of relating one's self to the trials, values, and adventures of others, and of projecting hopes and aspirations into the realms of tomorrow.

Improvement in the ability to read goes on continuously throughout life. No one can read with understanding everything that has been written. Pertinent experience and appropriate vocabulary development must be forerunners of reading achievement in new fields even though the mechanics of reading are almost automatic.

For the young child there must be many developmental activities before he is ready for the reading process. Well-rounded and interrelated physical, psychological, social, neurological, and emotional development, combined with a broad base of language growth, makes reading possible and rewarding. This development is explained in subsequent chapters. With such a background reading comes easily and with significance.

These objectives become his purposes for learning to read:

1. To be able to read the appealing books around him. (It is our responsibility to provide appropriate books that will entice him.)

2. To be able to read the many beckoning bits of reading that abound in his environment. (It is our responsibility to provide a stimulating environment.)

3. To accept the challenge and inspiration to learn the process of reading. (We have the responsibility of constantly providing that challenge and inspiration by helping him set attainable goals and be motivated by his achievements. In a sense, a teacher is saying, "This is how we can get to where you are wanting to go.")

4. To meet expectations. (The child comes to know that he is expected to read. We live in a reading culture. His parents expect him to read, the school and teacher expect him to read. He expects to read. He wants to read. He will and can read. This must be our attitude.)

For some unfortunate children, organic or neurological imperfections or impairments may create handicaps in developing their ability to read. These handicaps need to be detected early so that clinical diagnosis and expert help can be given. Emotional problems may cause reading problems, or inability to read may cause emotional instability. Faulty teacher-pupil relationships, poor teaching procedures, uninteresting or poorly developed materials, and constant pressures can cause fears and frustrations so that reading becomes distasteful and the child becomes rebellious or so docile and disinterested that he sits and daydreams. Thus, there is a wide range of factors that determine what reading means to children.

THE ELEMENTARY SCHOOL TEACHER

Reading is the most challenging and complex of all school subjects for the elementary school teacher. Success in nearly all other areas of learning depends to a large extent on the child's ability to read with understanding. A teacher knows the deep concern that parents have for their child's success in reading. She knows that achievement tests will be given. She knows that although tests have great value in diagnosing difficulties, too often they are used in making unfair comparisons: comparisons among children, among classes, among schools in a community, among communities, and comparisons on a nationwide basis. She knows that when test norms are established half of the school population is expected to be below the median and half above. She knows that for a school in which the enrollment is largely transient, where another language is used predominantly in the home, where homes are below economic standards, where children are deprived and opportunities are lacking, or where teachers' salaries are low, school facilities meager, rooms overcrowded and materials scant, it is reasonable to have low percentile scores, just as it is reasonable to expect schools in privileged areas with small classes, an abundance of materials, lavish facilities, high-salaried teachers, stable enrollment, and privileged homes with enrichment opportunities for children, well-spoken English, and affectionate encouragement to have extremely high scores. She knows that too often communities fail to understand the variables that make for "rightness" in comparative testing. She feels the pressures of a testing program and she knows that children can be harmed by incorrect use of tests and their results. She alone may be cognizant of all the variables within a group of children that must be taken into account as tests are selected and administered. She knows that it is just as reasonable for some children to begin reading in kindergarten as it is reasonable for certain other children to first feel the complete control of meaningful reading in the third, fourth, or fifth grade. She knows, too, that tests can never measure a child's attitude toward reading. Tests can never measure critical judgment of what is read in the out-of-school world; nor can they measure how much use of reading the child is making in his daily life, or how much reading may have affected his thinking, his values, or his interests.

To a conscientious teacher, reading affords continuous challenge throughout her teaching career. Never before has so much research been attempted. Never before have so many materials appeared on the market. Never before has so much money been available to buy, buy, buy. The well-informed teacher knows that there are many widely acclaimed approaches to reading instruction with varying degrees of emphasis on a variety of aspects of reading such as phonics, linguistics, rhyming words, and revised alphabets. She also knows that the whole of reading can never be accomplished by any simple formula. Yet occasionally she is the victim of an enforced approach or system of instruction selected by those who may be totally incompetent in making the selection for her particular group of children. She has to know how to work with the materials and still give the children the total program they deserve.

Reading is an area of the curriculum in which teachers, administrators, and schoolboard members need to educate parents and the lay public as well as children. It must be done reasonably, inoffensively, and with the assurance that every normal child can become an efficient and inspired reader—not by any quick and easy method, but with careful stimulation of interest, well-chosen techniques, and appropriate materials, along with good interpersonal relationships.

Young readers develop a feeling about the process. Children's interest in reading may be stimulated and nurtured or inhibited and destroyed. If children are guided to look upon reading as being delightful, if they are encouraged in their efforts, if they are supplied with appropriate materials and challenged in satisfying situations, the process of reading is likely to be looked upon favorably by them. Children then look forward with anticipation to more and more reading. However, if more is expected of children than they can achieve, or if there is no motivation, reading can become boring and frustrating. We might say that reading has emotional tone. With all that is known about children, with all that is known about the reading process, and with all that is known about the abundance of captivating reading materials, teachers have the opportunity of helping every child experience reading as a highly rewarding and enjoyable continuum of school and out-of-school experiences.

When schoolboard members and city school administrators spend time visiting the classrooms, they are better prepared to recognize school needs and to interpret the school to the community. (Photograph courtesy of the San Diego, California, Public Schools.)

Reading is more than what appears on the printed page. Language symbols cause us to think. How deeply or how broadly we think depends on our frame of mind, how free we are from distractions, and how much of an experience background we can use in our meditation. We interact with the thought content on the page. We accept, reject, or evaluate the content in terms of what we know. Sometimes we start to read with a definite purpose; sometimes we merely browse to see what might "strike our fancy." Sometimes a whole chain of thoughts we had not anticipated at all is set off by what meets our eyes in print.

Certain printed pages may inspire a reader to try hidden talents, to develop lofty ideals, to explore, or to create. Conversely, the amount of trash in books and magazines is deplorable. How much such reading contributes to delinquency in youth and crime among adults is not known. Certainly there is some relationship between trashy reading and trashy living.

Teachers attest to the value of therapeutic reading. It is a matter of finding the right book for the needy child. We have wonderful bibliographies to help select the "right" books. If the child can happen upon the book himself and glean from it the guidance he may need, it is much more effective than too much adult direction. In books children can find characters to admire, traits to value, goals to seek, solace in identifying with other children who have problems, vicarious experiences denied to him in real life, and nourishment for the thirst of curiosity.

Some children find so much solace or refuge in books that they tend to retreat into them. Such children may be considered recluse. Each is an individual case and must be studied as such with regard to causes and needs. Even so, the right books may help him to face life courageously and to see what is worthwhile within his realm of daily living. It is thus a matter of going beyond the contents of the printed page and making life more satisfying for having read.

Yes, reading affords many challenges to the conscientious teacher, but the rewards are great in terms of what can be done for the enrichment of young lives.

Educators Define Reading in Various Ways

This is a mere sampling of definitions by workers in the field of reading.

Reading is a subtle and complex act. It involves, more or less simultaneously, the following: sensation of light rays on the retina of the eye reaching the brain, perception of separate words and phrases, functioning of the eye muscles with exact controls, immediate memory for what has just been read, remote memories based on the reader's experience, interest in the content read, and organization of the material so that finally it can be used in some way. These various features operate more or less concurrently; but they can be analyzed into at least four successive stages: sensation, perception, comprehension, and utilization.[8]

Real reading means plucking out all the subtle threads of meaning from sentences, paragraphs, and pages and weaving them into your own personality.[9]

While reading is a single operation, we can distinguish four different steps in the total reading process—word perception, comprehension,

[8] David H. Russell, *Children Learn to Read.* Boston: Ginn, 1949, p. 74.

[9] A. Sterl Artley, *Your Child Learns to Read.* Chicago: Scott, Foresman, 1953, p. 7.

reaction, and integration—all of which reach back to meaning-background.[10]

Reading is a process of recognizing symbols which serve as stimuli to the recalling and constructing of meaning, accompanied by the manipulating of the reading meanings in thought processes so that his ensuing reactions are modified as a result of reading.[11]

In the broad view, reading is regarded as a manifold process that involves associating words with meanings and letter sounds with the printed symbols, thinking, feeling, acting, and becoming. Creative and thoughtful reading begins when the reader has learned how to find out what the author actually said.[12]

Reading is the deepening of perception and understanding through the intercommunication of minds using the medium of the written word. Reading is much more than mere word, phrase, or even sentence recognition. Reading involves not only the skills of word recognition (such as the use of configuration; contextual clues; and word analysis, which includes phonics as one of the basic means of word attack) but also comprehension, library, work-study, and appreciation skills. Reading includes the development of attitudes, abilities, and techniques whose interrelationships are many, varied, and intricate. Reading has dimensions that go far above and beyond the literal meaning of the printed word. Reading concerns context in which words expand into ideas and thoughts derived from past experiences. It involves the imagination, the thinking, and the feeling of both participants in the communicative process—the writer and the reader. Reading is a highly complex process, an expression of the total personality of the individual, and a vital facet of the language arts rather than a separate and discrete curriculum area. Mere word calling is to reading as snapping a photograph is to the painting of a beautiful picture—the one, a mechanical skill; the other, a life-giving art. Thus, all that one brings to the printed page plays a part in determining what he takes away from it.[13]

Perhaps an all-inclusive definition of reading might be stated as follows: Reading is recognizing and interpreting symbolic language and interacting with it. This interaction may be any degree of acceptance or rejection of what is stated; enjoyment of the language itself; retention of fact, feeling, or inspiration; stimulation to create; or any number of other positive or negative reactions. One never

[10] William S. Gray, *On Their Own in Reading*. Chicago: Scott, Foresman, 1948, p. 35.
[11] Lucile M. Harrison, *Reading Readiness*. Chicago: Houghton Mifflin, 1939, pp. 136–7.
[12] Ruth Strang, *Helping Your Child Improve His Reading*. New York: Dutton, 1962, p. 76.
[13] From "Sequential Levels of Reading Growth in the Elementary School," Advisory Committee of Assistant Superintendents, Division of Elementary Schools, New York City Schools, Feb., 1963.

knows for sure what may result from the act of reading. Indirect influences may be felt far into the future.

Reading is a pleasure of the mind, which means that it is a little like a sport: your eagerness and knowledge and quickness count for something. The fun of reading is not that something is told you, but that you stretch your mind. Your own imagination works along with the author's, or even goes beyond his. Your experience, compared with his, yields the same or different conclusions, and your ideas develop as you understand his.

Reading is like eating peanuts: once you begin, you tend to go on and on. Every book stands by itself, like a one-family house, but books are like houses in a city. Although they are separate, together they all add up to something; they are connected with each other and with other cities. The same ideas, or related ones, turn up in different places; the human problems that repeat themselves in life repeat themselves in literature, but with different solutions according to different authors who wrote at different times. Books influence each other; they link the past and the present and the future and have their own generations, like families. Wherever you start reading you connect yourself with one of the families of ideas, and, in the long run, you not only find out about the world and the people in it: you find out about yourself, too.[14]

—BENNETT CERF

Suggestions for Class Participation and Discussion

1. Make a record of the various situations in which you read in any one day. In other words, how did reading serve you?
2. Observe people around you and record the situations in which they were reading. What skills were involved?
3. Note the differences in thoroughness with which you read on five different occasions.
4. What are factors that might enter into a reader's obtaining thoughts far removed from an author's intent?
5. Do you have an aversion to any particular kind of reading? Why?
6. Explain the quotation by Bennett Cerf.
7. Ask three young children, "What is reading?" "Why do you read?" "Do you like to read?" Discuss in class.
8. From all the examples of "reading in life" in this chapter, list what you consider to be important skills in reading. Save your list and compare with other lists in class.
9. How has reading influenced your life?
10. What is your own definition of reading?

[14] Bennett Cerf, "The Pleasures of Reading," in *The Wonderful World of Books,* Alfred Stefferud, ed. New York: New World Library of World Literature, Inc., 1952, p. 25.

Resource Suggestions

Go to the library and look up "Reading" in the card file. Find the shelves where reading references are kept and do some browsing to become familiar with the types of books available. Also check the "Reserve" section.

Ask the librarian where the *Education Index* is kept. Each month the H. W. Wilson Company (950 University Ave., Bronx, New York) publishes an index to magazine articles in the field of education under various headings. At the end of each year these monthly publications are bound so that yearly indexes are available. Look up "Reading" and locate various magazines containing articles on various topics in the vast field of "Reading." Become familiar with this great source of current information. Refer to various topics throughout the course. Because many excellent articles on various aspects of reading are published each month, specific references to them have not been made in this book. Nevertheless, current magazines are a rich source of recent thinking and research.

Look up "Reading" in the *Journal of Education Research*. It, too, is an excellent source of current happenings in the reading field. Ask the librarian to see a copy of *Textbooks in Print* (R. R. Bowker Co., 1180 Avenue of the Americas, New York). Note the listing of professional books in language arts and reading. Then note the listing of readers: basal, supplementary, Skilltext, phonic, remedial, and programmed.

Find the "Curriculum Materials" section of the library and plan to spend a certain amount of time each week becoming familiar with the various reading materials available for inspection.

Go to the audio-visual section of the library or to that department on campus and plan to become familiar with the various teaching devices available. Visit classrooms and clinics to observe procedures, techniques, devices, and materials after they have been discussed in class.

Find the Supplementary Educational Monographs published by the University of Chicago Press and refer to the various titles as they relate to the forthcoming chapters. Find the Yearbooks of the various educational organizations and note the ones that relate to reading. Browse through the various courses of study and bulletins that are on file in the curriculum materials center.

Take note of the service bulletins from the various publishing companies. When you have a contract to start teaching, write to each of the following companies and ask that your name be put on their mailing lists for current bulletins as they are released.

American Book Company
55 Fifth Avenue
New York, N.Y.

Ginn & Company
Back Bay
P.O. Box 191
Boston, Mass.

Lyons & Carnahan
2500 Prairie Avenue
Chicago, Ill.

Houghton Mifflin Company
2 Park Street
Boston, Mass.

John C. Winston Company
1010 Arch Street
Philadelphia, Pa.

Row, Peterson & Company
1911 Ridge Avenue
Evanston, Ill.

The Macmillan Company
866 Third Avenue
New York, N.Y.

Scott, Foresman & Company
1900 East Lake Avenue
Glenview, Ill.

The following books provide material for stimulating seminars:

ANDERSON, VERNA, et al. Readings in the Language Arts (rev. ed.). New York: Macmillan, 1967.

DeCECCO, JOHN P. (ed.). The Psychology of Language, Thought, and Instruction. New York: Holt, Rinehart & Winston, 1967.

FIGUREL, J. (ed.). Vistas in Reading. Newark, Del.: International Reading Association, 1966.

HARRIS, ALBERT J. (ed.). Readings on Reading Instruction. New York: David McKay, 1963.

HOWES, and DARROW, HELEN (eds.). Reading and the Elementary School Child: Selected Readings on Programs and Practices. New York: Macmillan, 1968.

International Reading Association Yearbooks.

MAZURKIEWICZ, A. J. (ed.). New Perspectives in Reading Instruction. New York: Pitman Publishing Corp., 1964.

PIAGET, JEAN. The Origins of Intelligence in Children. New York: Norton, 1963.

SMITH, JAMES. Creative Teaching of Reading and Literature. Boston: Allyn & Bacon, 1967.

STEFFERUD, ALFRED (ed.). The Wonderful World of Books. New York: New American Library, 1953.

STEIGER, RALPH (ed.). New Directions in Reading. New York: Bantam Books, 1967.

University of Chicago Reading Conference Yearbooks.

University of Syracuse Reading Conference Yearbooks.

VAN DOREN, MARK. "In Praise of Reading." Explorations in Reading, June, 1962.

CHAPTER 2
The Scheme
of Reading Our Language

Language

Language is a learned arbitrary system *of vocal sound symbols with which people can communicate within a culture.*[1]

Language has been defined in many ways, but Gerd Fraenkel included the three words that are basic to its definition. Man is endowed with speech organs but the ways in which sounds are modified by throat muscles, tongue, palate, lips, and teeth are *learned.* As people banded together they *arbitrarily* established a means of communication by means of sound symbols. These symbols were understood by the person uttering the message and the person receiving it. To accommodate easy learning and use of a language, each tribe or group of people had a *system.* In some cases, as in Italy and Finland, there is a direct sound letter association. That is, each letter represents one and only one speech sound. In Chinese many symbols are pictograms and the symbol represents a word or idea.

[1] Gerd Fraenkel, *What Is Language?* New York: Ginn, 1965, p. 16.

Because many other languages had been established before our language came into being, we borrowed much of ours and it is somewhat lacking in any very definite system. Nevertheless, there are aspects of scheme to our way of talking, as shall be seen.

Ben Jonson once wrote, "Speech is the only benefit man hath to express his excellency of man above other creatures. In all speech, words and sense are as the body and soul. The sense is as the life and soul of Language, without which all words are dead. Sense is wrought out of experience, the knowledge of human life and action or of the liberal arts."[2]

Language is an aspect of culture which is common to all human societies. Languages are in a continual state of change, as social conditions change, as contacts between classes, peoples, and races touch and go, as ideas pass and repass. Language has been compared to the shifting surface of the sea; the sparkle of the waves like flashes of light on points of history.[3]

Some languages of the world do not have written counterparts. Communication can take place only on a person-to-person basis in such cultures.

It is impossible to achieve an accounting of world languages because of the many dialects and variations that occur in the very remote regions as well as such countries as India and China. The count of generally recognized languages runs into the thousands. Of these, Chinese leads with more than five hundred million speakers, India with more than four hundred million, and English a weak third with approximately two hundred ninety million speakers throughout the world. Russian and Spanish rank next, in that order. There are about three thousand identifiable languages in the world today, so one can see how impossible it would be to communicate a one-language message to all the people of the world.

Albert Schweitzer attempted a universal language for spreading civilization to remote areas of the world but it has not been far-reaching. Many of the political and social developments of the world today make a world language seem feasible, but it is difficult to initiate or to have it accepted. National pride is a strong factor.

If ever there is a world language, it will represent a world situation, a situation in which social, political, and linguistic circumstances have

2 Colin Cherry, *On Human Communication*. New York: Wiley, 1957, p. 75.
3 Cherry, *op. cit.*, p. 75.

combined to make a world language natural, not a situation in which a few people have concocted a world language and have tried to legislate it into being. To see this, one has only to consider what would happen if tomorrow the United Nations were to decide to compromise on a "dark horse" language, and names Nahuat, a language of the Mexican isthmus, as the world medium of exchange. Nahuat seems to be an excellent language, and it need occasion no Romanic-Germanic rivalry, no conflict of the East and the West. But what would happen? Nobody would learn Nahuat.[4]

One of the most interesting features at the United Nations is the almost instantaneous translation system that is in operation during all the meetings. A grave responsibility lies in the accuracy of such translations, and some languages do not have words equivalent in meaning to some that English-speaking people might use, and vice versa.

The Extensive Use of English

Many writers indicate that English is the fastest-growing language in the world. This growth can be attributed to a number of causes.

English is the native tongue of both the United States and the British Commonwealth of Nations. At this writing those two bodies of people control more of the sinews of language than any other in what we call the free world, incomparably more. These countries have more political prestige, more military strength, more international trade, more productive potential, more wealth, more of almost everything that goes to support language than have half a dozen of their nearest competitors. If, then, the future of the world is shaping at all as we hope it will shape, toward a free world following the lead of the English-speaking peoples, English has by all odds the best prospects of becoming a world language.[5]

Our armed services, scattered all over the world meeting people and spending money, our explosion of printed matter with its attractive formats and extensive use of pictures, and our relayed radio and television broadcasts no doubt have considerable influence on acceptance of the English language.

English is fast becoming a strong second language in many parts of the world and educators are likely to be faced with the challenge

---

4 Charlton Laird, *The Miracle of Language.* Cleveland, Ohio: World Publishing Co., 1958, p. 237.

5 Laird, *op. cit.,* pp. 237–238.

of helping teachers in various parts of the world to teach children to speak and read the English language.

The Development of the English Language

No one knows the true beginnings of language. We do know that English is a comparatively modern language. To trace its development is to trace the history of England with the addition of terms that come from scientific, industrial, political, and medical developments from all over the world. The Germanic tribes of Eastern Europe, which had been in and out of England for a long time, are largely responsible for the birth of the English language. The Saxons arrived in 477 and the Angles came in 547. The Germanic language, which became known as Anglo-Saxon, emerged in the seventh century. It was quite a different language from what is spoken today. The letters *g, j,* and *v* were not used; *c* was always hard; *f* had our *v* sound; and *h* had the German *ach* sound. Commonly used words such as *work, play, eat, arm, leg, nose, eye, ear, house, home, man, child, coat, yard, milk, hand,* and *head* are Anglo-Saxon. Each foreign invasion brought new words into the language. The Danes gave us words such as *steak, knife, dirt, fellow, window,* and *wrong.* We might blame them for some of our difficult spellings. They pronounced *knife* with the *k* sound. Somewhere along the way the pronunciation of the *k* was dropped but the letter remains. To add further complications, we have *no* from the Saxons and *nay* from the Norse; *rear* from the Saxons and *raise* from the Norse; we have *shirt* from the Saxons and *skirt* from the Norse; *whole* from the Saxons and *hole* from the Norse. We started with only present and past tense, but the Scandinavians gave us the future tense. *They, their,* and *them* are of Scandinavian origin. It is this influence that precludes any absolute reliance on phonics.

The French are responsible for many of our words. Words of French origin such as *soup, biscuit, fruit, beauty, grief, marriage,* and *grammar* add to the irregularities in our language and make reading and spelling extremely difficult for children.

The Dutch gave us *yacht, furlough, cookie, yankee, cruiser, schooner, freight,* and *switch,* words which add to a child's bewilderment in learning to read and spell by any rules or patterns.

From India comes *khaki;* from Arabic come *sugar, syrup, magazine, lemon,* and *candy;* and from Spain come *rodeo, tobacco, cocoa, potato, canoe,* and *mosquito.* All these words would violate most conventional rules of English spelling or pronunciation. The Italian contributions are equally complicating: *piano, vogue, design, broccoli, studio, alto,* and *cello.* From the Greek come *chrome* and *theater. Graph* and *gram* are Greek and to them we have added many Latin parts such as *photograph, autograph, telegram,* and many more.

Because of the church, Latin had a great impact on the English language. *Cheese, priest, school, circle, genius, necessary,* and *picture,* all of Latin derivation, are examples of words which further complicate our teaching of reading and spelling. Many of our prefixes and suffixes are Latin: *pre, pro, sub, super, anti* and *ate, ble, ic, ism, ize, ous,* and *ty.* They comprise a whole matrix of problems for young students.

Although 12,000 of the 20,000 most commonly used words in our language today are of Latin, French, or Greek origin, on any one page of most reading material one half of the words are likely to be Anglo-Saxon, because of the frequency of their use.

Our language is growing from day to day. How surprised our ancestors would be if they heard expressions like *goof off, get hep, hippies,* or *nylon net, coffee breaks, baby-sitters, atomic bombs, flying saucers, power steering, automatic shift, launching pad,* and *smog level.* Such slang words as *wisecrack, hi, dig, whodunits,* and *blitz* are in common use. Tomorrow will bring more and so will next week.

Thus, our ever-growing English language with its irregular structure and inconsistent word forms is facet number one in the teaching of reading. We must help children become aware of this linguistic aspect of reading with its myriad of complications.

Our Alphabet

Long before the advent of writing or printing, such symbols as smoke signals, flag signals, sand markings, and other types of hieroglyphics were used. In each case there was meaning attached to the symbols by the sender and by the receiver. The quality of the communication depended on the exactness of the meaning as understood by each person involved.

The first form of writing developed for use with our language consisted only of capital letters. It came from the Romans and in

turn had been patterned after the writing of the Greeks and Phoe-
nicians. The capital letter forms were stylized and designed so that
they could be carved. The original letters represented pictures, many
of them parts of the body. Most early alphabets were symbolic pictures. Chinese characters are still pictographic. The term *alphabet*
comes from the Greek *alpha* and *beta* the first two letters of the
Greek alphabet. It was the Roman influence that gave our letters
their present names.

It was the invention of the printing press by Johann Gutenberg
in the middle of the fifteenth century that gave our letters their
final form.

Paper had been made in Asia a long time before the Moors
brought it to Europe. Old rags were used by the Europeans in paper-
making, and sheets of paper were made one at a time. Today paper
is made largely from wood. It is cut into fine pieces, treated with
chemicals, and beat into a pulp. The pulp is mixed with water,
bleached, dried, rolled, and polished. The best quality paper is
smooth and highly receptive to ink without smudging.

In the first printing process, raised letters were coated with ink
and the impressions left on paper. This is known as the letterpress
process and is still used. However, we also have offset lithography
and gravure coming into general use. In early printing two pages
were printed at a time and about five hundred pages could be
printed in a day. Now over a hundred pages can be printed at one
time at the rate of many thousands an hour.

In our world of today where Telestar is only the beginning of
attempts at intercontinental radio and television broadcasts and
where few places on earth are truly remote, there is increasing need
for an international language. There is an International Phonetic
Alphabet, but it is used primarily in teaching a second language.
Music symbols, the Morse code, and numerals are more widespread
in their general use than are speech symbols. We therefore have an
antiquated alphabet of twenty-six letters with both capitals and
lower-case symbols, most of which are quite different from each
other. *C, k, o, p, s, v, w, x,* and *z* are the only letters in which size
is the only difference between lower and upper case letters. Thus,
in a sense, children have forty-three symbols to recognize in print
form in learning to read. Now, if they are going to be doing manuscript writing at the same time, consider the difference in form of
some manuscript letters in comparison with the printed form. The
a and *g* in lower case are very different, so we can add two more

Genealogy of our letters from the Phoenician alphabet. (From The Miracle of Language, *Charlton Laird.)*

Genealogy of Our Letters from the Phoenician Alphabet 1300 B.C.

Phoenician 1300-1000 B.C. Form, meaning, name	Greek 700-500 BC Form, name	Roman 50 BC Form, sound	Evolution of small letters 300 to 800 A.D	Gothic 12th AD	Italic 15th AD	Script 16th AD
= ox Aleph	A A Alpha	A Ah	a a a	a	a	a
= house Beth	B Beta	B Bay	b b b	b	b	b
= camel Gimel	Γ Gamma	C Kay	c c c	c	c	c
= door Daleth	Δ Delta	D Day	d d d	d	d	d
= window He	E Epsilon	E Eh	e e e	e	e	e
= hook Vau	F [Digamma]	F Ef	f f f	f	f	f
[*see footnote]			G g g	g	g	g
= fence Kheth	H Eta	H Hah	h h h	h	h	h
= hand Yod	I Iota	I Ee	i i i	i	i	i
				j	j	j
= palm Kaph	K Kappa	K Kah	k k k	k	k	k
= whip Lamed	Λ Lambda	L El	L l l	l	l	l
= water Mem	M Mu	M Em	m m m	m	m	m
= fish Nun	N Nu	N En	n n n	n	n	n
= eye Ayin	O Omicron	O Oh	o o o	o	o	o
= mouth Pe	Π Pi	P Pay	p p p	p	p	p
= monkey Koph	Ϙ Koppa	Q Koo	Q q q	q	q	q
= head Resh	P Rho	R Air	r r r	r	r	r
= teeth Shin	Σ Sigma	S Ess	s s s	s	s	s
= mark Tau	T Tau	T Tay	t t t	t	t	t
	Y Upsilon	V Oo	v u u	u	u	u
	Y	V	v v v	v	v	v
			wen 11th Cent Anglo-Saxon } W	w	w	w
= post Samech	X Xi	X Eex	x x x	x	x	x
	Y Upsilon	Y Ü	y y y	y	y	y
= weapon Zayin	I Z Zeta	Z Zayta	Z z z	z	z	z

* Until the Fourth Century B.C. the character C represented the sounds of both g and k when a bar was added to identify the voiced G.

In a table of this sort, dates, forms, and even meanings must be arbitrary. For instance, Koph can be spelled Goph or Qoph; He may have no meaning; Lamed (Lamedh) may mean "teacher's rod"; Samech (Samekh) may mean "fish" or "fulcrum;" Zayin may mean "olive" or "balance."

letters for a total of forty-five with which children must become familiar.

Only *I* and *a* have a meaning unto themselves and are used independently. In reading one says its name and the other does not. There is little relationship between the names of the letters and the sounds they make in words.

Latin, too, had an influence in our reading scheme. Latin was the language of scholars and especially of the church. It was phonetic, and whatever part of our language that can be considered phonetic is largely derived from Latin. However, we have maintained the original spelling of many French, Dutch, German, and Scandinavian words and of very commonly used Anglo-Saxon words. In phonics there are many more sounds than letters, as shall be explained in a separate chapter. In no other language is there so much inconsistency between letters and sounds as in English. Hundreds of common examples could be given, but perhaps one will suffice to stimulate readers to think of many more. Take the long sound of *i* and note how it is produced in each of the following commonly used words: *pie, try, ice, aye, bye, choir, height, line.*

According to George Bernard Shaw, *ghoti* is a perfectly logical way to spell *fish*. He got "gh" for the "f" from the word, *enough*. He got "o" for the "i" sound from *women* and he took "ti" for the "sh" sound from nation.[6]

Because the letters of the alphabet are basic in the development of words, some educators begin with letters in the introduction of reading to children. Some educators would introduce reading through a letter-sound approach.

Roman Johnny had an easy time of it, because he found that every consonant always had an unvarying value and every vowel had only two values, a long and a short. Oh, the blessings of a phonetic language! Roman Johnny had no trouble in pronouncing, no trouble in spelling rationally, and pretty soon he discovered that he could read. What is the lesson for us? Merely that we need to reform the English language. But this we are not going to do, despite the fortune left for the purpose by George Bernard Shaw.[7]

Some educators would start with the sounds represented by letters, but here again we find diversity of opinion. Some educators would

6 Franklin Folsom, *The Language Book*. New York: Grosset & Dunlap, 1963, p. 179.
7 Clarence A. Forbes, "Why Roman Johnny Could Read," *Classical Journal*, November, 1959.

start with initial word sounds, while others would start with final blends of words. Some educators would have children learn the letter names as they learn the sounds, while others would postpone the alphabet as such until later.

The letter or linguistic and various phonetic approaches are used in a number of series of readers published recently.

A movement began in England to simplify phonetic application to words by developing what is known as the Initial Teaching Alphabet, or i.t.a. It consists of symbols for forty-four speech sounds, lower case only and reading is taught through the use of these symbols. It has been in and out of use in various schools in England for several years and reports are underway to point up the strengths and weaknesses. It is being used in experimental situations in the United States also, but it is too early to determine how successfully children can make the transfer to an alphabet they must eventually accept with all the inconsistencies of which other children have already been aware. This and other approaches will be discussed further in later chapters. If our language had been one hundred per cent phonetic, both reading and spelling could easily be taught through mastery of the alphabet and the related sound of each letter, which is the case in such languages as Finnish and Italian.

Even though it is claimed that about eighty per cent of our words are phonetic, take any one page of reading material and see how many times the following words appear, none of which is entirely phonetic: *the, you, were, was, to, where, gone, come, who, they, does, from.* In fact, it is difficult to find many sentences in which every word is phonetic. This does not mean that phonics is not useful in reading, nor does it mean that the letter names should not be taught and eventually the alphabet in its proper order. It does mean that children need other word recognition techniques along with phonics. It does mean that time and patience are required to help children struggle with the letter-sound inconsistencies of our language. And so our alphabet is the second facet in our scheme of reading.

Words

To accomplish speech and reading, letters are grouped together into words to convey meaning. As we have seen, these words have been adopted from many languages and many cultures. To those thus acquired we are adding, daily, terms used in new discoveries, industrial developments, stage, screen, radio or television jargon, and teen-age lingo. There are over 500,000 words in the *Webster's New International Dictionary,* and a great many new words have come into common usage since its publication. No one could ever hope to know the meanings of all the words of our own language in our most commonly used dictionaries, much less all the words used in specialized fields such as medicine and law that have their own special dictionaries. It has been estimated that the average adult has an understanding of about 35,000 words but uses only about 5,000 in speaking. Many of these are used so infrequently that when a list of the most commonly used English words was made for foreigners who were attempting to learn English the list was cut down to 850 words. Even that minimum number could never be memorized without some clues. But along with the great number of words that we have in our language is the additional problem of many words having multiple meanings. The common word *run* has dozens of meanings. Look it up in a dictionary and you will be surprised. *Foot, can, yard, dance,* and *paper* call up various meanings in different situations. There are also words that have almost no meaning unto themselves. *A, the, very, among, toward,* and *through* are examples of words we expect to be followed by other words to give us a mental image. We modify meaning, we use shades of meaning— we sometimes even mean the opposite of what certain words appear to designate. We use poetic expression in which some words are omitted or implied. We use dialect and vulgarities to indicate the natural speech of characters in stories. Slang words are numerous and seem to be on the increase. But think of how many contextual meanings a single word like *form* may have. Add to that the number of meanings a word like *maybe* can have to a child if the mother grumbles, smiles, shouts, or is indifferent as she says it. Think of what his association with the word is likely to be when he reads it. People are never the same from day to day or even from time to time. Think of the meanings that the stamping of a foot, the raising of an eyebrow, the pointing of a finger, the set of the jaw, the clenching of a fist, or the fire in a person's eyes can add to words that are spoken. Words are magical, mysterious, amusing, revealing, and puzzling. Because the element of expression is lacking, it is more difficult to obtain an intended meaning from print than it is from speech.

Some educators introduce reading to the child through the word approach. A sight vocabulary is the initial goal. Series of readers have been built on this plan. Everyone would agree that children must eventually recognize printed words, but it is "when" and "how" that causes disagreement among educators. And so words are a third facet of our scheme of reading.

Sentences

In our scheme of writing, words are grouped together into sentences. to convey intended meanings. Because a word alone often fails to give adequate meaning, a scheme of grouping words to expand, qualify, describe, and clarify has come into use.

Punctuation marks assist in giving the sentence clarification. These markings assist in the use of pause and expression one would use if he were talking, and the reading material takes on a "written talk" significance.

Punctuation, literally "putting in points," has nothing like the orderly history which characterizes the alphabet. Early writing had no punctuation, not even in the sense that a space between words is punctuation: everythingwaswrittensolidandwassomewhathardertodeciperthanthiswouldbe. Some early languages used symbols resembling our punctuation marks as a part of the letter (they are still so used in Arabic and a number of related alphabets), and some early languages used no character at all for the vowel but only a mark which would look to us like a mark of punctuation. . . . Not until printing became widespread did punctuation approach anything like standard use; we have mainly the printers to thank for our modern system of punctuation.[8]

Even with the assistance of punctuation, we can have as many as eight meanings in a grouping of words:

SALLY is the stupid girl.	(Not Carol.)
Sally is the stupid GIRL.	(There may be boys more stupid.)
Sally is the STUPID girl.	(As opposed to clever or brilliant.)
Sally IS the stupid girl.	(There's no doubt about it.)
Sally is THE stupid girl.	(No one else could be as stupid.)

[8] Laird, *op. cit.*, pp. 178–79.

Sally is the stupid girl!	(I would never have thought it.)
Sally is the STUPID girl?	(She may be other things but I didn't think she was stupid.)
SALLY is the stupid girl?	(You must mean someone else.)

We have statements, declarations, questions, demands, assertions, and doubts expressed in mere sentences. It is the use of intonation, pause, and emphasis that adds to meaning and it must all be learned as a part of speaking and reading.

Because the sentence is a very common unit of thought, some educators would introduce reading through sentences composed by the children themselves. This has been commonly known as the language or writing approach. Others would introduce sentences written for children. Their argument is that most reading is for the purpose of getting the thoughts of someone else. Many series of readers are based on the sentence approach. Thus, sentences are a fourth facet of our scheme of reading.

Paragraphs

Many times a lone sentence is not enough to communicate much meaning. A sentence such as "The well was very deep" might bring to mind a variety of associations: To a child in the Midwest it would no doubt call to mind a water well with a windmill, a manual pump with a long handle or an electric pump attached to it drawing up water for family and livestock use. In Texas it might mean an oil well with a derrick over it or with a pump and pipes leading to a storage tank. In California it might mean an oil well out in the ocean with pumps along the shore. Some readers could reflect on the size of bore, the type of casing, and the likely amount of flow from certain types of wells, while other readers would depend largely on illustrations or other sentences within a paragraph to give it definite meaning. Therefore, some educators would start reading with a so-called whole approach wherein a child is first exposed to a meaningful paragraph or story that is eventually broken down into sentences, phrases, words, and letters. Whether we start with the smallest components and move toward the whole, or whether we start with the whole and break it into related parts, children must in time come to know all that goes into this complicated reading process. Thus, paragraphs may be considered a fifth facet of reading.

Format, Design, and Style

As adults we have been reading for so long that we scarcely remember when we became aware that in reading we move our glance from symbol to symbol and word to word or groupings of words along the line, from left to right, and from the end of one line to the beginning of the next and from the top of the page downward. (It it always interesting to children to know that Chinese children do not read in the same way.) At some time we learned that an indentation marked the beginning of a new paragraph. We learned the significance of titles, captions, an index, a glossary, a table of contents. We might refer to these as the *mechanics of reading*.

Certain areas of the curriculum have not only a vocabulary that is unique to that subject but also a syntax, a jargon, a structure, idioms, or cadence that need to be taught or brought to the level of awareness.

Arithmetic might be much easier for some children if a teacher took enough time to familiarize children with the relationship of such words as *addition* and *plus, sum, total, altogether, combined, addends; subtraction* and *difference, more or less than, subtrahend, minuend; multiplication* and *product, multiplicand, multiplier, if one costs* ———— how much will ———— *cost; division and quotient, dividend, divisor, if* ———— *cost* ———— *how much would one cost.* Certain words and combinations of words are direct clues as to what arithmetic process is required. Such help can pay big dividends to children as they move into the solution of story problems. (See Appendix H for helpful teaching devices.)

Many children also need help in knowing that words are sometimes omitted in music or poetry to maintain rhythmic quality. We cannot always "anticipate" consecutive words in poetry and song as we often do in prose. A sense of rhythm in words helps greatly in the reading of poetry and music, and often children catch on rather quickly if a teacher spends a little time introducing it.

Reading history is another area where a little teacher help can give students great assistance. Some historians depict history as a series of trends; others write it by making comparisons or contrasts. Sometimes history is written as a collection of historical facts. There are often wide gaps where facts are missing. Sometimes these facts are stated as if the author had been an eyewitness, but always they are facts. Then there is the approach where the author makes inferences from known facts and expands them in such a way as to reconstruct a pageantry, a period, or a lifetime, as with the life of King Arthur. History is sometimes compressed as in a time capsule; only selected significant events and documents are used and these may be summarized. Fifth- and sixth-grade children can be stimulated to want to delve into the exploration of examples of such an analysis after it has been explained to them. Each subject area has unique features that elicit analysis and exploration. John Jarolimek has written an excellent chapter entitled "Reading Social Studies Material,"[9] which is the kind of help teachers should have in all the content fields.

Just as there are recognizable formats in the various curriculum areas, there is also format in various types of literature. To know "about" literature can make it more comprehensible, more interesting, and more enjoyable as well as easier to read. Helping students to analyze an author's style of writing helps greatly in understanding the works and ultimately in appreciating and enjoying them. There is some danger, however, in carrying analysis too far. It could become boring. Analysis is not an end in itself but a means of achieving better understanding.

All such teaching can begin with its simplest form in the primary grades if teachers are alert to the hurdles children are about to encounter. In reading poetry to children, a teacher can help children to hear and understand the rhyming quality of words and to be able to say rhyming words long before they see them in print. The melodic quality of poetry can be experienced and understood without rhyming words. So too can certain poetic expressions be pointed out as they are enjoyed orally. The facility of reading comes much more easily when preceded by oral experiences in poetic design.

Children can be helped to *live* stories as they are told. They readily *become the characters* and *experience the events*. They become aware of the *who, what, when, where and why* within stories. The formats of stories need to be experienced before they are talked about. Then the discussion creates an awareness that assists in making reading more meaningful. Various authors have unique styles of writing. There is much evidence of this in the wide range

9 John Jarolimek, *Social Studies in Elementary Education*. New York: Macmillan, 1967, pp. 172–194.

A well-told or well-read story goes to the very heart of the listener, and what he retains may help to shape the destiny of the world of tomorrow. (Photograph courtesy of the Detroit Public Schools.)

of delightful books to read to children at each age level and they encompass many interests. (See Appendix O.) These concepts are all new to children and there must be a time and place for them to be a part of reading. Thus, format, design, and style comprise the sixth facet of reading.

Relation of the Process to the Person

A background of experience is necessary for any recognition of symbols. Consider the city child who reads the following: *It was milking time. The dog drove the cows down the dusty lane and into the barn. The farmer secured each stanchion. The new farm hand came in with a stool and bucket. "Don't sit on the wrong side of the cow," warned the farmer.* A city child might be able to decipher every word. He might be able to read the passage aloud quite eloquently. He might associate a stool with a bar stool or a step ladder kitchen stool. There is a great possibility that he would have no idea what a stanchion looks like. He might not know what a "farm hand" is although he can decipher the words quickly. Only a farm child might chuckle at what would be likely to happen to an inexperienced milker who attempted to milk from the left side if the cow had always been milked from the right side. If some city children were asked to draw a picture after reading such a short paragraph the results would be enlightening.

The above example presents a strong argument against teaching three- and four-year-olds to read. Consider how their limited backgrounds of experience would limit the meaning of what they read. Think about how few purposes reading could serve in their young lives. (Following chapters will throw more light on this subject.)

Even at the adult level we do not always comprehend all that an author has put on every page. For example, take this isolated statement:

From observations of animal behavior Lorenz postulated the innate or endogenous production of what he had called "action-specific energy."[10]

A young student teacher may pronounce every word correctly and know the meaning of each individual word (before or after using the dictionary), but the statement might still have very limited significance to him. On the other hand, an advanced student or worker in the field of pediatric psychiatry or in the field of animal behavior might call to mind immediately the work of Lorenz and know what he means by "action-specific energy." Sometimes dictionary definitions are not enough to help us gain adequate understanding. It takes broad experience and extensive reading to gain the fund of knowledge necessary to relate to such a statement. Reading can be a matter of expanding meaning at a highly professional or technical level.

We cannot always expect readers to have all the background they might need for complete understanding. There is challenge in exposing ourselves to some material that forces us to use the dictionary, atlas, globe, encyclopedia, and other references. In such cases pictorial or graphic illustrations may be an important part of the reference. Children, too, like to be challenged at times to higher and higher

[10] William Cruickshank, *The Teacher of Brain-Injured Children.* Syracuse, N.Y.: Syracuse University Press, 1966, p. 274.

levels of reading. If interest in the subject is great enough, golden opportunities are afforded to make reference books significant.

Any consideration of background of experience must include the reader's common use of language. A very large segment of our population has a background of vocabulary, sentence structure, and syntax that is very different from the middle and upper class usage, phraseology, and sentence structure used in most printed matter. Listen to some common bits of conversation of children as they leave a school in a deprived area.

"I gotta git goin'. Gonna peddle sale bills. Wanna come along? Yu c'n sit on the han'l bars an' hol' the bills if ya wanna."
"Naw! I'm gonna go swimmun."
"Hey, whadja git on that quiz? If it weren't fer one, Ida gotem all wrong."
"Where'dya put yer ball 'n bat? C'n I use ut?"

The questions among educators are: How can these children be helped to change their speech patterns? Should standards of English be lowered in education for these children? How can these children be expected to hear sounds in words when the words they use are different from those of standard English?

Just how the gap between slovenly English, or dialects of English, and the generally accepted printed form can be filled is a matter of concern to many educators.

Many times readers take from the printed page only what they want to take. A reader's convictions may be so strong that he will absorb only the material that supports his biases. In the case of young children, however, they are more likely to accept as fact anything that is read unless teachers and parents help them to challenge, to verify, and to ascertain authenticity. The highly competitive field of advertising, with millions of dollars being spent on inducing people to buy, makes the need for critical reading imperative.

Some readers may read page after page and not recall a single fact or incident after the book is closed; others may recall a fact or personality years later and know exactly the book from which it came. Teachers need to know children and materials well enough to determine how to make the most of challenging reading situations.

Thus, the seventh and final facet in the scheme of reading is the relationship of the process to the person, or reading to the reader.

Although our language is extremely difficult to read, and there are many language and personality complications, there are facts to prove that most children learn to read easily and well, despite publicity to the contrary.

> *The English language has been proliferating around the planet at a dizzying tempo since World War II. It has become in effect an international language. . . . The future of mankind may depend on a consensus of thought that can only be achieved by a precise use of English words and a reciprocal comprehension of what they mean. . . . The mechanical media of communication have evolved at a rate which presages the day, not far off, when nations will be able to transmit live television programs daily over the poles and across the seas. If the electronic highways of the air are to serve any useful purpose, however, the content of their signals, the ideas they transmit at the velocity of light, must be garbed in lucid and felicitous language. If English is allowed to degenerate into a babel of regional dialects, social stratifications, vulgarities, jargon, and juvenile slang, the hope of true understanding among the millions of English-speaking people around the earth is commensurately dimmed. In the health of the English language, the health of Western civilization may well reside.*
>
> *. . . Quintilian set a standard for precision of language when he declared: "One should not aim at being possible to understand, but at being impossible to misunderstand." And more than five centuries earlier the great Chinese philosopher-statesman Confucius expressed his views on the relationship between language and government. Asked what he should undertake to do first, Confucius replied: "To correct language. . . . If language is not correct, then what is said is not what is meant; if what is said is not what is meant, then what ought to be done remains undone; if this remains undone, morals and art will deteriorate; if morals and art deteriorate, justice will go astray; if justice goes astray, the people will stand about in helpless confusion. Hence there must be no arbitrariness in what is said. This matters above everything."*[11]

Suggestions for Class Participation and Discussion

1. What do you consider the most difficult facet of reading? Why?
2. Select five very commonly used words from any page in any book. Look up their derivation in the dictionary. Share them in class. Total the class findings. What percentage are of Anglo-Saxon derivation?
3. Do you think any drastic language or writing changes will come about in your lifetime? How could change come about? What would be the deterring factors?

[11] Lincoln Barnett, *The Treasure of Our Tongue*. New York: Alfred Knopf, 1964, pp. 293–294.

4. Do you think books should be written in regional dialects? Why or why not?
5. Is our system of punctuation adequate? Could you suggest any additional markings that would aid in conveying meaning?
6. Read any of the references on language and share some significant information.
7. Why is reading so closely associated with listening, speaking, and writing?
8. Can you recall the facets of reading and explain them?
9. Do you think that learning the names of the letters of the alphabet would be very helpful in learning to read?
10. What significance does the quotation at the end of the chapter have?

Suggestions for Term Projects

NURSERY, KINDERGARTEN, HEAD-START, AND FOLLOW-THROUGH PROGRAMS

1. Prepare a file of large pictures for oral language discussion. Be sure the details are not too small. Your file should include:

seasonal pictures	home and family pictures
holiday pictures	play-time pictures
activity pictures	concept expansion
health pictures	story starters
animal pictures	transportation
food pictures	work pictures

Clip on each picture a statement of your ideas for its use. Some suggestions for sources of pictures are *Sources of Free and Inexpensive Materials*; calendar publishing companies; magazines such as *Woman's Day* that offer cover pictures at a nominal cost; advertisements such as those for cat foods and baby foods sometimes offer enlargements of good pictures.

2. Explore the various kindergarten activity books, courses of study, readiness manuals, and kindergarten logs, and prepare a file of ideas and materials to enrich a reading readiness program.

3. Prepare story-telling accessories such as hand puppets, flannel board figures, and any others that would be appropriate for stories you intend to use with young children. (First-grade teachers, too, may choose this project.)

FIRST-, SECOND-, AND THIRD-GRADE TEACHERS

1. Select from the various teachers' manuals, logs, and bulletins practical suggestions pertaining to the development of the reading skills appropriate to your grade level. Prepare a card file of these ideas.

2. If you do not take a special course in children's literature, prepare a list of stories, picture books, and poems you intend to use at the grade level you will be teaching. The poems should be written on cards and filed under such headings as Weather, Fall, Halloween, Thanksgiving, Christmas, Easter, Spring, etc.

3. Read and summarize current magazine articles pertinent to topics in the eight chapters of this book most related to your teaching.

Fourth-, Fifth-, and Sixth-Grade Teachers

1. Browse through books on remedial reading, teachers' manuals, etc., and prepare a card file of ideas for practical ways of helping children who are behind grade level in reading.

2. Read and summarize eight articles from books of readings on the teaching of reading or language arts. (Choose articles that pertain most directly to your grade level.)

3. Prepare a large "Circle of Reading" chart and put in it the various interest areas appropriate for your grade. As you use it later with children allow them to place their initials in each area as they complete the reading of a book that fits the category. Prepare a list of books appropriate to each category at the reading level of your grade.

4. Collect materials for a unit on language or the newspaper. Prepare a bibliography of books children could read on the chosen topic.

Bibliography

ADAMS, J. DONALD. *The Magic and Mystery of Words.* New York: Holt, Rinehart & Winston, 1963.

ALEXANDER, HENRY. *The Story of Our Language.* Garden City, N.Y.: Dolphin Books, Doubleday, 1962.

BARBER, CHARLES L. *The Story of Speech and Language.* New York: Crowell, 1965.

BARNETT, LINCOLN. *The Treasure of Our Tongue.* New York: Knopf, 1964.

BAUGH, ALBERT C. *A History of the English Language.* New York: Appleton-Century-Crofts, 1957.

BERNSTEIN, THEODORE. *More Language that Needs Watching.* Great Neck, N.Y.: Channel Press, 1962.

———. *Watch Your Language.* Great Neck, N.Y.: Channel Press, 1958.

BLACK, MAX. *The Importance of Language.* Englewood Cliffs, N.J.: Prentice-Hall, 1962.

BODMER, F., and HOGBEN, LANCELOT. *The Loom of Language.* New York: Norton, 1944.

BRYANT, MARGARET. *Modern English and Its Heritage.* New York: Macmillan, 1948.

CARROLL, JOHN. *The Study of Language*. Cambridge, Mass.: Harvard University Press, 1959.

———. *Language and Thought*. Englewood, N.J.: Prentice-Hall, 1964.

CHASE, STUART. *Power of Words*. New York: Harcourt, Brace, 1954.

CHERRY, COLIN. *On Human Communication*. New York: Wiley, 1961.

DIAMOND, A. S. *The History and Origin of Language*. New York: Philosophical Society, 1959.

EPSTEIN, SAM. *The First Book of Words*. New York: Watts, 1954.

ERNST, MARGARET S. *Words* (1950); *In a Word* (1960); *More About Words* (1961). New York: Knopf. (These three books are simple enough for children in Grades 4 to 6 to read.)

FOLSOM, FRANKLIN. *The Language Book*. New York: Grosset & Dunlap, 1963.

FRAENKEL, GERD. *What Is Language?* New York: Ginn, 1965.

FUNK, CHARLES E. *Thereby Hangs a Tale*. New York: Harper, 1950.

FUNK, WILFRED. *Word Origins*. New York: Harper, 1950.

GARRISON, WEB B. *What's in a Word*. New York: Abbingdon Press, 1965.

GIBSON, WALKER. *The Limits of Language*. New York: American Century Series, Hill & Wang, 1962.

HAYAKAWA, S. I. *The Use and Misuse of Language*. Greenwich, Conn.: Fawcett, 1962.

HYMES, D. H. (ed.). *Language in Culture and Society: A Reader in Linguistics and Anthropology*. New York: Harper, 1964.

JESPERSEN, OTTO. *Growth and Structure of the English Language,* 9th ed. New York: Macmillan, 1948.

LAIRD, CHARLTON. *The Miracle of Language*. New York: Fawcett World Library, 1958.

LARSEN, ROY. *Communication and Education*. Boston: Boston University Press, 1960.

MARCHWARDT, ALBERT. *American English*. New York: Oxford University Press, 1958.

PEI, MARIO. *Language for Everybody*. New York: Pocket Books, Inc., 1960.

———. *The Voices of Man: The Meanings and Function of Language*. New York: Harper & Row, 1962.

SAPORTA, S. (ed.). *Psycholinguistics, A Book of Readings*. New York: Holt, Rinehart & Winston, 1961.

WYLD, HENRY. *A History of Modern Colloquial English,* 3rd ed. New York: Barnes & Noble, 1953.

CHAPTER 3
The Teacher
of Reading

Teachers Are Many Things to Many Children

A teacher is dedicated as a clergyman, selfless as a family doctor, sensitive as an artist, skillful as a master craftsman, ready as a good parent to understand, to sacrifice, to serve, to support, to forgive.

A teacher is committed to the faith that, while no child is exactly like another, for each the level of achievement can be raised, aspirations stirred, potential talents discovered and developed. A teacher is bound in conscience to help each child find his own worth, his own dignity.[1]

The twenty-one research studies conducted by the International Reading Association, started in 1965 and reported by Professor Guy Bond at the Dallas Reading Convention of IRA in the spring of 1966, concluded at that time that the greatest determining factor in the success of any reading program is the teacher. They found that outstanding achievement in each controlled method group was directly attributable to an able teacher. Teachers everywhere have tremendous responsibilities, opportunities, and challenges.

[1] Aleda E. Druding, *Improving English Skills of Culturally Different Youth.* Supt. of Documents, U.S. Govt. Printing Office, 1964.

Children enter school with their own individual expectations of what the teacher should be. These preconceptions are amalgamations of what their parents have been and what their parents and others have said teachers would be. Some children will be ready to offer their hands to feel the tactile warmth of a new mother substitute. Others will remain aloof or shy away from any close contact with this new symbol of authority.

Some children come expecting the teacher to do everything for them: tie their shoes, zip their jackets, open their milk cartons, put bobby pins back in their hair, and do countless other things an overly solicitous mother does for an only child. Others may be eager to show the teacher how much they can do for themselves. This is an opportunity for the teacher to give praise for "doing" in order to establish the respectability and expectation of self help.

Some children will come with a merry twinkle in their eyes, looking for an opportunity to see how far they can go with teasing antics before a voice of authority will intervene, and wondering what form the intervention will take. Other children may be anxious to show the teacher how well they can do what she asks them to do. They may sit spellbound with fright if harsh words or a stern manner suddenly alter the otherwise pleasant countenance of the teacher. They go home and tell about the "naughty" children who made the teacher angry.

Mostly, each child is waiting to see what the teacher interaction with him will be. It is the self image that must be enhanced through acceptance by the teacher. Each child will go home with a definite "feeling" toward the teacher, and sometimes first impressions are very lasting.

Teacher Guidelines

With twenty-five or more (sometimes many more) children suddenly descending upon her, a teacher has no easy task in meeting the expectations of every child. However, there are certain guidelines that may help.

HELP EVERY CHILD FEEL ACCEPTED

Teachers have heard this statement over and over again in various education courses, but seldom do they get specific answers when they question how this can be done. Perhaps some of the answers children have given when asked, "Do you think your teacher likes you?", will offer some clues:

"She knew my name right away."
"She smiles at me real often."
"She lets me help her."
"She even lets me help some of the other kids."
"She said so. She said she liked the way I rested and how I do my work."
"She talks to me and makes me feel grown up."
"Sure. And I like her a lot!"
"Of course, she does."
"She said I was a good worker and she likes good workers."
"Sure, cuz I'm good."
"I don't know. She never said."
"I think so. I get a good report card."
"Naw, I'm not as smart as the other kids."
"Not very good. I goof off too much."
"Sometimes, but not always."
"I guess so. She wouldn't be a teacher if she didn't like us kids. She could of got married."
"I don't know, but I'll ask her tomorrow."

These are a few of the several hundred responses we recorded over a period of time in several different school systems. Many children responded with a mere, "Sure," "I don't know," or "I think so," without any further comment, even though they may have been asked, "Why?" Most of the negative responses were related to misbehavior, poor work, or lack of ability. Perhaps teachers are a little too reserved in letting children know that they are liked.

It is a challenge to teachers to help children do their best, to accept ability limitations, to encourage desirable behavior without appearing to reject the child completely for misbehavior. There are delicate situations in which only a skillful teacher can stifle undesirable behavior and yet maintain the confidence of children that they are liked. It must be said and repeated that it is misbehavior, careless work, and laziness that a teacher really dislikes and not the child himself. The teacher must reassure the child that she knows and he knows that his behavior and effort can be worthy of praise whenever he wants them to be. This will be interpreted through the succeeding guidelines.

HELP EVERY CHILD TO SUCCEED AND TO FEEL THE THRILL OF SUCCESS

Goals must be set with the child and in accordance with his potentialities. Evaluation can only be made in accordance with his capabilities. In order to like going to school, to like any activity, a child must have successes. For a teacher to rejoice with the child in such successes is to afford him the best kind of motivation to set new goals and to work because he wants to work to achieve them. In practice this philosophy would work as follows:

If your class happens to be working on difficult vocabulary, after presenting each word carefully and giving the group as many clues to remembering the various words as possible and after conducting group drill and word games, you might say, "I've put these rather difficult words on flash cards that you may use individually. Jim, how many do you think you could learn in the next three days? You may take them home and you may work with other children in our class during free moments." A teacher sometimes needs to give a little guidance with regard to how many words a child can reasonably learn in the three days. When such challenges are made be sure to follow through on checking so the child has the satisfaction of evaluating his own progress. Express sincere pleasure with each accomplishment so that the child will want to repeat the process again sometime. Let him keep an individual chart to record his progress and be stimulated by it. Many other examples of setting individual goals, challenging, and evaluating will be given in subsequent chapters.

INSPIRE CHILDREN TO WANT TO LEARN

More tributes are paid to honored teachers for the quality of inspiration than for any other. A teacher who can assess potentialities of a child, determine his interests, and help him to aspire toward ever broader and more far-reaching goals is deserving of the highest honors. To cause a child to want to know, to want to be healthy, to want to be a worthy citizen, and to want to become all he is capable of becoming with dignity and honor is the essence of inspiration.

A fifth-grade teacher tells this story of a reluctant reader. An over-age boy in her class was not the least bit interested in reading from any of the books the room had to offer, and he was reluctant to pay any attention to the various types of reading instruction. The teacher observed that the boy was an avid baseball fan. He played on a boys' team and seemed to know much about major league baseball. The teacher secured much baseball information from a new paperback fact book and printed it on tagboard. She inspired the boy to want to read this interesting information to the class for a sharing period. She worked with him independently and was surprised at how some of the difficult words caused him no trouble at all. The teacher and the children appreciated what he contributed—spontaneously and sincerely. He was immediately eager for more baseball "stuff," as he called it. He was as pleased as she was with his accomplishment, and the search went on for more baseball information and baseball stories. Soon he was ready to try other subject materials, and his flight into reading was launched.

Other children have been inspired through animal stories, hero stories, mystery stories, and adventure tales. Sometimes these readings need to be simplified and adjusted to a level easy enough to make a good beginning.

BE FAIR

Most teachers in their own estimation are very fair. When a teacher is criticized for unfairness it is usually because she has been misunderstood. Frequently there is just cause for a teacher to make exceptions to rules, to expect more of one child than another, to grant special privileges, to show special attention. But the justification must be made clear to the children. If reasons are given, most children will respect the teacher even more because of her consideration. Children come to know that they, too, will be helped in accordance with special needs if an occasion arises.

Sometimes one child is given special help with work that other children are expected to do independently. Honest explanations can satisfy children and cause them to have greater respect for the teacher. Some children need more encouragement than others, some need repeated help with skills, some need stimulation in selecting a book to read independently, but all need recognition for their efforts. A teacher's expression of appreciation for initiative, appreciation for hard work, appreciation for achievement will help children to feel that "she's fair," regardless of the unequal distribution of her help. When a teacher senses that there is dissatisfaction among children in a class, it is a good idea to get the resentment out into the open and find out how the children feel and why. When both sides of the problem are presented there can nearly always be satisfactory conclusions. There must be free and easy avenues of communication between teachers and children to prevent bottled-up resentment.

Be Pleasant and Understanding

Often a reassuring smile can bolster a child's confidence in his attempts. Laughing with children when something really funny happens and chuckling with them as they enjoy the funny parts of stories strengthens children's ties with a teacher. Saving firmness for situations when it is required makes the firmness much more effective than when it is the teacher's usual countenance. Firmness on occasion is expected by children. The teacher is an adult and is expected to establish certain standards and to maintain them. Children know when they regress in their actions and they have respect for the teacher who expects the best in what they do. They want her to be consistent or else to know the reason for her inconsistency. Special warmth and understanding when children have experienced illness, defeat, or sorrow will always warrant the love and respect of both children and parents.

A certain teacher will never forget the agonizing week-end she spent wondering how to meet the situation of a first-grade child who was returning to school after learning that his father had been killed overseas. Monday came and the teacher was at the door with her customary smile and greeting when the child came up to her and gave her the tightest hug she had ever experienced. Words sometimes fail, but support and understanding are *felt*. Often a pat on the shoulder or a "Go ahead, I know you can do it" are what the discouraged child needs.

Every teacher should read *Dibs* by Virginia Axline. It gives the full impact of what an understanding person can do for a child who needs to be accepted and needs to know and accept himself. A friendly greeting and a personal inquiry when children arrive in the morning can start the day right for many children. Pleasant remarks to each individual child as he gets ready to go home and a warm "Good-by" keep the relationships warm and friendly.

Fourth-, fifth-, and sixth-grade children have the same appreciation for pleasantness and understanding, but it must be expressed in different ways. They want to be accepted in an adult relationship. No more sweetness or evidence of closeness between teacher and student—no, indeed! The peer relationship is such that among themselves they might say, "How about that new teacher? She's cool," or "A little bit of all right." There is always the precaution taken so as not to be looked upon as a "teacher's pet," and reference to school often takes on a negative aspect as do home associations. Respect is what children of this age really want. Showing interest in their fads and fancies and accepting their fluctuations between childhood and adolescence by tactful guidance in worthwhile reading materials and stimulating discussions can win their confidence and establish good rapport. Children of this age are not as interested in liking their teacher as in having a teacher they can "be like." It is what the teacher is, does, and knows that is important.

BE CAUTIOUS DETECTORS

Teachers are not qualified to diagnose illness, instability, or serious maladjustments. However, a teacher is in the best position to observe when such conditions exist. To detect an illness at the earliest possible stage, to report evidences of instability and seek out proper channels for securing help, to note impairments or malfunctions and refer them for clinical diagnosis and recommendations is to afford the child a very great service. It also protects the other children and saves valuable time for both the teacher and the afflicted child. A teacher should almost never make a diagnosis—leave it to those who are qualified. In the case of illnesses, it is important to remove the child from the group, secure the services of the school nurse, or call the parents to come and get the child. It is never wise to send an ill child home by himself. Be sure a parent is home and then send an older responsible child with the one who is ill if the sick child lives near the school and the parent cannot come for him. Sometimes a principal or nurse will take the child home. In cases of instability, it is best to consult the school psychologist, counselor, or visiting teacher and report all the symptomatic details you can gather. Problems of sight or hearing should be reported as soon as they are detected. A child who does not make the progress that a teacher considers him capable of making should be referred to a learning clinic as soon as symptoms of retardation can be assembled. Early diagnosis can often prevent failures, disinterest, and wasted time.

Have Broad Interests

Only as children's interests are created, stimulated, and broadened can reading have any great significance. Teachers can lead children into more and more paths of exploration as reading ability is developed. Here, a teacher's personal experiences—as a child in another part of the country—in travel, in reading, and in contacts with interesting people can enthrall fourth-, fifth-, and sixth-graders and open doors to new reading interests. It is the rich content of reading, sought after as curiosity is generated, that keeps children wanting to know more about the reading process. A teacher who can make nature a subject of endless wonder, who can introduce good literature with such a depth of appreciation that no one could help but want more and more of it, who can open the world of science to children with such fascination that they will eagerly devour more material on the subject with each new day, is giving to the child a lifetime of reading enjoyment, reading enrichment, and vital interest in improving his skills.

Teachers of students at fifth- and sixth-grade levels are dealing with a very sensitive group of individuals. Ideals are being established and the moral fiber of the oncoming generation is gaining its strength at this age. What kind of a person the teacher is, what beliefs she has (men teachers at this age level are especially effective), and what interests she reveals are scrutinized by each child every day. This is the age of heroes, stars, idols, and martyrs. Popular is the teacher who will play baseball and find good baseball stories, who will discuss camping, traveling, golfing, fishing, and hiking, and bring in books, travel folders, pamphlets, and brochures to nurture those interests. Good literature probably has more effect on the development of human values at this stage than at any other. Teachers have a tremendous responsibility not only to provide literature that will help children establish good values, develop the skills to read it easily but also to cause the reading of good literature to become a lifetime interest. Teachers who sincerely enjoy working with children and are familiar with their scope of interests, as well as having their own adult range of interests, will have no problem helping children to want to read and to see how each new skill that is introduced will help them to read more easily.

RELATING TO CHILDREN

To know and understand child development is not enough. A teacher must be able to "get behind the curtain of every child." To do this one must establish a rapport that elicits a child's confidence. The child's trust must be so well grounded that he dares to be himself, to speak freely, to bare his doubts and fears, and to know that there is someone who is a refuge, a resource, a guide, and a support. A teacher must see problems, conflicts, and challenges of daily living through the thoughts and feelings of the child. These feelings are present every day in the classroom and the teacher must develop a sensitivity to their symptoms. It takes considerable effort, a bit more time, and a keen awareness, but once the teacher has mastered the art of "getting behind the curtain" of each child there is a bond of affection and mutual understanding that establishes the kind of confidence in the teacher that will cause a child to want to please, to want to aspire, and to want to succeed. It is here that a carefully chosen book, in which the child can relate himself to another child also facing problems, can give him courage and confidence to face life courageously.

We must be very careful to avoid embarrassing a child. His home, his family, his friends are *his*. There is a loyalty and a sensitivity involved with regard to these things. If there is to be a striving toward something better it must come from within him and he must "feel right" about it. The teacher must accept and respect. New goals and new aspirations must come from within his feeling of wholeness and from within his loyalty structure.

A teacher works with children from all classes of society. She must remember that the values reflected in many of these children are not necessarily her own. A teacher's age, her cultural background, her total income, and her understanding of society as a whole influence the meaning she attaches to such terms as *a well-rounded student, moral and spiritual values, good literature, average income, a good diet, good living,* and *general well being.* It is difficult for many middle-class teachers to understand what goes on behind the walls of low-income or relief-family homes on a day-after-day basis. The principals of schools within such areas should schedule an experienced visiting teacher or relief worker who is familiar with the homes in the area, to give all teachers a detailed picture of the homes from which many of the school children come. Teachers cannot be cognizant of the needs of children unless they have such information. Such meetings also help teachers to know what personnel in the school and community can give help when it is needed.

Albert Rogers is an indefatigable shoeshine boy at a New York hotel whose rhythmic artistry with polish and brush leaves a shine that almost hurts your eyes. "Don't you ever get tired?" I once asked him. "No," he said. "But I would if I just shined shoes."

Albert has something in common with Will Edgers, a Vermont farmer who sells firewood. Some friends ordered half a cord last fall while we were visiting them. Will didn't just dump the wood from his truck. He made a small platform of stones, then carefully stacked the wood at a slant to keep rain water from standing on it. Then he surveyed his handiwork and said quietly, "Wood's a pretty thing now, ain't it? Growin', split or burnin'."

Albert and Will, each in his own way, have discovered a compelling secret that makes anything they do pay off in terms of greater satisfaction, deeper self-realization. Pablo Casals, the world-famous cellist, put it into words while giving a lesson to a young woman student. She played the notes just as they were written. Casals played the same notes, but they throbbed and glowed. He asked the girl to repeat the passage several times, each time demonstrating the special quality he wanted her to bring to it. "Bring to it the rainbow—always the rainbow," he said. When she finally did, her face lighted up in pure joy.

The "rainbow" is the glow that crowns an all-out effort to do a job, *any kind of job,* as well as it can possibly be done. It takes a shade more effort, a bit more time, but once you have experienced the mixture of elation, pride and relief that comes from creating rainbows, life is never quite the same. You can say with honesty, "This is good. It has a part of me in it."[2]

Through reading selections of this type in school, children of all classes can be inspired to experience enjoyment and satisfaction in the commonplace things of life. There are many books and stories that help to do this.

If teachers, too, can be inspired as they work with children, and if children in turn can be inspired as they are introduced to reading, self-sustaining endeavor with unlimited fruition will result.

CONTINUOUSLY GAIN MORE KNOWLEDGE ABOUT CHILDREN AND READING

1. To understand children with regard to growth and development and its relationship to reading.

2 John Kord Lagemann, "Bring to It the Rainbow." *Reader's Digest,* Nov., 1966. (Condensed from *Christian Herald,* Nov., 1966.)

2. To understand how children perceive, generalize, think, and learn to use language effectively in preparation for reading.
3. To know how reading becomes meaningful and significant in children's lives.
4. To know the clues of word recognition and how they are developed along with the many variables.
5. To understand phonics as a clue of word recognition along with its limitations.
6. To understand linguistics as it applies to reading and throws light on the inconsistencies and variables due to the way in which our language developed.
7. To know how to help children develop the skills of silent and oral reading.
8. To know how to help children be critical, creative, and appreciative in their reading.
9. To become interested in research and means of continuous professional growth.
10. To nurture an attitude of pleasure to help children grow and know.

Much muscular, sensory, and language development is antecedent to meaningful reading, and good teachers must be aware of the continuous and interrelated aspects of these developments even as reading instruction gets underway. (They will be discussed in the next chapters.) As James Hymes, who has done so much to help teachers and parents have a better understanding of young children, has written:

A direction indicator is set. An "automatic pilot" is at the controls. And a strong motor—call it growth—is purring smoothly inside each child. The motor powers a magnificent brain, an amazing body, a full, fine range of feeling. Your good teaching greases this motor and keeps it in shape. When your youngsters like you, when they like their work, when they like themselves, the motor hums and spins.

Your job is not an easy one. You never have all the tools you need. You have far too many motors to service. There are many pages missing from the "manual of instruction," and even when the directions are there in print, they are never completely clear. Nor are any of us old hands at this way of living with children; we are all puzzling and groping for the appropriate things to do. Hecklers are on the sidelines, looking for perfection, all too willing to remind you that you are feeling your way along.

Once you truly regard the child as human—caring, seeking, preferring, needing—you have to work. You have to think, to use your judgment and your sensitivity. But the motor is running, and the course is charted. How far will the human go? How fast? For how long? With your good treatment new records are possible: of reason and decency, of kindliness, of caring. The task is well worth the effort of your hands, the time of your head, and the searching of your heart.[3]

A teacher must develop her own individuality. After a teacher has completed a teacher education program and as she continues to learn from outside opportunities, she must proceed in accordance with her own convictions, with procedures that make her feel comfortable and secure. She must be fired with enthusiasm; she will discover that children respond to the dramatic, the enticing, and the colorful far better than to spiritless presentations. She must be ingenious in achieving variety in her procedures and techniques, just as she has access to variety in the materials she uses. A change in voice intonation, a change in pace, and use of surprise and anticipation add spice to the day's work. She wants children to be eager to try, to do, to read, and yet she must achieve this calmly so that the children do not become so excited that they want to run, jump, and shout. She must help children to know that reading requires restraint and quiet. Her personality must shine through as she inspires, guides, and assists.

There are many success stories of famous people who have attested to the fact that there was a teacher back in their formative years who inspired them with ambition and fired them with enthusiasm to do what had to be done each step of the way. A teacher is remembered for what she is, what she knows, what she does, and what she causes children to do and become.

It is sometimes considered an advantage to have one teacher work with the same group of children for several years because she gets to know the children so well. This would be true if she could inspire each child and maintain the kind of interaction that would permit maximum development all along the way, but this is seldom possible because personalities vary so much. A change of teachers from year to year affords children the advantage of experiencing the fine sense of humor of one teacher, the keen scientific interests of another, the great musical ability and inspiration of another, the artistic flair of another, the tenderness of another, and the charm and dignity of still another. We have only to reflect on the great teachers

3 James L. Hymes, Jr., *A Child Development Point of View.* © 1955. Reprinted by permission of Prentice-Hall, Inc., Englewood Cliffs, New Jersey. Pp. 144–145.

we have known to say with assurance—great, every one, but each in his or her own way.

I chose teaching because:
Children are the challenge and inspiration of today and are the hope, protectors, and champions of the future. Let the bankers take care of money, physicians take care of illness, lawyers take care of entanglements —important, yes, all! But, transitory, all!

Only parents and teachers can pass on a legacy that destines what the world of tomorrow will be.

Until parenthood and teaching are given the dignity and respect they deserve we cannot hope for an improved society.

—Verna Dieckman Anderson

Suggestions for Class Participation and Discussion

1. Recall two or three of the best teachers you ever had. List five qualities that set them apart from the others and be prepared to discuss them.
2. Might a favorite teacher of one child rate very low in the estimation of another? Is this good?
3. If there is a personality conflict between a teacher and a child, what do you think should be done? Do you know of any such cases? Why would the situation be a delicate one?
4. Ask three mothers of young children what qualities they consider most important in a teacher. Share your findings.
5. Classify in order of importance five qualities you think every teacher should have.
6. Ask three children if their teacher likes them. Record their answers and discuss them in class.
7. Ask three other children if they like their teacher. Record their answers with their reasons and discuss them in class.
8. Ask several children if they think teachers are fair and why or why not. Record their answers and discuss them in class.
9. Were you surprised to read that the teacher is the greatest determining factor in the teaching of reading? How would you account for this?
10. Explain the quotation at the end of the chapter.

Bibliography

Anderson, Verna, *et al. Readings in the Language Arts.* New York: Macmillan, 1964, pp. 468–74.

Anderson, Paul S. *Language Skills in Elementary Education.* New York: Macmillan, 1964, pp. 45–48.

BAUGH, ALBERT C. *A History of the English People*. New York: Appleton-Century-Crofts, 1957.

BRADFIELD, LUTHER. *Teaching in Modern Elementary Schools*. Columbus, Ohio: Merrill, 1964.

BROUDY, HARRY S., and PALMER, J. R. *Exemplars of Teaching Method*. Chicago: Rand McNally, 1965.

COLEMAN, JOHN. *The Master Teachers and the Art of Teaching*. New York: Pitman, 1967.

COLLIER *et al.* *Teaching in the Modern Elementary School*. New York: Macmillan, 1967, pp. 113–285.

FROMM, ERICH. *Man for Himself*. New York: Rinehart, 1947.

GAGE, N. L. (ed.). *Handbook of Research on Teaching*. Chicago: Rand McNally, 1963.

HARRIS, ALBERT J. *How to Increase Reading Ability*. New York: Longmans Green, 1952.

HIGHET, GILBERT. *The Art of Teaching*. New York: Vintage Paperback, 1963.

HOPKINS, L. THOMAS. *The Emerging Self*. New York: Harper, 1954.

HUDGINS, BRYCE. *Problem Solving in the Classroom*. New York: Macmillan, 1966.

HUMPHREYS, ALICE. *Heaven in My Hand*. Richmond, Va.: John Knox, 1950.

INTERNATIONAL READING ASSOCIATION. "The Role of the Reading Specialist." *The Reading Teacher*, March, 1967. (Several articles refer to personnel qualifications.)

JAMES, WILLIAM. *Talks to Teachers*. New York: Norton, 1963.

MEEKER, ALICE M. *I Like Children*. Evanston, Ill.: Row, Peterson, 1954.

OVERSTREET, H. A. *The Mature Mind*. New York: Norton, 1949.

PARRISH, LOUISE, and WASKIN, YVONNE. *Teacher-Pupil Planning*. New York: Harper, 1958.

PETERSON, DOROTHY. *The Elementary School Teacher*. New York: Appleton-Century-Crofts, 1964.

PETERSON, WILFERD A. *The New Book of the Art of Living*. New York: Simon & Schuster, 1963.

————. *The Art of Living*. New York: Simon & Schuster, 1961.

RIESMAN, DAVID, *et al.* *The Lonely Crowd*. Garden City, N.Y.: Doubleday, 1953.

RUGG, HAROLD. *The Teacher of Teachers*. New York: Harper, 1952.

SHEPPARD, LILA. *Dancing on Desk Tops*. Evanston, Ill.: Row, Peterson, 1960.

SILBER, K. *Pestalozzi, the Man and His Work*. London: Routledge & Kegan Paul, 1960.

SIMPSON, RAY. *Teacher Self-Evaluation*. New York: Macmillan, 1966.

SMILEY, MARJORIE B., and DIFKHOFF, JOHN S. *Prologue to Teaching*. New York: Oxford University Press, 1959.

TENNEBAUM, S. *William Heard Kilpatrick: Trail Blazer in Education*. New York: Harper, 1951.

CHAPTER 4

Getting Ready
to Read (1)

Toward Growing and Knowing

(This chapter is designed primarily for parents, workers in Head-Start, Follow-Through and Teacher Corps Programs, nursery school and kindergarten teachers, and any other students who have not had a course in Child Growth and Development.)

Child Development, the field of study, has three big concerns: It looks at normal children, at well children, at the run of youngsters just as they feed out of homes into schools, churches, camps, onto the play lots and the streets. It looks at what they typically do—at what they do just because they are children.

It looks at normal children and at well children of all ages—from the very start of life in the pre-natal period, into infancy, into the pre-school years, when boys and girls are in school, into adolescence and even beyond.

And Child Development is concerned with the whole *child:*

Whole . . . up and down, from his very start to his present and with at least a peek into his future.

Whole . . . across a child's middle and back again: a head, a heart, a body, a soul; his intellectual, his social, his physical, emotional, and spiritual growth.

Whole . . . the school child, the home child, the youngster in his club; the child with brothers and sisters and friends; with his parents and his teacher and neighbors; everywhere a youngster is in a day and with everyone he meets.

Whole . . . as an individual, but also as a human tied in to the total broad circle of all people—this child, boy or girl, ten-year-old or sixteen or six, as a person, acting in many ways as all other people do act and have to act.

As a field of study Child Development borrows a little from psychology, a little from psychiatry, a little from sociology. It takes some ideas from pediatrics, and some from nutrition. Anthropology chips in some of its findings. A great many disciplines—group work, religious education, industrial relations—all give something to Child Development.[1]

One of the finest experiences an educator can have is to develop a course in Child Development with an obstetrician, a pediatrician, a psychologist, a sociologist, a medical doctor, a nutritionist, an anthropologist, and a professor from a School of Social Work. It expands your outlook in many directions, and soon you are avidly reading books in each of the fields and your whole concept of the child changes. He is no longer an individual in a classroom. He assumes a "wholeness" comprised of all that has happened before he came to the classroom, all that has happened (or has not happened) in the home and continues to happen (or not happen) in the home, community, and school. It offers a challenge and inspiration to anyone interested in giving each child the opportunities he should have.

Plan to visit a classroom when school is in session and take a long look at the children in that room. No two will be alike. Even identical twins will have their differences. In the group as a whole there will be a wide range in height, weight, coloring, cleanliness, alertness, dress, manners, speech, and behavior. These are all observable evidences of varying degrees of difference. In addition, the children vary in what they think of themselves, in their relationships with their peers and with their parents, in how they get along with their teachers, in what they value, in their aspirations, in what talents and capabilities they possess, in the opportunities they have, in the fears and frustrations they possess, in the physical strengths and weaknesses with which they must live, and in the stamina and courage they have with which to fortify themselves in their encounters.

[1] James L. Hymes, Jr., *A Child Development Point of View.* Englewood Cliffs, N.J.: Prentice-Hall, 1955, pp. 2–3.

Each of these differences may be modified by good or poor health, good or poor nutrition, good or poor home environment, good or poor interpersonal relationships, and good or poor resources. There is a wide range between the two extremes of good and poor and a difference among individuals as to what they can tolerate. The older the group of children, the wider will be the range of differences and the more pronounced the problems are likely to be. To add to the complications of problems is the fact that some children are able to cope with a succession of difficulties and overcome almost overwhelming handicaps, while certain others show defeat through a wide range of undesirable behavior when even mild obstacles come into their lives.

Individual Differences

THE BASIC CAUSES OF DIFFERENCES

To gain an understanding of the more subtle causes of differences one must start with the very beginnings of the human organism. Four factors are basic to certain human differences:

GENETIC   The complexity of the combinations of genes in human reproduction is difficult to probe. It is generally known that certain characteristics, certain limitations, and certain tendencies are inherited. To what extent a favorable environment can prevent negative tendencies from developing and can foster positive tendencies to full development, and, on the other hand, to what extent an unfavorable environment might affect either case have been and still are vast areas for research.

PRENATAL   Much study is going on as to the influence of outside effects on the developing fetus during pregnancy. It is known that certain drugs can interfere with growth and cause malformations. It is known that a pregnant woman who is a drug addict will give birth to an addicted infant. The wide range of food influences is still being explored. In addition to body chemstry influences, there is a vast realm of emotional influences that is under scrutiny. Studies are being made about possible effects of depression and anxiety on the part of the mother as they relate to the unborn child.

Enough is known about good nutrition and prenatal check-ups to be reasonably sure of healthy children if mothers are willing to seek proper medical care and guidance.

Today, with the expert advice of gynecologists, pediatricians, and other medical specialists, and with the well-equipped and sanitary hospital facilities, expectant mothers have every opportunity to give birth to strong and healthy children.

BIRTH Continuous study is carried on to determine effects of prolonged labor, rapid delivery, caesarean section, and instrument assistance. Great care is taken to foresee any problems regarding the actual birth of the child. The trauma of birth is a subject with much substance for further research.

PHYSICAL, SOCIAL, AND PSYCHOLOGICAL ENVIRONMENT FOLLOWING BIRTH Never before has so much research been done and so much progress been made in detecting, diagnosing, and treating or correcting many retarding factors of infants that previously had been more or less ignored. What had been considered as facts with regard to native endowments such as intelligence, growth potential, and talent development are now under close scrutiny and we are bombarded with new hypotheses. Diagnosis, therapy, opportunity, improved self image, and better human relationships are keys that seem to have potentialities for unheard of changes in human adjustment and achievement.

Biochemistry, neurology, pediatrics, and all the subsidiaries of medical science are bringing about revolutionary changes in child growth and development. Teachers and parents can never hope to know all that these fields have to offer, but they can be aware that there are many specialists to make contributions to the welfare of children. Today, early detection of any type of imperfection or weakness can mean early and expert remediation to assure many children of normal development who, in the past, might never have been afforded classroom opportunities.

The newborn child is somewhat like a plant emerging from the soil. It needs proper nutrients and care, the kind of care that will enhance its greatest potentiality of full development. There must be protection against outward forces with which it is not yet capable of coping. The protectives and nutrients vary with the individual specimen.

Children have needs above and beyond those of plants. There is a whole system of locomotion that needs development. With locomotion comes ever greater control over one's environment and a need to communicate with other human beings. There is a self sufficiency that must emerge. Along with locomotion there is a capacity for performance and a potential to create. No one can predict the extremities of these capacities or potentials, but research is moving ahead rapidly in finding ways, means, and materials for facilitating such development.

Development is a term of many facets. It involves growth, dexterity, fulfillment, and facility. Maturity, as influenced by learning, is involved. Development takes place on many fronts simultaneously, and from birth throughout life, environmental conditions and personality contacts can change, retard, or inhibit well-rounded progression of the individual.

The home, in most cases, is the greatest environmental factor in a child's life. He spends more hours there than anywhere else. He must interact with family members for many years, and his language patterns, his values, his self image, and his whole outlook on life are influenced largely by home membership. Except in extreme cases little is done to remove a child from a poor home environment. Except in such extreme cases the law forces children to remain in the custody of parents even though they may do little to encourage or enhance the development of these children into worthy citizenry. Little is done to make demands on parents to meet certain standards of parenthood. Love, responsibility, and opportunity do not always accompany the begetting of children.

ENVIRONMENTAL CAUSES OF DIFFERENCES

Ideally a child thrives in the kind of home environment that provides the following elements:

PROTECTION Protection through vaccination against preventable diseases; protection against dangers with which the child is not ready to cope; protection against unscrupulous criticism, vicious or profane language, uncontrollable tempers, or other fear-inducing behavior should be a child's birthright. This is not a smothering kind of protection. A child must be supported and helped to face the ordinary dangers of existence and to know how to meet them. His protection must lead to self-preservation.

CARE Adequate rest in a clean, well-ventilated room; a nutritive diet in accordance with his individual needs; comfortable and appropriate clothing to accommodate his need for movement; cleanliness in body and in surroundings; constant vigilance for indications of illness or physical impairment that should be given immediate attention by those who can provide this care with love and understanding are essential to his well being.

FREEDOM   A child needs freedom to use each set of muscles as nature provides the urge for their development. He needs freedom to explore, to converse, to try, to become.

RESPONSIBILITY   A child needs to know that other family members have needs as great as his own. He needs to feel that he has jobs to do simply because he is a family member and that there is joy and satisfaction in the fulfillment of such obligations. He needs to know that time is of concern to everyone, that he has a responsibility to do certain things within the framework of a family time schedule. Routines are important in all lives, and while too much rigidity or pressure could be harmful, so could too much dawdling and care-free unconcern be retarding in the child's becoming a worthy family member and, later, a responsible school participant.

ENCOURAGEMENT   A child needs to feel the support of an adult who will rejoice with him in his successes and who will stand by to assist him when the going gets too rough. Such a person will help a child to withstand minor hurts but will give ready support when injuries or defeats are too overwhelming. Such a person will make new attempts seem venturesome, exciting, and worthwhile. A child can be inspired to want to try, to do, to achieve, and he can be challenged to continue because he wants to, and not because someone else is forcing him.

CONSISTENCY   There must be a uniformity in the expectations that are made of young children, both from time to time and among those in authority. A child is confused when a parent looks upon certain antics as cute one moment and a short time later proceeds to scold or punish him for doing the same thing. So, too, is it confusing if one parent tolerates certain behavior that the other parent forbids. Grandparents in the home can further complicate matters if they have still other standards of behavior that are expected of the child.

Expectations with regard to achievement should always be well within the child's range of accomplishment. To rejoice with the child when such achievements are made is to give him renewed incentive to go on. The child experiences a true challenge when he has the inspiration to make an accomplishment and he knows that *you* know and *he* knows it can be done. Consistency in such motivation pays big dividends in maintaining a child's confidence.

OPPORTUNITY   Most parents want the very best that life can offer for their children. Probably the greatest problem that faces them with regard to opportunities is to know what to provide and when.

A child in a playpen surrounded by expensive toys may not have as worthwhile an opportunity as a child who is allowed to creep around the room and take pots and pans from a cupboard and put his blocks into them. To understand the various types of opportunities children need, one must be aware of how learning takes place along with growth. This will be discussed later in the chapter.

Situational Causes of Differences

There are situations that arise from time to time within the lives of individuals that can cause temporary or prolonged differences among children.

DIVORCE, REMARRIAGE, OR PARENTAL QUARRELING   The full impact of disruptive home situations can never be predicted or estimated. A sensitive child may be so deeply affected that he is unable to concentrate on what is happening at school. Even his health may be affected. A remarriage, in some cases, may give a child renewed security. On the other hand, it could cause feelings of rejection. His self image may undergo serious change.

Quarreling in a home usually causes great insecurity on the part of children. Peace and tranquillity are basic in giving children a pleasant outlook on life. Happy times make for happy dispositions.

UNEMPLOYMENT OR OTHER ADVERSE HOME CONDITIONS   Children sense parent worries and are more concerned than parents and teachers realize. Worries and trouble can gnaw at a child's feeling of security. A prolonged illness of a parent can create anxiety among all members of the family, and little can be said or done about it. Taunts of neighbor children can add to the misery when poverty and its surrounding circumstances prevail.

FREQUENT MOVING   A child coming into a new school has a whole new adjustment to make. It is not only a matter of getting acquainted with classmates and a new teacher. He has to slip into routines that may be different from those in the school he left. Methods, materials, previous activities, and class level of achievement may not fit his needs at all. Both the child and the teacher may know that he will soon move again, and a "what's-the-use" attitude may result.

ILLNESSES   Besides depriving him of the continuum of learning experiences, many illnesses leave the child in a weakened condition that makes him more susceptible to other illnesses. It is not uncommon for children in the primary grades to have several of the common contagious diseases in the same school year. Frequent colds often follow whooping cough, and ear infections may follow measles or bad colds. Such conditions leave a child feeling less enthusiastic, and the fact that he is behind his classmates and has not experienced many of the things they are talking about causes further loss of interest. To prod a child to work double-time in order to catch up can add frustration to the total problem and a dislike for school. After an illness is the time when burdens should be light, when interests should be renewed, and when the regaining of strength and vitality are most important. A cognizant teacher will make a very gradual approach to pick up loose ends in helping the child catch up again. Only the most important segments missed because of illness may be really vital enough for concentrated effort, and these should be made up in stimulating ways.

UPSET ROUTINES IN THE HOME   When relatives come for long visits in a home, when a mother is called away to care for a sick relative, or when a mother goes to the hospital, there are many disturbing situational factors. Children may stay up much later than their usual bedtime. Their sleep may be disturbed by having to sleep with others when they have been used to sleeping alone. Meals may not be on schedule or may be lacking as far as the child's nutritional needs are concerned. Fear and loneliness may grip the young child. When he comes to school he may be wondering when his mother will return rather than concentrating on what the teacher is saying. Communication between home and school is essential.

SIBLING RIVALRY   To the child who is looked upon with glowing pride for his achievements and desirable behavior, praise may serve as a catalyst for continued success; but to the brother or sister who is taunted with negative comparisons, defiant behavior or an "I-can't-do-anything-right" attitude may result. The only self confidence some children can establish is through an understanding teacher.

PARENTAL PRESSURES   Because success in most areas of the curriculum depends on the ability to read, parents are especially concerned about the child's progress in reading. Parents need to know that providing a good stable home with rich broad experiences and good language communications does more to help the child with reading than any attempt on their part to assist with the actual reading instruction. Encouragement and praise of their attempts help children to want to read at home when they are ready for such activities. Negative criticism and too great expectations can cause anxiety and discomfort on the part of the child so that he will refuse to read at home. These anxieties can cause disinterest at school as well.

Individuality Causes of Differences

There is great variance among learners, even among those living in the same situation and encountering the same learning opportunities. The most significant differences with regard to implications for the teaching of reading are the following:

VARIANCE IN WHAT IS ACTUALLY TAKEN FROM AN EXPERIENCE   If you take two children on a picnic or to a show you may note that what seemed interesting and important to one child may have gone undetected by the other. What may be perceived as right or wrong by one child may not appear so to the other. Children can appear to be listening and not recall a word that was said. At other times they surprise you with how much they grasp, or you may be amazed at the individual differences in results on a test when you felt everyone would know the answers. Some children go home from school and give a complete account of the day's activities. Others seldom tell anything about what they do. This is not always because of faulty memory, but those who give an accounting have that experience as reinforcement for future recall. Some children remember for only a day or two, while others recall even minute details years later.

LEVELS AND INTENSITY OF FRUSTRATION   One child may sit for hours trying to lace his shoes and then very calmly ask for help. Another may make a quick attempt, and when the lace will not go through the eyelet he starts throwing the shoe and crying with rage. Some children are very dependent on help, and others would rather leave a task undone than seek assistance. Some children work well alone and will strive diligently to complete a task, but they may be quite frustrated in group work. Still others lose interest fast when they are left alone to work but participate enthusiastically in a group. Much research is being done in exploring the biochemistry of frustration and strong emotion. Differences in neurological structure and development may be factors. But regardless of the causes of frustration, children with quick tempers often have serious problems of adjustment to school situations, and teachers must know how to work with such children.

RATE OF MATURITY WITHIN THEMSELVES AND IN RELATIONSHIP TO OTHER CHILDREN   A child may learn to creep and walk at an early age, but he may be slow to talk in comparison with other children his age. Such differences are usually normal, and to exert pressures to hurry a child's maturation may only cause anxieties and frustration. Many records show that children may make very slow progress in reading in the first and second and even the third grade and then suddenly take hold or catch on with such interest and vigor that by the sixth grade their reading scores may be as good as other children who began well in the first grade.

VARIANCE IN TALENT, COORDINATION, AND ATTENTION SPAN   There is a relationship among good health, security, and attention span. Usually good things go together. A sound body and good health often go along with good coordination of large and small muscles. A child who is talented often has a longer attention span than one who is less talented. Children tend to enjoy doing what they can do well and thus their attention span in such situations is prolonged; conversely, deprivation along with lack of talent, shortness of attention span, and poor coordination can cause children to lag farther and farther behind those more fortunate.

VARIANCE IN THE SELF IMAGE FORMED OF THEMSELVES   Self images are closely related to the expectations expressed by the adults with whom the child lives. If the parents are critical and demanding and the child is frequently frustrated in trying to keep up with demands that exceed his ability to produce, he soon feels inadequate. As demands continue, he either becomes languid and does not care what happens, or he rebels. The rebellion may take various forms that may seem far removed from the area of reading achievement. Nevertheless, progress in reading and all other parts of the school curriculum is affected. Behavioral psychology is intensely interesting in this respect, and teachers should explore it as much as they can. A defeatist attitude may have been well established in a child before he starts school and he may expect to fail in learning to read as he has failed to fulfill many other parent expectations.

On the other hand, if expectations are kept within the child's range of ability to achieve, and if failures are accepted lightly and buffered with encouragement, a child becomes accustomed to trial and error and trial again before success may sometimes be achieved. Expectations need to be expressed with the child's understanding of exactly what, why, and when certain tasks are to be accomplished. These expectations should be his own goals as well as those of the adult. Expectations can be like rungs of a ladder with just enough space between the rungs for the child to take comfortable steps. He should have good personal motivation to climb, and he should feel satisfaction with each step. As with climbing the ladder and appreciating the broadening view with each step, so, too, in learning the child acquires a natural urge to go on when he is helped to use and appreciate the achievement he has made. He thus becomes satisfied with himself and acquires a healthy ambition to do more achieving, socializing, creating, exploring, and becomes a healthier, happier, well-rounded, and good-to-know individual. All areas of endeavor, whether social, scientific, academic, or creative, need the same "I want to," "I can," and "I will" approach, with understanding adults to inspire, to lend a helping hand when needed, and to rejoice in the achievement. Fortunate is the child who has such support.

Just as unfortunate as the child who lives in an environment of over-expectation is the child whose parents do everything for him and deprive him of the satisfactions of doing for himself. His attitude becomes one of "others must do for me—I can't do for myself." Doting parents, parents who are always in a hurry, and parents who get self satisfaction in always anticipating a child's every want are likely to deprive the child of the important early experiences of satisfaction in personal accomplishment.

Another aspect of doing something for one's self and for others is concerned with the matter of doing it to the best of one's ability. If parents would always encourage a child to recognize quality of effort within the range of the child's muscular and maturity levels, he can grow up with a sense of pride in worthy attempts. The practice of working to the fullest of one's ability is thus established. To do and do well is a worthwhile goal. Again, it is a matter of inspiring a child to want to do his best rather than pressuring him to do it over or merely expecting him to do it well without emphasis on the satisfaction it can bring.

There are children who come from homes where they experience no expectations, no opportunities, no stimulation. Such deprived children have come to the attention of educators all over the country, and the Head-Start program is an attempt to provide early experiences that will form a good foundation for later school programs. This and the following chapter contain many ideas for such programs.

Along with a child's self image is the variability in the images he establishes of others. If parent figures are harsh, punitive, and unapproachable, a child is likely to cower in the presence of adults. He is likely to avoid or even fear adult encounters. A kindergarten teacher once observed that one of the children in her class scampered to the far end of the room whenever she approached him. When the children came to the rug, this child always chose a far corner. When the teacher talked to the mother, an understandable explanation was given. All summer whenever young Jim did anything annoying, his father would say, "Just wait till your teacher gets a hold of you. She'll settle you good." If a child experiences adults as kind, helpful, and inspiring individuals, the outlook is far more advantageous.

Parents' attitudes toward others is often evident in their children's attitudes. If parents consider themselves inferior, unfortunate, and downtrodden, children will feel that way. On the other hand, if parents feel equal, enjoy sociability, cooperate, and give and take fairly with their associates and with the outside world, their children are likely to be that way.

A child's self image and the images he has of others are extremely important in his readiness to fit into the school situation and to learn to read. Manifestations of a child's self image are not always easy to detect. Sometimes the child with a poor self image strikes out at the world with both fists. He bites, hits, and scratches and produces all sorts of annoyances. Others with the same type of inner feelings may be docile and retiring. Teachers should always investigate the child who is always quiet, always withdrawn, always alone.

There are also degrees of variations within and among children. A child may be a star in athletics and his self image in this regard is lofty and bright, but he may feel inferior in the classroom when arithmetic or reading is taught. He may dread the dawn of a new school day unless someone can change his attitude and inspire him to discover new and rewarding interests in academic and creative areas of the curriculum as well as in athletics. Sometimes a relationship such as the reading of box scores and batting averages can become an incentive for an athlete to learn to read.

Yes, children vary in all known aspects of development. The range and degree of these variances broaden as children continue to operate under the same conditions and with the same personalities. Schools afford certain changes that may bring about greater opportunities for self enhancement and better relationships with others. A teacher's personality and depth of interest in children are extremely important. Every classroom should afford opportunities for every child to succeed in something and to become a hero unto himself in some area of the curriculum. Reading can be that area of success for many children.

Early Development

The task of science is to make the world we live in more intelligible. This world is filled with knowable realities. At one extreme is the Atom; at another extreme is the Child. In the Miracle of Growth these two extremes meet.

There are two kinds of nuclei—the nucleus of the physical atom and the nucleus of the living cell. Each contains energy derived from the cosmos through ageless processes of evolution. An atom can be pictured as a tiny solar system, composed of a central nucleus surrounded by electrons. In comparison, the fertilized human egg cell is transcendently complex, for its organic nucleus initiates the most miraculous chain reaction known to science—a cycle of growth in which a minute globule of protoplasm becomes an embryo, the embryo a fetus, the fetus an infant, the infant a child, the child a youth, the youth an adult, and the adult a parent.[2]

Going on from where Gesell left off, we might add that in each parent's realm of influence are the determining factors of how the next generation will use the knowledge of the atom, how they will use the wealth that seems to dominate the value structure of the present generation, and how reading with the help of dedicated teachers may have tremendous influence on shaping their destinies.

Gesell makes frequent mention of Charles Darwin in his lectures and writings. Darwin was as interested in child development as he was in his theory of evolution. He was the father of ten children and he kept copious notes on each child. When asked which years he considered the most "subject to incubative impressions," his emphatic answer was, "Without doubt the first three!"[3] More and more studies of adjustments, delinquent behavior, as well as reading problem cases, point to deprivations in early childhood as causes. That is why two chapters of this book are devoted to what constitutes the environmental, the interpersonal relationship, the precautionary, and the opportunistic aspects of child development in all the related areas that may help prepare each child to read.

[2] Arnold Gesell, *Studies in Child Development.* New York: Harper, 1948, p. 3.
[3] *Ibid.* p. 35.

Growing and knowing take place almost simultaneously. As a child gains use of various parts of his body he comes to know what he can do with regard to the how, what, when, and why of things of his environment. Each single impression—the feel of something hot, the sight of mother's face, the taste of orange juice, the scent of a flower is known as a *percept;* collectively they are known as *perceptions.* These are the beginnings of learning. It is these percepts and their relationships to many types of experiences that give meaning to what children read. Recognizing words would be useless if there were no funds of percepts to give the words true meanings.

Learning is largely muscular, multisensory, communicative, and attitudinal. As the unfolding or natural urge to use the various parts of the body occurs, the learning aspects can be either greatly enhanced or retarded by those within the child's range of contact and by the opportunities and physical aspects of the environment in which he exists. If people look favorably on the child's attempts, and if the environment is safe and yielding, the child is likely to gain satisfaction from his efforts and will continue them. He will, with such continued efforts, develop wholesome or positive attitudes toward the people involved and toward what he does, which in turn foster further development.

DEVELOPMENT OF MUSCLES

Many things are learned by doing. Large muscles are the first to feel the urge for use and the child produces random movement of legs, arms, and head. Sometimes legs and arms move so rapidly and persistently that mothers find it difficult to diaper, bathe, or feed the child.

Next, the child becomes able to roll over and over, and it is no longer safe to leave him on an unguarded bed. Locomotion takes place about the time his eyes are able to focus on near things in the environment, and there is a natural reaching out to explore. Again, it is the provision of a safe environment, encouragement, and support that will determine attitude and willingness to proceed.

Children experience a broken-front approach to learning. That is, few children have exactly the same experience involving the use of certain muscles at exactly the same time in the developmental pattern, or the same experiences with the various senses, or the same attitudinal influences, and few children have the same experiences at the same time. Even if they did, they are not likely to take the same percepts from those experiences. Fortunate is the child who has the opportunity to see, feel, hear, smell, taste, exercise, explore, and communicate within a safe, comfortable, encouraging environment. The world is so full of substance, fact, and activity that lack of wealth need not be too restricting. A child in a wealthy home restricted to a nursery and the care of a nursemaid whose responsibility it is to keep the child spotless and content may be more deprived than a child in a mountain shanty who is free to explore and whose contacts with many brothers and sisters afford countless seeing, hearing, tasting, smelling, doing, and becoming opportunities.

A child's readiness is the determining factor in the provision of opportunities. When his leg muscles are strong enough for standing, situations must be provided whereby he is helped to stand on his feet momentarily. There must be sturdy props for his support as he tries again and again to pull himself up and to take the first faltering steps. The reassurance he gets and the assistance when it is wanted will influence his attitude toward trying again and enjoying the attempts.

To prevent children from using muscles they have a natural urge to use is not only frustrating but may cause other types of retardation. There are those who feel strongly that some children who never had the opportunity to creep or somehow escaped having that experience may have failed to achieve proper bilateral body development. It is claimed by some authorities that lack of bilateral development has affected children's ability to read. Experimentation has been under way for some time on bilateral development and its relationship to learning.

Regardless of the direct influence of such development on reading, we do know that the child who gets locomotion under way as soon as he is ready for it has access to a much broader scope of new learning. Opportunities to develop left and right body coordination is important at all age levels. Creeping is only a beginning of such development. Walking, skipping, climbing, dancing, and skating are the next levels of such left-right leg-and-foot coordination. Sight, speech, and reading problems have all been to some extent attributed to lack of bilateral coordination.

In Appendix A are activities for young children that may be used in the home or in Head-Start programs, nursery school, or kindergarten. Even children beyond these age levels who appear to lack good left-right body coordination may benefit from such activities. Talk with children as they attempt any of these activities so that language is being developed at the same time. Encourage children to talk about what they are doing, to challenge one another, and to praise each other for trying as well as for achieving.

As children participate in these guided activities it is well to keep a chart with the children's names listed down the side of the chart and the various activities across the top. A key of symbols may be used as follows: *E* (excellent coordination), *H* (hesitation or awkwardness and some degree of error), *U* (unable to meet the challenge). Children in the second category are encouraged to keep trying and are given any needed help until they become proficient. Children in the last category are encouraged to start with the simplest activities, are given help, and move on as they are ready for the next difficult activities. This chart should be kept as a part of the child's permanent record.

There should be much opportunity for free play, especially active types of free play in the open air. Tag, horse-and-driver, partner tag, somersaulting, trapeze bar activities (with plenty of soft matting beneath and bars at a chinning height for children) are good.

"Statue" is a game in which he who is "It" swings each player gently by the hand, letting go when he is sure the player is standing on both feet. Each player is to remain rigid in the position he falls into when "It" has let go of his hand. After all players have been swung, "It" chooses the one who appears to be in the funniest position to become "It" for a new game.

"Pump-Pump-Pull-Away" is a good game to keep children active on the playground when it is cold outside. All players toe up behind a long line drawn on one side of the playground, or they may stand along a fence. Another line is drawn on the other side of the play-ground or at a reasonable distance. "It" stands half way between the two lines and calls out, "Pump-pump-pull-away. Come or I'll pull you away." At that command all players must run toward the other line and get behind it before they are tagged by "It." All the players he catches join him in being "It." The command is given again after all untagged players are toed behind the line. The last person caught is declared champion. The first person caught becomes "It" for the new game.

"Hop Scotch" is a good activity for body coordination, and it can be made simple or complex in accordance with the development of the children. They should be encouraged to hop on one foot in one attempt and on the other foot in the next attempt. It is better for them to compete with their own attempts than to compete with someone else who may be far better coordinated. Improvement in self achievement is always to be stressed.

Teeter-totters, swings, merry-go-rounds, and other reasonably safe playground equipment are fine, but safety precautions should be made in each case. No equipment is entirely safe, and each activity must be explained in detail and supervised carefully. Explanations of safety rules should be made and then followed rigidly. Guard lines should be drawn around swing, teeter-totter, and merry-go-round areas so that children will stay away while others are using the equipment. Each very young child needs to be shown how to hold on to a swing, teeter-totter, or merry-go-round. Challenge children frequently to set up any additional safety rules they think are needed and to review the old ones. An important part of learning is to foresee dangers and to regard their own and others' safety. An alert teacher should be on hand at all times when children are having free play.

Although a child may appear to be very well coordinated at the age of six, it is important that he continue to have coordinating experiences during every stage of rapid growth. Consider how awkward some children in their teens seem to be. Coordination is a continuing process as children adjust to increasing size and new proportions. Swimming, bicycling, tennis, skating, bowling, dancing, and surfing are excellent coordinating activities. See Appendix A for many specific activities for bilateral development.

DEVELOPMENT OF VISION

Claims have been made by the Gesell Institute of Child Development that "a child depends upon his vision for 75 to 80 per cent of his learning."[4]

If the use of the eyes is so significant in learning, it follows that they are equally important in all matters of daily living. With so much importance attached to this part of our body, it follows that extreme care must be given to these vital organs to retain their full potentialities throughout the span of life.

The more anatomic variability within an organ of our body the longer the maturation period. The eye is highly complex, and Gerald N. Getman tells us that the eyes of most children do not reach full maturity until they are seven or eight years old. His ex-

---

[4] Richard J. Apell, "Vision and the Eyes of Children." New Haven, Connecticut: Gesell Institute of Child Development, 1957.

tensive research in the field of sight and vision gives us some interesting statistics. This information from Dr. Getman should be reviewed frequently and shared with parent groups so that formal reading is not forced upon children when eye muscles are not ready.

Studies at Chicago University Hospital show that less than 2.4% of the infants had defective eyes. A study of 16,000 children in Texas showed that 20% had vision problems at the age of eight. This indicated that so-called eye defects—near-sightedness, astigmatism, and excessive far-sightedness—are related to the inadequacies of learning to use the visual mechanism in the first eight years of a child's life. Many studies show that neither eyes nor the entire visual mechanism are physically and physiologically ready for the school reading load until eight or nine years of age. Yet, our children are carrying a tremendously heavy load by six or seven years of age. It may not be possible to speed up anatomical and functional maturity of the visual mechanism; but it is possible to ease, and possibly avoid some of the stresses involved in the heavy near-point load by bolstering the skills and the abilities which the visual mechanism needs for achievement and efficient performance.[5]

Too often children are confined to tasks in which they must read fine print. Dr. Getman refers to this as "containment." He has made educators aware of avoidance responses and such physical distresses as tension in the muscles of the back, oscillation of the head and neck, high blood pressure, respiratory fluctuations, and galvanic skin reaction when too much pressure is brought to bear on containment in reading. In his own words, "Only recently has the idea emerged that the stress of containment can cause the child to observe, see, remember and learn less."[6]

There are many experiences for which young children are ready that serve to strengthen the eyes and which will eventually contribute to a child's success in reading. (See Appendix A.)

SIGHT AND VISION DEFINED

Dr. Getman defines sight as the response of the eye to any light that enters it. The eye will align with the light source to gain the most even distribution of light across the retina; the pupil of the eye will dilate or constrict according to the intensity of the light that is entering the eye. Sight is the "alerting process" that allows the eye to set itself in readiness

5 Gerald N. Getman, *How To Develop Your Child's Intelligence.* Luverne, Minn.: Announcer Press, 1962, pp. 18–19.

6 Gerald N. Getman and Homer Hendrickson, "The Needs of Teachers for Specialized Information on the Development of Visuomotor Skills in Relation to Academic Performance," in *The Teacher of Brain-Injured Children,* ed. by William Cruickshank. Syracuse, N.Y.: Syracuse University Press, 1966, p. 164.

for seeing. Acuity is the result of all the sensori-motor actions that take place in the end organ (the eye) that will provide for the clarity of the light pattern that strikes the retina. The two eyes align and the dioptic systems of the eye adjust to bring the most adequate light distribution across the retina for the most adequate "sign" of the pattern or object seen.

Vision is the learned ability to see for information and performance. Vision is the ability to understand the things we cannot touch, taste, smell or hear. Vision is the process whereby we perceive space as a whole.[7]

Not only is the eye capable of focusing at a distance but also close up. Our eye lens is somewhat telescopic in that we have a broad range of vision. Our eye also gives us a depth perception or what is known as a "spatial relationship." It is a three-dimensional perception that enables us to perceive roundness, distance perspective, and contour versus shape. Each eye can function alone and the two fuse as one. Often if sight is lost in one eye the other becomes stronger to compensate for the loss.

Eye movement patterns are established for walking, grasping, feeding oneself, and for the hundreds of activities where eye and other muscles of the body coordinate in almost involuntary action because we perform them so frequently. However, they are all learned, and repeated accomplishments give them the sensitivity of an assured or expected success. This is the way we control the environment about us and interpret it as to its usefulness. We know how to back into a chair to sit on it with the right amount of body drop, or how to step down to the next stair level (although when we make a slight miscalculation our body receives a jolt). This is all a part of spatial relationship that we comprehend through use of our eyes and their coordination with our bodies. Young children have all this to learn. Even our body balance is somewhat related to eye movement patterns and this spatial comprehension.

EYE CAPABILITIES AND DISABILITIES *Eye movement skill* includes the ability to see clearly far away and close up; to the left and the right; up, down, and diagonally; and to follow objects moving in all directions.

Eye-teaming skill includes the ability to focus both eyes on an object so that there is only one image as all or any of the above directional movements are achieved.

If a child complains of seeing double, repeats symbols when there

[7] Getman and Hendrickson, *op. cit.*, pp. 156–157.

is only one, closes one eye when looking, tilts his head frequently, or gives evidence of poor body posture and fatigue, you may suspect impairment in this skill.

Eye-hand coordination skill includes the ability of the eyes and mind to direct the hands in reaching out and grasping and manipulating both independently and as a coordinated team. It means getting the "feel" of differences in size, shape, texture, and spatial relationship that enables children to be conscious of likenesses and differences, an awareness that is so essential in learning to read. It takes many experiences for the eyes and hands to work so well together that they can almost subconsciously perform while the person's thoughts are on an anticipated accomplishment.

If after many opportunities to achieve this skill the child still appears to be very awkward and cannot guide his hands into simple eye-hand accomplishments, it is a good idea to refer him to a good clinic for a check-up.

Visual form perception (visual imagery, visual memory) includes the ability to establish a mental image so complete that recall might include form, texture, smell, weight, color, irregularity, and any discriminating feature that gives the impression identity. It includes all that goes into "knowing" insofar as concrete visual and tactual characteristics are concerned. It is a combination or culmination of the previous skills plus a next step of memorization and adeptness at immediate and accurate recall. True quality of visual form perception is lasting.

Refractive status (hyperopia, myopia, astigmatism, and other refractive problems) has to do with proper eye performance.[8] It is a physical aspect rather than a developmental one, although the cause may be related to actual experiences or lack of certain other experiences. Myopia (near-sightedness), hyperopia (far-sightedness), or any distortion of image gives children an abnormal perspective and they react to their environment in an abnormal manner. Comprehension is thus varied, and when pictures or print are substituted for the direct life experience the visual images are further distorted, and the visual perceptive form the child calls up in his thinking may be far removed from reality. Children experiencing such distortions cannot explain their problems and the casual observer cannot understand what is wrong with the child. Such children have great difficulty in trying to draw simple figures. They may keep trying to adjust their books to various distances from their eyes. They may

8 Getman and Hendrickson, *op. cit.*, pp. 162–167.

blink their eyes and show various symptoms of uneasiness, frustration, and despair. When parents or teachers observe children with such problems, they should make a referral to a good clinic at once.

A Snellen test is not enough to detect refractive problems. A child with these problems could test 20–20 (normal) at straight-ahead eye focus. A good clinic will use, in addition to the Snellen test, a tele-binocular test, an astigmatism test, a peripheral vision test, and a color blindness test. Following such diagnosis, expert advice will be given as to how correction and treatment may proceed. In our country today no child should have to struggle with vision problems since most of them can be corrected.

Dr. Getman and Dr. Hendrickson, both renowned for their work in visuomotor perception, suggest that school children be provided with "learning lenses" to protect their eyes from strain when doing close-up work such as reading. If such glasses cannot be provided, parents and teachers should make sure that young children are not subjected to close scrutiny of fine print. Reading readiness books and preprimers, primers, and first readers should contain bold print. In recent correspondence with Dr. Getman, he says with respect to learning lenses:

Before accepting my present position as Director of Child Development at Pathway School in Norristown, Pennsylvania, I have had thirty years of experience with reading glasses for children in first grade. We in optometry would rather call them school lenses or achievement lenses because they are not prescribed on the basis of ocular defect! They are prescribed on the basis of least stress, most physiological effectivity, greatest cognitive rapport in a loaded visual activity. The clinical evidence is overwhelming—those children who are protected, supported, and assisted by such lenses are characteristically more successful, and not only become the higher achievers, but avoid the ocular deteriorations that can result from overloading any physiological structure.[9]

Parents and teachers should be aware of the following symptoms of eye problems:

Considerable head movement when reading
Rubbing of the eyes
Facial contortions
Blinking

[9] Gerald N. Getman, Section Chairman of the Optometric Extension Program (International), a nonprofit foundation for education and research in vision, in a summary statement, March, 1967.

Frequent attempts to move the book into better focus
Watery or bloodshot eyes
Red eyelids
Crusted eyelids or discharge from the eyes
Holding the book too close or too far away from the eyes
Tension or frustration during visual work
Tilting of the head as if looking with only one eye
Complaints of blurred vision

Be sure that more than the Snellen chart is used when a child's eyes are checked. It is well to remember that children usually are not aware that their faulty sight is different from that of other children. They have learned to live with it and assume that it is as it should be. Only the wary adult can become conscious of the child's problems through observable symptoms. An early diagnosis may open a new world of learning to the child.

DEVELOPMENT OF EYE-HAND COORDINATION   As soon as a baby can focus his eyes on people and things, he begins to reach out into the world beyond himself. By this time he has discovered his fingers and toes and has been occupied for long periods of time playing with them. Now his spatial relationships expand to include concepts of distance, timing, and coordinative movement. In the simple matter of grasping something that is offered to him a child has to see the object, estimate the distance his hand must travel to reach it, direct his arm muscles to move the required distance, and at the same time direct his finger muscles to expand and contract to accommodate the size and shape of the object. If the object is moving, as in the case of a rolling ball, an allowance for that movement must be made in "knowing" when the grasp must be made. All of this is a part of eye-hand coordination and a part of the child's total visual perception. Many of the activities of muscular development involve eye coordination with the hands and with other parts of the body as well. Not only direct but peripheral vision is important in most body movements. A child who appears to be awkward may have the direct focus capability, but a clinic would be able to ascertain whether or not he has peripheral problems in seeing. Again, a Snellen chart test would not be sufficient. (See Appendix A for eye-hand coordinating activities.)

STRENGTHENING EYE MUSCLES   In reading, much depends on the eyes' rapid movement along the lines of the page and the return sweep to the beginning of the next line. We are told that many children having 20–20 (normal vision at twenty feet) may have serious peripheral vision problems that cause serious reading disability. Eye muscles that control the peripheral vision need strengthening and developing as do all body muscles. (See Appendix A for activities strengthening eye muscles.)

One of the greatest services a teacher can render any child who is having difficulties is to detect any weaknesses or impairments of vision and to refer the child to a good clinic for a thorough check-up and diagnosis.

Work that is too intricate or too confining is not good for very young children. Be conscious of their eyes at all times.

DEVELOPMENT OF TOUCH

Helen Keller would attest to the fact that the sense of touch is the greatest avenue of learning, but hers is a special world deprived of sight and hearing. Only when we are deprived of one or more of the senses do we realize how much the others can compensate for the loss. I doubt that enough attention in most schools is given to an acuity of touch and its significance in learning—what is often referred to as the "tactile" approach to learning. Marie Montessori established a school with an entire program in which much emphasis was placed on tactile learning. Some children seem to need the 'feel' of objects to get a lasting mental image. Getting the feel of what we see can be advantageous to most of us. However, we must be sure a child gets more from a tactile experience than the blind men and the elephant (the fable which points up the need to get the whole of a mental image and not be content with a small part). There seems to be a natural urge for children to reach out to grasp whatever they see as soon as eye-and-hand coordination begin to take place. Young children not only feel with their fingers, but their lips and tongue seem to be part of the intake of the sense of touch. The coldness and hardness of ice, the smoothness of glass, and the softness and coldness of snow are sensations that children frequently experience with their lips and tongues. Some children like to put their cheeks against something that appears to be soft or against a smooth windowpane. Helping children to know what is safe to touch and what is not to be touched is part of learning.

As soon as leg muscles permit locomotion there is a strong tendency to go after things. This exploration, seeking, wanting to feel, and wanting to put things to the cheeks and mouth are the natural avenues for giving the things of life more and more meaning. (See Appendix A for suggestions for developing the percepts of touch.)

DEVELOPMENT OF THE SENSE OF SMELL

The phenomenon of smell is another aspect of perception. No environment is devoid of smells, but some children are more aware or more sensitive to them than are other children. Quick recognition of the smell of smoke or gas could save both lives and property. Appreciation of the fragrance of flowers and perfume adds to the enjoyment of life. Children may be helped to develop, use, and appreciate the sense of smell. (See Appendix A for suggestions for developing the sense of smell.)

DEVELOPMENT OF THE SENSE OF TASTE

At a very young age children become conscious of taste. They tend to like sweetness and reject what is sour or bitter. As speech develops, children come to associate taste with terms such as *salty, hot, spicy, sour, sweet, bitter, bland,* and *tart.* They come to have favorite foods because of taste. Taste also helps us to know when food is spoiled or when it is in need of seasonings. It is a part of total perception.

Forcing children to eat often causes distaste for certain foods. A gradual approach to new foods is more likely to meet with acceptance. Good advice at the school cafeteria is, "Take enough to taste it, even if you think you don't like it. Sometimes you are surprised at what you have been missing. We all grow into liking more and more foods." Discussions of how foods taste helps to develop vocabulary and language facility.

DEVELOPMENT OF HEARING, AUDING AND LISTENING

Although it has been estimated that eighty per cent of learning comes through seeing, there is much overlapping of hearing and seeing in a great many learning experiences. To say that seeing is by far the more important intake of learning is like saying that food is much more important than water in sustaining life. The deaf have been taught to read and so have the blind, but both require very different teaching techniques from those we use with children who have both sight and hearing. It is as important to check and be sure a child does not have impaired hearing as it is to check and be sure he does not have impaired sight.

There are two important aspects of hearing: the range of softness and loudness, and the range of low to high pitch. The physical act of transferring sound pressure and frequency waves to the brain is known as hearing.

The sound pressure units are known as decibels, and they measure or indicate degrees of loudness. The measuring scale used is from 0 to 140. About 20 is a whisper and beyond 100 is unpleasant to human ears.

The frequency wave cycles are indicative of pitch. The voice range is from 125 to 400 cycles per second. Hearing loss of high frequencies is most detrimental in reading because they are associated with many of the consonant sounds.

Auditory perceptual skills include the recognition of single letter sounds in the context of the word. This highly developed sequential auditory skill evolves during the fifth to seventh years of life. Thus, very young children cannot be expected to have all the auditory skills necessary for a successful reading program before they are about seven years old.

To read, the child must perceive and fuse auditory and visual stimuli. That is, he must see the letters in their sequence within the word and associate sounds with the letters or combination of letters and associate meaning with the whole. Faulty hearing can be a serious detriment to the whole process.

Frequently there may be a temporary loss of hearing caused by severe colds, diseases such as diphtheria or scarlet fever, or as a result of mastoid or other ear infections. Sometimes these conditions are not pronounced enough for the child to complain, but they can be frustrating to him.

For example, Dwayne was a happy, energetic and friendly kindergartner until after Christmas when he seemed to be a very different child. He became more and more inattentive and lost interest in the stories about which he had previously been so enthusiastic. He retired from play activities in which he had at one time afforded friendly leadership. The parents could not account for this change in his behavior, and prodding only seemed to cause outbursts of resentment. Finally, one day the teacher observed the child turning his head far to one side as she talked to him. She sent him to the school nurse with the note, "Please check his hearing." The nurse reported that Dwayne was able to hear with only one ear. When the parents were informed, they explained that the child had had a very bad cold and a throat infection during the holidays. The family doctor soon effected a complete recovery, and Dwayne once again became a happy, well-adjusted boy. Unless their ears ache children often are not aware of hearing loss.

Teachers need to be aware of the following indications of defective hearing:

Poor attention span
Frequent requests to have directions repeated
Failure to repeat correctly speech sounds, words, or sentences after hearing them
Monotonous speech patterns (a monotone usually has a narrow auditory frequency range).
General disinterest
Turning the head to one side when spoken to
Earaches
Complaints of humming or buzzing sounds in the ears or head
Ear drainage
Poor communication with others

A watch test is not enough to check a child's hearing. A hearing specialist or clinic will check on the auditory frequency range, auditory acuity, auditory vocal sequencing, and neurological aspects of hearing.

Listening is the willful or deliberate attention to the hearing act. Birds may be singing and the sounds may strike our hearing organs, but human beings are capable of "tuning out" sounds in the environment. With the confusion we have about us in this busy world, it would be a sad state of affairs if we could not tune out certain sounds that would otherwise be very distracting. But when we single out certain sounds and give them our attention we call it *listening*. We listen to music, news, and many environmental sounds. When we interpret these sounds and react to them with appreciation, criticism, or analysis, we refer to the procedure as *auding*. In other words, auding is putting listening to use in our thinking and living.

It is important that we help children become good listeners and carry their listening into the realm of auding. Some children shut out almost everything. Consider the child who is spoken to only when a command or reprimand is given. He comes to know that by not responding, no further disturbing request or hurting comment will be made. Or, there are mothers who repeat everything they have to say over and over again so that the child knows he can "tune in" any time he chooses. If sounds directed at a child are disturbing and unpleasant he may react negatively to other sounds as well, and hearing or listening becomes an unappreciative experience that seldom reaches the level of auding. (See Appendix A for suggestions for improving listening and auding.)

When visual steering, coordinated bilateral motor actions, audition, touch and speech are integrated, elaborated, reinforced and repeated, the children are being physiologically prepared for the world of school. This is readiness in action.[10]

Suggestions for Class Participation and Discussion

1. Observe a group of children at play. Make a list of the differences you note and discuss these in class.
2. What types of differences are likely to be most serious in a classroom?
3. What deprivations do you consider to be most disadvantageous to young children?
4. What sudden changes within a home, in addition to those mentioned in this chapter, might affect a child at school?
5. Read parts of a book on neurology or biochemistry and share some pertinent facts with the class.
6. Read from references on heredity and environment. Share pertinent statements with the class.
7. What advantages do most parents today have in bringing children into the world that your parents did not have?
8. Why is a child's early development so significant to a teacher of reading?
9. Is there any part of a child's early development that would have no bearing on his learning to read? Explain.
10. What is your reaction to the quotation at the end of the chapter?

Bibliography

ASSOCIATION FOR CHILDHOOD EDUCATION INTERNATIONAL, *Basic Human Values for Childhood Education,* 1963.
————, *Creating with Materials for Work and Play,* 1957.
BARCLAY, DOROTHY. *Understanding the City Child.* New York: Franklin Watts, 1959.

[10] Gerald N. Getman and E. R. Kane, "Programs to Accelerate School Success," in *The Physiology of Readiness.* Minneapolis: 1964, p. 40.

BLOOM, BENJAMIN, DAVIS, ALLISON, and HESS, ROBERT. *Compensatory Education for Cultural Deprivation.* New York: Holt, Rinehart & Winston, 1965.

BOWER, ELI. *Fostering Maximum Growth in Children.* National Education Association, 1965.

BRECKENRIDGE, MARIAN E., and MURPHY, MARGARET N. *Growth and Development of the Young Child.* Philadelphia: Saunders, 1963.

BRUNER, JEROME. *On Knowing.* Cambridge, Mass.: Harvard University Press, 1962.

CLARK, DONALD (ed.). *The Psychology of Education, Current Issues and Research.* New York: Macmillan, 1967.

COMBS, ARTHUR. *Perceiving, Behaving, Becoming: A New Focus for Education.* Association for Supervision and Curriculum Development, 1962.

CROW, LESTER, and CROW, ALINE. *Child Development and Adjustment.* New York: Macmillan, 1962.

DEUTSCH, MARTIN. "The Disadvantaged Child and the Learning Process," in *Education in Depressed Areas,* ed. by A. Harry Passow. Teachers College Bureau of Publications, New York, 1962.

FLARELL, J. H. *The Developmental Psychology of Jean Piaget.* Princeton, N.J.: Van Nostrand, 1963.

GETMAN, GERALD N. *How to Develop Your Child's Intelligence.* Luverne, Minn.: Announcer Press, 1962.

GORDON, IRA. *Children's Views of Themselves.* Association for Childhood Education International, 1959.

HAMMOND, SARA LOU, et al. *Good Schools for Young Children.* New York: Macmillan, 1963.

HAWKES, GLEN R. *Behavior and Development from 5 to 12.* New York: Harper & Row, 1962.

HOPPOCK, ANNE. *All Children Have Gifts.* Association for Childhood Education International, 1958.

HOSTLER, PHYLLIS. *The Child's World.* Baltimore: Penguin Books, 1953.

JENKINS, GLADYS, et al. *These Are Our Children.* Chicago: Scott, Foresman, 1954.

MARTIN, WILLIAM, and STENDLER, CELIA. *Behavior and Development.* New York: Macmillan, 1967.

MELTON, A. W. (ed.). *Categories of Human Learning.* New York: Academic Press, 1964.

MILLER, CARROLL H. *Education for the Disadvantaged.* New York: Macmillan, 1967.

MURPHY, LOIS. *The Widening World of Childhood.* New York: Basic Books, 1962.

NOAR, GERTRUDE. *Living with Difference.* Anti-Defamation League, New York, 1965.

NOLL, VICTOR H., and NOLL, RACHEL F. *Reading in Education Psychology.* New York: Macmillan, 1963.

OHIO STATE UNIVERSITY. *How Children Develop.* Columbus: Ohio State University Publications Office, 1964.

PIAGET, JEAN. *Play, Dreams, and Imitation in Childhood.* New York: Norton, 1951.

————. *The Origins of Intelligence in Children.* New York: Norton, 1963.

RADLER, DON H., and KEPHART, NEWELL. *Success Through Play.* New York: Harper, 1959.

RIBBLE, MARGARETHA. *The Rights of Infants: Early Psychological Needs and Their Satisfactions.* New York: Columbia University Press, 1943.

SEARS, ROBERT, MACOBY, ELEANOR, and LEVIN, HARRY. *Patterns of Child Rearing.* Evanston, Ill.: Row, Peterson, 1957.

SMART, MOLLIE, and SMART, RUSSELL C. *Children: Development and Relationships.* New York: Macmillan, 1967.

SPEARS, HAROLD. *Don't Push Me.* Association for Childhood Education International, 1960.

STRANG, RUTH. *An Introduction to Child Study.* New York: Macmillan, 1959.

TODD, VIVIAN, and HEFFERNAN, HELEN. *The Years Before School.* New York: Macmillan, 1964.

See Bibliography for parents at end of Chapter 14.

CHAPTER 5
Getting Ready to Read (2)

Speech and Language Development

(This chapter is especially for parents, teachers of Head-Start, Follow-Through, and Teacher Corps programs, Nursery School and Kindergarten teachers.)

Speech and hearing factors are contributory causes in 18% of reading disability cases and dyslalia (faulty articulation of speech sounds due to causes other than brain damage) was considered one of the causes in 14% of the cases. Faulty speech not only interferes with progress in reading but creates personality problems as well.[1]

The importance of detecting hearing problems early in a child's life so that they can be corrected has already been stressed. Because a child cannot be expected to reproduce speech sounds he cannot hear, one can readily understand the importance of accurate hearing.

---

[1] Helen M. Robinson, *Why Pupils Fail in Reading*. Chicago: University of Chicago Press, 1946, pp. 227–228.

Equally important is the accuracy of the speech sounds and patterns the young child is to imitate. A child's speech is usually patterned after the speech of those with whom he lives. Even after a child starts to school, the number of hours he spends at home and the amount of communicating he needs to do with family members during that time are a continuous influence on his speech development.

Sometimes a child's incorrect attempts at certain speech sounds are regarded by parents as "cute," and family members may encourage this baby talk by using it with the child. The child must eventually learn the correct speech sounds, and it is much better if he learns them correctly at the start. As with all learning, it is more difficult to overcome a faulty habit than to learn correctly in first attempts.

The formative period of speech development continues into kindergarten and first grade, and the child should not be considered retarded in speech if he has a few remaining imperfections in letter sounds as late as the third grade. This is the period, however, when strong emphasis must be placed on correcting faulty speech but without emotional stress.

In a study made by Mildred Templin in 1957, it was found that most children did not correctly produce the sounds of *th* (voiced), *z, zh,* and *j* until they were seven years old (Table 5-1).

Irene Poole, in an earlier study, found many children of up to seven-and-a-half years having difficulty with *s* and *r* sounds.[2]

Correct speech consists not only in the ability to reproduce the speech sounds correctly, but also in blending sounds within words, correct accent, intonation, pronunciations, patterning of phrases and sentences in accordance with our cultural usage, and rate of speech. All of these constituents of good speech are a part of good reading for, after all, reading material is printed language. Children must acquire the components of correct speech in order to read effectively. Of course, some speech refinement is acquired while and after a child learns to read, but the earlier and better the control of language is acquired, the easier will reading achievement be possible.

Speech skill is a positive activity involving the whole person. It involves thinking, imagination, sensitiveness in listening, accuracy in the adjustment of the organs of speech, high standards in effort, a critical

---

[2] Poole, Irene, "The Genetic Development of Consonant Sounds" (doctoral dissertation, University of Michigan, 1934), p. 61.

Table 5–1. Comparison of the Ages at Which 75 Per Cent of the Subjects Correctly Produced Specific Consonant Sounds in the Templin, the Wellman, and the Poole Studies

Sound	Age Correctly Produced			Sound	Age Correctly Produced		
	Templin	Wellman	Poole		Templin	Wellman	Poole
m	3	3	3.5	r	4	5	7.5
n	3	3	4.5	s	4.5	5	7.5†
ng	3	. .*	4.5	sh	4.5	. .‡	6.5
p	3	4	3.5	ch	4.5	5	. .‡
f	3	3	5.5	t	6	5	4.5
h	3	3	3.5	th	6	. .*	7.5†
w	3	3	3.5	v	6	5	6.5†
y	3.5	4	4.5	l	6	4	6.5
k	4	4	4.5	th	7	. .‡	6.5
b	4	3	3.5	z	7	5	7.5†
d	4	5	4.5	zh	7	. .‡	6.5
g	4	4	4.5	j	7	6	. .‡
				hw	. .*	. .*	7.5

* Sound was tested but was not produced correctly by 75 per cent of the subjects at the oldest age tested. In the Wellman data the "hw" reached the percentage criterion at 5 but not at 6 years, the medial "ng" reached it at 3, and the initial and medial "th" and "th" at 5 years.

† Poole, in an unpublished study of 20,000 preschool and school-age children reports the following shifts: "s" and "z" appear at 5.5 years, then disappear and return later at 7.5 years or above; "th" appears at 6.5 years and "v" at 5.5 years.

‡ Sound not tested or not reported.

Source: Mildred C. Templin, *Certain Language Skills in Children*. Minneapolis: University of Minnesota Press, 1957, Table 24.

attitude toward self, and a release and sense of power with accomplishment.[2]

Influences of the Home

Few parents realize the tremendous amount of education a child gets in the home long before he is ready for school. His whole language and speech patterns are well established by then. There are meanings behind the words he uses, relationships among them, and experience associations with them. What is more important, there is feeling about everything he does: what he thinks of himself, and what he thinks of others. Parents are creating his whole outlook on life. But many mothers get bored with the simplicity of such early beginnings of learning—there is so much routine and monotony in caring for little children. As James L. Hymes has said:

2 Los Angeles City Schools, *Speech in the Elementary School*, Los Angeles, Cal., 1949, p. 1.

One factor in our life is that American women are well-educated. They have high standards, ambitions, drives. Many mothers have real trouble feeling right about simply relaxing with their babies: nursing them, bathing them, singing to them, playing. In our great productive country often women feel: "I ought to be *doing* something. Just loving a baby is not doing enough." Mothers in many other parts of the world have nothing more important open to them. To be with a child, to hold the youngster, to care for him, is their life.

An additional problem is arising in an increasing number of families: There simply is no time. Mother works. She is out of the house on a job. She has outside interests, friends. The baby has a substitute—a nurse, a maid or just some other woman who "keeps babies"—but rarely does the substitute do "mothering" with any real enthusiasm. Yet mothering is what very young children need.[3]

A mother must develop her own attitude toward the significance of her responsibilities. She can sense a thrill with each new response the child makes. She can win smile after smile and see an emerging happy child if she smiles as she talks to, sings to, and fondles him. She can accept the mundane tasks as contributing to the welfare of the world's most priceless treasure—a child. She can enjoy sharing stories, rhymes, and jingles to make childhood a happy time. She can find new interests in books on all aspects of child care and learning and in books the child himself will enjoy. She can be sustained by rewards such as gleeful laughter as little games are played; eyes that show surprise, delight, and wonder at each new experience; a vocabulary that is often amazing as it grows by leaps and bounds if opportunities exist; new capabilities and more expressions of love and affection. She can know that hundreds of other mothers are having the same problems that accompany the pleasures of early childhood. She needs association with other mothers and the time to be alone and with other people. All this can make for satisfying, contented, and rewarding motherhood. On the other hand, she can allow herself to be bogged down with self pity, boredom, a longing for other activities, and a relationship with the child that is seldom rewarding to either her or the child. A child is very sensitive to the true feelings of his mother.

Unless we can help mothers understand, appreciate, and enjoy their role, we had better provide Head-Start programs for all "kept" children.

Head-Start teachers should not be selected on the basis of academic

[3] James L. Hymes, Jr., *A Child Development Point of View*. Englewood Cliffs. N.J.: Prentice-Hall, 1955, p. 22.

achievement. They must be young women who love children, who are patient with the minute details of learning, and who relate well to children. They must know what constitutes the important first steps of developing, learning, and being.

What follows in this chapter will seem very simple (simple indeed!). But if every child coming into the primary school brought with him the background suggested in this and the preceding chapter, he would be ready to accept, use, and enjoy reading.

SPEECH AND LANGUAGE DEVELOPMENT

Language to the child is a tool he employs to impose himself upon his environment. This assertion of the self through words may or may not involve communication with others. Words are not symbols of varying degrees of accuracy: They are magic. Life is impoverished for child or adult, when the words lose their magic. The most serious single criticism that can be made of the schools—all schools everywhere, but especially American schools—is that they operate systematically, especially through the reading program, to destroy prematurely the child's sense of the power of words.[4]

Speech and language are inseparable. The speech sounds of our culture constitute the language, and speech sounds are learned in the context of meaningful words and phrases. As soon as a child starts to notice people and begins to make babbling sounds, there is an attempt on the part of adults to prompt him to say, "Mama," "Daddy," and other words. He is molded into speech patterns from babyhood. There is evidence that some children begin to respond to certain words as early as nine months.[5]

Several studies indicate that some children have a vocabulary of about 2,500 words when they enter school, which is only a small part of all the learnings that take place through the influence, direction, and opportunities of the home during the time before a child comes to school.

Language should be a part of all the activities mentioned in the preceding chapter.

Regardless of where a child lives, his environment is rich in first-hand experiences that make language meaningful. Facilitating learning is a matter of attaching language to, stimulating interest in, and answering questions about what the child sees, tastes, smells, hears,

4 Martin Mayer, *The Schools*, Garden City, N.Y.: Doubleday, 1963.
5 M. M. Lewis, *How Children Learn To Spend*. New York: Basic Books, 1957, p. 62.

and does. His likes and dislikes are giving meaning to such terminology as: "m-m-good! " "more! " "too much," "not so much," "enough," and to words that go along with recognizing, relating, controlling, using, and expanding his environment. For example, the opportunity to use a perfume atomizer to give himself one squirt of perfume gives a young child the "feel" of using an atomizer and gives him meaning to the words *squirt, squeeze, atomizer, perfume, fragrance, smell,* and so on. Squirting, squeezing the bulb, smelling, feeling the cool moisture on his skin, hearing the sound of the atomizer and seeing how it works, all help to develop a concept of these objects, sensations, and an appreciation for them. Thus percepts take on relationship.

The relationship of these percepts and association with the word *perfume* is known as *generalization* and the end product is a *concept.* It is these percepts and concepts with which children think. The percepts and concepts are the substance of *thinking.* Children soon begin to note more advanced relationships—cause and effect, classification, wholeness and parts—and soon adults are bombarded with endless queries of What is this? What is this for? What's in it? Can I take it apart? Why? Why? Why? Conversing while an activity is experienced can utilize many words that could not possibly be foretold or anticipated. Neither can words be explained as meaningfully as when they are used along with an activity.

Piaget believes strongly that knowledge comes from operation:

Knowledge is not a copy of reality. To know an object, to know an event, is not simply to look at it and make a mental copy, or image, of it. To know an object is to understand the process of this transformation, and as a consequence to understand the way the object is constructed. An operation is thus the essence of knowledge; it is an interiorized action which modifies the object of knowledge. For instance, an operation would consist of joining objects in a class, to construct a classification. Or an operation would consist of ordering, or putting things in a series. Or an operation would consist of counting, or of measuring. In other words, it is a set of actions modifying the object, and enabling the knower to get at the structure of the transformation.[6]

The child may ask questions and questions may be asked of the child to stimulate thinking. The keenness of his interest, the clarity of the mental image he forms, the language involvement, the in-

6 Jean Piaget, "Cognitive Development in Children" (the Piaget Papers), in *Piaget Rediscovered: A Report of the Conference on Cognitive Studies and Curriculum Development,* ed. by R. E. Ripple and V. N. Rockcastle. Cornell University School of Education, Ithaca, N.Y., March, 1964, p. 8.

tensity of his feelings all determine the lasting effect of the experience. Thus, "knowing" is established. How long he retains each tidbit of knowledge will depend on how often the experience is called up for association with other experiences, how strongly he felt about the experience, whether he is frequently afforded the same or similar experiences, and whether he is given opportunities to talk about them. Just how much of the ability to retain is based on heredity is difficult to estimate, but the environmental influences are the only ones parents and teachers can hope to influence. Retention is extremely important in the teaching of reading.

To find out what a child knows about anything we rely heavily on language. It is our primary means of communication. Countless cases are on record of children who have been rated low in I.Q. and achievement tests because of poor language facility.

One can readily see how opportunity for simultaneous sensory, motor, and language experiences are basic to the development of intelligence and the ability to communicate it. In language and intellectual competencies the greatest development probably occurs between conception and the ages of three and four. We are not sure what limitations are placed on a child at conception and during pregnancy and at the process of birth, but we are becoming more and more aware of what can happen or fail to happen in early childhood. At age four, something can be done but not as much as at the preceding stage. At age six, something can be done but not as much as at age four. Less and less can be accomplished as children grow older, as far as intellectual development is concerned.

"According to Benjamin Bloom, fifty per cent of the variance in intelligence takes place between conception and age four; thirty per cent between the ages of four and eight, and twenty per cent after eight."[7] These statistics put emphasis on the importance of "growing and knowing" opportunities in early childhood.

A disadvantaged child not only lacks a wide variety of involving experiences but, because of it, he also lacks the vocabulary to express himself. Such vocabulary as he may have may not only be inadequate but faulty by comparison with the expected manner of speaking and usage of the school. These children need a rich stock of experiences in which they can become wholeheartedly involved so that language is required in the on-going activities. Thus they

7 Kirk, Samuel. "Language, Intelligence, and Education of the Disadvantaged," in *Language Programs for the Disadvantaged*, edited by Richard Corbin, and Muriel Crosby, National Council for the Teachers of English, 1965, p. 267.

gain self confidence and poise in using the school-accepted type of English. This is a task for Head Start and Follow-Through Programs.

LANGUAGE AND EMOTION

A very young child expresses frustration, want, fear, or discomfort by crying. A little later, he strikes out at the offender and points to indicate his desires. He may scratch, bite, pinch, or kick as an expression of frustration or displeasure, or to gain attention. Smiles, cooing, snuggling, hugging, or cuddling may show pleasure. Because a young child meets so many obstacles in the adult environment in which he lives, negative reactions are often more prevailing than positive ones. This is especially true where there are no understanding adults to comfort, reassure, support, or encourage the groping child. The child, in order to learn from frustrating experiences, must be helped to see how he can overcome obstacles, redirect interests, or otherwise acquire what he is seeking. If such procedures are accompanied by language interaction with the child, he comes to express his emotions more and more in words rather than in actions—that is, he will ask for help when he knows an adult is likely to provide it, rather than cry or kick at the obstacle. He will learn to talk about a problem rather than use his fists to get what he wants. Children can be helped through experiences to know that politely asking another child to share produces better results than snatching it away from him. He learns that saying "I'm sorry" when an infringement on another's rights is made can prevent an irate explosion, and that discussing rules of the game and going on with the play is better than getting angry and quitting or attempting physical violence.

Thus, language development enhances social development and both contribute to an understanding of concepts such as fairness, sportsmanship, courtesy, sharing, and feelings such as anger, helplessness, desire, happiness, and satisfactions, which in turn make reading more meaningful.

Talking and Correct Speech

To demand or expect quiet of nursery school or kindergarten children is to deprive them of rich language experiences. It is not enough for them to hear the teacher use words, phrases, and sentences; children have to get the feel of language as lips, tongue, teeth, and throat produce sounds and as meanings are experienced.

Only fifteen per cent of those said to have speech defects have any physical basis for them, and only ten per cent more have defects that could be classed as complicated. According to several authorities, about seventy-five per cent of all speech defects are the result of bad habits based on poor listening, carelessness, or imitating poor models. With this information it behooves teachers and parents to meet the challenge.

It is the responsibility of parents and teachers to detect faulty speech and to refer such cases for clinical diagnosis. If causes are physical, such impairments can usually be corrected before the child approaches the hurdles of formal reading. Often hearing and bilateral incoordination causes are uncovered in clinical study. Here again medical science and physical therapy can give assistance that will prevent reading problems in the child's later schooling. If no physical causes of imperfect speech can be found, other corrective procedures are outlined by the clinician, and parents and teachers are guided in therapy for the child that will assist him in substituting correct sounds for those he has habitually formed incorrectly.

There is much that a parent or teacher can do in an incidental way that is very helpful without producing pressures, fears, or frustrations in the child. Too much emphasis on what is wrong with a child's speech can cause stuttering, or it can cause the child to be so fearful of having his manner of speaking criticized that he is reluctant to speak at all.

STUTTERING AND STAMMERING

Almost any type of hesitant speech is more of a personality problem than a speech defect. As sneezing may indicate a cold, stuttering tells us that the speaker is not on free and easy terms with the world around him. People or situations are too threatening for him to have the assurance he needs to speak up without misgivings. There is tension or anxiety behind the flow of speech that acts as a constant interference. The following are some of the common causes of stuttering:

1. Loss of status, as when a new baby, or a step-parent, comes into the home, or a sibling is considered too superior.
2. A home situation in which the child is under pressure to hurry

with his eating, hurry in putting on his clothes, hurry in what he is asked to do, and hurry to say the things he would like to say.

3. Emotional involvement in toilet training, family strife, family criticism, habits such as thumb-sucking or nail-biting.
4. Lack of a security figure in the home or in school with whom the child can feel comfortable and relaxed.
5. A shocking experience, such as death in the family, sudden illness of a parent, an accident, or moving into an uncomfortable new situation.
6. Inconsistencies in what is expected of the child, nagging, etc.
7. Parents' impatience when a child is trying to tell something and they constantly interrupt or try to help.
8. Too high standards for the child to meet.
9. Tense personalities in the child's family circle; uncontrolled tempers and harassment create inner tensions in the child.

Each stutterer must be studied as an individual, and many times remediation depends on home cooperation. The following are suggestions for helping the child who stutters:

1. Always approach the child calmly and pleasantly.
2. Never refer to his stuttering, but accept what he has to say.
3. Be very patient and give him ample time to complete his tasks and communicate his ideas.
4. Try to find out what may be disturbing him, and refer the case to the visiting teacher if the home is involved.
5. Never get hasty or emotional when the child begins to stutter. Give him a reassuring smile or act very unconcerned.
6. Do not call unexpectedly on children who stutter. Be sure they have had plenty of time to think about what they want to say.
7. Help the child to forget himself by placing importance on his particular contribution and, if possible, help him to prepare it in advance.
8. Prevent any kind of failure and help him build up his self image by paying particular attention to his strengths and achievements.
9. Protect a stutterer from criticism or teasing. A child must understand that he has worthwhile things to say and that he can say them easily if everyone cooperates by being good listeners.
10. Help the child to know that you are his support, his friend, and you have the utmost confidence in him.

GENERAL SPEECH IMPROVEMENT

A very positive approach to correction can be made once a teacher is aware of a clinician's diagnosis. If a child says, "Him makes good pictures," a teacher might respond with, "Yes, he does make good pictures. Would you like to tell Mary that he makes good pictures, and the two of you might like to watch how he does it." Then listen to see if the child has followed the correct pattern in talking to the other child. Rather than refer to anything the child has said as wrong, it is better to help him substitute in subtle patterning. (See Appendix B for speech-sound check.)

If no hearing or speech organ defect is present but the child habitually says *w* for *r* and *d* for *g,* an understanding teacher can find many situations for reenforcing the correct sounds. In playing "Pump-Pump-Pull-Away" on the playground she can take the child by the hand and suggest that they say, "Run, run, run," all the way across the playground. Hearing all the children say it and participating with them should enable the child to hear the sound correctly and afford many opportunities for using it correctly. After a while, the children might be encouraged to say, "Go, go, go," as they run across the playground in the same game. Sometimes help must be given the child in proper placement and use of lips, tongue, teeth, and throat in making the various sounds. Emphasis must be on the correct sound, and nothing should be said about the incorrect one the child has been using. The following charts give directions for making the various speech sounds.

Description of Sounds of English[8]

VOWELS AND DIPHTHONGS

Caution: For vowels and diphthongs the tongue tip is never any higher than the cutting edge of the lower teeth. "High" or "low," referring to tongue position for vowels or diphthongs, are comparative terms, as the tongue is never very high in the mouth for any vowel.

[8] Adapted from *Speech for the Retarded Child, A Teacher's Handbook* by permission of the Board of Education of the City of New York.

Sometimes children need individual help with the placement of the tongue in making certain speech sounds. Good speech paves the way for an association of speech sounds with letters that represent them. (Photograph courtesy of the Cincinnati, Ohio, Public Schools.)

The following are two groups of sounds that are effectively taught first because they are frequently used and are basic to word-building.

LONG SOUNDS

ah—a "yawning" sound. Drop the jaw, lower tongue, unround lips.

arm	car	market
barn	father	farm

ay—a diphthong formed by the combination of the short vowels *e* (as in end) and *i* (as in it). Drop the jaw slightly and spread the lips easily.

ate	made	play
bake	cane	away

ee—a "smiling" sound. Spread the lips easily, drop the lower jaw very slightly so that there is little space between the teeth.

eat	feed	people
machine	clean	cedar

aw—a round, open sound. Lower back of tongue, drop jaw, round the lips.

*a*ll	*wa*ter	qu*a*rter	b*ou*ght
b*a*wl	s*aw*	t*a*lk	c*au*ght

oh—a diphthong formed by the combination of the vowels, *o* (as in p*o*lice and *u* (as in f*oo*t). Drop the jaw and round the lips for *o*, raise jaw very slightly and increase rounding for the *u*.

*o*pen	c*o*ld	*o*cean
c*oa*t	gr*ow*	sh*ou*lder

oo—roundest of the vowels. Open mouth slightly, round lips well.

m*oo*n	fl*ew*	tr*u*e
r*oo*f	r*u*de	l*o*se

SHORT SOUNDS

a (as in *a*pple)—a "relaxed," open sound. Be sure to relax while lowering the front of the tongue and jaw. *Avoid a nasal sound.*

*a*pple	m*a*n	fl*a*g
c*a*t	h*a*nd	l*a*mp

e (as in *e*nd)—a very short "smiling" sound. Spread the lips and drop the jaw a little more than for *ee*.

p*e*n	r*e*d	s*ay*s
fri*e*nd	s*ai*d	f*ea*ther

i (as in *i*t)—another short "smiling" sound. Lower the tongue and drop the jaw a *little* from the position for *ee*, relax, and keep the lips spread. For this sound the tongue position should be a little higher than for *e* (as in *e*nd).

h*i*t	b*ui*ld	pr*e*tty
c*i*ty	b*u*sy	w*o*men

o (as in *o*ffice)—an open, rounded vowel. Lower the back of the tongue and relax the jaw as though you were going to say *ah,* then round the lips a little.

c*o*ffee	d*o*g	w*a*nt
c*o*llege	g*o*t	w*a*tch

u (as in *u*p)—open low vowel. Lower middle of tongue and the jaw.

*u*nder	d*o*ne	s*u*n
c*o*me	c*u*p	j*u*st

OTHER VOWELS

a (as in b*a*sket)—made with a lower tongue position than *a* in *a*pple. Drop the front of the tongue and the jaw a little farther than for that sound. If pupils have difficulty mastering this sound the *a* (as in *a*pple) may be used instead. The most important thing in teaching this sound is to aim for pleasant voice quality and avoid nasality.

*a*fter	cl*a*ss	p*a*st
*a*sk	d*a*nce	gr*a*ss
*a*nswer	h*a*lf	Fr*a*ncis

ur—er—ir—or (as in t*ur*n, b*er*th, f*ir*st, w*or*m)—a vowel frequently *mispronounced* by addition of the consonant *r* (as in *r*ed). Keep the tongue tip down on the back of the lower front teeth, drop the jaw slightly, raise the middle of the tongue to a high position and spread the lips a little. *Avoid pronouncing r.*

f*ir*m	m*er*cy	*ear*th
w*or*st	b*ir*thday	*ear*ly

oo (as in b*oo*k)—a rounded, short vowel. Lower the tongue from the position for *oo* (as in m*oo*n), relax the lips and jaw, round the lips. *Avoid confusing this sound with the vowel in "up."*

l*oo*k	g*oo*d	p*u*t
w*oo*d	st*oo*d	w*o*man

o (as in p*o*liceman)—a *very short,* round vowel. Lower the back of the tongue farther than for *oo* (as in b*oo*k), drop the jaw slightly, continue lip rounding.

*o*bey	N*o*vember
h*o*tel	p*o*lice

The indefinite vowel—a short vowel used *only in unstressed syllables,* as in *a*gain, moth*er*, sof*a*, *A*merica, c*o*rrect, p*a*rade, anim*a*l, etc. Drop jaw a little, have lips and tongue in neutral position.

OTHER DIPHTHONGS

i (as in I)—a "smiling" sound formed by combining the vowel sound *a* (as in *a*sk) and *i* (as in *i*t). Start to make the sound with the tongue on the lower front teeth lifting it a little as you spread lips slightly. *Avoid confusing this sound with ah* (as in Southern speech) *or pronouncing ah as the first element of the diphthong.*

m*y*	d*i*me	r*i*de	b*uy*	ch*oi*r
t*i*me	t*i*de	*ai*sle	cr*y*	h*eigh*t

oi—oy (as in b*oi*l b*oy*)—formed by combination of *aw* (as in s*aw*) and *i* (as in *i*t). Begin with jaw low and lips rounded as for *aw*, then spread lips for *i*. Avoid confusing this sound with *ur* (as in t*ur*n).

*oi*l	enj*oy*	r*oy*al
t*oy*	sp*oi*l	s*oi*l

ou—ow (as in *ou*t, d*ow*n)—formed by combining *ah* (as in *a*rm) and *oo* (as in b*oo*k). Lower the back of the tongue and the jaw for *ah* (a "yawning" action) then round the lips for *oo*.

*ow*l	t*ow*n	l*ou*d
c*ow*	m*ou*th	r*ou*nd

ea—ee—ei—ere (as in d*ea*r, d*ee*r, w*ei*rd, m*ere*) formed by combining *i* (as in *i*t) and the indefinite vowel (as in moth*er*). It is frequently *mispronounced* by adding the consonant *r* (as in *r*ed). Lower the tongue as you say this sound, keep lips relaxed and in a neutral position. *Avoid pronouncing r unless a vowel follows.*

ear	f*ear*	m*ere*
h*ear*	n*ear*	ch*eer*

ai—are—ea (as in *ai*r, f*are*, t*ear*)—formed by combining a vowel (not ordinarily used alone in New York City speech) for which the tongue is slightly lower than for *e* (as in *e*nd) and the indefinite vowel, (as in the final syllable of chin*a*). *Avoid pronouncing r unless a vowel follows.*

f*air*	wh*ere*	p*are*nt
m*are*	d*are*	th*ere*

oo (as in p*oo*r)—formed by combining the round vowel *oo* (as in b*oo*k) with the indefinite vowel. Lower the tongue as you move from the first to the second element of the diphthong. *Avoid pronouncing r unless it is followed by a vowel sound.*

t*our*	s*ure*	d*oor*
y*our*	c*ure*	ch*air*

oo—or—ou (as in st*ore*, d*oor*, p*our*)—formed by combining the *aw* (as in s*aw*) with the indefinite vowel. Lower the back of the tongue and round the lips as for *aw*, relax and lower the tongue for the second element of the diphthong. *Avoid pronouncing r unless it is followed by a vowel.*

fl*oor*	sh*ore*	*oar*s
m*ore*	p*our*	w*ore*

Caution: Final *e* that is silent is not considered a vowel. In words such as mere, where, sure, store, and tore the *r* is *not* pronounced unless the word is followed by one beginning with a vowel as in: "The store *is* open" or "Where *is* he?"

CONSONANTS

The terms "voiced" and "whispered" used below in describing consonants refer to vibration or lack of vibration of vocal cords. A "voiced" sound has vibration; a "whispered" or "voiceless" sound has not.

b (voiced)—Press the lips together lightly and quickly separate them by the force of breath—feel vocal cord vibration.

*b*oy	tu*b*	*b*a*b*y

p (whispered)—Press the lips together lightly and separate them expelling breath as in puffing a pipe—feel puff of air expelled while saying this sound.

*p*encil	cu*p*	*p*a*p*er

m (voiced)—Close lips gently and hum through the nose—feel the "hum" on either side of nose.

*m*an	co*m*e	ha*mm*er

w (voiced)—Round the lips and separate them quickly expelling voice —use a mirror to watch lip rounding.

*w*inter	q*w*eer	t*w*ice	any*w*one

h (whispered)—Open the mouth and sigh—feel the puff of air expelled.

*H*arry	*h*im	*h*ouse

d (voiced)—Press the tongue tip against the ridge behind your upper teeth, then take it away suddenly (as though knocking sharply on a door), making a plosive sound—feel vocal cord vibration. Use a mirror to check on correct tongue placement.

*d*ig	*d*i*d*	gla*d*ly
*d*og	ba*d*	la*dd*er

t (whispered)—Press the tongue tip against the ridge behind the upper teeth, then take it away suddenly expelling a puff of air that sounds like the tick of a clock. Use a mirror to check on tongue placement.

*t*able	ha*t*	bu*tt*er

n (voiced)—Place the tongue tip on the ridge behind the upper teeth and let the sound hum through your nose, making a sound like a motor "warming up"—feel the vibration on either side of the nose.

*n*ose	te*n*	pe*nn*y

g (voiced)—Raise the back of the tongue to touch the soft palate and then release it quickly expelling a plosive sound. *Avoid giving pupils detailed directions*—if they substitute *d*, direct them to lower the tongue tip, feel vocal cord vibration.

*g*o	do*g*	bi*gg*er

k (whispered)—Raise the back of the tongue to touch the soft palate and release it, expelling a plosive sound (if pupils substitute *t,* have them lower the tongue tip)—feel the puff of air.

candy	key	tack	lucky

y (as in *y*ellow) (voiced)—Lift the front of the tongue, feeling it slide lightly against the roof of the mouth as you voice the sound. If pupils substitute *j* (as in *j*am) direct them to spread lips for *ee* and lower tongue tip.

*y*es	*y*ou	stu*d*ent	few

ng (as in si*ng*) (voiced)—Raise the back of the tongue until it presses lightly against the soft palate and hum through the nose—feel the hum by touching the sides of the nose.

ng

si*ng*	bri*ng*	lo*ng*	ha*ng*er
si*ng*er	bri*ng*ing	you*ng*	ga*ng*
si*ng*ing	wro*ng*	stro*ng*	swi*ng*

ng plus *g*

lo*ng*er	stro*ng*er	you*ng*er	a*ng*ry
lo*ng*est	stro*ng*est	you*ng*gest	la*ng*uage
E*ng*land	hu*ng*ry	si*ng*le	fi*ng*er

f (whispered)—Place your upper teeth lightly on your lower lip, blow air through the narrow space between teeth and lip—feel the air stream. Use a mirror to observe position of teeth on lips.

*f*ast	cal*f*	rou*gh*	a*f*ter
*f*ather	hal*f*	cou*gh*	co*ff*ee

v (voiced)—Place your upper teeth lightly on your lower lip, blowing through the narrow space between teeth and lips as you voice the sound—feel the vocal cord vibration. Use a mirror.

*v*alentine	li*v*e	o*v*er

sh (whispered)—Proceed as for the sound above but blow breath without voice—feel the air stream. Use a mirror to prevent any tendency to protrude the tongue.

*sh*e	wa*sh*ing	pu*sh*
*s*ure	ma*ch*ine	fini*sh*
*Ch*icago	o*ce*an	di*sh*
	atten*ti*on	
	ti*ss*ue	

s (as in plea*s*ure) (voiced)—Raise the tip of the tongue toward gum ridge, draw the tongue back slightly until the sides of the tongue contact the upper side teeth, blow through the space between the front of the tongue and the gum ridge as you voice the sound. Teeth are close together.

measure   pleasure
treasure   garage

l (voiced)—Press the tip of the tongue against the ridge behind the upper front teeth, feel air escaping over the sides of the tongue as you *hold* the tongue position and make a voiced sound.

*l*ady   ba*ll*   he*ll*o

th (as in *th*umb) (whispered)—proceed as for the sound above but blow a voiceless sound—feel the air stream. Avoid pressure.

*th*ree   bo*th*   bir*th*day

th (as in *the*) (voiced)—Allow the tip of the tongue to touch the edge of the upper front teeth, *blow* a voiced sound through the narrow space between the teeth and the tongue—feel the air stream. (Avoid *pressure* of tongue on teeth as this will produce a plosive *d*.)

*th*e   fa*th*er   brea*th*e

s (whispered)—Point tongue tip toward (but not touching) the ridge behind the upper teeth with sides of tongue lightly touching the sides of the upper teeth, keep teeth close together, but not clenched, and blow a stream of air gently, through the narrow space between tongue tip and gum ridge—feel the air stream. Use a mirror.

*s*ee   *c*ereal   cat*s*   i*c*e

z (voiced)—Proceed as for the sound above but add voice—feel vocal cord vibration. Use a mirror.

*z*oo   plea*s*e   buz*z*   freez*e*   ea*s*y

r (voiced)—Turn the tongue tip up and slightly back, keep the sides of the tongue in easy contact with the edge of the upper side teeth, and blow a voiced sound over the tongue tip. *This sound is pronounced only when followed by a vowel.*

*r*ed   *r*ead   car*r*y   ve*r*y   spar*r*ow

ch (whispered)—Join *t* and *sh;* proceed as for the sound above but whisper this sound. If pupils substitute *sh* for *ch,* have them feel the tongue tip touch the ridge for *t*, then quickly pull it away, expelling the sound *sh*.

*ch*air   tou*ch*   *ch*ur*ch*   rea*ch*ing

j (as in *J*ane), *g* (as in *G*eorge) (voiced)—Join *d* (as in *d*oll) and *s* (as in plea*s*ure) by touching the tongue tip to the ridge behind the upper teeth for *d*, pulling away quickly as you widen the space between tongue tip and ridge and blow a voiced sound—feel the vocal cord vibration.

*j*am	*J*une	hed*g*es
*j*elly	ed*g*e	reli*g*ion

If children do not soon begin to practice all of the phonemes in the English language, eventually they will not be able to make some of the phonemes, as, for instance, Yugoslavs cannot make our "v" or "w" and North Americans have great difficulty with the Spanish "r." Children must practice early.[9]

Use can be made of sentences containing a preponderance of the sounds needed for reenforcement. Finger plays, poems, and jingles that are fun for the child are better than meaningless sound ditties. (There are many fine speech handbooks such as the one developed by the Los Angeles City Schools and Montebello County Schools of California that give a variety of exercises, games, etc.)

To help young children hear all speech sounds clearly and produce them accurately is a great stepping stone toward success in reading. The speech test in Appendix B is good for individual diagnosis.

The sounds that seem to cause the most trouble in children's speech are *s, r, l, th, g,* and *k.* The blends *dr, cr, bl, cl* and *tr* are sometimes difficult. If children can be helped to hear and to reproduce all speech sounds correctly, they will have a tremendous advantage in learning to read.

THE PROBLEM OF DIALECT

If a child's dialect is so different from standard English that the speech sounds of his words do not correspond to most standard English, then there can be no phonetic relationship to printed words and reading is still another language. In Negro speech there were found to be ten phonetic and thirty-six phonemic differences according to a Chicago study. There is controversial thinking with regard to standardization of school children's dialect. Some say, "Sometime during his schooling the child should master English dialect, but it does not matter when, and thus nothing is wrong with a gradual, drawn out approach to teaching it."[10]

However, if standard English is going to be an asset in social and employment situations, and if the child's dialect is going to be a deterrent when reading is presented, it would seem that the earlier

9 Walter Loban, in "A Sustained Program of Language Learning." National Council for the Teachers of English, 1965, p. 226.

10 Bereiter, *op. cit.,* in "Academic Instruction and Preschool Children," p. 198.

his standard English becomes habitual the better. Parental programs in standard English would seem to be extremely important. Parental speech improvement would be very advantageous for children in all homes because so much of language patterning is accomplished in the home. If, at the earliest possible age, children can have standard English labels attached in all they experience and all they communicate, then thinking and speaking will be in that form, and the way is paved for an easier approach to reading. Studies made by linguists of various dialects can be very useful to teachers in helping children not only with the speech sound differences but also the differences in verb forms, syntax, and accent. A child cannot be expected to read easily in standard English when his pattern of speaking is almost like that of another language.

Vocabulary and Concept Development

Experience is the substance of language and language is the instrument or medium of learning, thinking, and, eventually, reading. Words become the labels for all that is seen, heard, felt, smelled, tasted, done, or experienced in any way. The meanings are more permanently established if we help children to associate all that goes into the meaning of a word with what he already knows, so that the association is very broad. For example, the word *orange* should have the following associations for a child: a distinctive color, a distinctive shape, a surface texture that can be seen and felt, a spatial relationship that he comes to know so he can adjust his hand to grasp it and to know the distance his hand must travel and the approximate weight of the orange as he anticipates grasping it. He knows about how much effort it takes to hold an orange. It has a distinctive aroma. He has seen it peeled and he may be able to do the peeling himself after observation and experimentation. He has seen the sections, the pulp, and the seeds. He comes to recognize the taste. He may have seen an orange cut and squeezed, so that he knows what it looks like inside as well as out. He may have put his tongue and fingers on it as well as looked at it. He may have had fresh or canned orange juice to drink. He may have tasted a very sour orange and later recalls the unpleasant taste so that he isn't enthusiastic about tasting another; in time, however, he comes to know that oranges vary in degree of sweetness. He may have been given medicine with orange juice, which may give the word *orange* an unpleasant connotation. He may have seen a grove of orange trees in California or Florida in bloom and smelled the fragrance of orange blossoms, observed the maturing process, or picked the fruit. If he lives where oranges are grown, he may come to know the difference between Valencia and Navel oranges and the time of the year that they ripen. Pleasure or frustration may have been a concomitant emotional part of any of the preceding experiences. The child may have had various kinds of orange-flavored candy, gelatin dessert, marmalade, cake, icing, sherbet, etc. He may become familiar with various shades of the color orange through crayons, paints, clothing, etc. He becomes aware that other things in his environment are orange in color, such as pumpkins, some kinds of squash, etc. Thus, one word becomes an ever-broadening concept, and there is no limit to the types of experiences that go into the facets of understanding and feelings toward just such a word.

In good teaching, clear-cut mental images must be established by bringing as many of the senses into play as possible and by bringing to a level of awareness and significance the qualities and relationships within the experiences children have. Later such imagery will be evoked as children recognize words in phrases and sentences in reading. This is the substance of reading. As stated before, *it is not what a writer puts on the printed page but what the reader brings to it that determines what constitutes the product of the reading act.*

DEPRIVED CHILDREN AND CONCEPT DEVELOPMENT

The development of the concept of the word *orange* is a good example of what conceptual background a deprived child may lack. *Orange* is a word used in one of the intelligence tests, and frequently there are children who cannot respond to it. Deprived children do not necessarily come from financially poor homes. They come from experience-deprived situations. Children left to the care of a housekeeper whose only concern is to get the work done and keep the children out of mischief are usually the most deprived. If the housekeeper uses poor English and is irritable and neglectful, the children are actually in a detrimental situation.

The school tries to compensate for such deprivation and the Head-Start program is especially intended to compensate for the lack of opportunities of underprivileged children. Backgrounds of experiences must be provided before reading can be meaningful. All the foregoing experiences related to muscular, sensory, and speech growth must be checked and carried on at the child's individual stage of readiness. It is difficult at age five to make up for all that has been lacking for more than four of the child's most formative years. Yet, attempting to start such children with reading is like giving a needy family material for a roof before a foundation is laid or walls have been erected.

Learning experiences can be planned for a child only insofar as he can be inspired to want to be an active participant. To tell a child, "Do this; now do that; see this; feel that; listen to this," is little better than turning a child into a barren play yard to amuse himself day after day. Opportunities must be opened to the child, along with stimulation toward nurturing an attitude of enthusiasm to see, hear, feel, do, and find out.

A good teacher with a true zest for living soon captivates children with the wonders that any environment holds. She helps them to have eyes that envision, ears that listen, touch that detects, and minds that inquire, respond, appreciate, reflect, and project—not because the teacher merely asks for these responses but because she has caused the children to want them and to feel good about every attempt to achieve them. She guides, stimulates, challenges, encourages, and recapitulates as plans are made, activities proceed, and conclusions are drawn. She helps children initiate, develop, and evaluate activities so that they become increasingly able to carry on for themselves. Such activation leads to the need to read and an understanding of the purposes reading will serve.

Suggestions for Developing Concepts

TALKING   A Head-Start teacher can begin a class with a question such as, "What did you see on your way to school?" (possible answers: birds, cars, grass, buildings, trees, sky, clouds, people, trucks, insects, rain, store window displays, flowers). It might be well for the teacher to start the discussion with what she saw, stimulating enthusiasm and inquiry as she talks. At first most children are likely to make very simple statements. With such prompting as, "I wonder if you noticed what kind of a truck it was?" or "What do you think that trucker was delivering?" children soon begin expanding what they have to say. They begin to observe more carefully, and soon it is apparent that they are forming clear-cut mental images with more and more detail, which helps expand vocabulary and establish language patterns in real-life situations. Use a positive approach to

any kind of correction. "It might sound better if we said————."
Encourage children to comment about what is said. When they are
critical ask them to help say it in a way that would sound better.
Always be careful not to correct speech or usage so much that children stop talking.

Many young children, in telling about what they have seen, go
off on a tangent of make-believe. It is difficult to know whether
these fabrications are what they actually think they saw as a result
of poor mental images or whether they are the result of stories they
have heard. Regardless of the reason, it is during the primary grades
that teachers must help children to differentiate between fact and
fancy. This must be done without causing the child to feel guilty
or self-conscious. When you know that what the child is saying is
definitely a flight of imagination, let him know that it is make-
believe. *And to Think That It Happened on Mulberry Street,* by
Dr. Seuss, is a good book to use for a discussion of what is real and
what is make-believe in a child's telling about what he saw as he
walked along a street. Sometimes it is fun to tell make-believe stories,
but we should have special times for them. In a kind but definite
manner help children separate the real from the unreal.

Encourage children to ask questions of one another to satisfy and
nurture their curiosity. Each observer will sense the need to look
more carefully, use all of his senses, and be prepared to tell his experience so well that everyone will understand. Many words come into
use, and syntax becomes speech patterning. Language will then flow
naturally when children start to read.

EXCURSIONS Take a walk around a city block, down a country
road, or around a neighborhood. You might suggest watching for
birds, animals, flowers, or pretty leaves. Do not be distraught if the
children find something far more interesting (to them) along the
way than what you had suggested. Let them determine the topics
for discussion when you and the group return to the classroom.
Praise children for careful observations, and let use of language
expand as it will from interest in, curiosity about, and problems
arising from the expedition.

Suppose the children see a dog on the street. One child says,
"That's a fox terrier. I know it because I've got one at home."
Another child says, "No, it isn't. It's a Scottie." Other children express opinions and there is a lively discussion. Instead of offering her
opinion the teacher might say, "Let's take a very good look at this
dog so we can find out what kind of dog he is. Look at his hair. See

how curly it is. Look at the color. What about his size? Take a good look at his face. What about his ears and his tail? Are his legs long or short?" Again, children are experiencing the need for very careful observation and the forming of clear-cut mental images. Now the children are ready to be helped to know how to resolve their problem. They are encouraged to find out all they can about dogs by asking questions at home. The teacher looks up pictures of fox terriers and Scotties that evening. She may ask two children the next day to go down the hall to the library to ask the librarian for a book about dogs (that children their age could understand). (The teacher may need to write a note for the children to take until they have had enough of such experiences to feel capable of telling the librarian what they want.) Children should be given an opportunity first to tell what they found out at home. They may have enough information to identify the dog, and the book and pictures may only serve to verify their findings. Anyway, they come to know that books are important for obtaining many kinds of information. As the children report what they learned at home, rather than have many children repeat the same thing simply ask, "How many others found out the same thing? Fine, Jim, Nancy, Carl, and Susan, that's what we call research—when we seek answers to our problems from many people and places."

In using pictures let the children decide through careful inspection which one looks like the dog they saw. Then read what it says below the picture and read from the book what is pertinent. They will be delighted with their own solution of the problem, and they have participated in many worthwhile experiences that are better than that of the teacher merely telling them what kind of dog they saw. Point out the fact that their being able to read someday will help them to know what it says below pictures and in books and then they can solve many of their own problems.

Excursions provide many first-hand sensory experiences, encourage the use of much language, lead to questions and problems that in turn give opportunities for research, further expansion of vocabulary, more concepts, and more opportunities to see how books are extremely useful.

A walk to observe all that is displayed in a store window (bakery, pet shop, toy store, hardware store, drug store, small grocery are best) sharpens observations and stimulates visual memory. Challenge the children to see how many things they can recall about the display. Again, the discussion can do much to broaden concepts (uses of many items, prices, varieties, brands, etc.). Discussion might lead to bringing in items about which there is disagreement, special interest, or a particular use that may be made of the item. Buying a coconut at the grocery store and a bag of assorted nails at the hardware store can add further delight to the excursion. Sorting the nails as to size and discussing their use, counting and finding a good place to keep them are good related learnings. The coconut can be lifted and felt by every child, and the monkey face at one end of it will be intriguing; the children can decide what sized nail should be used to punch the holes to drain out the milk. Every child will get to taste the milk and eat a piece of the coconut meat. Conversation is likely to include their having seen shredded or flaked coconut in packages or cans that mothers have used in cakes, cookies, or candy.

A box of tissues may be purchased at a drug store at little cost. Back at school the box may be passed around for each child to pull out a tissue. A demonstration on how to cover one's nose and mouth when a sneeze comes on can be followed by each child attempting it. Attention is called to the soft quality of the tissue, how one sheet is folded into the next so that they are easy to pull from the box. The word *absorbent* may be explained as children observe how moisture is soaked up into the tissue. Children's remarks such as, "My mother makes flowers out of tissues," and "We wrapped my model airplane in tissue when we moved," expand the concept of tissue. Further discussion of various brands of tissues and a comparison of prices and number of sheets in the box leads to an awareness of what goes into careful buying.

Excursions through a bakery, a zoo, a park, a fire station, or a garage afford further variety in rich concept development. It can include other related learning such as respect for various types of work, an appreciation of a clean park, kindness toward animals, respect for neighborhood yards, and responsibility for expressing thanks for conducted tours. Attitudes and values are related parts of the learning process as well as the language involvement.

Forming concepts, in the broadest sense, involves more than the statement "This is a dog." It is what else a dog is, what it is not, how it is related to many other concepts by being alike and different in form, color, use, and so on. For instance, a kitten is an animal; it is also a pet; it is not a toy unless it is a stuffed one; it may be friendly or it may scratch; it has feelings and needs; there are various kinds and colors and sizes; it can be compared with other pets, and so on. Many of the above concepts can be elaborated considerably. There is scarcely an end to such ever-broadening concepts, but the extent is limited by the attention span and interests of the children. Nevertheless, an enthusiastic teacher grasps every semblance of interest and carries the group on with real enchantment in their growing knowledge. She uses every possible situation to point up the fact that someday being able to read will help them find out more and more about all the wonderful things that are in the world to explore.

OPPORTUNITIES TO GUESS   Bring in a surprise paper bag and pass it around for the children to lift, shake, smell, and feel. Sometimes they might need to "handle with care." Then encourage guessing and talk about plausibility of guesses without condemnation of poor guesses. Help children to think carefully of the limitations of being in a paper bag. Guessing and the possibilities afford good language and thinking experiences. The bag might contain such things as a yo-yo, a hand puppet, an envelope scales, a compass, a magnet, a bag of balloons (one for each child), a very large box of crayons, a sweet potato, a package of seeds—all have significant uses that can be discussed and demonstrated. It is interesting to note how the children will become better and better in their guesses. They can give each other reasons for the why or why not of certain choices. The follow-through of concept and language development is tremendous because the teacher has the undivided attention of all the children in their interest in a surprise package. Sometimes a wrapped box or covered basket may be brought in for greater variety in what it might hold.

NUMBERS   Use numbers in all possible situations, both numerals and ordinals. For example, count how many children are present: how many girls, how many boys. Help children grasp the one-to-one relationship when counting—have them wait until you touch a child's head before he is counted. Refer to first, second, third, etc., in referring to position. Keep game scores on the chalkboard and challenge children to count them with you. Write figures in large size whenever they relate to on-going activities. Make such terms as: *more than, less than, as much as, altogether, how many,* and *how much* meaningful in the things you do from time to time. Many situations can be utilized to help children know the meaning of the monetary units of pennies, nickels, dimes, quarters, half-dollars, and dollars. When the class goes to a store let a child be responsible for the money transaction. Such transactions may involve buying a box of crackers that can be passed around at milk time; a package of seed or a sweet potato to be planted; a box or two of animal crackers to be passed around, identified, and eaten; a stalk of celery or a bunch of carrots to be prepared and served at snack time; a package of gelatin; a loaf of bread and a jar of peanut butter.

Much discussion should take place about anything that is purchased—its price, utility, quality, quantity, amount, texture, taste, form, production, packaging, and development of an interest in what is printed on the package.

MEASUREMENT Introduce items of measurement such as cup, pint, quart; ruler and yardstick; teaspoon and tablespoon; pound; and others that are meaningful for the children in the situations in which they live. Sand or grain in a large box, in the classroom in cold climates or outside in warm climates, affords wonderful free-play activities of measuring, hauling, buying, and selling, etc. Such terminology as *level, heaping, rounded, equals, deliver, cost in terms of weight or measurement units* are all a part of on-going play that will involve many concepts and utilize much language. The able teacher will be at hand to give much guidance and to expand learnings. Disregard the inch markings on rulers and yardsticks; they are too small for the stage of eye development of children under seven. Express delight when children discover that two cups fill a pint measure and two pints fill a quart. Encourage children to use a ruler to level off measures. Encourage them to share their findings with classmates so all will feel a satisfaction in discovery of facts in learning.

TIME The time concept begins with the here and now. Today is the appropriate beginning. Yesterday and tomorrow soon take on meaning as children talk about what they did and are going to do. *Soon, later, before, after, morning, this noon,* and *this afternoon* are concepts which come into use in the planning. Before children go home from school at the end of the day frequent mention is made of "this evening" and "tonight." *Early* and *late, daytime* and *night-time* take on meaning before *weeks* and *months.*

Frequent mention of the days of the week can be made: Today is Monday; who can tell me what day tomorrow will be? Does anyone know what the next day will be? and the next?" etc. On Friday, "We don't come to school tomorrow or the next day. Do you know what day tomorrow is? the next day?"

The month of December is a good time to introduce the calendar. Children are eager for Christmas and they can count the number of weeks and days. They can be shown how each big number is a day.

The days of the week are across the top and each row of numbers is a week. It is fun to make a ceremony of crossing off a number each day and counting the remaining days. Encourage children to go up and explore the calendar when they have free time. They may discover that there are twelve months. They may look for their birthdays. Some may note that all the months do not have the same number of days, that months may start on different days. The stage is set for introducing a new calendar when they return after Christmas. Select one with very large numerals. Coming birthdays may be circled; spring vacation may be indicated; and toward the end of the year remaining days may be counted. The intent is not to teach everything there is to know about the calendar, but to engage in meaningful counting and to extend vocabulary.

Time can be mentioned frequently: time to go home, time for rest, time for milk, time to clean up, etc. Comments involving time concepts (we go home one hour after outdoor play; we'll be going home in five minutes; it is just ten minutes until recess so let's see if we can finish our work in that time) and their experience association help to give children a sensitivity to time.

Discussing age at the time of birthdays gives children a first experience with the concept of years. Carrying the discussion farther by talking about the ages of brothers and sisters makes it more meaningful. The time between one Christmas and the next, one birthday and the next, one Halloween and the next, and one Thanksgiving and the next is very long in a young child's living and thinking. Few young children can remember that long.

CONCEPTS OF ACTIONS AND THE LANGUAGE INVOLVED Young children need much large muscle activity. They cannot be expected to sit quietly for long periods of time. However, much language development can take place along with activity. Children enjoy rhythms, and there are many fine records for skipping, running, galloping, marching, and walking that can be accompanied by remarks such as: "Now we are marching. Let's say 'left, right, left, right' as we go marching around the room"; "Isn't it fun to gallop like horses? Let's say 'Here we go galloping, galloping, galloping' as we gallop around the room"; "This time let's say 'I skip, I skip, I skip' as we do it to the music." In making plans for the work period a teacher might say, "Who painted yesterday? Who would like to paint today?" "Jean, what did you do yesterday?" Thus, children become familiar with the present and past tenses of such words as *play, work, rest, draw, finish, bring, follow, sing, dance, hop, clean, clap, tip-toe,* and many others. A teacher will use special care to involve children who need help with present and past tenses.

"State-of-being" terms such as *is, are, was,* and *were* require much contextual usage to establish them as speech patterns. At this stage of development, what is known as "structural grammar" can have a sound foundation. When a child misuses a word form—for example, "I seen a dog yesterday"—a teacher might say, "Jane saw a dog yesterday" (with emphasis on *saw*) and "Bobby, what did you see?", and she would call on a child who would be likely to use the correct form. Then she might call on several others who would be likely to use the correct form before calling on someone who needed the reinforcement of having heard the correct form used a number of times and who would now be likely to use *saw*. If the incorrect form is used the teacher might quickly correct it without losing the thought content of what was said. It is always much better to point up the correct form and provide opportunities for using it than call attention to an incorrect form. Some children who use the correct form may become confused after hearing too much mention of an incorrect form. It is best to avoid reference to any speech pattern as being "wrong." It may be the form used consistently in some children's homes. If the teacher says, "It sounds better to say '————,' " it is not offensive and is far more effective.

It is a very real challenge to teachers who work with the underprivileged to make correct substitutions for "I ain't got no," "them there," "him don't got," etc. A teacher needs to work calmly, inoffensively, and gradually so as not to inhibit the speaker or lose the significance of the content of his statement. She must help the child feel secure in knowing she has a kind accepting attitude toward the content of what he is saying and is genuinely interested in helping him to say it in a better way.

CONCEPTS OF SPATIAL RELATIONSHIPS AND CORRESPONDING LANGUAGE DEVELOPMENT

Everything known about language suggests that the improvement of writing and reading must be built upon instruction in oral English.[11]

With children sitting close at hand a teacher may use a bean-bag and challenge children to see if they can do exactly as someone says. She might start by saying, "Please put the bean-bag *on* the table,

11 Richard Corbin, in *Language Programs for the Disadvantaged.* National Council for Teachers of English, 1965, p. 28.

Joyce." Then Joyce will tell someone where to put it in the same polite way. In this way words such as *on, under, beside, between, below, beneath, above,* and *in* are used.

CONCEPTS OF QUALITIES, CONDITIONS, AND IDEALS WITH LANGUAGE ASSOCIATIONS It takes much living and much awareness of interactions with people, places, and things to grasp the concepts of beauty, kindness, courage, fear, sympathy, appreciation, and caution. The wary teacher will make use of every possible situation to use these terms in various appropriate experiences the children are having. For example, on a bright spring day the teacher might greet the children with, "What a beautiful morning. The sun is shining, the birds are singing, the temperature is not too hot or too cold. It is a truly beautiful day. What other things do you know that are beautiful?" You may be amazed at some of the observations of children. The importance of such a discussion is that it helps more children to be aware of beauty, to look for it, and to appreciate it. Under-privileged children especially need to realize that there is much beauty in life that is not bought or sold. Some homes afford little experience that would enable children to understand love, kindness, or sympathy. School can never in any sense be a substitute for parental love, but acts of kindness and consideration may be as important to the over-indulged child as they are for the deprived child is establishing "self" and "other" relationships. Many deprived children have never experienced a closeness with anyone. Helping them to find satisfaction in being friends with one another through smiling at each other, sharing, going hand in hand to the playground, choosing a partner to take a message to the principal, inviting someone to look at an achievement, sitting beside a friend to listen to a story, to sing or participate in a game or rhymes all serve to give meaning to friendship. Further happiness can come from having many friends. "To have a friend is to be a friend" is a good slogan for young children. Children can suggest what causes them to like people and these reasons become the basis of their own standards or friendship values.

Stories can point up or reinforce the above-mentioned qualities. Stories and poems "get inside" children. Each child relates himself to the characters and the events. A story carries a message far better than anything else. It is not the teacher or the parent saying, "think this way," "get this meaning," or "understand that." It is the appeal of Caddie Woodlawn and her fine philosophy in action, the regard for animal life that Robert Lawson so charmingly develops in *Rabbit*

Hill, and the joy of sharing the simple things in life brought out in *Ask Mr. Bear,* that carry messages to children—lasting messages that give language deep and abiding meanings. Poems sing to children; they are the music of literature and help children to know and appreciate that our language has rhythm. Affectionate child-to-child, children-to-teacher, and teacher-to-children relationships foster open, relaxed, and joyous avenues of communication that will in turn give the child reassurance when he is ready for the tasks of reading. It is well to get the idea across to children that one can never have too many friends and that to cut someone out from a friendship circle is really hurting oneself as well as the person left out. Some children, however, must rely heavily on a teacher's friendship, and the teacher must sometimes struggle to help the child gain acceptance by his peers. Rejection is very debilitating at any age, and a teacher renders a great service if she can help each child to be worthy of acceptance and all children to be receptive in the belief that there is something good in every person if they seek it out.

Reading about courage, affection, kindness or any of the other qualities, conditions, or ideals and their opposites can never have true meaning for the reader unless he has had certain related experiences in his background to make them real.

Critical Thinking

Because critical thinking is so vital in our culture, and because it is an important part of reading, we need to take advantage of opportunities to help young children use it as they listen, see, and respond.

A group of kindergarten children listened to the story of *Katy No-Pocket,* a story of a mother kangaroo who had no pouch for her baby and kept him in the pocket of a carpenter's apron. One child asked, "Could a baby kangaroo live that way?" Instead of answering the question, the teacher responded with, "What do you boys and girls think?" Such replies as, "He wouldn't be warm enough," "He couldn't eat," etc., brought about excellent thinking and led to other skepticism and queries.

"Do you think that's a good title?" or "Do you think you would do what he did?" or "What would you have done?" are good thought-provoking questions to follow the reading of a book.

Critical thinking about news items, advertising, etc. can be initiated as soon as interest can be developed. There should be many opportunities for continuous growth in critical thinking.

Language Refinements

Conversation is the most natural, vital, and significant activity possible for the development of vocabulary and speech patterns. Children should be encouraged to carry on running conversations while they work unless it is a listening experience. Asking questions and listening intently to answers and thinking about them in relation to what they are doing is one of the most natural day-by-day language learning experiences that people of all ages can have. Too often in classrooms of young children, conversations are largely from child to teacher and teacher to child. Too seldom is there conversational give-and-take among children, and yet conversation is carried on in life more frequently than reading. If only parents were as anxious to improve children's ability to converse interestingly and well as they are to hurry them into reading, the latter would come more easily and be more meaningful. The child would be far better equipped for getting along in the world of people. Even after children are able to read, there is no better way of checking comprehension than stimulating children to converse about what they read.

It is parents' and teachers' responsibilities to foster growth in language through conversation. Merely being permissive in allowing children to converse freely at appropriate times is not enough. She needs to note and call attention to descriptive and qualifying words, phrases, clauses, and figurative language. Words can be fun, and children like to twist the unusual ones around their tongues and experiment in their usage. A word of praise for complex sentences motivates others to try to make more than simple statements.

Suggestions for Expanding Children's Language Facility

1. Challenge children by such remarks as "Let's think of all the words and phrases that would describe or tell about this kind of day" (*cloudy, hazy, balmy, mild, warm, chilly, cool, gray, foggy, crisp, damp, fall, spring, cold, autumn, wintery, windy, makes you want to hurry, makes you feel good, beautiful, rainy, umbrella weather,* etc.). "Let's think of all the words and phrases that would

describe how we went to the bakery" (*walked slowly, looked all around, walked with partners, talked softly, were polite*, etc.). "Let's think of all the words and phrases that would tell about what kind of person the baker was" (*short, fat, jolly, clean, kind, funny, hustled and bustled, had a nice voice, explained everything carefully, quick*, etc.). If a child comes up with an unusual word like *efficient* give him much encouragement and have him explain its meaning to the class. Expect more and more of the unusual as children progress. Make use of many such situations so children become aware of more and more descriptive, qualifying, and enchanting words. Children having many such experiences in oral language have little difficulty later in obtaining meaning from reading, understanding grammar, and writing creatively with ease, fluency, and charm, and they will enjoy doing it.

2. Read many types of literature at the children's level of understanding, pointing out interesting use of words, making sure they get the meanings and share a real appreciation for the materials used. (See Appendix O.)

3. Use rhymes, jingles, and finger-plays so that they are regarded as fun. Encourage children to share them at home. After much use, help the children hear the words that rhyme. Challenge children to give words that rhyme with: *it, in, all, nest, at, day, me,* and *sing.*

4. Challenge children to retell favorite stories. They may challenge the other children to guess what story it is. They may sometimes tell about a favorite storybook character and ask the class to guess who it is. A series of clues may be given for a book.

5. Play "Fun with Words" games in which children are challenged to give words that rhyme with a certain picture as: *car, fan, bee, bed;* other words that mean much the same as a given word; words that mean the opposite; words that have many meanings.

6. Challenge children to bring in a new word with its meaning every Friday morning. Then see whose word can be used the most times the next week. Record them on the chalkboard.

7. Bring in pictures and challenge children to tell all they can about the picture. Sometimes ask them to state only facts and sometimes use make-believe.

8. Give children opportunities to tell about activities, drawings, and any other types of classroom work, including evaluations and summarizations of work activity.

9. Challenge children with riddles and share simple jokes.

10. Involve children in discussions of cause-and-effect relation-

ships. For example, when problems come upon the playground or in the classroom or on the way home from school, involve the class in a discussion to determine the basic causes and then involve them in determining remedies.

11. Dramatizations. Start with very simple enacting of well-known favorites such as *The Three Bears, Three Billy Goats Gruff,* and *The Three Little Pigs.* Peep-through puppet faces are very good in helping children overcome timidity. The child holds the cardboard caricature with both hands and thrusts his head through the opening to play the role of the character. Hand puppets are also good in giving children moral support as they speak for the character. Most finger puppets are too small for young children, but third-graders can create them for stories they think could be "played." Dramatizations give children poise and self-confidence along with practice in voice modulation, good expression, wide use of language, and recognition of direct quotations. All this oral language paves the way toward making printed material meaningful and helping the child to read well both silently and orally. Flannel board stories serve the same purpose. They may be told by the teacher until children are ready to participate.

This chapter and the preceding one present in detail what constitutes a child's physical, mental, social, emotional and linguistic readiness for reading. (See Appendix G for a good summary of growth factors at various ages.) The various aspects of each have been discussed separately, but in reality they all take place simultaneously and in an interrelated manner. For example, a child is learning the social amenities of give-and-take as he builds blocks and converses with his classmates. In the same activity his coordination and speech development are being enhanced, and he learns to control his emotions when things go wrong. (See Appendix C for a kindergarten inventory.)

Much of what has been suggested seems like mere play, and in many instances, play it is! Play is a child's world of living. In it are all the problems he faces at home and in the world about him and with the people with whom he must abide. But in his miniature world of play he can resolve all conflicts, set things to right, and be himself in the kind of world he wants. Much perception, much problem-solving, much critical thinking, and much use of language are paving the way for easing into meaningful and useful reading. Lawrence K. Frank has this to say in defense of play:

When play seems to the casual observer to be most purposeless, a child is orienting himself, endlessly rehearsing what will later become directive in all his activities. He learns what no one can teach him. If the child had only to master the physical world, his task would be relatively easy since like other organisms he has inherited capacities for such neuro-muscular learning and sensory discrimination. But the infant organism must be humanized—learning to live in our symbolic cultural world; learning to recognize and respond to the meanings of things; events and people; learning the complicated and subtle problem of human relations; and learning goal seeking, purposive striving. Hence through play the child continually rehearses, practices and endlessly explores and manipulates whatever he can manage to transform imaginatively into equivalents of the adult world. He experiments with and tries to establish the meaning and use of a variety of symbols, especially language, as he tries to cope with this often perplexing grown-up world. In his imaginative use of play materials and games as surrogates or models, or miniature replicas

Playtime is the time when a child may be himself or someone else and feel good about it. Play affords many opportunities for language and concept development. It often improves the quality of oral expression. (Photograph courtesy of the Cedar Rapids, Iowa, Public Schools.)

72638

of this adult world, he creates a microcosm more amenable to his limited strength and skills and understanding. Through verbal play he tries the varied combinations of words and phrases, discovering and mastering the meaning of these verbal symbols and practicing communicating, both verbal and non-verbal.[12]

James L. Hymes has said of play:

It is clear that much intellectual development comes through the senses. The essential means is: Play. As youngsters: see, touch, feel, etc., they do things in their own imaginative way. They use language as they play. They act out, they try on for size, all the bits and pieces of information that have come in to them. Play is threatened in the times we live in. Our society seems hellbent to end it and to move youngsters much more quickly into a talky-talk kind of learning that has form, and right and wrong, where progress is tested and measured, where standards are established and rigid, where one task must be accomplished before the child can move on to the next.[13]

Play fosters individuality, togetherness, and social competencies. In addition to play the extensive use of suggested activities in the various areas of development is to indicate that readiness is not mere waiting for children to grow up, but it is the teacher's and parents' responsibility to provide rich and varied experiences that give children opportunities for well-rounded development. Professor Almy has said in defense of some "direct instruction" and "organized information":

Much has been made of late of the importance of children's finding out, or "discovering," new ideas or new relationships for themselves. From one point of view, this is the essence of Piaget's theory—the child comes to an understanding of the world through his own efforts. While he may accommodate his thought to the ideas of others, it is only as he tries those ideas out within the context of the ideas he has previously acquired that he makes them his own.

But there is no reason to believe that a discovery is more meaningful if the child has had to flounder aimlessly for a period before making the discovery. The essence of Piaget's method, it might be said, is the assessment of the child's readiness to make a particular discovery, and the pacing of his educational experience to that readiness so that he will have both the intellectual content and the cognitive abilities needed to make it. There is nothing in either the theory or the method to imply

[12] Lawrence K. Frank, "Play and Child Development," in *Play—Children's Business.* Association for Childhood Education International, 1962, p. 4.

[13] James L. Hymes, Jr., "Intellectual Development of the Pre-School Child," in Maryland Child Growth and Development Institute Proceedings, Baltimore, Md., 1959.

Dramatic play is often a very effective means of improving speech. Good diction, proper inflections, and wide use of words must precede expectations of good oral reading. (Photograph courtesy of the Cincinnati, Ohio, Public Schools.)

that there is no place for the giving of direct instruction, or for the supplying of organized information. The implication is, rather, that the curriculum should be so arranged as to organized information so that it is within the grasp of the child, once he has sufficient opportunity to explore and manipulate it.[14]

14 Millie Almy, Edward Chittenden, and Paula Miller, *Young Children's Thinking.* New York: Teachers College Press, 1966, p. 139.

READINESS BOOKS

Many readiness books have detail that is too small for the young child. They develop and check on rather restricted aspects of eye-hand coordination and other prereading skills that can be accomplished more satisfactorily through activities that will be presented in the next chapter. Some kindergarten children may be ready for and benefit from certain types of readiness materials if their eye development has been given basic consideration.

Proportionately, a child does more learning from birth to five years than any other time in his life. By providing worthwhile opportunities, a stable emotional climate, congenial playmates, inspiration, and challenge, mutual respect and the reassurance that he is important and is doing well we can give him the best preparation not only for reading but for all of life.

—VERNA DIECKMAN ANDERSON

Suggestions for Class Participation and Discussion

1. Listen to the speech of several young children. Record the speech sounds that were made incorrectly. Also note any unusual speech patterns these children seem to make. To what do you attribute them?
2. What good reasons would you give a parent for developing good speech and expanding language development before starting formal reading?
3. Present arguments for and against attempting to change the dialect of young children.
4. Can you think of two kindergarten situations where children might be challenged to do some critical thinking?
5. Share with the class some interesting information gleaned from a reference on speech.
6. Reflect on how you were helped with speech and language development as a child.
7. Discuss how a "Friday Word Time" session could be made interesting and enlightening for children at the age level you intend to teach.
8. What are the most common speech errors you are inclined to make? Plan a course of action for correcting them.
9. Are there adult classes for the improvement of speech and language in your community? Are they needed? How might they be provided?
10. Discuss the full significance of the quotation at the end of the chapter.

Bibliography

ALMY, C. MILLIE. *Children's Experiences Prior to First Grade and Success in Beginning Reading.* Teachers College Bureau of Publications, New York, 1949.

ANDERSON, VIRGIL. *Improving the Child's Speech.* New York: Oxford University Press, 1953.

Boston Public Schools, *ABCD, Boston Pre-Kindergarten Program,* Boston, Mass.: 1964. (This publication contains many practical suggestions for teachers of young children.)

BRYNGELSON, BRYNG. *Speech Correction Through Listening.* Chicago: Scott, Foresman, 1959.

BURTON, WILLIAM H. *The Guidance of Learning Activities.* New York: Appleton-Century-Crofts, 1962.

CHURCH, JOSEPH. *Language and the Discovery of Reality.* New York: Random House, 1961.

CORBIN, RICHARD, and CROSBY, MURIEL. *Language Programs for the Disadvantaged.* Champaign, Illinois: National Council for Teachers of English, 1965.

EMIG, JANET, FLEMING, J. T., and POPP, H. M. *Language and Learning.* New York: Harcourt, Brace & World, 1966.

FRAIBERG, SELMA. *The Magic Years.* New York: Scribner, 1959.

Fresno Unified Schools, *The Compensatory Program, Pre-School Guide,* Fresno, Calif., 1965.

GOLDEN, RUTH. *Improving Patterns of Language Usage.* Detroit: Wayne University Press, 1960. (Available from National Council for Teachers of English, Champaign, Ill.)

HENLE, PAUL. *Language, Thought and Culture.* Ann Arbor: University of Michigan Press, 1958.

HILDRETH, GERTRUDE. *Readiness for School Beginners.* New York: Harcourt, Brace, 1950.

HOLBROOK, DAVID. *English for the Rejected.* New York: Cambridge University Press, 1964.

HUNT, EARL. *Concept Learning: An Information Processing Problem.* New York: Wiley, 1962.

HYMES, JAMES L., JR. *Before the Child Reads.* New York: Harper, 1958.

JOHNSON, WENDELL. *Speech Problems of Children.* New York: Grune & Stratton, 1957.

———. *Toward Understanding Stuttering.* The National Society for Crippled Children & Adults, 1958.

LAMBERT, HAZEL. *Teaching the Kindergarten Child.* New York: Harcourt, Brace & World, 1958.

LEWIS, MORRIS. *How Children Learn to Speak.* New York: Basic Books, 1959.

LIN, SAN-SU C. *Pattern Practice in the Teaching of Standard English to Students with a Non-Standard Dialect.* Teachers College Bureau of Publications, New York, 1965.

LOBAN, WALTER. *Problems in Oral English*. National Council for Teachers of English, 1963.

LORETAN, JOSEPH, and UMANNS, SHELLEY. *Teaching the Disadvantaged*. New York: Teachers College Press, 1966.

Los Angeles City Schools, *Speech in the Elementary School,* Los Angeles, Calif., 1949.

Montebello Unified School District, *A Guide for Speech Improvement in the Primary Grades,* Montebello, Calif., 1954.

REDL, FRITZ. *Understanding Children's Behavior*. New York: Teachers College Bureau of Publications, 1949.

RIESSMAN, FRANK. *The Culturally Deprived Child*. New York: Harper & Row, 1964.

ROBINSON, HELEN F., and SPODEK, BERNARD. *New Directions in the Kindergarten*. New York: Teachers College Press, 1965.

ROOT, SHELDON. *Source Book on English Institutes for Elementary Teachers*. National Council for Teachers of English, 1965.

STAUFFER, RUSSELL. *Language and the Higher Thought Processes*. National Council for Teachers of English, 1965.

TEMPLIN, MILDRED. "Certain Language Skills in Children, Their Development and Interrelationship," in Institute of Child Welfare Monograph Series, No. 26. Minneapolis: University of Minnesota Press, 1957.

WANN, KENNETH, *et al. Fostering Intellectual Development in Young Children*. New York: Teachers College Bureau of Publications, 1962.

Regarding preschool language programs: The following school systems have helpful bulletins: New York City Schools: Merced, California Schools; Cincinnati Public Schools; Oakland, California Public Schools; Austin, Texas Schools; Los Angeles City Schools; Denver Public Schools.

See also the Bibliography for Parents at end of Chapter 14.

CHAPTER 6
The Beginnings of the Reading Act

Research shows that it is fatal to "push" young children along in the initial stages of learning to read, particularly if there have not been activities to create a functional language background beforehand. Many children fail in reading because they are plunged into formal reading with an over-analytic method employing abstract symbols before they really understand what words and sentences mean in spoken, let alone printed form. Young immature minds need opportunity and time to "sort things out," to understand what they are doing, and to see the purpose in the operations with which they are confronted. My strongest plea in the teaching of reading is, don't hurry children, don't expect too much in the early stages—do all you can to provide a language background. This slower, wider approach will repay doubly later on.[1]

Some of you may not recall how or when you started to read. It may have been so much a part of on-going activities that there was no crucial moment when it began. Others of you may have a vivid memory of a certain teacher, of sitting on your father's or mother's

[1] Sir Fred J. Schonell, *The Psychology and Teaching of Reading.* New York: Philosophical Library, 1961.

knee and being helped to read, or struggling for a long period of time before you felt that you had any real control of the reading process. Nevertheless, each of you learned to read. Sometimes learning to read comes in spite of, rather than because of, certain methods or techniques. The desire to know may be so strong that any kind of help gives the child enough clues so that he can go on through efforts of his own to make further discoveries about words and their relationships. With more help when he asks for it, his strong motivation carries him along to satisfy his interests and curiosity. Our culture makes such heavy demands on the ability to read that each individual eventually feels that he *must* read.

If children are helped to have the kind of background proposed in the preceding chapters, they are ready to slide right into the act of reading with anticipation, ease, and pleasure. There are hundreds of specific ways in which reading can be accomplished with varying degrees of "rightness" or "wrongness" depending on the individuals involved, the situation, and the motivation. If children were machines they could be put on a production line of recorded, programmed, machine-checked lessons, and all would come out with the same capabilities. But because children are human and few retain the same things from a given experience, any successful reading program must be geared to individual needs and interests rather than machine procedure. Basic requirements are inspiration, determination, and understanding. Some children may learn a word after a single exposure, while others may require hundreds of exposures and then, when it suddenly becomes important to the child and he interacts with it, the word is his and, we hope, with meaning, significance, and retention.

Children may read a phrase or even whole sentences as first reading experiences. In fact, if they understand that reading is language written down, it is better for them to read thought units of varying lengths right from the start. Children will differ as to how they catch on to reading. Some will almost move ahead of the class in their ability to associate likenesses of sound units from known words to new ones and to figure out new words from the meaningful context of the sentences. Others have to be helped to use every possible clue that unlocks words and phrases and their meanings. For some it is difficult learning and easy forgetting. It is a real challenge to a busy teacher to offer these children fresh stimulation and challenging approaches day after day in order to make even the most minute bit of progress, but sometime, somehow, each child (with the preceding elements of readiness) can and will learn to read.

Most of what follows should happen simultaneously. Some of it may have been happening at home and will continue through successive stages of reading. There must be overlapping, reinforcement, renewed enthusiasm, and continuous support as children proceed. There is always far less danger of too much review than there is of frustrating children by expecting more than they are ready to achieve. Delight in each accomplishment is wonderful motivation for continued efforts.

Invitations to Read

We live in a "you-must-read" culture, so it should not be difficult to introduce children to it. In fact, many children will have been reading from television, in restaurants, in Sunday school, and on the street before they come to school if an interested adult has ever answered the question, "What does this say?"

A statement of caution to be repeated often throughout the discussion of beginning reading is *Do not introduce very young children to ordinary book size print. Their eyes are not ready for it until they are six or seven years old.* There is much about reading that can be taught before book reading is introduced, and children will read books much more easily and with greater pleasure and understanding if correct preliminary steps are taken. The following are suggestions to be used as encouragement for reading.

ENVIRONMENTAL READING

SEQUENTIAL PICTURE STORIES Buy two good picture books with large details of a story with which children are already familiar, such as *The Three Bears, Peter Rabbit, The Three Little Pigs, The Gingerbread Boy, Jack and the Beanstalk,* and others that may be purchased at any dime store. First, read it to the children, showing them the title and running your hand under it from left to right as you read it. Then read or tell the story showing the pictures page by page as you proceed with the story. The next day challenge the children to tell it with you as the pages are turned. When you feel that the children know the story well, and before they become tired of it, explain that you are going to put the pages along the chalkboard (use the type of paper tape that holds well and can be pulled off easily from both the book pages and the chalkboard) just high enough for them to see the pictures at their eye level as they walk along. While they are watching, in your best large manuscript writing print the title of the story just above where the pictures will be placed. Give them several opportunities to read the title as you sweep your hand along under the words you have written. Explain that *they are reading*. They know what it says and their eyes are moving from left to right as they see the words. At their leisure, children may then follow the sequence of the story in pictures from left to right (cut off the print as it is too small for them to attempt to read). The next day challenge a child to move a hand along under the words you have written and read the title of the story. The delight of the teacher at such an accomplishment gives children further satisfaction in feeling able to read. The story may be told from picture to picture with a different child telling about each page. After several days the teacher may introduce a second large picture book in the same way. When she takes down the pages of the first book (two copies are required in order to have front and back sides of each page), these pages may be used as a challenge to children to put them in the right order. It is a good idea to paste a sheet of light colored paper under the front cover and manuscript the title in letters about 1½ inches high. Thus, children become familiar with the title of books and the print is large enough so that it doesn't strain their eyes. Separate the pages of the two books because one is enough of a challenge to put in correct order. This is a good way to help children know the mechanics of reading from left page to right page, turning the page over, and moving again from left to right. Children are also learning to keep in mind a sequence of ideas, which is an important aspect of reading. The pages of each book may be kept in a large envelope or large flat box with the title printed in one-and-a-half-inch letters. When a child has been checked to be sure he has arranged the pages correctly he is then challenged to mix the order of the pages before putting them into the envelope for the next child to rearrange. Keep introducing more picture stories as long as interest can be maintained.

BULLETIN BOARD MATERIALS A bulletin board can be made so interesting to children that they will rush to it when they come to school in the morning to see what new treasure it might hold. The bulletin board may relate to an excursion, to special interests of the class, to science, to a holiday, or to the current season. The

Stimulating room environment can help children to want to read. (Photograph courtesy of the San Diego, California, Public Schools.)

caption at the top should be in very large letters—preferably about three inches high—because it appears above the eye level of the children and they will be observing it from a distance. If the material lends itself to subtitles these should be introduced so that reading will be from top to bottom of the bulletin board and always from left to right.

For example, before the Christmas holidays the title of the display might be "Merry Christmas"; there could be pictures, with captions below them, of Santa Claus, angels, toys, dolls, book, puzzle, ball, game, carols, reindeer, and sleigh. The lettering may be done on strips of paper and mounted on the bulletin board with tape or pins. Other holidays may be featured this way, too. On the first morning when the display is new it is well to take time to enjoy it with the children and help them *read* the various captions starting with the top and working down and across from left to right. The children will have no trouble reading from the picture clues and will feel very good about it. Tell children to look at the pictures and captions frequently when they have time during the day. Refer to them and read them again before the children go home in the afternoon and tell them that several days later you will take down all the words and see how many they know without the pictures. In a second grade, those who are ready may be challenged to write a story using some of these words; the bulletin board serves as a dictionary with reference to spelling. (By Christmastime some first graders will have had enough common words to be ready to do some independent writing.) Be sure to give them a chance to read the stories they create. For each holiday the bulletin board can serve as a very good spelling reference for words pertaining to both the holiday and season. Sometimes second- and third-graders need such help, and this is one way they can get it without disturbing the teacher. Advanced kindergarten children can be challenged with a few such pictures. It is important to discourage looking at fine print; keep young children's reading interests on large-sized print.

Occasionally a bulletin board may be used to advantage in helping children with a cluster of common phrases such as *on the table, under the table, by* or *beside the table, above* or *over the table.* It is easy to use large sheets of brown construction paper and cut the tables all at one time. Colorful balls may be made and placed appropriately and the captions placed beneath on strips of paper. Always use a bulletin display as soon as it is put up and be enthusiastic about it. Children will read from the picture clues. Then the phrase strips may be taken down and the children challenged to read them without the picture clues. After trials, one or two children can be challenged to find the right places for them as they are returned to the bulletin board. At the very beginning of such experiences a second set of phrase strips may be used and children may be challenged to match the phrases, then to read them independently with a look at the bulletin board for verification.

Early in October a second-grade bulletin board might have a caption such as "Pumpkins Everywhere." Illustrations and captions below might be of pumpkins on fence posts, pumpkins beside fence posts, pumpkins under fences, pumpkins made into jack-o-lanterns. Another bulletin board with such illustrations and captions as "Signs of Halloween," ghost, witch, goblin, broomstick, magic brew, and skeleton give children an excellent reference for use in reading and writing stories independently.

USING PICTURE BOOKS   Feature each new book that comes into the classroom. A teacher's enthusiasm for a book is very contagious. A course in children's literature should be a requirement for every student preparing to become an elementary school teacher. In this course teachers gain a wonderful background of knowledge about books, and from the vast number published and in libraries she can make wise selections in accordance with her tastes and the interests of children. Using the books effectively with children can do much to enhance their love of books.

When a lovely picture book is brought into the kindergarten the teacher holds it up reverently and refers to the loveliness, the mystery of content, and the fun of anticipating a good story. She moves her hand along under the title of the story and after reading it herself challenges the children to read it with her. After completing the story and showing the pictures as she goes along, she explains that the book will be put on a table, on top of a cupboard, or in some other conspicuous place where the children may go to look at it independently. At the beginning of the year the teacher should demonstrate how to handle a book, impressing the importance of having clean hands, looking at the cover and thinking about what the book is going to be about, how to turn pages carefully, how to start at the front of the book, how to look from top to bottom of each page and from left page to right page, and to put the book back where it should be. This kind of instruction is known as *the mechanics of books* and should be demonstrated again and again.

In the first grade the children occasionally may be challenged to read the title of the book the teacher brings in if the title contains words they know, if the picture on the cover might be revealing, or if they have had enough phonetic or linguistic clues to figure it out by themselves. Always let children have the thrill of reading something new and challenging when they can. Such activity is very stimulating and calls up all they have learned and the need for learning more.

At all grade levels teachers should continue to read occasionally to the class. They should demonstrate the best qualities of oral reading. There is no better way of helping children to want to read than to have them experience the joys of reading. In second and third grades a teacher may start reading a story and challenge the class to finish it themselves. The only problem in doing this is that every child will want the book at once. It is best to select a book of which several copies may be borrowed from the library. In fact, it is good motivation for second- and third-grade children to obtain library cards and be frequent customers of the local library. Sometimes several books may be started by the teacher and placed on a display table for leisure or free-time reading.

Poetry, rhymes, and jingles may be read or recited by the teacher with enough charm so that the children will want to be able to read them, too. After a short poem or jingle has had a good class response, the title of it may be printed on the chalkboard or on a chart; when children are ready for more than the title, the entire verse may be printed and put up in the room where children may go to read it. Second- and third-grade children may want to copy it to take home to read.

Here are some guidelines for reading to children:

1. Select stories and poems with care, making sure that the length corresponds to the attention span of the age level of the children in your class and that the content is within their ability to comprehend and will be of interest to them. (The bibliographies in Appendix O may assist you.)

2. Make sure you have the attention of every child before starting to read. Sometimes a finger play such as "Here are Grandma's glasses; here is Grandma's cap; this is the way she folds her hands and puts them in her lap," may help children to be ready. If you are having to wait for several children to join the group it might be a good time to introduce a new finger play or tension-releasing exercise (see Appendix E) or give individual children a chance to recite some of their favorites. Never expect young children to sit still with nothing more to do than wait.

3. Hold up the book with delightful anticipation, saying, for example, "We never know what exciting adventure will be between the two covers of a book."

4. Be sure everyone is seated comfortably where they can see and hear well. Seat any potential troublemaker beside you where you can put your hand on his head or shoulder without distracting the other children's attention.

5. Using a calm, soft, pleasant voice read the title of the book as you show the cover, giving all a chance to see it. Whet their appetites for the story by indicating just a little of the content, by challenging them to listen for answers to one or two questions, or by telling why you happen to like the story.

6. Read or tell the story simply and directly. Look up from the book as often as you can and look into the eyes of as many children as possible so that they feel the story is being read to them. If a child's attention seems to waver, draw him back by a remark such as, "And, Jim, the next thing that happened was ———" and go on with the story.

7. If one or two children become too obnoxious, send them away

from the group but be sure they have something to do. Be disgusted enough so other children will not want to join them or misbehave.

8. If the group as a whole seems disinterested in the story, stop reading and explain that you probably chose the wrong book and next time it will be one you are sure they would enjoy. Frown upon discourteous behavior. Make storytime a very special privilege and praise good listening.

9. Even though some children say, "Read it again," do not prolong story time to the extent that children get tired of listening. It is much better to end a story period with desire for more than to have children get too tired. It is seldom wise to read the same story a second time in one day. There are so many wonderful stories for all grade levels that only occasionally would we reread a favorite on request.

10. Facial expression, change of pace, and voice inflections can help hold attention and make the story more meaningful. A feeling of suspense will often bring the group to almost spellbound attention.

11. Use flannel board characters and hand puppets for certain stories that lend themselves to such portrayal. Children may be challenged to retell stories, to help retell by playing a part, or by merely holding or manipulating the props. Your rendition of the story will be the likely pattern they will use when they do the telling. A pleasant well-modulated voice is a great asset to a teacher.

12. Let the story stand on its own merits. Do not moralize. Children themselves will note that the Old Witch gets what she deserves or that kindness is rewarded or that it pays to tell the truth. A story can be somewhat depreciated by too much follow-up. Giving children a little chance to react to a story if they show inclinations is enough. They will savor it and long afterward may reveal what it did for them.

USING LABELS IN PURPOSEFUL WAYS IN THE ROOM   Introduce one label at a time and never clutter the room with too many labels. There is no good reason for using a label if the child will have no use for the word in his reading. There are many objects in the school room that will appear frequently in much reading material, and here the prelearning will be valuable. *Paste* will appear in many instances so it is a good idea to put that label on the shelf where the paste is kept and to examine the word and talk about it before it is put on the shelf. With a marking pen, the word *paste* may be put in bold letters on each jar, bottle, or tube.

Every label should be introduced to the children very carefully so that they have an opportunity to form a mental image of it before it is placed for reference use. Because *scissors* is rarely used in reading material there is no need to use that label. The word *cut* is used in reading directions, but since it is phonetic and very easy there is no need to use either *scissors* or *cut* on labels. *Draw* might be placed on a cupboard door where drawing materials are kept since it is so frequently used in independent seatwork, workbook, and reading test exercises. In fact, the sentence, "We write and draw," might appear on a cupboard where writing and drawing materials are kept since all those words will be used commonly.

When words such as *table, chair, window,* etc. are to appear in stories children are to read, it is a good way to introduce them and to have them for easy reference by presenting them as labels. These labels would be used for only a few days and then a careful check made to be sure children know the words as the labels are removed.

CHALKBOARD EXPERIENCES Every kindergarten and first-grade classroom should have a large section of chalkboard ruled 1½ inches apart with white paint. If a teacher cannot have this done she might use white crayon to make the lines. For mature children in the last half of kindergarten and for first-grade children there are many uses for ruled chalkboard space. Children can be learning much about reading, but it need not be the confining type where children are forced into reading type that is too small for the development of their eyes.

The following are suggestions for making use of the chalkboard:

Use of names. Manuscript a child's name and suggest that he write it below your copy. Molding clay around a stick of chalk sometimes makes it easier for the young child to grasp. He should be encouraged to start with the first letter only. In fact, it is a good idea to write only the first letter for him to copy until he can do it well. Then add the next and then the next, and so on. In this way the child is sure to work from left to right and establish that pattern from the beginning.

When the child can write his name well on the chalkboard, give him a name card to use at his seat (these cards should be heavy tagboard with three-fourths-inch ruling and the names should be two spaces high in bold lettering). Give him a sheet of ruled paper (three-fourths-inch ruling) and a pencil with soft lead. When he has accomplished this challenge he is ready to write his own name on his drawings and other paper work and should be encouraged to do it carefully.

After most of the children can write their first names the teacher might introduce the phrase, "I am _____," using a child's name. After *reading* this several times they can write it and take it home to read. It is a good beginning sentence and contains words that are used very commonly, are very different from one another, and have true meaning to the child and those to whom it is read. It yields great satisfaction in both reading and writing to the child, his parents, and the teacher. The rapid learners may write "You are _____" and become familiar with other children's first names. After many children can write "I am _____" and their names, these strips can be mounted at one end of the chalkboard or on a bulletin board with the caption "I Can Write My Name." Children are helped to read the caption and then to read each sentence as each child's strip is posted. Then the children may be challenged to practice writing any time they have free time, and whenever a sentence looks better than the one posted it may be exchanged. This is excellent motivation for children to compete with themselves and to want to do better. It can establish good work habits that will stay with the child if each teacher helps to nurture such values. Just before report cards are sent home in first and second grades, each child may be challenged to write, "This is my best writing," and sign his name. This is sent home with the report card for parents to keep and to compare with the sentence the child brings home the next time. The child will read what he has written and it will serve several good purposes. In second and third grades the children could write sentences such as, "The quick brown fox jumps over the lazy dog," which contains all the letters of the alphabet.

Sentence reading. The teacher might write a sentence such as, "I can walk" (moving her hand along from left to right under the words as she reads the sentence). "Now I am going to write, 'You can walk' " (and she reads that with a sweep of her hand). "Now let's read both sentences, all of us."

Explain that people sometimes read with only their eyes. They "think" the words that they see and do not say them out loud. They do not use their throats or their tongues or their lips—only their eyes. Challenge the children to read the sentences in this way as you move your hand under the sentences from left to right. Explain that they can now read *silently* like grown-ups.

"What else can we do?"

Limit the sentences to three or four with the common action words children suggest. They might be *work, play,* and *jump.* The teacher would write, "I can play," "You can play," "I can jump," "You can jump," etc. Be enthusiastic about their ability to read the lines silently with you. Now challenge them to read whatever line you point to. You might make a game of it by having the child who reads a line correctly become the teacher and choose a child to read another line. The teacher may have prepared matching sentences on strips of tagboard (the same size lettering as on the board) and challenge children to find other matching sentences. Now challenge children to find other words that look like a given word. You would have children sitting in front of the chalkboard for this activity, but when you feel that interest is waning it is time to stop. Challenge each child to read a line as he or she leaves the area. Thus, we start with meaningful wholes—whole short sentences, phrases, and words that are significant.

As Piaget has stated, "In a word, the line of development of language, as of perception, is from the whole to the part, from syncretism to analysis, and not vice versa."[2]

Another day, talk about "things we can do." Manuscript sentences such as "We can write," "We can paint," etc., limiting the new words to about three. Then add such review sentences as "I can play," "You can run," "I can work." At first challenge a child to read any line he feels sure he can read correctly. Then do some sentence matching with your tagboard cards of duplicate sentences. Note word likenesses. Finally, challenge the group to read all the sentences from top to bottom and left to right. There should be a good feeling of accomplishment. Thus, more short sentences using common words can be introduced each day.

Introduce a family for story building. Preferably this family might have the names of characters that will appear in the first preprimers the children will be reading, if such is to be the procedure. Rather than take the characters from any one series, the following are suggested: Mother, Father, Bess, Jim, Larry (the baby), and Scamp (the dog). It is well to use names that look very dissimilar. We want children to think of word meanings and not have to be too perplexed by words that look too much alike. These characters may be cut from magazines or old workbooks. They may be used on the flannel board or mounted on cardboard. The teacher might tell a story using these character names, but should present their names on the

---

[2] Jean Piaget, *The Language and Thought of the Child.* London: Routledge & Kegan Paul, 1952, pp. 133–134.

chalkboard before she starts to tell the story. The character names would be enough of a reading lesson for one day. After the story has been told she could go back and review the character names and ask each child to point to one name and read it before returning to his own seat. The next day the character names may be reviewed. If there is some confusion the teacher will have to work for better mental images of the words. Let children who are having problems come up to the board and trace around the letters of the problem names with their pointer finger, which is known as the kinesthetic or tactile approach. The sense of touch combined with looking at the word and saying it help some children to form a better mental image. They get the "feel" of the word.

Following recognition of these names, two- and three-line stories may be introduced. The first one might be on the board as children come to the reading area. The teacher must show vital enthusiasm about a story and exhibit pleasure in their ability to READ something all by themselves. It is wonderful, and she and they know it! As attention is called to the story on the chalkboard or flannel board, the teacher says that she will read it but they may help with any words they know. She may give them a chance to look for words they know before starting the reading. A story such as the following may be used: Start with a few sentences they know—*Bess can run; Jim can run*—then add new material such as:

> *Mother has a birthday.*
> *She has a birthday cake.*
> *Happy birthday Mother.*

A picture of a birthday cake may be used.

Always keep new words at a minimum and limit the reading to about three lines of new material, or to four to six when review sentences are included. It is always more interesting if at least one sentence is introduced in a challenging way—for example, say, "I really think you might be able to figure out this sentence all by yourselves. You know all the words but one, and I wonder if someone might be able to figure it out:" *Scamp wants birthday cake.*

The teacher might have flannel-board figures of Scamp and a table with a birthday cake on it, or she might have a large picture showing a dog looking up at a cake. Children should be helped to obtain a thrill from reading something independently, and the understanding teacher will help to maintain that delight. In the sentence, *Scamp wants birthday cake,* the children know all the words from previous reading except *wants*. They are in fact using the context clue if they can figure out what word would make good sense when filled in with those they know. Some children might suggest *sees,* which would not be a bad choice, but the teacher might explain that there should be another little word, *a,* to make it sound better if *sees* were used; then it would read, *Scamp sees a birthday cake.* However, children should be encouraged and credited with making a logical intelligent kind of guess. Using the context clue is not mere guessing —it is intelligent reasoning that insures that the child is getting meaning from what he reads. Context with phonics is what adults use most frequently in reading difficult material.

The children may be challenged to complete the story after the above sentence has been read. They may suggest: *Mother gives birthday cake to Scamp. Scamp likes it.* Avoid long sentences and help the child with rewording when necessary. Children are getting help with language as well as reading in such experiences. Thus, children see that reading may be what they compose or it may be what someone else has written. In all cases, it has a meaning. They can anticipate some of the words from those they already know.

USE OF WORD CARDS   After children have been reading sentences, phrases, and words from the chalkboard and the bulletin board, the most commonly used words may be put on word cards. The lettering should be on tagboard cards about 4½ inches by 10 inches. The ruling should be 1½-inch spaces between lines and the tall letters should be double-spaced.

For a good beginning, to assure many children of success in a new learning experience, about four words such as the following might be placed along the chalk tray: *I, play, we, work.*

Several of the most immature children might be asked to come up and trace around the letters with the pointer finger of the right hand to get the feel of the letters, moving from left to right. Then the children might be challenged to say the words with you as your hand is placed under each word. They may then be challenged further when you say, "I wonder who can find a word that tells what we like to do on the playground." Who can find a word that means you and me." "Now, who can find a word that means something we all have to do sometimes." "Can you find a word that you call yourself?"

Riddles. Challenge children with such as the following after many of the words have been used: (Accept many plausible answers):

I like water.
I can swim.
I eat bugs.
I am _____.

I can run.
I can fly.
I eat bugs.
I am _____.

I can swim.
I eat bugs.
I swim and swim.
I am _____.

We like candy.
We like to play.
We are _____.

I can hop.
I eat carrots.
I have long ears.
I am _____.

I can run.
I can jump.
I can play.
I can work.
I am _____.

In this process, children are thinking of word meanings, which is the essence of reading. The words may be mixed and a child challenged to recognize them as they are flashed. If the child can do this without mistakes he goes to his seat feeling very satisfied with his achievement. If he has difficulties he remains to watch while others try and he has another turn later. Usually each child can learn four such words, and with teacher enthusiasm will feel very satisfied and should be encouraged to go home and tell mother and father that he knows four words.

Each day a few new words are added such as *can, you, mother, father,* etc., according to what has been presented in sentences as from previously mentioned activities. When ten words have been learned, it is well to bind the word cards with a rubber band into a pack that will be numbered and referred to as "Pack I." Each child may be checked to be sure he knows all the words in that pack. Duplicate word cards are made of any words the child misses when tested and he may take these home or use them with a helper at school. A child who knows the words but with slight hesitation may serve as a helper to reenforce his own learning, but watch closely to be sure he is helping correctly. A chart is made with the children's names down the side and pack numbers across the top. In this way a continuous record of vocabulary recognition can be kept during the first few months of beginning reading. It is especially useful when children are absent and need to pick up from where they left off.

Children may be challenged to build sentences with the pack of word cards and ask another child to read them. Word games may be played such as those listed in Appendix I. Words may be sorted into "action" or "do" words and "name" words, and a third category for those words that are neither "do" or "name" words.

Children who know the words well should be doing other things. When it is observed that a child forgets easily it is a good idea to have him go back over the word packs frequently. Word games, sentence building, word classifying, tactile tracing, and writing are all means of helping each child find a way of learning that may be best for him in forming lasting mental images.

Before books are introduced it is a good idea to have all the words from the first few pages of pre-primers on word cards, but present them in a context that is different from the book. By knowing the words but reading them in a new context, the first books give children a great thrill. Presenting new words on flash cards and keeping ahead of the vocabulary development in the books are good practices throughout much of beginning first grade. Then complete attention can be given to comprehension and fluent reading when children have their books. Only the most commonly used words are put on cards. Only during the very early stage of reading would words be presented on the chalkboard before reading them in a book. After children have learned the various word recognition techniques (presented in the next chapter) it is better to use new words orally if there is any doubt about children knowing their meaning before meeting up with them in a book.

TEMPLATES OF LETTERS   Plastic letter forms of words that are used on the chalkboard may be used by a child at his seat for additional help in forming mental images of the word or words that seem to be difficult.

INDIVIDUAL CHALKBOARDS   Eighteen-inch-square pieces of sheet metal may be bound with heavy gummed tape and painted black. White crayon lines may be ruled on them and children can work individually on names and words. A large sheet well bound may be used on an easel. Word cards with tiny magnets glued on them can be used for sentence building; word, phrase, and sentence matching; and story composition. Cards with the various punctuation markings (periods, commas, question marks, and quotation marks) may be introduced as they are needed. Children can manipulate the cards and understand the use of the marks in sentences they compose.

USE OF CHARTS   Sheets of tagboard may now be purchased with lines already drawn for use in making charts. For the very first chart work it is best to use 1½-inch spacing. Make the tall letters two spaces tall. Newsprint is the least expensive material and is the most satisfactory for stories that are not going to be used very long. Very large tablets with wide ruling are available and could be considered as storybooks. They could be put on the chalk tray or easel for use with the class.

Here are some guidelines for making charts:

1. Plan to have a balanced border of space at top, bottom, and sides.

2. A picture or pictures, if appropriate to the material on the chart, always makes the chart more attractive and appealing to children. Sometimes the pictures may be centered at the top, spaced along the border, sometimes along the top and bottom. Sometimes children may be challenged to find a picture in magazines to use on the chart. Sometimes pictures from dime store books are appropriate to what you are doing.

3. One-and-a-half-inch spacing is good for beginners, using two spaces for tall letters. Make the caption a little higher and bolder, and be sure it is centered (count the letters in the title and put the middle letter in the center of the title line, then work in both directions in writing the title).

4. Be sure to use perfect manuscript with good spacing and correct punctuation.

Chart reading can be one of the earliest reading experiences of first-graders. Many children leave kindergarten with the knowledge that when they get to first grade they will learn to read. In fact, many first-graders come to school expecting to read on the first day. If such is the case we must make sure they are not disappointed with the first day's program. A reading experience may be provided that will be satisfying and not cause eye strain. We know that the best quality of learning takes place when there is enthusiasm for it. The first group experience to be recorded and read may be as simple as a brief record of play, such as:

> *We played Dodge Ball.*
> *It was fun.*

A large round ball would be easy to draw for an illustration at the top of the chart, and the two lines could be quickly printed. Or this little story could be printed on the blackboard that day so the children would have the satisfaction of reading it, and the chart could be introduced the next day for an interesting review. The words *we, play, It,* and *was* might be put on word cards. Use only the words that recur frequently for word card work.

The teacher will need to create the brief statements of the very first recorded experiences. Very soon, however, children catch on to the idea and there is ready response to the question, "What might we record about what we did?"

The span of attention of first-graders at the beginning of the year is very short, so that care must be taken to get a few brief statements on the chalkboard rapidly. Then the teacher reads each line. She slides her hand along under the words as she does it a second time. Children know what is written, and their eyes follow along as the teacher's hand moves from the end of the first line to the beginning of the next and on across the page from left to right. They are observing the mechanics of reading as they participate. There is no stopping at any one word. It is read as thought units. In this case, reading is "speech put down in writing." The symbols may be as unfamiliar to some of the children as the markings on the Dead Sea scrolls might be to many adults. Children are told what the symbols say. Some children will remember after one telling and others will need to be told again and again. The repetition, however, is achieved through new short compositions.

After the class has read the two lines several times, the teacher might say, "Now when you go home, you can say that you have been reading in school. And wasn't it fun?" Her enthusiasm and pleasure will add to the children's enjoyment of the experience. That would be enough for one time, and the group would proceed to other activities. Just before they leave for home, they might review the two-line story and leave with a feeling of accomplishment that makes school seem worthwhile to them and to their parents. Each day a few more experiences may be recorded, and soon children will notice words that look alike. Strips of tagboard with matching sentences may be used, and certain common words may be isolated for careful scrutiny and learned as sight words. These "experience charts" would include brief recordings of excursions, play activity, art work, or anything else in which the group had been involved and which would have meaning for each child. In these "experience charts" meaning precedes the reading.

Cutting the top off a carrot and placing it in a shallow dish of water affords a good classroom experience. After watching it sprout and grow a teacher might suggest making a story about it. It might develop as follows:

TEACHER: It was fun to watch our carrot-top grow. We might write two or three lines about it. Can you think of a short title?

1ST CHILD: *Our Carrot Plant.* (Teacher writes it on the board.)

2ND CHILD: *Jean brought a carrot to school and then she cut off the top and Bobby put water in a dish and—*

TEACHER: I couldn't put all that on one line, could I?

CHILDREN: No. It has to be short sentences.

TEACHER: Margery, try again, and tell us one thing about our carrot-top.

2ND CHILD: *It looks pretty.* (Teacher writes it on the board.)

TEACHER: Can someone tell us in a short sentence what happened first?

3RD CHILD: *I brought a carrot to school.* (Teacher writes *Jean brought a carrot to school.*)

4TH CHILD: *She cut the top off.* ("That's a very good sentence," and teacher writes it on the board.)

5TH CHILD: *Bobby put it in water.* ("Now isn't that a good sentence! It tells just what he did in a very few words," and she writes it on the board.)

6TH CHILD: *We watched it grow and it got pretty.* ("Fine," says teacher, adding it to the board.)

TEACHER: Now let's read our story and see how we like it.

If this experience comes after children have been making chart stories for some time, a child is likely to suggest leaving out the sentence, *It looks pretty,* just under the title. Otherwise, it is well for the teacher to explain, "We couldn't see that it was going to be pretty until after the carrot-top had been put in water and we watched it grow, could we? And we have Margery's idea in our last sentence, don't we? So, Margery, your idea is at the end of Tom's sentence and we'll take it away from up here where it doesn't belong. Now let's read our story again."

It is important not to prolong such compositions and not to reread them to the extent that children become bored. It is not the intent to learn many of the words on the chart. A few very commonly used words are enough. Words such as *our, it, I, to, school,* and *pretty* would be good for word-card activity.

There is wonderful opportunity for development of language, proper usage, and sentence structure in creating experience charts. Again, do not detract from thought content by being too fussy about exactness. Experience charts serve the following purposes:

1. Children make frequent use of the mechanics of reading:
    a. They recognize the use of a title.
    b. They read from top to bottom.
    c. They read from left to right.
    d. They use sentences.
    e. They observe use of capitalization.
    f. They observe use of punctuation.
2. They learn to recognize frequently used words.
3. They understand that there is meaning in whatever is written.

After such chart reading has become a familiar activity, the words of the sentence may be put on cards with the period on a separate card. The cards are distributed to children who are challenged to stand up and form the sentence with the period at the end. It can be explained that the period is a stop sign and that we lower our voices when we come to that symbol. Later, when a question appears in their reading, this approach can be used. Then children should be given an opportunity of asking questions of one another with a questioning intonation.

These experience charts may be kept as a record of the year's activities and may be brought out from time to time for review. During the last month of first grade the children may decide on a title for the cover, such as "What We did in First Grade"; rings may be put at the top and children may enjoy reading all the pages. This book might be passed on with the children for good review reading at the beginning of second grade. The new teacher would be interested in hearing about the activities the class had in first grade. Later, the book could be given to a children's hospital.

Other types of charts that are useful in the primary grades are the following:

Picture Charts. One type of picture chart serves as a dictionary or reference chart for young children. A caption or title might be, "Things We Can Do." Beneath it would be words such as *paint, color, paste, run, walk, jump, hop,* and *skip,* with an appropriate picture above each word. When doing independent seatwork exercises, a child can go to this chart for help with a word rather than disturb a reading group to ask the teacher. Another would be a "Color Chart" showing the various common colors with its name beneath each one. This is good for reference, too, until the children know the color words very well. Another might be a "Number Chart" with objects and the corresponding figure and word for each amount. These charts aid toward the initial understanding of references.

Another picture chart would be one showing a large detailed picture with a story below. It could be introduced as a surprise story every once in a while, kept under cover until the teacher was ready to use it. Children could be helped to anticipate it eagerly. One such chart might show a group of children having a birthday party, titled "The Surprise Birthday Party." The picture would give children clues regarding the new words. The story might be as follows:

The Surprise Birthday Party

> *It was Jim's birthday.*
> *He was seven years old.*
> *Mother made a cake.*
> *It had seven candles.*
> *Seven children came to the party.*
> *It was a big surprise.*

Word cards of commonly used words such as *The, It, was, a, to, big, He,* and *came,* could be matched with words used in the chart story. Be sure the children are saying the words as they match them so that they are not merely matching forms but are matching meaningful words. Sentence cards, too, may be read and matched.

Sometimes the sentence cards can be distributed at random. The child holding the card with the first sentence gets up, stands in front of the group, and reads it. Then the child with the next sentence stands up beside the first child and reads his sentence, and so on. The children who remain without cards are challenged to read the whole story from the cards the other children are holding. Such activity provides for much rereading. Lastly, challenge each child to read a line as he goes back to his seat.

Stories that children create are fine, but children should be helped to know that reading is more often what someone else writes. They need to be helped to obtain the thought from print without knowing the thought content in advance. We should challenge children to figure out as much of the content as they can and then give help when they are ready to give up. We do not attempt to teach all the words in each story, but we pull out some that are most frequently used and check on the ones that are already known. The stories do not get boring this way, and each new story reveals that the children

Our Weather

Our Helpers

Attendance Slip
Milk Slip
Pass out napkins and straws
Take out tricycle
Take out wagon
Pick up toys
Check paint corner
Straighten books

Bob
Bobby
Denise
Becky
Randy

know more and more words and are becoming able to use both picture and context clues.

Sometimes children can be challenged to compose a story about a picture that has interesting subject matter. Signs of fall would be an example of such a stimulating picture, and any child could make a contribution to such a subject. Stories created this way on both group and individual bases comprise much of the writing or language arts approach to reading to be explained in a later chapter. Sometimes a small group of children can be challenged to create a story for the other children to read.

Weather Charts. In kindergarten, a weather chart may be entirely pictorial. A dial with a pointer hand, much like a clock, may be made on a large sheet of tagboard. Around the outer edge of the dial might be a shining sun, clouds, a cloud with a face that looks as if it were blowing to indicate wind, streaks of broken lines for rain, and white crayon marks on a piece of gray paper for snow. A child may move the dial to indicate the kind of weather. In kindergarten, children would talk about the days of the week and later about months.

In first grade, the chart might have the title, "Our Weather Chart." Beneath it might be a calendar pad; try to get one that has the name of the month, the names of the days of the week, and large clear numerals. Children need to be helped to see that a calendar is read as a story chart is read—that is, from top to bottom, from left to right, and line after line. Beneath the calendar pad might be the words:

Today is _____. (Make two slits into which a strip of tagboard would fit. Make strips with the days of the week.)
Yesterday was _____. (Make two more slits as above.)
Tomorrow will be _____. (Make two more as above.)
Today is a _____. (Make slits and cards with kinds of weather common in your area.)

At the bottom of the chart would be two pockets with the word cards. Each day a different child would have the privilege of finding the correct words and placing them on the chart. At the time the chart is presented the words should be taught carefully. They would

Charts help children to use and enjoy reading for many significant purposes. (Photographs courtesy of the Cedar Rapids, Iowa, Public Schools.)

note that *Saturday* and *Sunday* start with the same letter and they can hear the *s* sound at the beginning of each word. They also would note that *Tuesday* and *Thursday* start the same way, but the beginning sound is not the same. An explanation could be given that the *Th* at the beginning of *Thursday* says *th* so that they know early in their experience with reading that they must be wary of the many peculiarities in our language. Such situations as this bring up opportunities for an incidental teaching of phonics, but a more systematic study will come later. Often the best quality of learning occurs when children are curious and alert to explanations that are given when they ask, "Why?"

The best time to take care of the weather chart is during opening exercises. Choose the children who need help with the words to participate most often. When a child has difficulty, help him trace the word with his pointer finger as he says it and then point out any peculiarities. Soon all the children will know the days of the week and such weather words as *cloudy, clear, windy, foggy, rainy,* etc. In second grade, a thermometer and barometer reading might be added. Direction of the wind may also be noted. A very short period of this weather study is enough for third grade as a review as it would no longer be a learning activity. In second grade, too, the weather chart would serve a purpose only until everyone knows the words or until children become disinterested.

News-Item Charts. As children share news with the class a teacher may record such items as:

Sue has a baby brother.
John has new shoes.
Kirk found his jacket.
Ellen has a birthday today.
Mary's grandmother came last night.

After the news has been reread children may be challenged to find two words that look alike and to tell what they are. Challenge them to find the longest word, the shortest word, and to listen while they are said. They can hear many sounds as the teacher says "grand-mother," so it has to be a long word. *A* is just one sound so it is a short word. "Do you know another word that has just one letter?" (*I.*)

A little phonics may be taught as children notice similarities and become curious about the beginning sounds. If a teacher expresses surprise and pleasure with each new learning accomplishment, children become curious about more and more things in their eagerness to learn.

As the year progresses or in second and third grades, short summaries of local, national, and international happenings might be put on a chart and reviewed during the week, or news clippings may be mounted. Children should be encouraged to listen to the news as soon as it has meaning for them and before they are able to read it. Sharing news at school helps to stimulate interest in it, and with a teacher's guidance children can become selective in what is appropriate for sharing. We emphasize the things that make people feel good about what they hear: new discoveries, interesting and unusual things that people or animals do, and new records or achievements that are made (this eliminates the crime and accident news).

Planning Charts. If children are to go on an excursion, a set of group rules for conduct may be developed and written on the chalkboard and later transferred to a chart. These rules are important for the success of a trip. A list of things the group hopes to see might be recorded. Upon returning, the lists would be reread and checked. A science project might be planned and recorded. A diary might be kept of the development of seeds or bulbs that were planted. A name list with individual responsibilities might be changed each week. The directions for a new game might be presented or kept for reference on a chart. Rules for fair play or safety should be made and reviewed frequently. Plans for a party, for the work period, for study time, for recess, or for game time might be recorded so children can see the need for variety, for taking turns, and for trying many different things. They see from these planning charts that school has much to offer, and parents and other visitors note this, too.

Record Charts. It is always satisfying to note what has been accomplished—not only for children but for the teacher and parents as well. A child should be encouraged to compete with his own record, whether it be vocabulary development, quality of handwriting, or any other endeavor. A good way to help a child set his own goal is to look at a chart with the child and say, "You have been checked on six packs of words, and that's fine. Now, how many do you think you might be checked on at the next report card time? I'll be interested in seeing how well you can do." A child should know what every comment or mark on his report card means and what he can do to improve. A teacher's interest and confidence in the child helps greatly in his aspirations. Seeing evidence of progress, such as putting check marks on a chart or watching his line of progress move along or up, is stimulating to increased effort. Doing more than is expected can be looked upon as very thrilling, therefore keep expectations well within a child's ability range but inspire him to keep reaching.

INDEPENDENT ACTIVITIES

It is much easier to work with a small group of children who need the same kind of help or who are ready for about the same type of experiences, but it is always a problem for a lone teacher in a classroom of about thirty children to keep the other children occupied with a worthwhile activity that does not require her direct help or supervision. In many instances, teachers have hurried to teach children a few basic words so that worksheets could be used to keep children busy and quiet. Although worksheets, carefully prepared in accordance with children's needs, serve a worthy purpose later in the reading program, the size of print is usually too small for the very young in kindergarten or beginning first grade. The following suggestions are made with consideration for children's early eye development, short span of attention, and readiness:

FINDING PICTURES FOR CHARTS   At the beginning of the school year every primary teacher should ask the children to bring magazines with pictures from home. It is best to give them a note explaining to parents that such magazines as *McCall's, Ladies' Home Journal, Saturday Evening Post, Good Housekeeping, Woman's Day, House and Garden, Ideals, Look, Life,* or any other magazine or catalog with good pictures will be cut apart and used in many ways at school. When the magazines come to school they are put together in a cupboard and no longer belong to any one child or children who may have brought a great many. No child is to feel that he must bring magazines, but all will share.

Following a discussion of "Members of the Family," a group of children could be seated on the floor with a pile of magazines and a box of paper strips. It would be their job to look for large pictures of mothers, fathers, brothers, sisters, babies, grandmothers, grandfathers, aunts and uncles. They would put a slip of paper next to the binding as a marker whenever an appropriate picture is found. This is good prereading experience because children are doing in pictorial form what adults do in printed language form when they skim for desired information. After school the teacher would draw a red line around each figure she felt appropriate and leave the markers in those pages, removing the other markers. The next day the children in one of the groups would cut out the pictures along the red lines where the markers were left. Thus, the pictures would be ready for use on a "Family Chart" or for mounting on tagboard for use with word cards designating family members.

Another time, following a discussion of fruits, the children in a group could find pictures of fruit and put markers in the magazines. Some pictures could be used on a large chart and the teacher would manuscript the word beneath each picture in three-inch letters. Some pictures could be put on cards and the corresponding

The listening post has many uses. Records, tapes, and radio or television programs may be used at the "listening post." Children may enjoy well-read poetry or prose, or they may receive individualized instruction. They may also listen to recordings of their own reading and be helped with self-evaluation. (Photograph courtesy of the Cincinnati, Ohio, Public Schools.)

word put on another card; the children would be challenged to match them and to check against the chart. This could be done for vegetables, clothing, furniture, toys, and various foods as well. Do not introduce too many words at one time. Take it slowly so many children can enjoy the accomplishment. A record chart could be kept for packs of three words as a beginning kind of goal. If about three words are introduced at one time and two or three days are spent on helping children to know them and to be checked, the procedure should be very satisfying.

LISTENING POST Good records or tapes of stories and poetry should always be available. These should be exchanged frequently so children may hear an abundance of good literature appropriate to their level of understanding, in addition to what the teacher tells or reads at other times during the day. Children's programs on radio and on television may be enjoyed this way without disturbing other children.

MAKING PICTURE BOOKLETS After children have learned how to cut out pictures and to paste independently, they can make little booklets as an independent activity. Newsprint can be cut into 12"-by-6" sheets and folded over to make the pages of the booklets. These pages may be tied or stapled. Titles such as "My Family," "Toys I Like," "Foods I Like," "Colors I know," "Things I Like to Do," may be suggested and each child chooses one. He selects one picture to go on each inside page of his book and pastes it at the top of the page. The teacher might have him make his selections with markers the first day, then cut them out and paste them the second day. She would print the word under each picture in large lettering, and he could read it to the other children and in turn listen to them read their books. Simple sentences may be included. Later children may make such books independently and copy the words from word cards. They might be allowed to take their books home one evening to read and bring them back the next day. With more vocabulary development, more content can go into the books. These may be put on the library shelf for all to enjoy. Pictures may be found to illustrate favorite short poems, and these may be made into books, too.

EACH ONE TEACH ONE Children work in pairs. One day one child is the teacher and the next day the other child is the teacher. Words used on word cards are ones that appear beneath pictures on the bulletin board, on a chart, or in previously described class-made picture books. The child who is teacher attempts to help his partner learn from three to ten words (the teacher determines with each child what the goal should be). The child who is teacher may check against the bulletin board, chart, or book if he is not sure of the words himself. The learner may trace the word with his pointer finger, say it to himself several times, take a good look, and then close his eyes to try to envision it, and note any particular configuration that may help him remember it. This kind of one-to-one relationship in learning is sometimes very beneficial. If there is a record chart on which children note their progress for being checked on vocabulary packs of five or ten, this teamwork helps in more rapid accomplishment.

CHALKBOARD WORK   Most children enjoy working on the chalkboard. The teacher can manuscript on the board:

I am ————.   *I* ———— ————.
You are ————.   *You* ———— ————.
We are ———— *and* ————.
            can,   run,   jump,   see,   read.

Children fill in names in the first three sentences and select words for the last two sentences.
Children enjoy creating simple sentences for another child to read, it gives them much opportunity to learn common words and many names and to use them in meaningful context. New words may be added frequently, especially commonly used words such as *were, want, they,* and *saw.*

In the initial stages of learning to read, any experience with writing benefits reading, no matter what methods are used in reading instruction. With more emphasis on writing paralleling the reading experience, fewer children would reach an early plateau in reading and be unable to learn at a normal rate.[3]

DEVELOPING NEW CONCEPTS   It is good to have many kinds of catalogs and picture dictionaries with illustrations such as toys, furniture, food products, cars, general merchandise, and others that would afford children the opportunity of gaining new understandings. Three children may sit together and thumb through such books naming the items as they look at them. If they come to one they do not know, they are to put a marker in the place and ask the teacher for help when she is through helping others. (Children come to know that they must speak softly to one another, or after one warning the offender must work alone.) This plan helps children identify many items that had previously not been a part of

---

3 Gertrude Hildreth, "Early Writing As an Aid to Reading," in *New Perspectives in Reading Instruction,* ed. by A. J. Mazurkiewicz. New York: Pitman Publishing Co., 1964, p. 156.

their vocabulary. Frequently there needs to be a general discussion of some of the items that appear to be unfamiliar. In fact, it might be well to bring such items into the classroom so that they can be seen, felt, and used. A popcorn popper was an item that children in one classroom inquired about. The teacher brought in a popper, some popcorn, and butter, and the children quickly learned all about popping corn. The teacher introduced the poem, "Song of the Popcorn," and the children wanted to memorize it. She also wrote "Pop, pop, pop" on the chalkboard. The children decided that the words almost sounded like kernels of popcorn exploding in the pan. They listened to the little "exploding" sound at the beginning of the word. In the development of a concept there are usually many accompanying learnings, and one never knows how many facets of interest there will be or how far children will be ready to explore any one of them.

OVERHEAD PROJECTION   An extremely useful piece of equipment in any schoolroom is the overhead projector in which the page of a book or any similar material can be projected on a screen so that children view it easily. In beginning reading it has these uses:

1. All children may see the pictures of a story as it is read or told much more easily than when a book is held up for them to see.
2. Pictures may be used for concept and language development.
3. Pictures with words, phrases, or sentences below may be used for children to determine the ones that go with the picture and in what order. A child is given a pointer to make the selection.
4. A great variety of commercial or teacher-made learning aids may be used as needed.
5. Many topics for discussion can be opened by first showing a picture, a diagram, or key words.
6. Book jackets of new books may be projected for all to see as stimulating comments are made to make them appealing.
7. Transparencies may be used. Many book companies have them for beginning reading materials. Refer to current catalogs for listings to go with many stories, etc.

Thus, without using print that would be too small for undeveloped eye muscles, young children may have many experiences that make reading meaningful, satisfying, and enticing. Through such experiences children learn many commonly used words and become familiar with the following mechanics of reading:

1. Stories have titles.
2. We read from the top of the page to the bottom.
3. We read from the left to the right of each line.
4. We make the return sweep from the end of one line to the beginning of the next.
5. Reading is made up of words and sentences.
6. Sentences begin with capital letters and end with a period or question mark.
7. Some words are short (*a* and *I* consist of only one letter) and others are long (*grandmother*).
8. We can hear many sounds in long words.
9. Words that start with the same letter or letters usually have the same first sound.
10. We open a book with the binding on the left side.
11. We turn pages by taking hold of the right-hand page and turning it over to the left side of the book so that we can look at the left-hand page and then the right-hand page.
12. Books are to be handled carefully and with clean hands so that they can be enjoyed by all.
13. Many simple sentences can be created and read with understanding and satisfaction.

A twelve-year-old boy was once asked how he would go about teaching his dog a new trick. After a moment of deliberation, he replied:
"Well, first I'd have to know what it was I wanted him to learn. Next, I'd figure out just how he'd like to learn it. Then I'd teach him that way."
After a slight pause, the lad added, "Of course, I know my dog awfully well!"[4]

Suggestions for Class Participation and Discussion

1. When and how did you start to read? Did you like it? Why or why not?
2. How were you taught to read in first and second grades?
3. How many of you have had to wear corrective glasses since starting school? When were you fitted for glasses? Was it at the time you started to read?
4. Do you think that wearing learning lenses would be good in every first grade? Why or why not? What problems would arise?
5. How could the various experiences in this chapter give children a

[4] Roy A. Kress, "Directing the Reading Lesson." *Controversial Issues In Reading,* April, 1961.

better reading background than introducing them from the start to
preprimers and merely following through with the succeeding books
of a series?

6. What purposes for reading could young children be helped to know
and understand?

7. Prepare a chart for the grade level you intend to teach. Show and
discuss it in class.

8. Explore some of the references pertaining to this chapter and share
with the class three other experiences that children might have in
beginning reading that would not involve the use of book-size print.

9. Read or tell a story to a group of children. Discuss the experience in
class.

10. What significance does the quotation at the end of the chapter have?

Bibliography

ANDERSON, IRVING H., and DEARBORN, WALTER F. *The Psychology of
Teaching Reading*. New York: Ronald Press, 1952.

ARTLEY, A. STERL. *Your Child Learns to Read*. Chicago: Scott, Foresman,
1953.

AUSTIN, MARY C., and MORRISON, COLEMAN B. *In the Modern Elementary
School*. New York: Macmillan, 1963.

BLAIR, GLENN. *Diagnostic and Remedial Reading*. New York: Macmillan,
1956.

BOND, GUY, and TINKER, MILES. *Reading Difficulties: Their Diagnosis
and Correction*. New York: Appleton-Century-Crofts, 1957.

BOND, GUY, and WAGNER, EVA BOND. *Teaching the Child to Read*. New
York: Macmillan, 1966.

BROOM, MYBERT B., *et al. Effective Reading Instruction*. New York:
McGraw-Hill, 1951.

CARILLO, LAWRENCE. *Informal Reading-Readiness Experiences*. San Francisco: Chandler, 1964.

Dallas, Texas Independent School District, *Primary Education—Curriculum Guide,* Dallas, Texas, 1964.

Fresno Public Schools, *The Kindergarten Year,* Fresno, Calif., 1965.

HEILMAN, ARTHUR. *Principles and Practices of Teaching Reading*. Columbus, Ohio: Merrill, 1961.

HUBER, MIRIAM B. *Story and Verse for Children*. New York: Macmillan,
1965.

KOEHRING, DOROTHY. *Getting Ready to Read*. Extension Service, State
University of Northern Iowa, Cedar Falls, 1965.

KOTTMEYER, WILLIAM. *Teacher's Guide for Remedial Reading*. St. Louis:
Webster, 1959.

LANGDON, GRACE, and STOUT, IRVING. *Teaching in the Primary Grades*.
New York: Macmillan, 1964.

LEE, DORRIS, and ALLEN, ROACH V. *Learning to Read Through Experience*. New York: Appleton-Century-Crofts, 1963.

Long Beach Public Schools, *A Teacher's Guide for Kindergarten Education*, Long Beach, Calif., 1959.

McKEE, PAUL. *Reading a Program of Instruction for the Elementary School*. Boston: Houghton Mifflin, 1966.

McKIM, MARGARET, and CASKEY, HELEN. *Guiding Growth in Reading*. New York: Macmillan, 1963.

MONROE, MARION. *Growing Into Reading*. Chicago: Scott, Foresman, 1951.

Nevada State Department of Education. *Reading Readiness, a Developing Guide for Teachers at the Primary Level*, 1950.

Primary Education—Changing Dimensions. Association of Childhood Education International, 1964.

Roseville Schools, *Kindergarten Guide*, Independent District 623, 1261 Highway 34, St. Paul, Minn. Include all, 1963.

San Bernardino County Schools, *Let's Make Charts*, San Bernardino, Calif.

San Diego Public Schools, *Kindergarten Course of Study*, San Diego, Calif., 1963.

San Jose Unified School District, *Kindergarten Curriculum Guide*, San Jose, Calif., 1963.

STONE, CLARENCE. *Progress in Primary Reading*. St. Louis: Webster, 1950.

STRANG, RUTH. *Helping Your Child Improve His Reading*. New York: Dutton, 1962.

YOAKAM, GERALD. *Basal Reading Instruction*. New York: McGraw-Hill, 1955.

Many counties and cities have excellent courses of study, guide books, and bulletins with practical teaching suggestions for kindergarten and each of the grades of the elementary school. Also explore the materials in the curriculum materials library.

CHAPTER 7
The Clues
of the Reading
Process

With a basic sight vocabulary and sufficient mastery of word recognition skills, the child will be able to experience the excitement of having words tell him what the characters are saying and what happened next.[1]

When children are first introduced to the reading process they are exposed to symbols as strange to them as the black markings on a Chinese scroll would be to most of us. As adults, we would probably seek to find the relationship between the Chinese symbols and our own so that we could apply or translate them through association with what we know. Children do not have such a fund of reference. They need to develop clues that will unlock word recognition so rapidly and easily that their minds can focus on word meanings rather than on merely decoding words. Some children may know the names of the letters of the alphabet, but in many instances this is a handicap rather than an assistance. Letter names have almost no relationship to letter sounds in words. The alphabet will serve in

[1] Ruth Strang, *Helping Your Child Improve His Reading.* New York; Dutton, 1962, p. 16.

filing purposes and using the dictionary later, but first reading experiences do not require knowledge of the alphabet or recognition of letter names.

The "clues" or "cues" of reading are often referred to with use of various terminology, and writers in the field of reading place varying degrees of emphasis on any one or all of the clues. This is also true of the proponents of various systems of methodology in the teaching of reading. It is the complete understanding of all possible aids to word recognition that may serve any and all children that concerns us most. One child may rely heavily on one type of clue, and another may find them all useful in various situations. It is well to give each child an opportunity to understand all clues and to enable him to choose what he finds most helpful in various reading situations.

The basic clues of word recognition are *sight, configuration, context, picture, word analysis, phonics, and linguistics.*

Sight Words

The English language is comprised of many words that are not phonetic and do not lend themselves to any type of regular analysis; some of them do not fit into any particular language pattern. We must rely almost wholly on memorization of such words. In beginning reading we introduce some such words and we also introduce the ordinary words children use in speaking as sight words to form the basis for the relatedness that is necessary to understand some of the other clues. The following are some words that might be introduced early:

a	boy	egg	had	me	saw	us
am	bring	every	have	mother	see	very
an	brother	father	he	my	she	walk
and	brown	for	her	not	skip	want
apple	by	friend	here	on	some	was
are	cake	from	I	over	store	we
at	can	fun	in	party	table	went
baby	chair	girl	is	paste	the	were
ball	come	go	it	play	they	will
banana	color	gone	jump	presents	this	with
big	cut	grand-father	keep	put	to	yellow
birthday	did	grand-mother	like	ran	toys	you
black	do	grapes	little	red	under	your
blue	draw	green	look	run	up	

These are words that have meaning for all children and that can be used in a variety of situations in the classroom. All have been used in one way or another in the projects outlined in the previous chapter. Teachers should be flexible in helping children know the words that come most naturally in classroom situations to give reading meaning and importance.

Names are very important to children and should be included in the listing of known words, each child starting with his own first name. He learns to write it on the chalkboard with the help of the teacher, as explained in the preceding chapter. Children will try to read what other children have written and thus become familiar with other children's names. The experience of distributing a few papers according to the name on the paper helps in wanting to know more and more of the names. Also, reading names from the board when work assignments are made helps too.

A teacher should check against the words in the back of the first preprimer that children will be reading to be sure she has introduced many of the words that will be required for reading that book. Most first preprimers have from eleven to thirty words.

Now some extremely easy first preprimers are being written. Some have very few words. For the following reasons, such a book would be especially good:

1. Children are extremely eager *to read a book.*
2. Parents are equally eager to have their children read.
3. It gives both parents and child a feeling of satisfaction that *the child is reading.*
4. The lightness of the vocabulary load enables the teacher to concentrate more on establishing good habits of handling books properly, using the mechanics of reading, and reading with fluency and expression.
5. *All* children get the motivation or stimulation that comes from having read a book. No child is denied the thrill of reading from a book along with the entire class.
6. It enables the teacher to allow the fast learners to move on to other more challenging books while the slow learners spend a little more time (without too much prolongation) on a book that is still new, colorful, and satisfying.

The characters' names may be the only new words in the preprimers, and they can be introduced with picture figures and on word cards. The advantage of having learned all the words previous to presentation of the books is that children have the delightful experience of being able to read the book immediately, and all look upon reading as fun.

There are few greater thrills in first grade than that of the growing anticipation of soon being able to read from a book. Then, when most children are physically ready and have the required meaningful sight vocabulary, the long-awaited moment comes and they find that they *can read a book*.

Because it is such a long-anticipated experience, no child should be deprived of this first preprimer reading regardless of total readiness. Perhaps this will be the only book the class as a whole will be reading at the same time, but it is a special occasion.

The teacher should be comfortably seated with the books at hand. She should demonstrate how to hold the book because the little paper-covered preprimers are difficult to manage especially if they are new. She can demonstrate by placing her thumb between the pages, spreading her other fingers behind the book, and using the right hand to turn the pages. Do not keep the children waiting too long. They are anxious to "read from a book" and now is the time. Distribute the books and let the children have the thrill of being able to read at their own rate and to enjoy the pictures.

Markers may be offered to help children read the lines, and it may be explained how they can be held with the right hand. Dr. Gesell states that although the six-year-old is very interested in words and sentences, he "has difficulty in holding to a horizontal line." There are the following advantages of using markers:

1. They make horizontal reading easier.
2. They give the teacher an opportunity to watch the child's reading procedure more closely.
3. They keep the child's right hand occupied and he is more captivated to keep his attention fixed on his book.
4. They help many children become accustomed to the line-to-line procedure of reading.
5. They keep children from pointing at individual words.
6. Children give them up easily when they no longer need them.

It may be suggested that each child find one page to read that he has read and is sure he can read well. "When you are ready, come to me if no one else is here, and after you have read you may leave your book and go back to your seat and get a picture book from the library." A pleasant comment about each child's reading gives the experience added delight. (When children leave their books be sure they are stacked with the bindings all on the left side. Establishing such procedures can save much time and avoid unnecessary confusion.) The next day the teacher might start with the first story in the preprimer and use suggestions from the teacher's manual in accordance with what the children may need. If all the words had been taught well in advance the children will be able to move along in the book rapidly, which is a great advantage because interest runs high and success begets interest in sharing their great accomplishment with their parents. As soon as the book has been completed the children should have a chance to take it home in a large envelope with instructions on the envelope to return the book the next day.

Before reading from the book each day some new word presentation should take place. One group of children may need help with old words, and new games may give them incentive for learning. Games with accent on meaning are always best. For example, "Find and Do" is a word game in which nouns and verbs are printed on the chalkboard. A child may read as many words as he can, and he can do what the words tell him to do or touch the things they tell him to touch. Words such as *run, skip, hop, jump, walk, look, see, table, chair, book,* and *girl* may be used. When he comes to a word he does not know he takes a word card to his chair, is told what the word is, and traces over the letters from left to right as he says the word to himself. Then some other child has a turn. "Find a Word that Means" is an especially good word game in which the teacher gives the meaning and the child finds the word.

For children who are ready to move on to another book, present new words that will be appearing in that book and use them with the same meaningful approach. Children need frequent changes in approach; therefore, try other word games as explained in Appendix I and from sources in the bibliography at the end of this chapter. *The Grade Teacher* and *Instructor* magazines often suggest activities for word recognition.

After the first preprimer has been completed all the words listed in the back may be printed in large manuscript on the chalkboard and the game of "Mushpot" may be introduced. The teacher points to a word and each child in turn says what it is. If the child misses he must sit on the floor in front of his chair—that is the "mushpot."

He may be given a word card with the word on it to trace with his finger as he says it to himself. Frequently she will call on him again, and if he knows the word he gets out of the "mushpot" (that is, returns to his chair). Children try to see if they can stay out of the "mushpot" throughout the game. The teacher is alert to which words each child misses and makes word cards of them for the child to use. She finds time when he can work on them with another child. Some children may continue with the first book or another book with easy vocabulary after others read from more difficult books.

Words to which most of the word recognition clues do not apply can often be learned through word games such as these. (Photograph courtesy of the San Diego, California, Public Schools.)

Configuration

When children work on their names at the chalkboard they will soon begin to make comparisons: "Your name is longer than mine." "You have lots of tall letters in your name." "Your name has that crooked letter [*s*] at the beginning." "My name [*Lillian*] has lots of straight letters." This reference to how a word looks with regard to distinguishing features that will help the observer remember it is known as the *configuration clue*. Thus, we immediately have an overlapping of word recognition clues. One child may remember *ball* as a sight word, and another may refer to it by saying, "The first letter looks like a bat with a ball lying beside it, and the last two letters look like high fences to keep balls from getting out."

While children will continue to have additional sight words, they will also note similarities, peculiarities, word contours, and other features that assist in recall. The following are specific examples of the configuration clue:

look	We look with our eyes and the two round *o*'s or circles look like eyes looking at you.
balloon	The two circles look like balloons that had been taken off the sticks right beside them.
bed	The two ends are tall and it is low in the middle just like a bed.
I	*I* looks like one person standing alone.
girl	The first letter looks like a little girl with a hair ribbon in her hair.
orange	*Orange* starts with a letter that looks like an orange.
furniture	All long words are relatively easy because of their length. There are so few in beginning reading. It is the short, "look-alike" words that cause trouble.
snake	The first letter makes a sound like a snake and it looks like a snake.

Do not encourage children to note configurations that do not relate to the meaning of the word. Such observations would be very confusing. For example, one child might note that the word *bad* looks like a bed, too, which would be a misleading association.

The Context Clue

The context clue is extremely important because the only way it can be used is by thinking of the meaning of the sentence. As adults we use it almost unconsciously, not only in recognizing words but in determining meanings of unfamiliar words. For example, the word *run* has more than fifty very common meanings. In the sentence *The batter brought in four more "runs"* few people in our country over twelve years of age would have any problem knowing exactly what had happened. No mention would need to be made of a *home run*. The use of the word *runs* with *batter* and the number *four* establishes the fact that the bases were loaded and the batter got home to make the fourth run. It would take a background of knowing the game of baseball to give meaning to the words in this context. *Context* means the way in which the word is used in the sentence or passage to give it a particular meaning. *Our neighbor plans to run for office,* is another example where the word *run* depends entirely on the rest of the sentence to determine which of its many meanings is the correct one. So many words in our language have multiple meanings that this clue is highly significant.

The context clue is not only used for words with multiple meanings. It is also used to determine what an unknown word might be by reading what comes before and after it. Syntax or the patterning of our language is helpful. Through knowing language form children come to learn more and more about language.

Using the context clue is not mere "guessing." It is intelligent guessing. The mind of a person using the context clue has grasped the significance of the balance of the sentence and from this knowledge he determines what the word might be to give complete plausibility to the passage.

As children mature they may be helped to know that if they are reading about boats, for example, an unknown word is likely to relate in some way to that topic. They can anticipate, too, through reasoning what kind of word they need, whether it be a descriptive word, an action word, or a name word.

READINESS FOR THE USE OF CONTEXT CLUES

Teachers of nursery school or kindergarten children can prepare the way for use of context clues by oral language experiences. Children can be challenged to supply the missing words as the teacher uses sentences such as the following: (See Appendix D for more) (The pause should be about as long as it would take to say the word, then finish the sentence and wait for the children's responses.)

Mistress Mary ———— contrary.

We plant seeds and watch them ————. (*Sprout* or *grow* would be acceptable.)

We need a ———— to mail a letter.

The ———— sells eggs and butter. (Accept all plausible answers.)

Mother baked a ———— for Jim's birthday.

Funny ———— are seen on Halloween.

Clowns ———— at a circus. (Encourage more than one response such as *perform, act, wink, strut,* etc.)

Trains travel on a ————.

Cars travel on a ————.

We should be ———— when we cross the street.

During the showing of a film, a teacher may be writing fill-in sentences that would be a good review of the film content as well as provide excellent practice in using context clues. They also help greatly in familiarizing children with our language patterns. They develop and expand vocabulary and keep children concentrating on sentence meanings as they listen. Children become so conscious of context that often when a teacher begins writing sentences on the chalkboard they can anticipate the next words the teacher will write. It is a worthwhile experience for children if teachers will challenge them to think ahead in this way. Reading comes much easier for children with such background. Even after reading gets under way, it is good for children to have oral language challenges once in a while.

When children get into book reading, to use the context clue the child is encouraged to read the rest of the sentence when he comes to a word he does not know. Then he thinks of what word could be put in that place in the sentence to give it meaning. Phonics is often used with the context clue, and the range of possibilities becomes more narrow. Often the first letter sound with the context possibilities are all the child needs to go on with his reading. Later, when he is ready to use the dictionary, he can be helped to know that there are times when we must verify our guesses or ascertain the correct meaning through help from the dictionary.

Now this is the method used by the child. He lets all the difficult words in a given phrase pass by, then he connects the familiar words into a general schema, which subsequently enables him to interpret the words not originally understood. This syncretistic method may of course give rise to considerable mistakes, some of which we shall presently examine; but we believe it to be the most economical in the long run, and one which eventually leads the child to an accurate understanding of things by a gradual process of approximation and selection.[2]

The greatest value of the context clue lies in the fact that the reader's thoughts remain with the content of what he is reading when using the clue.

Picture Clues

As adults we often look at illustrations in books and magazines to get a mental image that word explanations alone cannot give. It is a mistake to think that children use pictures only to guess at what is printed below them. If such is the case, the children have not been helped to use pictures correctly.

Some writers of children's readers have gone so far as to delete pictures from books so that children will have to decode words without relying on pictures. If the purpose of reading is merely to independently decode words, then such deletion might be significant. However, if the purpose of reading is to obtain meaning, and if an important aspect of reading is the expansion of concepts, then children's readers should be selected with the best possible illustrations. Some qualities of good illustrations are as follows:

1. The details should be large enough so as not to cause eye strain.
2. The colors should be true to what is illustrated.
3. The details should clarify concepts developed in the printed material on that particular page.
4. There should not be too many extraneous details.
5. There need not be pictures where no purpose is served.
6. Avoid distorted, impressionistic, or cluttered pictures in readers for young children. To obtain true concepts, children must see objects in their most natural setting and in their most common usage.

2 Jean Piaget, *The Language and Thought of the Child*. London: Routledge & Kegan Paul, 1952, pp. 133–134.

7. Some pictures may serve the purpose of intriguing children to read what is on the page to find out something about the picture.

Children should be helped to know the purposes that pictures serve and to refer to them before or as they read. Sometimes a teacher may ask, "What did that picture help you to know?" It is our aim to help children use every possible clue and not to force them to rely wholly on any one clue.

It is good experience, too, after a group story has been written, to challenge one or two children to look through magazines to find an appropriate picture to use with the story. Story content must be kept in mind as they look for a suitable picture. Sometimes interesting pictures are found first, and then stories are composed to go with the pictures. In either case, there is help in relating pictures and content. It is very good nursery school and kindergarten experience for children to look at very large pictures and tell all they can about them. In a sense, it is a form of reading—they are getting thought from picture symbols instead of printed words. The pictures call to mind real-life activity. Picture study and related oral language should be a part of every kindergarten day. Picture book enjoyment is good home activity too.

Word Analysis Clue

Children are not ready for the word analysis clue until they have a large sight vocabulary and the reading process is well established. Word analysis is the process of taking words apart in a way that will enable the reader to put the known parts together to make a meaningful whole. Perhaps two of the first words that a young child could be helped to know in this way would be *grandmother* and *grandfather*. Children already know *mother* and *father* very well. They also know *and*. These words, however, seldom cause any trouble; they are such long words that their configuration helps children to remember them. Calling children's attention to known words at the end of new words could confuse children into paying too much attention to word endings, which could result in some reversal tendencies. To point out a known word that appears at the beginning of a new word is much more consistent with the orderliness of the reading process. Words like *handsome, something, shoestring, nowhere, dishpan, forehead, partridge,* and *anything* are good examples of two words put together to make a new word. However, even a word like *nowhere* might be analyzed by a child as *now-here*. Attention must be focused on meaning assistance in the sentence. From the beginning children must be helped to know that any one clue is not entirely reliable As, for example, in words like *beat* (not pronounced as *be* and *at*), *season* (not *sea* and *son* or *seas* and *on*), *dragon* (not *drag-on*), but children can be helped to use this clue along with the context clue.

Children develop many concepts from pictures long before the printed symbols are recognized. (Photograph by R. H. Stagg, San Diego, California.)

Common word endings such as *s, es, ing, ed,* and *est* are used so frequently by the end of the first grade that they can be discussed as common word endings. Children can be helped to see that when *am* and *are* are used with action words, the action words nearly always have *ing* at the end. This, too, is a part of language pattern. Oral language exercises calling for such words help to clinch the learning. The *s* at the end of known words would be noticed by some children and then called to the attention of all as an ending that signifies more than one object, as *caps,* or doing something, as *runs.*

To understand *structural analysis* one must first understand the meaning of a *root word.* A root word is an uncompounded word or element without prefix, suffix, or inflectional ending (this is not a definition for children).

Children come in contact with words that are derived from root words very early in their language and reading experiences. *Play* is a *base word* and *plays, playing,* and *played* are all derived from *play.* Becoming familiar with endings such as *s, ed,* and *ing* would be an introduction to structural analysis. Then using knowledge with regard to these endings in recognizing other words that have such endings would be utilizing the *structural analysis clue.* The *s* at the end of such nouns as *boy's, girl's,* etc., showing possession, are also instances where the structural analysis clue can be used.

Not until after children have learned many words with these endings would we present them as endings. Then we would take those words with which they are familiar and help the children to generalize on the pronunciation of the commonly used endings. For example, these might be listed as follows:

play	played	playing	plays
look	looked	looking	looks
skip	skipped	skipping	skips
book	books		
girl	girls		
	girl's		
boy	boys		
	boy's		
box	boxes		
dish	dishes		
glass	glasses		

From these words children can be helped to listen for the common endings and to know what letter and groups of letters make up the sounds they hear. However, children should not be introduced to this procedure too early. The idea of looking at words from left to right must be well established first; as should much of beginning phonics. We also need to help children realize that we cannot always change words to mean more than one by adding *s* or *es,* and a word like *run* is not changed by adding *ed.* Children must always be helped to be wary of the irregularities of our language.

Structural analysis is also noting that some words are made up of a known word and other letters, and sometimes of two known words such as *playground, dollhouse, into,* and *sandbox,* at the first-grade level. Again, too much emphasis on known words occurring in larger words can cause trouble. Consider the problems of a child attempting to use this clue in words such as *rather, father, Catherine,* and *balloon.* Always the emphasis must be on meaning so that the sentence will make sense.

In second and third grades structural analysis elements such as the following may be taught through known words:

Contractions: *it's, let's, don't, you'll* (sometimes one and sometimes two letters are omitted)

Plural forms: changing *y* to *i* and adding *es* (some children may note that the plural of many words ending in *f* or *fe* is *ves*)

Possessive forms: *Mary's, mother's,* etc.

Suffixes: *er, est, less, ful, y, ly, ed, en, tion*

Of course, all first-grade work on structural analysis should be reviewed. All teaching must be repeated for those who need it and with some children many times.

In fourth, fifth and sixth grades, it is more important to be sure children have the very basic elements of structural analysis than to burden them with too many less commonly used bits of analysis. All this must be regarded as a means to easier reading and not as a fund of knowledge in itself. The time to teach any of this material is when it is the most meaningful and useful.

Teaching the meanings of prefixes and suffixes is especially important. Some commonly used ones are:

Prefixes meaning *not: dis, im, in, un, non*

Other prefixes: *trans, semi, fore, tri, under, com, con*

Suffixes: *ist, ible, ern, ment, ness, able, ish, ive, ous, ize*

More of this will be discussed in Chapters 8 and 11.

Syllabication

Phonics is much more helpful as a clue than is word analysis. In fact, to understand syllabication one must first know the vowel and consonant sounds and blending. One must have a keen ear for breaking words apart much as one phrases words in sentences—that is, in accordance with a language pattern. Syllabication must be heard before it can be understood.

Long before a child sees plural forms of words in print he can be helped to hear that when we talk about one ball we say *ball,* but when we mean more than one we say *balls.* However, when we talk about more than one house we say *houses.* Other plurals are formed by changing the word completely, as in the case of *mouse* and *mice.* Then when Christmas comes along and children speak of reindeer they must be helped to know that *reindeer* means both one and more than one. More peculiarities? Yes, indeed. Children who live in desert areas know that they speak of cactus when they mean one but cacti when they mean more than one. Thus we cannot teach word endings without developing awareness of exceptions to any rule.

Children must also be helped to know that some words like *pretty, big,* or *funny* can be used comparatively as in *pretty, prettier, prettiest;* but other words, such as *beautiful, huge,* or *peculiar,* would never have such endings.

A *syllable* might be defined as a vowel or a group of letters containing a vowel sound that form a pronounceable unit. The vowel sound may consist of two vowels making only a single sound. Much listening experience must precede any mention of syllables, and initial phonic instruction should precede this type of word analysis.

The following are rules for dividing words into syllables:

1. Because prefixes and suffixes are recognizable syllables, look for them first.

2. There are as many syllables in a word as there are vowel sounds that can be heard within the word.

3. A word is usually divided into syllables between double consonants or between two separately sounded consonants (*en ter tain, com mand*). However, when the root word ends in a double consonant, it is usually divided after the last consonant when a suffix has been added. (*spell ing, roll ing, call ing*).

4. A single consonant between vowels usually goes with the second vowel (*be gin, re turn, im prove*).

5. Digraphs and consonant blends should not be separated. If children were not made conscious of this generalization they might attempt to pronounce words according to the third rule and get into difficulties (*im pro per, both er, tea cher*).

It is hoped that through teaching syllabication children will be able to pronounce new words through applying the rules that might be relevant, arrive at correct spelling, and break words at the end of a line of writing in accordance with syllabic principles.

It can be seen that some rules serve one purpose better than others. For example, the word *preamble* might be pronounced *preem ble*. The *ea* in most words would be a single vowel sound. However, if it is a known word that must be divided at the end of a sentence, hearing division of the word would enable the writer to divide it easily. In fact, having it divided as *pre-amble* would enable subsequent readers to recognize it more readily.

It is well to help children understand these rules through generalizing about what they know, but going into complicated lessons in syllabication is time poorly spent. Dictionary usage can give children all the help they need in the more involved use of syllables.

Linguistics and phonics are valuable clues in word recognition, but they will be dealt with in following chapters because of the lengthy content of each subject.

Accent

Accent is vocal stress or emphasis. Vocal stress on certain words within sentences and on a certain letter or letters within words are important parts of our language pattern. Children have been using both through patterning ever since they learned to talk. Children are heard to say, "Look at *me*. Watch me *somersault*." They say *car* penter and *lolly* pop.

When they are ready to use many long words with several syllables in reading, the element of accent must be brought to the level of awareness. As in most things we teach, this can be done by using words they know and indicating how the accent mark placed on the indicated part of the word is used to indicate vocal stress.

Professor Carol K. Winkley of Northern Illinois University produced evidence of value showing that teaching accent generalizations as a word recognition technique is valuable to children. That is, the teaching went farther than mere introduction of the dictionary aid of marked syllables. Such teaching gave pupils greater power in the ability to attack unknown words, vocabulary development, and comprehension. After concluding that children having average or above reading ability should be taught accent generalizations, she proceeded to find out which generalizations were most useful. Her conclusions were as follows:

1. When there is no other clue in a two syllable word, the accent is usually on the first syllable (*ba' sic, pro' gram*).

2. In inflected or derived forms of words, the primary accent usually falls on or within the root word (*box' es, un tie'*).

3. If either *de, re, be, in,* or *a* is the first syllable in a word, it is usually unaccented (*de lay, ex plore*).

4. Two vowel letters together in the last syllable of a word may be a clue to an unaccented final syllable (*com plain, con ceal*).

5. When there are two like consonant letters within a word, the syllable before the double consonants is usually accented (*be gin', let' ter*).

6. The primary accent usually occurs on the syllable before the suffixes—*ion, ity, ic, ical, ian, ial,* or *ious* (*af fec ta' tion*)—and on the second syllable before the suffix *ate* (*dif fer en' ti ate*).

7. In words of three or more syllables, one of the first syllables is usually accented (*ac' ci dent, de' ter mine*).

No research has been conducted with regard to using such generalizations with pupils of below-average ability.

The time to introduce assistance of this kind is after students are reading material in which long and unfamiliar words appear. One child or a small group of children may be introduced to such generalizations as soon as there is recognizable evidence that such teaching would be useful. Later, other children would be helped in the same way. The time for teaching is when there is apparent need.

In attacking an unfamiliar multisyllabic word, children may be helped to use the following procedure:

1. Divide the word into syllables, following the general rules.

2. Decide where the accent should be.

3. Apply phonics rules to the syllables as you would to words. (Watch for digraphs and diphthongs.)

4. Pronounce the word. Read the sentence and decide whether it makes sense. If it does not, try variations of your pronunciation with emphasis on the consonants, digraphs, and accented syllable.

To me, the first three grades are everything.
—Hugh C. Riddleberger, Headmaster,
Trinity School, New York City [3]

Suggestions for Class Participation and Discussion

1. As a child, what clues did you use in attacking new words in independent reading?
2. Ask three children what they do when they come to a word they do not know when they are reading. Discuss their answers in class.
3. Why is it important to help children with all the clues of word recognition?
4. Be alert throughout one day for the situations in which you use any of the clues discussed in this chapter. Discuss them in class.
5. Secure the teacher's manual of two different preprimers. Note how children are first introduced to the reading. Discuss how you feel about the various suggestions. Could you be flexible in your own procedures regardless of what series you might use?
6. How important do you feel that syllabication has been to you?
7. Find other "Most Commonly Used Word Lists" and make comparisons. (Dolch, Thorndike, Durrell, Gates, Stone, and others have compiled such lists. Look for them in the index of various references on reading.)
8. Read about word recognition clues from one or two references suggested for this chapter and share some of the ideas that impressed you.
9. Study Appendix I and outside suggestions for establishing sight words, share these suggestions in class, and start a card file for your own use when you become a teacher.
10. React to the quotation at the end of the chapter.

Bibliography

Anaheim, California, City Schools, *Teachers' Guide for the Reading Program,* 1963.
Artley, A. Sterl. *Your Child Learns to Read.* Chicago: Scott, Foresman, 1953.
Botel, Morton. *How to Teach Reading.* Chicago: Follett, 1959.
Brogan, Peggy, and Fox, Lorene. *Helping Children Read.* New York: Holt, Rinehart & Winston, 1961.
Des Moines Department of Public Instruction. *Reading, Iowa, Elementary Teacher's Handbook.* Des Moines, Iowa.
Developing Children's Word Perception Power. Chicago: Scott, Foresman, 1954.

[3] Martin Mayer, *The Schools.* Garden City, N.Y.: Doubleday, 1963.

DURRELL, DONALD. *Improving Reading Instruction.* Yonkers-on-Hudson, N.Y.: World Book Co., 1956.

FERNALD, GRACE M., *Remedial Techniques in Basic School Subjects.* New York: McGraw-Hill, 1943.

FLINT, MICHIGAN, COMMUNITY SCHOOLS, *The Primary Cycle—Reading Guide,* 1961.

GRAY, LILLIAN. *Teaching Children to Read.* New York: Ronald Press, 1963.

GRAY, W. S. *On Their Own in Reading.* Chicago: Scott, Foresman, 1960.

HARGRAVE, ROWENA. *Building Reading Skills.* Wichita, Kan.: McCormick-Mathers, 1960.

HARRIS, ALBERT J. *How to Increase Reading Ability.* New York: Longmans, Green, 1961.

HILDRETH, GERTRUDE. *Teaching Reading.* New York: Holt, 1958.

JAMESVILLE-DEWITT CENTRAL SCHOOL. *The First R, A Reading Guide K–6.* New York City, 1966.

KIRK, SAMUEL. *Teaching Reading to Slow Learning Children.* Boston: Houghton Mifflin, 1950.

NEWTON, J. ROY. *Reading in Your School.* New York: McGraw-Hill, 1960.

NATIONAL SOCIETY FOR THE STUDY OF EDUCATION. *Reading in the Elementary School.* Chicago: University of Chicago Press, 1949.

Reading in the Elementary School. 48th Yearbook, Part II, National Education Association, 1939.

ROWLAND SCHOOL DISTRICT. *Let's Consider Reading.* La Puente, Calif., 1963.

RUSSELL, DAVID. *Children Learn to Read.* Boston: Ginn, 1961.

SMITH, NILA BANTON. *Reading Instruction for Today's Children.* Englewood Cliffs, N.J.: Prentice-Hall, 1963.

STRANG, RUTH, MCCULLOUGH, CONSTANCE, and TRAXLER, ARTHUR E. *The Improvement of Reading.* New York: McGraw-Hill, 1961.

WHEELER, ARVILLE. *Teacher's Question-and-Answer Book on Reading.* New London, Conn.: Croft, 1955.

WITTY, PAUL. *How to Become a Better Reader.* Science Research Associates, Chicago, 1953.

———. *Reading in Modern Education.* Boston: Heath, 1949.

CHAPTER 8

Phonics

The use of phonics did not enter American reading instruction until after the Revolutionary War, and then it came in as a patriotic, rather than a pedagogic measure. Noah Webster, who wrote the first series of American readers and who was highly activated in terms of patriotic motives, sought some means of unifying the diversity of dialects which existed in the United States following the Revolutionary War. Unity was an essential aim at the time because on it depended the future existence of the young nation. The idea of teaching all children in the country to give the same sound to each letter and to each of the important groups of letters occurred to Webster as a means of teaching all young Americans to pronounce words in the same way. And so phonics was introduced vigorously in his Blue Back Speller *and taught for many years for the purpose of unifying spoken language in America.*[1]

Phonetics is the science of speech sounds and *phonics* is the application of phonetic elements to the teaching of reading. It consists largely of associating letters with the speech sounds they represent. In languages that are one hundred per cent phonetic, every letter is

[1] Nila Banton Smith, "What Research Tells Us About Word Recognition." *Elementary School Journal*, Vol. LV, April, 1955.

associated with only one sound. When children learn each speech sound and the corresponding letter, they are ready to read or spell any word from their language that they care to use. Establishing word meanings and expanding concepts is the major task of teaching in countries such as Italy and Finland that have purely phonetic languages. We should never compare techniques of teaching reading in those countries with our own techniques.

Take a page from any book, or use this page for convenience. Count the number of words that are purely phonetic. Every letter must make the sound most commonly associated with it, and all must be heard when the word is pronounced. What is the proportion as compared with the total number of words? It is sometimes stated that our language is slightly less than eighty-five per cent phonetic, but that figure is misleading. If one considers the repetition of the many common words that are unphonetic and the many words that are only partly phonetic, the percentage of purely phonetic words would be much less. Children have no way of knowing which parts of unknown words may or may not be phonetic, and that makes the use of phonics even more confusing. However, phonics is useful to a degree if children are striving for words that make sense in the sentence. The words must be in the reader's hearing and understanding vocabulary, otherwise phonics is a key that opens a door to nowhere. With conscious emphasis on meaning, phonics becomes a tool that we use when and if it helps.

Many of our most commonly used words (*is, you, the, was, were, one, once, do, said, want, where, word, are, your*) are used over and over in daily reading, and to approach them phonetically would be a waste of time and effort. Such words must become sight words. Children must be told from the beginning that sounds are helpful in some but not all words.

Because phonics is a letter-sound relationship it is based on a listening-saying background of experience. That is why the subjects of hearing and correct speech received so much emphasis in an earlier chapter (see Speech-Sound Check, Appendix B).

A child with a dialect requires help with speech before he can be expected to use the letter-sound relationships of phonics. The speech of children in the Deep South is accommodated by teachers who use the same speech variations, but a child from the Deep South coming to the North has a problem.

Nicholas Silvaroli and Warren Wheelock of Arizona State University conducted a study in which it was found that auditory training of lower socioeconomic group children helped them considerably to discriminate thirty-three basic speech sounds more effectively. It would seem that auditory training would be an important part of Head-Start programs (see suggestions in Appendix A).

Children should have a knowledge of about seventy-five to a hundred sight words before general instruction is given in phonics or sound make-up of words. However, some incidental enlightenment might come about as they become curious. They have, in the course of chalkboard work, experienced the writing of their names and the names of other children. Thus, they begin to get the feel of various letter forms, and they become conscious of likeness and differences. A teacher mentions that each name starts with a big capital letter. Children will quickly be aware of anyone else's name that starts like his own. If Betty announces, "Look, Bobby's name starts like mine," it is a good time to say, "Listen while I say your names: Betty, Bobby. Do you see how my lips are placed together when I start saying both names and how I make the same first sound? Watch and listen again." This much of an introduction will probably start many children to being conscious of similarities in first letters of words. Whenever interest is shown, the teacher has an opportunity to help children hear more likenesses in beginning word sounds, which will constitute an incidental teaching of phonics that should be utilized whenever there is an opportunity.

While the sight word vocabulary is being acquired the children will have read little experience stories, used word cards, learned words on the bulletin board, played games with word cards, traced over some of the words that caused difficulty, and will have come to know that words have meanings and sentences give them more meaning. The "meaning" idea should be well established.

A Linguistic-Phonetic Approach to Word Recognition

When most of the children in a class know about fifty words by sight, some will know as many as a hundred or more. Some will already be conscious of similarities in word beginnings, and many actually know many initial word sounds from the incidental teaching that has interested them. A little help in an incidental way is sometimes all that is needed to make the necessary associations that give linguistics or phonics meaning. However, those who are not as fast to catch on need help in using a linguistic-phonetic clue. Children may be challenged to dictate all the sight words they know. The list should include children's names for two reasons. First, most children will be familiar with the names of children in the class through chalkboard and chart experiences and through helping to distribute papers. Second, it is good to include words with capital and small letters because they need to become familiar with both. Dictating the words they know and then saying them once or twice, or spending a little time finding words that start with the same first letter, would be enough for one day. The next day the teacher should have them alphabetized on a chart, something like this:

a	candy	father	he	make	pretty	up
am	car	find	her	Mary	put	us
and	Carol	for	here	me	quick	Vicki
Ann	cat	Frank	his	mother	red	walk
are	color	from	I	my	ride	want
baby	come	fun	in	name	Robin	was
ball	cut	Gary	is	Nancy	said	we
balloon	David	get	it	not	Sally	went
be	did	girl	Jerry	off	saw	were
Betty	dog	give	jump	open	see	will
big	Donna	go	keep	paste	she	Wilma
black	down	grand-mother	Kippy	Patty	take	with
blue	draw	grass	let	Paul	Terry	work
boy	egg	green	like	play	the	write
came	Evelyn	Harry	little	please	this	you
can	every	have	look	Polly	to	your

It might be explained to children that up to now they remembered words because they looked different from each other in length, size, and shape of letters, and by getting the feel of the word. Many words look almost alike. Now, by becoming familiar with first letters of words, these letters can be used in figuring out new words in sentences. Challenge them to find the letter with which the greatest number of words begin.

INITIAL WORD SOUNDS

Dr. Gesell has this to say about the six-year-old and his observance of the initial letter of words:

The 6-year-old is beginning to read words, as well as letters. He identifies familiar words on the cereal packages and in magazine advertisements. He shows new facility in memorizing stories read to him. His ability to pick out words which he knows at random is correlated with his reading ability. In recognizing words, he makes major use of the initial letter, a trait which is characteristic of his increasing interest in beginnings. While reading, he has difficulty in holding to a horizontal line. This difficulty is another symptom of his immature but growing orientations to structured space, in minute as well as in gross aspects.[3]

Children are likely to note *w, b,* or *c.* Choose one child at a time to come up and find a word starting with the letter selected. After the words are encircled the teacher might rewrite them quickly on another area of the chalkboard so they can be referred to easily.

If children have agreed on the letter *w* as being the most common beginning letter of the words they know, the list would be:

we	with	were	was	went	write
work	will	want	walk	Wilma	

Have the children read the words with you. Ask them to watch your lips while you say all the words from the list. Then ask them if they can see your lips make the same sound at the beginning of every word. Now they are ready to conclude that it is the *w* at the beginning of each word that makes that sound. For the first time isolate the sound, say it several times, and have them say it with you. Thus, we are helping children become aware of speech sounds at the beginning of words they already know. This is "linguistic" in that the speech sounds are retained within the words. Children are gaining this knowledge through generalizing about what they know.

Now, as we isolate the initial sound from these known words to use it as a clue in recognizing other words, we are using a phonetic element. Therefore, this may be known as a linguistic-phonetic approach. The primary emphasis remains on reading for meaning as we now proceed in using the generalization we have helped children to make. Now children are ready to be challenged to think of other words they know (but may not have read) that start that way. Any child who gives a wrong word should be helped to hear the difference. After children are proficient in relating the sound to many words, it is well to relate this knowledge to use in context. Such sentences as the following might be used orally (write the *w* on the board and point to it each time you come to a blank space; make the w sound).

[3] Gesell, Arnold, Ilg, Frances, and Bullis, Glenna, *Vision: Its Development in Infant and Child.* New York: Harper, 1949, pp. 137–138.

The w——— was blowing.
Some houses are painted w———.
The w——— was hung on the line.
Plants need w———, light, and food.
The children w——— to school.
Mother w——— from the window.
We might see w——— on Halloween.
Some places have cold weather in w———.
One day of the week is W———.
You make a w——— when you blow out birthday candles.
We w——— and play at school.

Children might then be asked to volunteer sentences to challenge their classmates. Give them several minutes to think of good sentences. Stop immediately when interest wanes and attention wavers. Keep the list of words on the board for use the next day or transfer the *w* words onto a chart sheet. Help children to feel the joy of achievement now that they can associate many meaningful words with the initial sound of *w*.

The next day all the children whom the teacher is sure know the sound of *w* and can associate it with many words are sent to the magazines to find a good picture of a *w* word. Each child is to paste the picture in the upper half of a page of paper the teacher has provided (half-sheets of the least expensive paper the school provides are adequate). Beneath the picture the child may write any words he knows that start with that sound. More words may be added from day to day. The teacher will have made one for a sample. The children are to print "W w" at the top of the page. This will become a "Letter-Sound Book." Each child is to put his completed page in his own large envelope. These pages will later be arranged in alphabetical order before being stapled or tied together. Then the teacher works with the remainder of the class on the *w* sound. If some children are absent and others extremely slow to learn, she will have to give individual or small group help.

Now is a good time to start a "Word File." The teacher might bring in a card-size file box. On the first index file card she would print *A a* in manuscript, and so on through the alphabet. She would then make word cards to fit the file box.

Now children have need for the alphabet. (See suggestions for teaching the alphabet in Appendix L.) Let a different child be responsible for filing the word cards after each letter has been learned.

Children might check each other on the words behind any letter
card when they have free time. As new words are learned they are
added to the "Word File."

The *b* is another initial sound of frequent usage. Usually there
are many children whose first names start with *B,* and they should
be included with an explanation of the capital letter each time a
name appears. Lip placement can be shown and all the *b* words in
the list encircled and read. The following sentences are suggested:

Two boys' names are B———— and B————.
Two girls' names are B———— and B————.
It is fun to blow up a b————.

There need be no prescribed order for introducing initial letter
sounds, but it is best to start with those used most frequently and
those that look very different from each other. It is confusing to
some children to have *d* introduced right after *b.* Let the *b* become
very well established first. In fact, as the teacher writes it she might
repeat, "Straight line first, then the round part."

Letters in which children can see the lip placement necessary for
making the sound are helpful to children as first letters—for example, *w, s, b, l, m,* and *p.*

From the list of words children will find the following *s* words:
see, said, Steve, she, saw, something, Sally, stop. Some classes may
have a Shirley or a Sharon. After the words are listed and the teacher
says them as she writes them, someone may observe that *she, Shirley,*
and *Sharon* do not sound the same way as the others, even though
the first letters look alike. Praise children who listen so well. If no
one makes the observation, ask the class to listen while you say, "*See,
said, Sharon, Shirley.* Do they all sound alike at the beginning?"
Now is the time to give the explanation that sometimes two letters
together make a new sound. These are called digraphs. *Sh* makes
the *sh* sound that we sometimes hear when water rushes out of a
hose. Now they are ready to think of other words that start with *s*
and other words that start with *sh* but list them separately. Index
cards for the file box must be provided with the digraphs as they
are introduced.

The following sentences are good to keep thoughts on meanings:

Two numbers that start with *s* are s———— and s————.
Sometimes when we look up at the s———— it is very blue.

We send things over the ocean in a sh————.
Hippety-hop to the barber sh————.
A first name might be Sh————.

When children are challenged to mention other words that start with the *s* sound, a teacher may get such suggestions as *Cindy, city,* or *cent.* Here is another opportunity to introduce a peculiarity of the language. We must explain that *c* at the beginning and in some words makes the sound of *s.* More commonly, however, it makes the sound that can be heard at the beginning of *car, can, come,* and *cat.* Challenged for more words starting with *c* children may submit *clean, clear, carry, cup,* and *clay.* Some child may mention a name such as *Charles* or *Charlotte* or *Charlene.* Here is the opportunity to teach the *ch* sound at the same time as the *c* so that children are alert for an *h* after the *c.* Make up a list of *ch* words as the children dictate them. They would be likely to include *children, church, chimney,* etc. Sentences with fill-in words keep attention focused on context meanings so that the new knowledge becomes a clue.

Rabbits like to eat c————.
It is fun to c———— a tree.
Crayons come in many c————.

Many people go to ch———— on Sunday.
Smoke goes up the ch————.
I like to ch———— a story to be read.

When children are challenged to think of *c* words someone is likely to mention *kite, kick,* or *king.* It is well to teach the sound of *k* as being the same as *c* and make listings of both.

The k———— wears a jeweled crown.

While these learnings are going on, children will be expanding their vocabularies and recognizing more words through other experiences throughout the day.

When *g* is introduced some child is likely to mention *George* if that happens to be his name or if he has a brother with that name. Help the children to hear the difference in sound but to know that sometimes the *g* does make that sound as in *age, page,* and *ranger,* and at the beginning of such words as *George* and *gentle.* Tell them that there is another letter that makes the same sound as the *g* in George and that is the *j*. Perhaps such names as *Jack, Jean, Janet,* and *Joyce* will be known to many of them.

A first name might be G——— (Gary, Glen, George).
Grass is g———.
We keep cars in a g———.
We like to play g———.
We like to eat bread and j———.
The boy's name was J———.
Two girls' names are J——— and J———.

It is often best to start the introduction of a sound with the first names of children in the class, if there are any, as these children rarely forget that particular sound. A name association is a strong one.

The *m* sound can be seen as well as heard. It is a voiced sound because the voice can be heard as the sound is made. The *p* has the same lip placement, but it is voiceless. Sometimes it is good to give children this additional clue but let them hear and experience voiced and voiceless sounds. M is very easy to teach as children are helped to place their lips together and think of the words that start that way. *Me, my, many, mother, monkey,* etc. may start a list of considerable length.

I like to drink a glass of m——— with my breakfast.
It takes m——— to buy things at a store.
We find pictures in m———.

I would like a p——— of pie.
He made a jack-o-lantern from a big p———.
The rain rolled down the window p———.
We cut p——— from magazines.

It is easy to show the lip placement for *l* and for children to start words that way. *Little, like, lay, look* will start a list. Encourage children to think of sentences, too.

For a jack-o-lantern I would like a l——— pumpkin.
A bird can stand on one l———.
The funny story made me l———.

FUSION

An important part of the phonics clue is the ability to put sounds together in words, to fuse them. When sounds are taught apart from words some children have great difficulty putting them together.

With the *l* sound children can be helped to put *b* and *l* together in what is known as a *blend*. They can also put *s* and *l* together, *p* and *l*, and *g* and *l* in words such as *black, slow, play, glad*.

Then to put the clue in its most useful setting, play a game such as the following:

I'm thinking of a word that means a color and it starts with *bl* (*blue* or *black*).

I'm thinking of something we can do with our feet and it starts with *sl* (*slip* or *slide*).

I'm thinking of something that is a fruit and starts with *pl* (*plum*).

I'm thinking of a word that means a funny man in the circus. It starts with *cl* (*clown*).

I'm thinking of a word that means happy and it starts with *gl* (*glad*).

Challenge children to think of others. Such exercises keep attention on word meanings as they begin to use blends.

T and *d* may be introduced as a voiceless and voiced pair. The tongue is placed behind the teeth to make both sounds, but we use our voices when we make the d sound.

I like to d——— milk.
If I try to carry too much I may d——— something.
There was a deep d——— along the side of the road.
Please shut the d———.
Two names are D——— and D———.

When children look through their list of sight words for words beginning with the *t* sound, someone is likely to mention *the* and *this,* and the teacher will have to explain that we have another sound when there is an *h* after the *t*. In fact, we have two sounds. Then children need to be helped with the voiced and voiceless sounds of *th*. If they place their tongue along the edge of their upper teeth they are ready to make either sound. Say many words starting with the *th* sound. Ask children to clap when the *th* is voiced. Watch for children who do not seem to hear the difference between voiced and voiceless *th*. Lists of words might be made and then sentences used for context.

Many stories start with, "Once upon a t———."
Many times we can do it if we t———.
One day of the week is T———.

Put the books over th———.
You may use th——— pictures.
Do not do th——— work for th———.
We must do th——— work today.
Th——— pencils are not mine.
To sew we must use a needle and th———.
A pitcher must be able to th——— a ball well.
One day of the week is Th———.
It is easy to hit your th——— with a hammer.

Be careful not to proceed too fast. If children get confused, take time to set them straight and to regain their confidence. *F* and *v* is another pair of voiceless and voiced consonants. The *v* is not used frequently, but it can be associated with the *f* for teeth and lip placement. The upper teeth are placed on the lower lip and the *v* is sounded or voiced, while the *f* is voiceless.

Two numbers are f——— and f———.
With a pole, line, hook, and some bait, we can go f———.
Cows live on the f———.

Grapes grow on a v———.
I like ice cream v——— much.
A name is V———.
When there is no school we call it v———.
We get v——— so we will not get small pox.

The *r* sound opens the way for many word recognitions when combined with other known sounds. Start first with the initial *r* sound. Let children get the feel of making the isolated sound and then saying words starting that way, such as *run, ride, rope, ribbon, right, ran, rest, road,* etc. Then challenge them with sentences such as:

It is fun to jump r———.
She wore a r——— in her hair.
He drove the car down the r———.

Challenge children to find things in the room that start with the *r* sound. Then challenge children by putting other known sounds with the *r* to make blends.

I'm thinking of something that means what will happen to a glass if we drop it—it starts with *br* (*break*).
I'm thinking of a word that means what children sometimes do when they get angry. It starts with *cr* (*cry*).
I'm thinking of a word that means what we sometimes do when we sleep and it starts with *dr* (*dream*).
I'm thinking of a word that means what we pay, and it starts with *pr* (*price*).
I'm thinking of a word that means something we use when we fly a kite and it starts with *str* (*string*).

The *h* sound is common; it is voiceless and made by emitting a short puff of air from the throat. The voiced sound would be *a* as in *away, about, among, around, again, alarm*, etc.

Birds fly away up h———.
We went up the h——— to fly our kites.
When I haven't eaten for a while I begin to feel h———.
Tell us a story a——— witches and black cats.
The fire a——— sent the firemen away in a hurry.
He rode a——— the block on his bicycle.
Sometimes we must try a———.

Some children are likely to mention such words as *are* and *at* when *a* words are listed. Now is the time to help them know that there are many sounds associated with *a*. *At, am, and, add*, and *after* are all examples of the short sound of *a*. This will be discussed later. However, introduce it when children are ready and interested.

The *n* sound is not so common, but it can be introduced quickly as it is not easily confused with any other sound.

Squirrels can crack n——— with their teeth.
People who live next door to us are called n———.

In arithmetic we talk about n————.
At n———— we go to sleep.
At n———— we eat lunch.

The sound of *y* is different at the beginning of a word from the sound it makes at the end of a word. We call it a consonant at the beginning of a word when it makes sounds such as those at the beginning of *you, year, yesterday,* and *yellow.*

Some flowers have y———— centers.
We finish work today that we started y————.
Sometimes we measure with a y————.
She was seven y———— old.
Mother wants you to play in your own y————.

Q is a peculiar sound because it always has a *u* after it when it is used at the beginning of or within a word. We can hear that *u* when we say *q*. It is like saying *c* or *k* with *u*. You might present *qu* together as that will always be the phonetic word clue. Only at the end of a word does it make the *k* sound alone (*Iraq*).

I felt very qu———— when I got up.
The Qu———— was seated on a throne.
Two children got into a qu———— on their way home from school.
Sometimes we need to be qu———— to hear what someone has to say.
If we do our work qu———— we will have time for a story.

X, y, and *z* might be put on the same page of the children's "Letter-Sound Book" because they will have difficulty finding pictures to go with those letters. They might make a big zero on that page and write the word "zero" below it. It might be explained that *x* sounds like *c* and *s* together, and we have it only in words such as *box, fox,* and *oxen.* The *z* sound is like a saw buzzing, and the word *buzz* helps us remember it.

Consonants

Children may be told that the single-letter sounds they have learned except the *a* are known as consonants. These letters form a kind of framework for words.

Consonant Blends

Some children may frequently need to be made aware of blends. Sometimes blending helps children to fuse sounds for more fluent reading if they tend to become too letter conscious. Children coming from schools where letters and letter sounds have been introduced before words and sentences sometimes have problems of fusing and fluent reading.

The following blends are most commonly used:

bl(black)	gl(glad)	st(stay)
br(bring)	gr(grass)	sw(swing)
cl(clay)	pr(price)	scr(scrap)
cr(cry)	sk(skate)	str(street)
dr(drink)	sl(sled)	spr(spring)
fl(flag)	sm(smell)	
fr(frog)	sn(snap)	

Digraphs

Two consonants that lose their own identity and make a new sound are known as *digraphs*. The digraphs are especially important because they are very constant. Unless the child remembers the constancy of digraphs he is likely to have problems in syllabication. A word is almost never divided when two consonants that ordinarily make a digraph appear together as in the following:

ch(*ranch* er)	wh(no *where*)
sh(friend *ship*)	ph(tele *phone*)
th(*slith* er ing)	
th(*loath* some)	

An interesting study was conducted by twenty-one teachers and administrators at Fort Atkinson, Wisconsin, in which children were tested on the use of the following phonics clues:

1. Four word choices were listed from which to choose the word that had been omitted from the sentence.

2. The beginning and final letter of the missing word were given.

3. The initial letter only was given for the missing word.

4. All the consonants appeared in the missing word.

5. Only a line appeared in place of the missing word, and it had no relationship to the length of the word.

6. A line appeared in place of the word, and it was in accordance with the length of the word.

The results showed greatest success when all consonants were given. Four word choices was second. Beginning and final letter rated third.

It is interesting to try to read sentences with only the consonant sounds:

Th– b–ll r–ll–d d––n th– str––t. Th– g–rl r–n –ft–r th– b–ll.

Knowing only the consonant sounds is a very helpful clue in reading, especially when meaning is sought.

Many exercises like this help to draw children's eyes along the print so that they can glance at known consonant sounds in words and read quickly and easily. This much phonics is as much as many children need.

Prolonged study of the many vowel sounds can be a waste of time, and effort might be better spent on purposeful reading.

VOWELS

The *vowels* are *a, e, i, o, u,* and sometimes *y.* They are voiced sounds produced by modification of the intonation jet by the throat, palate, tongue, and lips. (This is not a definition for children. They do not need to be bothered with such definitions. Understandings through use must come first.)

It is the vowels that cause great variation in speech patterns from one section of our country to another. Each vowel has many variations in sound within words and a few rules can give only slightly dependable guidance. Look at the vowels with their diacritical markings at the bottom of any large dictionary page. It is wise to help children to be alert to exceptions to long and short vowel rules.

These vowel rules are most commonly used:

1. A single vowel within a three- or four-letter word is usually short.

man   sled   big   hot   cup

2. An *e* at the end of a short word makes the vowel within the word long, and the final *e* is silent.

tape   here   nice   note   tune

An *e* at the end of a long word makes the vowel in the last syllable long and the final *e* is silent.

inflate   recede   decline   compose   refuse

3. When two vowels appear together in a short word, the first is long and the second is silent. Children may be helped to remember this rule by expressing it as follows: When two vowels go walking the first one does the talking.

pail   dream   dial   coat   fuel

The long sound may be referred to as "saying its name." There are many exceptions to these rules as in:

weight   post   come   was

It is enough to teach first- and second-grade children the long and short vowel sounds in short words and to alert them to many exceptions.

Several research studies show that there are about as many exceptions as applications of these rules in the total vocabulary of adults. However, as there are large groupings of words used frequently by children in which the rule applies, they are considered worth teaching.

To complete the children's book of initial word sounds the following pictures might be used. These booklets may be stapled and used for reference when a child forgets any letter sound. They are a first picture dictionary. Other words can be added to each page and the picture is the sound guide. (They can be easily drawn if the children cannot find magazine pictures.)

Long *a*	ape, apron, acorn
Short *a*	apple
Long *e*	eagle, Easter basket, easel
Short *e*	egg
Short *i*	Indian, igloo, ink
Long *i*	I, ice cream
Long *o*	oh, oval
Short *o*	ostrich
Long *u*	United States
Short *u*	umbrella

The *y* is a consonant at the beginning of a word, but it is a vowel at the end of a word.

Stone made an interesting study of sound-symbol frequency.[4] He

---

[4] David R. Stone, "A Sound-Symbol Frequency Count." *The Reading Teacher*, April, 1966, p. 498–504.

took the 6,000 sounds from the vocabulary of the primary grade books of five basal reading series and analyzed them. He found that about 89 per cent of the consonant sounds were regular whereas only 54 per cent of the long vowel and about 85 per cent of the short vowel sounds were regular. He excluded the short *u* sound in the short vowel computation or the percentage would have been much lower. The short *u* had more irregular sounds than regular.

His study revealed that the long *a* was produced by the final *e* in 43 per cent of the cases; by the *ai* combination in 20 per cent; *a* alone in the word, 18 per cent, and by *ay* in 11 per cent of the cases. Other variations (*ey, ea, eigh*) accounted for less than 1 per cent. The long *e* sound was produced by a final *y* in 31 per cent of the cases. (In words like *pretty* the *y* was considered as long *e* rather than soft *i* as in many dictionaries.) The *ea* and *ee* combinations each accounted for 21 per cent of the cases; the single *e* for 19 per cent of the cases; and *ie, ey, i, eo,* and *ei* accounted for the remaining 1 per cent. The long *i* sound was produced by the final *e* in 46 per cent of the cases; by *i* alone in 17 per cent; by *ie, y,* and *igh* each in 11 per cent, and *ey* and *ig* each appeared once. The long *o* sound was produced by *o* alone in 34 per cent of the cases; by final *e* in 32 per cent; by *ow* in 18 per cent; by *oa* in 12 per cent, and in 6 per cent by *oo, ou, oe,* and *ough*. The long *u* appeared only in five words. Two were at the beginning of words such as *usual;* two others were *view* and *few;* the other word was *beauty*. The short vowels were regular, except the short *u,* it was made by *u* in 35 per cent of the cases; by *e* in 20 per cent, *a* in 16 per cent; *o* in 22 per cent, and in 6 per cent of the cases by *i, ou,* and *ai*.

The vowels make many other sounds besides the long and short, but it is better to postpone explanation of them until fourth grade when the dictionary and diacritical markings are taught. Children who make good use of context, who are conscious of the length of words, and who become familiar with consonants, consonant blends, and digraphs have little trouble in independent reading. They can spot enough sounds in a word to be able to fit the vowel sounds in automatically. Too much letter-by-letter analysis of words can be inhibiting rather than helpful.

Try reading a sentence with only the vowel sounds: ––e –a–– –o––e– –ow– ––e –––ee–. They are not as useful as the consonants. Do you see why it is important to place more emphasis on learning the consonant sounds as clues for reading?

Mildred Bailey, in her doctoral study at the University of Mississippi, discovered these generalizations to occur the most frequently:

1. When *c* and *h* are next to each other, they make only one sound.

2. When the letter *c* is followed by *o* or *a* the sound of *k* is likely to be heard.

3. When *c* is followed by *e* or *i*, the sound of *s* is likely to be heard.

4. When two of the same consonants are side by side, only one is heard?

Robert Emons, Professor at Temple University, found that the following generalizations occur frequently:

1. The letters *oo* usually have the long double *o* sound as in *food,* or the short double *o* sound as in *good*. They are more likely to have the double *o* sound as in *food*.

2. The two letters *ow* make the long *o* sound or the *ou* sound as in *out*.

3. When *y* is used as a vowel, it most often has the sound of long *e*.

4. The letters *io* usually represent a short *u* sound as in *nation*.

5. When the first vowel is *o* and the second is *a*, the *o* is usually long and the *a* is silent.

6. When the first vowel in a word is *a* and the second is *i*, the *a* is usually long and the *i* silent.

7. When a vowel is in the middle of a one-syllable word, the vowel is short, except that it may be modified in words in which the vowel is followed by an *r*.

8. When the vowel is the middle letter of a one-syllable word, the vowel is short.

Diphthongs

The *diphthongs* are vowels or vowel and consonant groupings in which individual letters lose their identity and a new sound is made. Some common diphthongs are *oo, ou, oi, oy, ough, tion, ing, ow*.

The time to introduce them is when children have learned enough words to generalize from those words they know what the diphthong sounds would be. Then they can use this general knowledge in attacking unfamiliar words. There are several problems, however. The *oo* makes one sound in *book* and *look* and another in *room* and *too*. Which will it be in a new word? Again, avoid problems by keeping attention focused on word meanings as the basic clue.

Consider the variety of sounds *ough* makes in words such as *though, tough, bought, trough, cough, through,* etc.

Phonics in Grades Three Through Six

The reading inventory in Appendix F will assist third- and fourth-grade teachers in determining what help children need in basic phonics. If there is any doubt about a child's ability to use initial consonant sounds, it is a good idea to include him in the group that is getting help. Make up a chalkboard list of sight words the children suggest, and from them proceed as suggested earlier in this chapter.

Place much emphasis on digraphs and consonant blends. When longer words come into focus, the clues that seemed so effective with short words begin to lose their value. For example, in two- and three-letter words most of the vowels within the words are short if there is only a single vowel. Now consider these words: *between, pathetic, fathom, rather, Catherine, mathematics, bathroom, pathway.* Children know the first three letters as words. Now they need to look for digraphs and blends for help in pronunciation. Children find phonics a much better clue if they follow from left to right through the word with the consonant, digraphs, and blends as clues along with the context clue. The meaning association and those sounds are usually all they need. The consonants that follow sometimes have sounds not usually associated with them. They are presented—not because children should be expected to memorize them all—but to help children to be alert to the many variables that might show up at any time in their reading.

The following are consonants having more than one sound:

c The letter *c* is most frequently associated with the sound of *k*. However, sometimes when followed by *e, i,* or *y* it makes the sound of *s* as in *rice, bicycle, cider, cyclone, cell.* When it is followed by an *h* it becomes a digraph as in *church, chair, which.*

d The letter *d* is most frequently associated with sounds appearing in *doll, dish,* and *did.* However, in such words as *soldier, gradual,* and *individual,* it makes the sound of *j.*

g The letter *g* is most frequently heard as in *guess* and *game.* However, frequently it makes the sound of *j* as in *gypsy,* and *gymnasium.* In *rouge* it makes the sound of *zh.*

q The letter *q* is most frequently heard as in *quiet* and *quest,* in which it sounds like *kw.* However, in *antique* it has only the *k* sound.

s The usual sound of *s* appears in such words as *some* and *sister.* However, it makes the sound of *z* in *his* and in many plurals formed by adding *es* to words such as *boxes, bushes,* and *wishes.* It makes the sound of *sh* in *sugar, tissue,* and *sure.* It makes the sound of *zh* in *decision* and *treasure.* When it is followed by an *h* it becomes a digraph, as in *shall* and *ship.*

t The most frequent sound of *t* appears in such words as *take, tent,* and *test.* However, with an *h* following it, it becomes a digraph in such words as *this, that,* and *throw.* In the combination of letters *tion,* it becomes a diphthong in such words as *attention* and *mention.*

x The most frequent sound of *x* is *ks,* as in *box* and *extra.* However, in *examination, exalt,* and *exempt* it makes the sound of *gz.*

The *schwa* is an unaccented vowel sound that is so influenced by the consonant following it that it can scarcely be discerned.

u in *burn*	*i* in *pupil*	*a* in *mortar*
e in *cover*	*o* in *bottom*	*y* in *martyr*

Ng is referred to as a *nasal digraph.* Children can feel the air moving up through their noses rather than through their mouths as they say *ing, ong,* and *ung.*

Chalkboard exercises in which important words are left out and only the first consonant appears are good to help children use the context and initial sound clue and is often as much as they will need. Sometimes it also helps to insert little dashes so that they can see how long the word is. Then putting in all the consonants gives them a real thrill when they find how helpful they are. Exercises from some of the commercial phonics workbooks may be useful for those children who need additional reenforcement in use of phonics.

The *consonants, digraphs,* and *blends* are by far the most useful elements of phonics as far as reading is concerned. Further analysis has questionable value because of the many variables. However, many reading authorities go farther in the teaching of phonetic elements.

COMMON DIPHTHONGS

ou and *ow*	(town, about, ground, frown)
oi and *oy*	(boy, oil, enjoyment, soil)
oo	(broom, stool, bloom)
oo	(book, wool, good)
ew and *eu*	(few, feud, new)
tion	(direction, election, mention)
ing	(bring, sing, wing)
ough	(enough, though, thought, cough, trough, tough)
ould	(would, could, should)

Table 8–1. Common Vowel Phonograms[5]

Phonogram	Example	Symbol
ar	b(ar)bed	/är, ár/ (sound of the name of the letter *r*)
ear	sp(ear)	/ir/ (*ear*)
air	f(air)	/ar, er/ (*air*)
or (stressed)	t(or)ch	/õr/ (*or*)
ore (stressed)	st(ore)	/ōr õr/
oor (stressed)	d(oor)	/ōr õr/
er (stressed)	h(er)self	/ər/
ir (stressed)	b(ir)d	/ər/
ur (stressed)	c(ur)tain	/ər/
ou	h(ou)nd	/aū/
ow	cr(ow)n	/aū/
ow (stressed)	kn(ow)	/ō/
ow (unstressed last syllable)	shad(ow)	/ö/
oi	app(oi)nt	/ói/
oy	destr(oy)	/ói/
au	c(au)se	/ó/
aw	j(aw)s	/ó/
a (before l)	st(a)ll	/ó/
u (stressed)	(u)mpire	/ə/ (short *u*)
a (unstressed)	(a)bout	/ə/ (short *u*)
ay	dism(ay)	/ā/ (long *a*)
y (last syllable)	fort(y)	/ē/ (long *e*)
syllabic l (unstressed)	gigg(le)	/-l/
syllabic m (unstressed)	rhyth(m)	/-m/
syllabic n (unstressed)	drag(on)	/-n/
syllabic r (unstressed)	fev(er)	/-r/
	col(or)	
	coll(ar)	

[5] Source: Emmett A. Betts, "Controversial Issues in Reading," April, 1961.

*Homograph*s are words that are spelled the same but pronounced differently depending on meaning in the sentence, as in:

I will *read* this book. I *read* that one yesterday.
I must *wind* the clock. The *wind* was blowing.

Challenge the children to think of others and to use the dictionary in their search.

Homonyms are words spelled differently but pronounced the same:

This is the *right* way to open the   I will *write* a letter.
book.
The *maid* cleaned the house.   She *made* a cake.

To stimulate interest in a review of consonants and digraphs challenge the children to make a listing of voiced and voiceless consonants and digraphs with word examples.

Voiceless Consonants and Digraphs

p (put, play, pick)
t (took, time, train)
k (kind, king, kangaroo)
f (find, finish, far)
th (thing, throw, three)
s (same, salt, scratch)
sh (share, shall, shop)
ch (church, chair, chime)
x (box, six, mix)
h (here, have, hurry)
c (come, carry, cart)

Voiced Consonants and Digraphs

b (baby, basket, bring)
d (dog, did, drink)
g (give, gate, glad)
v (voice, victory, vine)
th (they, this, there)
z (zoo, zebra, zipper)
j (just, jury, jam)
r (river, rain, raise)
w (wig, women, wagon)
q (quick, quack, quiver)
y (you, yet, your)
l (little, lake, long)
m (many, much, monkey)
n (never, not, name)

Fun with Words

To keep children wary of the many words in our language that are not phonetic, it is fun and a good learning experience to spend a little time occasionally (opening exercise on Friday or Monday morning) challenging children to find three common words to which phonics would not apply. Soon they will be chuckling about "our funny language," and it is surprising how many words will be learned from this "fun" type activity. Children soon draw their own conclusions as to the need for many clues to word recognition and that the most important is the meaning or context clue (what word would make sense when used with the other words).

Children enjoy the challenge presented by having a teacher write a sentence on the board with a difficult word in it. It may or may not be a phonetic word. The child who is able to determine what the word is independently explains what clues he used, and it is a good learning experience for the whole class. Sometimes a list of sentences may be put on the board as a challenge, and the children are given until Friday to try to read them without teacher help.

Phonics is not an end in itself; it is only one of five word recognition techniques in reading used most effectively with the context clue to assist children in decoding words quickly and easily with the thought of the complete sentence foremost in the child's mind.

—VERNA DIECKMAN ANDERSON

Suggestions for Class Participation and Discussion

1. Did you learn much about phonics when you learned to read? Did you learn it before or after word meanings were established?
2. Is there any letter that is sounded only one way in each and every word in which it appears? Be wary of silent letters.
3. Some authors put much stress on final blends. Why are initial blends better clues?
4. Examine any preprimer. From the list of words in the back of the book, how many are one hundred per cent phonetic?
5. Look at the bottom of any dictionary page and note how many different sounds are given for each of the vowels. Bring this listing to class.
6. Think how many letter combinations might make the sound of short *i* in various words. Do this for long *a,* too.
7. What do you consider to be the right amount of phonics?
8. Consult other references on phonics. Do you think that further phonetic analysis is necessary than has been included in this chapter?
9. What arguments would you give to parents against the study of too much phonics?
10. React to the final statement at the end of the chapter.

Bibliography

ANDERSON, VERNA, *et al. Readings in the Language Arts.* New York: Macmillan, 1967.

BEALE, LOUISE. *Phonics Fun*. Lemon Grove Public Schools, California, 1959.

BETTS, E. A. *Foundations of Reading Instruction*. New York: American Book, 1954.

BOTEL, MORTON. *How to Teach Reading*. Chicago: Follett, 1962.

CORDTS, ANNA. *Phonics for the Reading Teacher*. New York: Holt, Rinehart, & Winston, 1965.

DOLCH, EDWARD. *Teaching Primary Reading*. Champaign, Ill.: Garrard, 1950.

DURKIN, DOLORES. *Phonics and the Teaching of Reading*. Teachers College Bureau of Publications, New York, 1965.

GRAY, WILLIAM S. *On Their Own in Reading*. Chicago: Scott, Foresman, 1960.

HEILMAN, ARTHUR. *Phonics in Proper Perspective*. Columbus, Ohio: Merrill, 1964.

————. *Principles and Practices of Teaching Reading*. Columbus, Ohio: Merrill, 1961.

HERR, SELMA. *Phonics Handbook for Teachers*. Smith & Holst, 1961.

Kent County Schools. *Word Attack Skills Beyond First Grade*. Chestertown, Md., 1959.

KOTTMEYER, WILLIAM. *Handbook for Remedial Reading*. St. Louis: Webster, 1947.

TERMAN, SIBYL, and WALCUTT, CHARLES C. *Reading: Chaos and Cure*. New York: McGraw-Hill, 1958.

Union School. *Phonics Rules*. Orinda, Calif., 1961.

WEINBERG, JOEL S. *Word Analysis* (Reading Spectrum). New York: Macmillan, 1964.

Look up "Phonics" in the *Education Index* for many articles on the subject.

CHAPTER 9

Linguistics

Most of us have had little training in the linguistic concepts which now clamor to be recognized. We have been flying on one wing. Somehow, now, in mid-air, we must assemble that other wing—of appropriate size and shape and timing to provide balance and efficient progress in flight.[1]

The Vastness of Language

Linguistics is generally referred to as the science of language. It is a term as broad as oral and written communication. From mankind's first attempts at vocalized communication someone had to be interested in the form and structure of communication through vocal sounds. Today there are sixty-nine languages, each of which is spoken natively by five million or more people. Add to these the more than 2,000 languages spoken by fewer than five million. Consider the vast number of dialects within many of these languages.

[1] Constance M. McCullough, from the Fifth Edith P. Merritt Memorial Lecture given at San Francisco State College, June, 1966.

Consider further the variety of ways in which some of these languages are transcribed into written form. Linguists are engaged in studies of these languages, in dialects and in hieroglyphics.

Now, let us take a look at English, which is spoken by about 300 million people—about a tenth of the world's population. Consider the variations of English as spoken in England and in the United States. Some linguists have been analyzing the differences in English as spoken in the various English-speaking countries.

And let us look at English as spoken in the United States. Consider the regional dialects of the South, Brooklyn, Boston, the Ozarks, the Midwest, etc. Some linguists have been analyzing these speech differences.

Consider, if you will, the more than 500,000 accepted words in the English language, plus the multiplicity of meanings attached to many words (the word *run* has eighty-two specific meanings listed in *Webster's New International Dictionary*), plus the changes in tenses and number with variations (for example, the change of *run* to *ran* is one of fifty-two possible modifications of the inflectional system for the past tense in English).[2] Add to this, poetic expressions, song word innovations, and literary word usage (compare Shakespeare, Chaucer, Shaw, and Burns). Consider, too, colloquial expressions that are commonly used and understood but that have not reached dictionary status. Give thought to the wide range of jargon—teen-age, radio and television, space, industrial, and professional. And lastly, take into account the slang and vulgarisms of large segments of our population, along with the slovenly diction and careless sentence structure that constitutes almost another language.

In the Detroit study conducted by Gertrude Whipple and graduate students, it was found that fifty per cent of the vocabulary of commonly used basic readers differed from that of children in the Head-Start programs.

New words and word groupings come into use with each passing day.

Words! Words! Words! Some have meaning within certain geographical areas, some have meaning within certain social strata, some within certain professions, some within an industry, some within an age group, and some have meaning to nearly everyone. Some words have meaning within themselves, and others are specific only when

2 George H. Owen, "Linguistics: An Overview," in *Readings in the Language Arts,* ed. by Anderson, Verna L., *et al.* New York: Macmillan, 1964, p. 21.

in the context of a phrase or sentence. Many have changes of meaning when used in various contexts. Some cause us to know that the following word will be a noun and it will be singular (*a* and *an*), others reveal that the word that follows must be more than one (*many, few*), and still others indicate that the word that follows may be singular or plural (*the*) or that it belongs to someone (*his, her, your, my*). Words can cause us to anticipate next words and anticipate with bits of knowledge about our language that yield meaning.

Words, when spoken, take on added meaning, in accordance with inflections, intonation, facial expression, and gestures. The stamp of a foot, the raise of an eyebrow, the set of the jaw, the wink of an eye, or the volume or pitch of the voice can give added meaning to a word, phrase, or sentence. Figures of speech and exclamations further enhance but complicate the understanding of communication. Some linguists are interested in these aspects of language.

The words and phraseology we use are largely habitual. They originate in the home, are modified by the school and community, and are passed on to the next generation. Some linguists have been attempting to discover an order or structure in the scheme of language and to describe it. Because our words have come from nearly all the well-known languages of the world, the inconsistencies are tremendous, and because the dialects within our own country are so perplexing, the task of creating order out of chaos is overwhelming.

The subject matter of linguistics is astoundingly broad, and many scholarly approaches are being made to study parts of the whole. Leonard Bloomfield is usually credited with initiating interest among educators in American linguists nearly thirty years ago with his book entitled *Language*. Since then Fries, Soffietti, Lefevre, Barnhart and others have written books on the subject, and they and many others have prepared many magazine articles. Within the last ten years some of them have prepared reading books for children incorporating a linguistic approach.

Linguistic Terminology

Linguistic science is understood to be a body of knowledge and understanding concerning the nature and functioning of human language, built up out of information about the structure, the operation, and the history of a wide range of very diverse human languages by means of those techniques and procedures that have proved most successful in establishing verifiable generalizations concerning relationships among linguistic phenomena.[3]

Language is an arbitrary system of articulated sounds made use of by a group of humans as a means of carrying on the affairs of their society.[4]

Historical linguistics is the study of the changes that have taken place in any language from the earliest record of its beginnings. The origin of words and expressions would be a part of this study, where they came from and how they have undergone change. Chapter 2 contains many examples of what has come from historical linguistic studies.

Comparative linguistics is the study of differences and similarities in various languages and dialects. For example, a *cookie* in the United States is a *biscuit* in England. *Petrol* in England is *gasoline* in the United States. With countries drawn closer today and chances of their being drawn even closer in the future, such studies when made available can be both interesting and useful.

Descriptive linguistics is the study of the significant features of the speech of people in a certain geographical area. It is not speech as it should be spoken but as it *is* spoken. Such studies should help speech clinicians and teachers to understand the problems faced by children coming from homes where dialect and regional speech is spoken in the home. These children must learn a somewhat new reading language.

Structural linguistics is the seeking of patterns, an orderliness and a structure in language, which has been found in some languages. Within the subject of structural linguistics there are several subgroups with special interests.

One group is especially interested in the structural form and function of words as they are used in sentences. They start in their analysis by considering what the word does, what other words may be clustered about it, and the function they serve in speech. Structural grammar or formal grammar comes within the scope of this group.

Another group is more interested in starting with a word and adding certain other words to "generate" a sentence. By adding or extending according to formulas we have what is known as *transformational* or *generative* grammar.

---

[3] Charles C. Fries, (Professor of Linguistics, University of Michigan), from a lecture given in San Diego, Calif., 1966.

[4] W. Nelson Francis, *The Structure of American English*. New York: Random House, 1958, p. 13.

Still another group is especially interested in *phonology,* or the structure of words with a continuous search for patterns of structure. Intonation or patterns of stress, pitch, and juncture have varying degrees of emphasis within this group.

To understand the definitions of terms used by linguists one had best forget any association with reading momentarily. Remember that the linguist is primarily interested in language. It is the oral conveyance of communicative thought through speech sounds in which he is primarily interested. Any recording that is done is for the purpose of preserving the conveyance of speech patterns and language design.

One term of linguistics is the *utterance,* which may range from one speech sound to a lengthy monologue. It is defined as "any stretch of speech by one person before which there was silence on his part and after which there was also silence on his part. Utterance units are thus those chunks of talk that are marked off by a shift of speakers."[5]

In working with young children we generally refer to such an utterance as a direct quotation, and we help children to become familiar with quotation marks. Linguists refer to a meaningful unit of speech as a *morpheme,* which can be either *free* or *bound.* A *free morpheme* can stand alone as a word, whereas a *bound morpheme* produces a meaningful change upon a free morpheme; for example, in the word *childish, child* is a free morpheme and *ish* is a bound morpheme. Some words may consist of several free morphemes (*playground, dollhouse*) or a free morpheme and several bound morphemes (*carelessness: care* is a free morpheme and *less* and *ness* are bound morphemes). Certain bound morphemes are also called *affixes,* such as the plural *s* or the possessive *'s.*

Phonemes are the speech sounds as heard within words that make a difference in meaning within words. For example, *rat* and *hat* differ in only one sound, the initial consonant, but that phoneme distinguishes the one word from the other. The phonemes of our language have been developed from all the different variations of sound within the words of our language. Because linguists found the letters of our alphabet inadequate to designate all these significant sounds, phonemic symbols were proposed. Tables 9–1 and 9–2 show the phonemes and their spellings.

5 Charles C. Fries, *The Structure of English.* New York: Harcourt, Brace & World, 1952, p. 23.

Table 9–1. The Phonemes of English and Their Spellings*

Phonemes	Spellings	Examples†
/i/	ee, e, ea, æ, eo, oe, ei, ie, i, ey, ay	see, be, sea, Cæsar, people, amoeba, receive, believe, machine, key, quay.
/ɪ/	i, ie, e, ee, o, u, a, y, ui	it, sieve, England, been, women, busy, village, hymn, build
/e/	e, ei, ea, ey, a, ai, ao, au, ay	eh, veil, steak, obey, gate, pain, gaol, gauge, gay
/ɛ/	e, ea, æ, ei, ie, eo, oe, ai, a, u, ay	ebb, leather, æsthetic, heifer, friend, leopard, foetid, said, any, bury, prayer
/æ/	a, ai	hat, plaid
/u/	u, ue, ui, eu, ou, ew, o, oe, oo	rule, flue, fruit, maneuver, group, grew, move, canoe, moon
/ʊ/	u, ou, oo, o	put, should, book, wolf
/o/	o, oo, oa, oe, oh, ou, ow, eo, au, eau, ew	note, brooch, road, doe, oh, soul, flow, yeoman, hautboy, beau, sew
/ɔ/	o, oa, ou, a, ah, al, au, aw	order, broad, ought, tall, Utah, talk, fault, raw
/a/	a, e, ea	father, sergeant, heart
/ə/	u, o, ou, oo, oe, a, ai, ia, e, ei, eo, i, oi	cup, son, couple, flood, does, alone, mountain, parliament, system, mullein, dungeon, easily, porpoise
/p/	p, pp	pen, stopper
/b/	b, bb	bed, robber
/t/	t, ed, ght, th, tt	two, talked, bought, thyme, bottom
/d/	d, dd, ed	do, ladder, pulled
/k/	c, cc, cch, ck, ch, cq, cque, cu, k, qu	cash, account, bacchanal, back, character, acquaint, sacque, biscuit, keep, liquor
/g/	g, gg, gh, gu, gue	give, egg, ghost, guard, demagogue
/f/	f, ff, gh, ph	feel, muffin, rough, physics
/v/	v, vv, f, ph	visit, flivver, of, Stephen
/θ/	th	thin
/ð/	th, the	then, bathe
/s/	s, ss, sc, sch, c, ce	see, loss, scene, schism, city, mice
/z/	z, zz, s, ss, sc, x	zone, dazzle, has, scissors, discern, Xerxes
/š/	sh, ce, ch, ci, psh, s, sch, sci, se, si, ss, ssi, ti	ship, ocean, machine, special, pshaw, sugar, schist, conscience, nauseous, mansion, tissue, mission, mention

Phonemes	Spellings	Examples
/z/	si, g, s, z, zi	division, garage, measure, azure, brazier
/č/	ch, tch, te, ti, tu	cheap, patch, righteous, question, natural
/ǧ/	ch, d, dg, dge, di, g, gg, j	Greenwich, graduate, judgment, bridge, soldier, magic, exaggerate, just
/m/	m, mm, mn, mb, lm, gm, chm	mile, hammer, hymn, comb, calm, paradigm, drachm
/n/	n, nn, gn, kn, pn	not, runner, gnat, knife, pneumatic
/ŋ/	n, ng, ngue	pink, ring, tongue
/l/	l, ll	love, call
/r/	r, rr, rh	red, carrot, rhythm
/y/	y, g, i, j	you, lorgnette, union, hallelujah
/w/	w, o, u	well, choir, quiet
/h/	h, wh	hit, who

Phonemic clusters	Spellings	Examples
/aɪ/	ai, ay, ei, ie, ey, i, uy, y, ye	aisle, aye, height, tie, eye, ice, buy, sky, lye
/aʊ/	ou, ough, ow	out, bough, cow
/ɔɪ/	oi, oy	oil, toy
/ɪu/	u, eau, eu, eue, ew, ieu, ue, iew, ui, yu, yew, you	use, beauty, feud, queue, few, adieu, cue, view, suit, yule, yew, you
/ər/	er, ear, ir, or, our, ur, yr, ar	term, learn, thirst, worm, courage, hurt, myrtle, liar

Source: James P. Soffietti, "Why Children Fail to Read: A Linguistic Analysis," *Harvard Educational Review.* Vol. 25, No. 2, 1955, pp. 63–84.

* From a theoretical point of view, linguistic scientists are not agreed as to the number and classification of the phonemes of General American. This should in no way disturb the reader: physicists are not agreed as to the number and identity of the prime elements in the universe. While theoretically inclined to accept Roman Jakobson's views, this writer believes that Fries' list of thirty-five phonemes is a more practical classification since it comes closest to corresponding to the sound units that are usually recorded in a broad phonetic transcription of General American.

† Many of these examples have been taken from the Table of Common English Spelling on p. xxxix of the *American College Dictionary.*

It must be remembered that linguists start with language as it is spoken and represent that spoken language through the scheme of phonemes.

A phoneme is a class of sounds, any one of which is heard as the equivalent of any other. In the variety of American English used in the Middle

Table 9–2. English Vowel-Letters and Phonemes They Spell

Letter(s)	Phonemes spelled	Examples
a	/a æ e ɛ ɔ ɪ ə/	father, hat, ate, any, tall, village, sofa
e	/ɛ a i ɪ ə/	ebb, sergeant, equal, England, system
i	/i ɪ aɪ y ə/	machine, it, ice, union, easy
o	/o ɪ ɔ u ʋ ə w/	note, women, order, move, wolf, son, choir
u	/u ɛ ɪ ʋ ə ɪu w/	rule, bury, busy, pull, cup, use, quiet
ee	/i ɪ/	keen, been
eo	/ɛ i o ə/	leopard, people, yeoman, dungeon
oe	/ɛ i o u ə/	foetid, amoeba, toe, canoe, does
ei	/e ɛ i aɪ ə/	veil, heifer, receive, height, mullein
ie	/ɛ i ɪ aɪ/	friend, field, sieve, tie
ey	/e i aɪ/	obey, key, eye
ca	/e ɛ ə i/	steak, feather, heart, team
æ	/ɛ i/	æsthetic, Cæsar
ai	/æ e ɛ aɪ ə/	plaid, rain, said, aisle, mountain
ay	/e ɛ i aɪ/	ray, says, quay, aye
au	/e o ɔ/	gauge, hautboy, fault
oa	/o ɔ/	road, broad
ou	/o ɔ u ʋ aʋ ə/	soul, fought, troupe, should, out, couple
oo	/o u ʋ ə/	brooch, moon, look, flood

Source: James P. Soffietti, "Why Children Fail to Read: A Linguistic Analysis," *Harvard Educational Review*. Vol. 25, No. 2, 1955, pp. 63–84.

West there are, for example, twenty-six consonant phonemes and thirteen vowel phonemes, or loosely twenty-six consonants and thirteen vowels. The study of individual speech sounds, or phonetics, and the study of the patterning of the sound-classes in a given language, or phonemics, provide the basis for linguistic analysis.[6]

Linguists do not agree as to exactly what the representation should be so that we have several phonemic representation charts. Included here is the one designed by James Soffietti, Professor of Linguistics at Harvard. Another has been designed by Charles Fries and appears

[6] Anderson, Verna L., *et al.*, *Reading in the Language Arts*. New York: Macmillan, 1964, p. 36.

in *Linguistics and Reading* (pages 66–67 for the vowels and pages 196–98 for the consonants). Still another was designed by Paul Roberts and appears in *Patterns of English* (pages 224–225).

Graphemes are the written or printed counterparts of phonemes. If you refer to the chart of phonemes you can establish a relationship between phonemes-graphemes and phonics-letters. You will know how irregular our language really is when you become aware of how many spellings many of the phonemes have. *Vowel clusters* are what we ordinarily refer to as diphthongs.

Phoneme-Grapheme Correspondences

Paul R. Hanna, Professor of Education at Stanford University, and his wife and graduate students have been analyzing phoneme-grapheme relationships in American speech, using 17,310 of the most frequently used words. The data was put on computer cards so that it could be analyzed in many ways by computers. (The complete word analysis has been bound in three volumes of about 1,700 pages each and they are available through the U.S. Office of Education, Washington, D.C.) A 62-phoneme classification was used at the beginning, but this was reduced to 52. Symbols were also used for stress assigned to syllables: primary stress, secondary stress, and unaccented. This information is in code. A frequency code number appears on each card. Forty-nine plus per cent of all the words in the study can be spelled on a phonological bases. The relationship of vowel sounds to symbols is 62.27 per cent and consonants 83.99 per cent.

Many linguists believe that there are no isolated sounds for such letters as *b, p,* or *d*—there are only names for them. Therefore, they suggest that the alphabet be taught first. Some linguists would teach only the capital letters first; others teach both the capital and small letters, and still others would start with the small letters. The phonemes, or sound units, do not exist in isolation; they exist only with other phonemes in words—that is, one phoneme is influenced by another with regard to sounds they produce in words. The symbol-sound correspondence is taught within words. Linguists who have stressed the system of language on a phoneme-grapheme basis are Charles Fries, Robert Allen, Robert Hall, Henry Smith, and Paul Hanna (a renowned educator engaged in linguistic research).

Linguists emphasize the fact that language is made up not only of phonemes and words that are somewhat patterned, but also that these words are put together into sentences with what is referred to as *intonation*. According to Trager and Smith, *intonation* consists of four significant levels of pitch, four significant degrees of accent or stress, and four significant junctures or ways of interrupting or terminating the voice stream. Linguists such as Le Fevre would place major emphasis in beginning reading on a sentence approach to ascertain the establishment of intonation from the very start in the teaching of reading. Of course, all intonation cannot be represented in writing or printing. It is definitely a part of oral language and further establishes the importance of developing well-established patterns of speaking before introducing children to reading. It also reinforces the importance of the context or anticipation clue in reading sentences. It establishes further the need for oral reading.

Linguists believe that thoughts are generated in the language familiar to the person and expressed through speech. Speech is symbolic of language. Writing is in turn symbolic of speech. Thus, the linguist believes that writing is twice removed from thought. Because this is the order of expression, they feel that the order of impression, or reading, is the converse, or that first the written or printed symbols are transferred into speech and then the speech symbols enter into the thought process. Linguists engaged in directing a reading program put primary emphasis on decoding. Some go so far as to use nonsense symbols for the child to decode into speech in early stages. There are several different linguistic approaches set forth in readers, as we shall see in the next chapter.

Psychologists and educators have (since the time of the Cordts and Beacon Readers) recognized the importance of introducing reading as a meaningful thought process. Children learn speech, not as any patterning of sounds, but as a means of getting what they want or telling what they want to say. Reading must serve their purposes in the same way. They are not content to take a long, arduous, patterned approach. Reading must serve immediate goals and satisfy interests. The reading symbols must represent thought with no concern for speech in between.

What is the difference between phonics and phonemics? *Phonics* is a *word recognition* technique; it is a means of helping the reader recognize words through association of speech sounds with the letters he sees in the word. (Letters may or may not match the phonemic sounds of a word.) *Phonemics,* on the other hand, is a system of encoding (writing) and decoding (reading) speech sounds as they are heard within words.

What Does Linguistics Have to Offer Elementary Teachers?

1. Linguistics makes us more conscious of language and all the relevant problems stemming from the irregularities and inconsistencies in it. Elementary school children can be helped to understand why our language has so many irregularities. At about the fourth-grade level, developing an interest in word origins can be helpful to children in coping with some of the irregularities. It is helpful to know that *kn* words come from the old Anglo-Saxon at which time the *k* was pronounced; we have now dropped the sound but retained the *k* in our spelling and have words such as *knit, knight, knock, know, knife, knee, knack, knap*. Such knowledge is helpful in both reading and spelling.

2. Linguistics makes us more conscious of the fact that adequate speech must precede any kind of helpful sound-letter association.

3. Descriptive linguistics can give speech clinicians and teachers assistance in helping children with dialects by pointing out the specific speech peculiarities of the dialect.

4. Linguistics helps us to be more conscious of the syntax of our language and its relationship to reading. We can help the child be aware of *"where* phrases," *"when* phrases," etc., for more fluent reading.

5. Linguistics helps us to become more conscious of the patterns of accent in words and sentence forms that can be an aid in better reading. Intonation can be brought to a level of awareness.

6. Linguistics makes us conscious of certain patterning within words of which children may be made aware as they become ready for it. We would not teach a child to speak by introducing him to a patterning of language and a knowledge of phonemes. Instead we start with meanings and give him words to express his wants. He becomes used to our sentence structure, and vocabulary, phrase, and sentence structure become habitual. So, too, with reading. After meaning is well established, then he is ready to take a look at both speech and written structural analysis that may assist him further in his reading, speaking, and writing activities.

Let us be sure that what we teach has utilitarian value to the child in what he is trying to do—that is, to express orally ideas important to him, to write what is significant to him, and to read what he is interested in reading. The influence of linguistics has been felt in new proposals for the teaching of English and spelling as well as for reading. However, linguistic analysis must be a means to an end—better speech, better written communication, and better reading—but not an end in itself. It must follow—not precede—beginning, meaningful, and significant reading.

7. Maybe linguistics will lead to more general recognition in our society of the need for spelling reform, the need for a sound-to-letter relationship in language and spelling.

There is one very real danger to be avoided vigorously in applying findings of linguistics to the teaching of beginning reading. It is the danger of engaging in practices which can encourage the first grade or second grade pupil to center his attention, as he reads, on form and structure rather than on meaning and content and can lead him to conclude that reading is much more analytical and difficult and much less satisfying than it is or should be.[7]

Suggestions for Class Participation and Discussion

1. What is your understanding of the scope of linguistics?
2. Were you aware of any of the elements of linguistics when you went through elementary school? Discuss.
3. Bring in to class the derivation of five words that are commonly used and explain how the derivation might help children recognize them and later assist with their spelling.
4. Think of a sentence that could have at least three different meanings in accordance with the way it is read (for example, *Did I tell you that?*).
5. If you have some friends who speak another language, notice the construction of their sentences. Bring in some examples. Might children from such homes have problems with our language? In what ways?
6. Are these occasions when the expected organization of sentences is varied? Explain.
7. Would you consider any of the aspects of linguistics as basic or as supplementary knowledge in the teaching of reading? Discuss.
8. Do you think it would be better to teach a child to read in his own dialect, or would you attempt to change the dialect first? What factors would you consider?

[7] Paul McKee, *Reading, A Program of Instruction for the Elementary School*. Boston: Houghton Mifflin, 1966, pp. 192–193.

9. Summarize your thinking with regard to linguistics and reading.
10. React to the statement at the end of the chapter.

Bibliography

BERKO, JEAN. *The Child's Learning of English Morphology*. New York: World, 1958.

BLOCH and TRAGER. *Outline of Linguistic Analysis*. Linguistic Society of America, Waverly Press, 1942.

BLOOMFIELD, LEONARD, and BARNHART, CLARENCE. *Let's Read*. Detroit: Wayne University Press, 1961.

BLOOMFIELD, LEONARD. *Language*. New York: Holt, 1933.

BLOOMFIELD, MORTON, and NEWMARK, LEONARD. *A Linguistic Introduction to the History of English*. New York: Knopf, 1963.

CHOMSKY, NOAH. *Syntactic Structures*. The Hague: Mouton, 1962.

FOLEY, LOUIS. *How Words Fit Together*. Melrose, Mass.: Babson Institute Press, 1958.

FRIES, CHARLES. *American and English Grammar*. New York: Appleton-Century-Crofts, 1940.

————. *Linguistics and Reading*. New York: Holt, Rinehart & Winston, 1963.

————. *Linguistics: The Study of Language*. New York: Holt, Rinehart & Winston, 1962.

GLEASON, HENRY ALLEN. *An Introduction to Descriptive Linguistics*. New York: Holt, 1955.

GRAVES, ROBERT, and HODGE, ALAN. *The Reader Over Your Shoulder*. New York: Macmillan, 1961.

GREENOUGH, JAMES. *Words and Their Ways in English Speech*. Boston: Beacon Press, 1962.

HALL, ROBERT. *Linguistics and Your Language*. Garden City, N. Y.: Doubleday, 1960.

HARRIS, ZELLIG. *Structural Linguistics*. Chicago: University of Chicago Press, 1960.

HILL, ARCHIBALD. *Introduction to Linguistic Structure*. New York: Harcourt, 1958.

HOCKETT, CHARLES. *A Course in Modern Linguistics*. New York: Macmillan, 1958.

HUGHES, JOHN PAUL. *The Science of Language: An Introduction to Linguistics*. New York: Random House, 1961.

JOOS, MARTIN (ED.). *Readings in Linguistics*. New York: American Council of Learned Societies, 1958.

LEFEVRE, CARL. *Linguistics and the Teaching of Reading*. New York: McGraw-Hill, 1964.

PEI, MARIO A., and GAYNOR, W. *A Dictionary of Linguistics*. New York: Philosophical Library, 1954.

PIKE, KENNETH. *Phonemics, A Technique for Reducing Languages to Writing*. Ann Arbor: University of Michigan Press, 1947.

ROBERTS, PAUL. *Patterns of English.* New York: Harcourt, Brace, 1964.

ROBINSON, H. ALAN. *Reading and the Language Arts.* Chicago: University of Chicago Press, 1963.

STURTERANT, E. H. *Linguistic Change.* Chicago: University of Chicago Press, 1961.

Look up "Linguistics" in the *Education Index* for many magazine articles on the subject.

CHAPTER 10

Approaches
to the Teaching
of Reading

There is no such thing as an interesting book: there can only be interested readers.[1]

Our great-grandparents remind us of times when all reading was taught from a single book. If a teacher could read she was expected to be able to help children to read, and no thought was given to criticizing her for how she went about it. Great-grandma tells of how the class read in unison, and she recalls with delight some of the stories with their moralistic lessons. A book was a prized possession in those days, and perhaps that is why the old McGuffey Reader is still looked upon with nostalgic reverence by that generation. After we have learned anything successfully it is only natural that we would defend the method by which we had been taught. It is difficult to accept new and startling changes when the old and tried have served us well. However, times change. Scientific research in many areas of learning, greater production of materials, more edu-

[1] A. B. Herr, "A Teacher Looks at Reading," in *The Wonderful World of Books* (ed. by Alfred Stefferud). New York: Mentor Books, 1952, p. 85.

cators interested in producing them, and affluent school budgets give us an abundance of material. Teachers and administrators today have many sets of readers with various approaches from which to make selections. School budgets afford more books, and children today are soon able to read widely and well. What is more, children today have much leisure time in which to read, and the need for worthwhile leisure time activity is great.

Teachers today know much more about children—their needs, their interests, and their tastes—besides knowing much about the reading process so that various approaches to reading can be investigated with intelligent discrimination. Intensive research is being reported every month to help in evaluating these approaches. New approaches are likely to make appearances at any time, and research and intelligent discrimination must be continuous as time goes on.

Basal readers no longer comprise a single book to last all year. A company pours millions of dollars into getting experienced educators who in turn spend many months writing stories and securing many of the "gems" of good literature to achieve a rich and varied well-balanced reading diet. The manuals and workbooks are designed to include every reading and phonic-linguistic skill with many practical suggestions for flexible use. To compete in today's market, reading books must be attractive, durable, based on a sound teaching philosophy, and give teachers many teaching aids that they may take or leave in addition to containing quality reading for children.

In summarizing the "Basic Reading Series Approach," Leo Fay has this to say:

THE BASIC READING SERIES APPROACH

A recent estimate suggests that over 90 per cent of elementary classrooms in the United States use a basic reading series as the foundation for their reading instruction. Marked differences in programs exist within this wide pattern of usage. Different series represent different points of view in regard to the nature and pacing of instruction in word study, the utilization of phonics or linguistics principles, the nature of story content and of vocabulary control, the use or not of an augmented alphabet such as i.t.a. and several other factors.

Nevertheless, the various basic reading series share a common rationale. Series authors insist that a basic reading series represents only part of a total reading program. A well-conceived reading program consists of three major parts:

—A systematically organized presentation of the basic skills of word study, comprehension, and study.

—Refinement of developing reading skills in directed research and enrichment reading.

—Highly individualized reading for the primary purpose of utilizing reading for personal development.

The first of these represents the learner's growing edge in reading and hence needs to be well-organized and carefully directed by the teacher. The learner is highly dependent in this phase of the program. The teacher's guides and the skillbooks of the basic reading series are developed to provide the teacher with instructional plans and exercises for skill development. The basic reader provides initial practice in the use of the skills being developed. As they use these materials teachers are encouraged to use diagnostic teaching procedures selecting from the activities suggested in the guides and the skillbooks those that are appropriate for the children they are teaching. Through grouping and adjustment of instruction, basic reading series can be used to provide differentiated instruction.

The second part of the reading program is introduced by the basic reading series but extends beyond it. Selections in the child's text are used to introduce a variety of kinds of reading materials and activities in which reading skills may be practiced. Enriching materials, other than the textbook, are also read and reacted to as a means of introducing the children to a wider range of reading activities. The teacher's direction is less specific and the children are encouraged to assume a larger responsibility for their own learning than is possible in the skill development program.

The third part of the total reading program stems from the first two. As the children grow in their maturity to read they are encouraged to read widely for their own purposes. The teacher is present to guide but the child assumes a major responsibility for his development as an independent reader. Thus the basic reader series approach is concerned ultimately with the development of good readers who indeed *do* read.[2]

Linguistic Programs

During the last ten years several series of basal readers have been written based on linguistics. Although each series has certain unique characteristics, they have these features in common:

1. The letters of the alphabet are learned by letter names.

2. The emphasis is on decoding.

3. There is a systematized patterning of initial phonemes and selected word endings.

4. Sounds are never isolated from the words.

[2] Leo Fay, Professor of Education at the University of Indiana, author of the Curriculum Motivation Series, and editor of the new Lyons and Carnahan basal reading series, in a summary statement, March, 1967.

5. Associated learning activities are for the purpose of developing skill in decoding.

6. Other clues of word recognition are ignored in most of the linguistic approaches. Pictures are disparaged as an aid in word recognition; some series do not have pictures in the first books.

7. Syntactic systems of English are a part of the reading instruction.

The series vary in that all capital letters are used in some books, while in another series the lower case alphabet is used. Some series put more emphasis on a sentence approach to reading.

Compared with other approaches to reading, linguistics-oriented books have the following characteristics:

1. There is much less emphasis on reading for meaning in beginning reading.

2. There is less regard for basic reading vocabulary based on words most commonly used by children.

3. Other approaches use additional word recognition clues in beginning reading.

4. There is little or no story content in beginning reading.

The i.t.a. Approach

i.t.a. (initial teaching alphabet) originated in England. It was conceived by Sir James Pitman and introduced into the United States by John Downing. It consists of a phonemic alphabet of forty-four lower-case letters, which reduces reading to a consistent letter-sound relationship. If the whole English spelling structure could be changed to this or any other system with a letter-to-sound relationship, reading and spelling would be easy for children and adults alike.

It is a medium rather than a program. Most proponents of i.t.a. media have a read-for-meaning philosophy, and the materials published in i.t.a. expand children's concepts "as far as outer space." There is emphasis on self concept, human experiences, and meeting children's needs and interests. Various types of illustrations are used, and the various word recognition clues are included in many programs.

At first children were seriously handicapped by having little other material to read except the basic program materials. Now many children's books have been translated into i.t.a.

The very real existing problem is the fact that children live in a society and community environment that has not and is not likely to change the traditional spelling of words. The child must sooner or later learn to read as countless other children have done from the start. How readily he can make the change and how much effect this early experience will have on later reading and spelling remain to be seen. Research studies have been and are being made. Testing must be done after these children have transferred to the traditional reading alphabet so that they can read the tests without being handicapped. The question many educators raise is: Why teach another alphabet when children must eventually use the established one and when everything in their environment is printed in the established form?

The following questions also are to be answered: Can children learn to read much more easily? Can they make the transition easily? Are they delayed or accelerated by using the simplified approach first? What effect does it have in spelling?

UNIFON

John R. Malone designed what is known as UNIFON. Like i.t.a., UNIFON is a new alphabet with a sound-letter relationship—that is, each letter represents one speech sound. UNIFON is printed in block capitals and all material for children appears in this form. Because of recent advances in photographic printing it is now economically feasible to have materials reproduced in whatever letter forms an author may devise. It promises an earlier transfer to regular spelling and reading than i.t.a. does (most children make the transfer from UNIFON at the end of four months, from i.t.a. in eight). Both i.t.a. and UNIFON systems are undergoing experimentation in several of the large city school systems and evaluations are being made.

Words-in-Color

Words-in-color is a linguistic-phonic system developed by Caleb Gattegno in 1957. The traditional alphabet is used, but shades of colors are used for the forty-seven sounds of English. The shades of color vary with the different vowel sounds, but each vowel sound has its own color regardless of what letter or letters represent it in a word. For example, the *a* in *rain, ran, ago,* and *call* would all be represented in different colors; in *they, day, wait, great,* and *vein,* the letters responsible for the *a* sound would all be the same color. Such clues would be helpful, but children must eventually learn to read without them. There are no books used with the color clues, and children learn to write with only a mental association with the colors.

Adults as well as children have been taught with this method. It is a technique for introducing the sounds to those for whom English is a second language. It proved so effective with adults that Gattegno feels it should be equally effective with school children. Some school systems are experimenting with this approach.

Various Phonic Approaches

About fifty years ago reading was taught with a large overdose of phonics. Children were drilled on "family" endings and isolated sounds with stories attached to them, with pictures supporting the stories. Such was the Beacon Series of readers and the Cordts system. In some respects they resemble some of the linguistic materials.

Then it was discovered that children were comprehending poorly, and psychologists helped educators to see that meaning did not come from starting with sounds but rather by starting with meaningful wholes. Then the pendulum swung completely away from phonics until educators began to see that an awareness of initial letter sounds could be a valuable clue along with other clues in word recognition. Along with the context clue it did not take away from the fluent quality so necessary for thought continuation. Now nearly all of the recognized basal reading series include linguistic-phonic instruction when children are ready to use such help.

There are several phonic approaches that start with word sounds. Some start with final blends, some with initial sounds, some with the vowel sounds, and there are other variations. In some cases the program is designed to parallel any other reading series. If a child rates low on word recognition in a diagnostic test, some help with phonics may be just what he needs. If, however, he rates high in vocabulary and low in comprehension he may be too letter-sound conscious and he needs to be helped to move his eyes along on consonants and digraphs and pay less attention to each and every phonic element.

Various phonics systems are those of Aiken, Carden, Sister Caroline, Daniels and Diack, Eaton and James, Hay-Wingo, and Mc-Cracken. The Lippincott program is a link between the phonics systems and basal reading; it has heavy emphasis on phonics.

Phonovisual Method[3]

The Phonovisual Method is not intended to be used instead of sight reading, but as parallel teaching. It is based on the use of pictorial charts arranged on a scientific phonetic foundation, together with a definite plan for training in auditory and visual discrimination. There are 26 sounds on the Consonant Chart and 17 sounds on the Vowel Chart.

Some of the values found from its use in specific cases are as follows:

1. It provides a quick and easy means for teaching all initial and final consonants and vowel sounds.

2. It teaches the pupil that a consonant sound at the beginning of a word is identical with the same sound at the end of a word.

3. It teaches him to distinguish easily between letters often confused, such as *p* and *q, m* and *n, b* and *d.*

4. It trains him to read from left to right by emphasizing the beginnings of words, thus preventing "reversals."

5. It gives the child, in the first few months of his reading experience, tools with which to attack new words. He does not have to stop and acquire each tool as the need arises, and does not confuse similar words such as *funny, bunny, sunny.*

6. It corrects minor speech defects without making the child aware of being corrected.

7. It gives security to the child who has failed in reading or who is slow.

8. It produces marked improvement in the reading and spelling of remedial cases.

9. It enables even a first-grade child, after mastering the consonants and vowels, to read and spell hundreds of words without study.

10. It provides a short-cut to reading and spelling of the twenty-

3 From *Phonovisual Method* by Schoolfield and Timberlake with permission from Herbert H. Mack, General Manager of Phonovisual.

The Phonovisual Consonant Chart and the Phonovisual Vowel Chart are reproduced by permission of Phonovisual Products, Inc., 4708 Wisconsin Ave., N.W., Washington, D. C.

Phonovisual® Consonant Chart

By Lucille D. Schoolfield and Josephine B. Timberlake

p—   b—   m—

wh-   w—   qu-

f—   v—
ph

3 th-   this th-

t—   d—   n—   l—

s—   z—   r—
c   s

sh-   y—

ch-   j—
tch   g

k—   g—   -ng   -x
c   n(k)
ck

h—

[2] The Phonovisual Consonant Chart and the Phonovisual Vowel Chart are reproduced by permission of Phonovisual Products, Inc., 4708 Wisconsin Ave., N.W., Washington, D.C.

Phonovisual® Vowel Chart

By Lucille D. Schoolfield and Josephine B. Timberlake

a–e	ee	i–e	o–e	u–e
ay	-e	-y	oa	ew
ai	ea	igh	ow	
			-o	

-a-	-e-	-i-	-o-	-u-
	ea	–y		

aw		oo	ur
au			er
a(ll)			ir
o(r)			or

a(r)

oo
u

ow
ou

oy
oi

nine initial consonant blends, thus avoiding days, perhaps even weeks, of laborious teaching.

11. It recognizes the importance of stressing comprehension and fluency.

WHAT IS A PHONIC APPROACH TO READING?[4]

Let me begin with some definitions. First, there is coming into clear perspective a distinction between *phonic* and *phonetic*. *Phonetics* is properly defined as the science of speech sounds, or the scientific study of speech sounds. It has to do with language and speech, not reading; all languages are, incidentally, 100% phonetic. *Phonics* is coming to be understood as a system of representing word sounds by letters; conversely, it is used to label the approach to reading through the attention to how letters represent word sounds.

Next, what is reading? I would answer this important and controversial question by saying that *reading* has three meanings which must be seen as existing *simultaneously* in the word as we normally use it in the context of a book. Or perhaps I should not say "normally" but rather as the person who advocates a linguistic-phonics approach to reading uses it. Everything depends on this definition, as I shall try to show. How we teach reading depends exactly upon what we think reading *is*.

The three meanings which I say exist simultaneously in the word *reading* may be designated reading 1, reading 2, and reading 3—and I shall try to show why the phonics-linguistic approach sees these numbers as indicating the proper steps toward mature reading achievement. [This definition is more fully expounded in "Reading—a Professional Definition," *Elementary School Journal,* April, 1967.]

Reading 1 is the skill of decoding print into sound. In other words, it is converting writing into language, for language is *spoken sound*, which existed for many thousands of years before writing was invented. It is the spoken sound of language that carries the meaning, as it always has done, since pre-history.

Reading 2 is *understanding the language* that has been decoded from the printed page. It is, of course, the goal of reading 1–2–3, but there's a puzzle here: whether I read a paragraph of difficult philosophy on a printed page, or whether you read it aloud to me, my problem of understanding the language is exactly the same. If I read it on the printed page and fail to understand it, we might say that my reading was at fault; but when we consider that I have the same problem hearing it, with my eyes closed, we see that this matter of understanding language is not actually reading at all! Yet the only purpose of decoding the language-sounds from the printed page is to understand the language so decoded, and this is what we mean by reading 2.

Reading 3 is what we get from books: the style, sentence-structure, organization, vocabulary, and the beauty and quality of thought that

---

[4] Charles C. Walcutt, Professor at Queens College, New York, and co-author of *Basic Reading* (Lippincott), from a summary statement, March, 1967.

come in good books on any subject—these have been developed through writing. The literary artist is a *writer*, not a talker, for it is with writing that he develops, refines, and enriches his expression. Reading 3, then, takes us into a cultural world that is not accessible to the unlettered. Today even the drama would not be understood by an illiterate person because he would not have developed an adequate vocabulary through his experience with the spoken language.

A phonic-linguistic approach to reading begins by developing, as rapidly as possible, a mastery of the decoding process of reading 1. But it does not devote any time to isolated soundings-out or drill with letters and syllables. It learns the phonics in regularly-spelled words right from the beginning; and as soon as the very first steps in mastering the code have been taken, it makes sentences and stories from the letter-sounds available. Emphasis on meaning comes very soon, but psychologically (as distinct from temporally) it is shown to depend on the prior step of decoding the printed word into the sound-symbol (i.e., speech) that carries the meaning. This order soon leads to instant whole-word recognition and thus takes the child straight into the realm of literature, where, as I have indicated, he is getting a quality of thought, imagination, and even vocabulary that he does not find elsewhere.

I would urge, in conclusion, that a linguistic-phonic approach to reading makes use of all the valid advances in motivation, learning psychology, and teaching techniques that have been made during the present century.

Programmed Reading

As with many reading innovations, programmed instruction was conceived as a technique for teaching in the army, Job Corps, etc. Its success depends largely on the individual case. Some children who feel challenged by a step-by-step procedure might fit into such a developmental approach very well with varying degrees of flexibility. Some children—especially those who are immature and have short attention spans—need much teacher help and stimulation. They are easily frustrated, and the alert teacher knows how a change of approach, a change of materials, and a change of activity may be needed frequently.

The danger in any kind of programmed instruction is in the tendency to put children on a production line—if they fit, well and good. The psychological approach is to get to know the child and select ways and means of helping him.

There is a wide variety of film strips and other learning devices available. It is important to know them well and to use them as they fit the situation. For example, the Sullivan materials and others coming on the market in rapid production should be examined carefully with regard to the purposes they can and cannot serve.

Language-Experience Approach

For many years teachers have helped children to record some of their experiences and to write little stories as part of their language development. During the past ten years such an approach to reading has been advocated, and some schools are implementing it. R. V. Allen, Professor of Education at the University of Arizona, and his wife (authors of *Language Experiences in Reading*) have developed materials to support such a program of reading.

First the child expresses an experience in a drawing or painting. Then he explains the picture to the teacher and his classmates. He dictates his story about the picture to the teacher. In time he can write stories with less and less help from the teacher. He can then read his stories to the class and can eventually read the stories other children have written. His reading and writing vocabularies increase, and he is gradually introduced to commercially prepared books. He gathers more ideas, which he can speak or write about. Most important, he's learning to use reading, writing and speaking as tools to collect and transmit ideas.

Alphabet understanding, phonetic analysis, spelling and other reading and writing skills are developed as a natural part of this over-all experience and communication. Each child builds vocabulary as he speaks, listens, writes and reads. There's no pat formula.

The act of teaching reading is viewed as the art of raising levels of sensitivity of each child—to his environment, including his language environment; to relationships between oral language and printed symbols; to the variability of oral-written relationships in English spelling; to writing as a means of making reading materials and of preserving ideas; to books as sources of information and recreation; to the personal usefulness of writing-reading in effective communication.[5]

Individualized Reading Approach

Idealistically, conscientious teachers aspire toward helping each child develop the maximum of his potentialities at the optimum rate, nurturing his interests and arousing new ones, finding materials that will benefit him most, appreciating his efforts and accomplishments, and stimulating him to set next goals to move ever onward.

[5] R. V. Allen, with permission of the author.

An ungraded classroom allows children to work at their levels of achievement regardless of age. (Photograph courtesy of the Boston Public Schools.)

The term *individualized* is somewhat misleading. It is good common sense to know that in the interest of economy of time and effort there are occasions when group work is not only practical but advantageous. Most of the enthusiastic supporters of an individualized approach would accept the need for some group work in the following situations.

1. Giving children some common experiences upon which a group story could be based.
2. Developing initial sight word vocabulary.
3. Helping children to understand the mechanics of reading.
4. Chalkboard and chart work developing basic word recognition clues.
5. Helping individuals who have needs in common with certain other individuals—working together can be more stimulating.
6. Sharing and discussing good books much as a group of adults would get together to discuss what they had read.
7. An occasional working together on a common problem, a common interest, or a chosen project (see under heading "Using Reading for Many Purposes," in this chapter).

Although the schools at one time favored extreme use of group work—that is, units in every subject much of the time—we need to be careful now that each child is not off in a corner operating a machine or reading a book day after day. We need to be sure that he is not left to operate on a plateau and mark time instead of being inspired to stretch his capabilities. With these precautions in mind we are ready to consider how and when individualized reading can be most effective:

1. When the purpose of a group session is to present a new clue, new vocabulary, a study skill, or bring to a level of awareness the scheme of sentence structure, we should invite those children who are ready for such help to join the circle. As soon as any child is observed to have gained the help he needs, invite him to leave the group and go about his individual work. Not only is this better for the individual, but the group work is more effective for those who are left.

2. When group work is largely review, only those children who need such review should be invited to the circle.

3. There should be times when children have a chance to use their reading skills in a free choice of pleasurable reading. This is where the teacher needs to bring in carefully selected books within the range of reading abilities within her group. She should have the books grouped into reading levels so the child can practice "self selection" within the framework of his ability to read. This is where good bibliographies help teachers provide for a wide range of interests at the various reading levels (more of this in a later chapter). (See bibliographies in Appendix P.)

Modern technology can greatly assist but never replace a competent and understanding teacher. (Photograph courtesy of the San Diego Public Schools.)

4. Reading is definitely an *individual* process. We can only help a child bring more to it, use it more effectively and widely, and thus gain more from it. We can determine his individual needs through:

a. Diagnostic tests;
b. Observation of his silent reading habits;
c. Hearing him read orally;
d. Conferences with the child;
e. Clinical reports.

5. A child can be helped individually by:

a. Setting a goal with him and making sure he understands what he is to do and how he is to do it.
b. Word and phrase cards for more rapid and fluent reading.
c. Tactile assistance in which the child traces over the letters of a word as he says the word to himself to get the feel of it and thus form a more lasting mental image of it.
d. Providing him with the help that diagnostic tests show he needs.
e. Supplying books or other materials that will reenforce the learn-

ings you are helping him to achieve. (Skills to be retained must be used.)

f. Providing for the child who needs language development (the "listening post" with recordings of stories, poems, words, and phrase tapes, etc. may provide opportunities for growth).

g. For the fast learner, newspapers, magazines, travel guides, "Wonder" books, and carefully selected books in all fields of interest offer rewarding reading experiences.

h. Providing a confidence-inspiring approach. He should be put "on his own" to reach a goal, to accomplish a task, or to read what he has selected and is eager to read.

A move toward individual competencies, self selection, critical judgments, and ever-broadening reading satisfactions should be the goals of individualized reading.

To be sure that children are achieving all that is necessary for reading competencies it is a good idea for teachers to refer frequently to a chart such as in Figure 10-00 as individualized reading proceeds.

Books have been written on this approach and they contain many practical suggestions that would help any teacher in implementing worthwhile procedures regardless of what basic program she may be using. (See Bibliography at the end of this chapter.)

Individualized reading, like any other method of instruction, is no panacea, no "perfect" solution. Its success depends upon teaching skill, as does the success of any method. For teachers who believe strongly in working with the individual on his unique level of learning, for those who do not rigidly adhere to traditional assumptions popularly followed but unsupported by research, for those who have faith in teacher judgment and creativity, individualized reading opens the door to limitless opportunities for pupil and teacher growth. Freedom to grow and to learn is a fundamental characteristic of the individualized method of teaching reading.[6]

An Eclectic Approach to Reading

An eclectic approach to reading can be whatever the teacher wants it to be. She must first of all be thoroughly familiar with what the various approaches have to offer by reading teachers' manuals, study-

[6] Helen Darrow, and Virgil Howes, *Approaches to Individualized Reading*. New York: Appleton-Century-Crofts, 1960, p. 100.

ing the guidebooks, examining all the books and related materials, and going to various classrooms where the programs are used. By talking to the teachers, reading many research studies found in current magazines, and knowing her own situation, she can determine what *she* wants to use. Certain materials, techniques, and ideas may be taken from various approaches and used flexibly by discerning, creative teachers.

A Checklist Criterion for Teachers

As a dedicated and informed teacher, it is your responsibility to know the various approaches and materials involved in teaching reading and to pick and choose in accordance with the individual and group needs you recognize. With the help of any approach and supporting materials, you should try to accomplish the following:

1. Help the child know the purposes that reading serves and how to read effectively for each purpose.
2. Help the child read at a rate appropriate to the purpose and material, but also appropriate to the emotional composure of the child.
3. Make sure that every child knows the basic word recognition clues: sight, configuration, context, phonetic-linguistic, picture and word analysis.
4. Make sure that every child has opportunities for growth in comprehension of various types of materials.
5. Give specialized guidance in reading in content areas such as social studies, science, mathematics, music, literature (prose and poetry).
6. Operate flexibly so that the needs of both the extremely slow and the rapid learners can be met.
7. Help children to appreciate the skill of oral reading, to acquire it, and enjoy using it.
8. Help the child to appreciate and use good work and study habits.
9. Help children appreciate the services of librarians and use reference and resource materials effectively.
10. Help children to evaluate their progress and to want to improve.
11. Help children to develop broad interests in reading and taste for quality in literature.
12. Help children to be critical and appreciative in their reading.

OAK PARK STUDY SKILLS CHART — READING SKILLS

SKILL	GRADES K–2	GRADES 3–4	GRADES 5–6
Ability to follow printed directions	Acts out simple written directions; finds name and duty on helper's chart; plays game with direction cards	Reads to perform science experiment; follows directions for seatwork; interprets directions given in narrative form; does double-step math problems	Understands written regulations; carries out an art process from direction card; interprets written assignment correctly; does more complicated math problems
Ability to read to find answers to questions	Selects words that answer questions; does simple true-and-false tests; supplies answers other than direct recall	Justifies answers by reading aloud; takes notes that answer question; answers multiple-choice questions	Uses more than one source to find answers; understands how to find appropriate references; gives answers requiring application of information
Interpretation of figurative language	Separates fact from fantasy; recognizes unreal quality of giant and fairy tales	Recognizes figurative language in prose and poetry; selects unusual descriptions to read aloud	Identifies similes; reads fables or allegories and interprets them; distinguishes between literal and figurative speech
Increased vocabulary	Uses words met in reading in regular speech; tries new words or words in different ways; keeps list of new words	Plays vocabulary games such as crossword puzzles, Scrabble, multiple meaning, or matching words and definitions; recognizes new words in other content	Plays such games as anagrams; shows interest in word origins; recognizes homonyms, antonyms, synonyms, compounds; uses words in speech that are read and understood

Adaptation of reading method to purpose and content	Reads silently and orally	Reads for various purposes, such as to tell a story, get ideas in sequence, determine author's purpose verbalizes differences in how he reads; does simple skimming	Recognizes different types of reading; shows differences in speed according to purpose; skims familiar material; easily uses a variety of reference materials
Ability to use reference material	Uses picture dictionary	Knows parts of a book; selects key word to look up; takes simple notes; makes use of encyclopedias	Selects appropriate sources for reference; uses different types of materials; works independently; acquires concepts as well as facts
Recognition of paragraph organization	Identifies a paragraph in book; has simple definition of it	Gives main idea of paragraph in single sentence; recognizes relative roles of headings and subheadings	Composes telegram as a paragraph summary; reads series of paragraphs and gives topic sentence
Ability to read for comprehension	Understands content of experience charts; reads silently and sees what he reads	Selects specific sentences which refer to pictures; finds solution to problem in story	Summarizes a selection; identifies cause-and-effect relationship; reads and interprets poetry
Ability to read for deeper meaning	Identifies with characters or settings in stories	Can suggest setting for story he hears or reads; tells how a character feels; makes inferences from pictures and title before reading; suggests additional events that might occur	Discusses characterization; recognizes implied meanings; enjoys poetry

OAK PARK STUDY SKILLS CHART — READING SKILLS (continued)

SKILL	GRADES K–2	GRADES 3–4	GRADES 5–6
Ability to move eyes from left to right	Forms letters of own name; adds to series of shapes; places letters one by one to form name of object; follows pointer; reads in groups of words rather than single words	Speed for silent reading gradually exceeds oral reading	Sees longer blocks of words at a time
Transition from picture to word symbols;	Matches pictures to symbols; labels objects in room; matches like figures; matches labels or captions with correct pictures; recognizes own name; builds sight vocabulary	Recognizes larger words on television and in signs; adds words from other subjects	Associates meaning and synonyms with new words; builds vocabulary substantially
Understanding the importance of sequence of ideas	"Reads" stories by arranging pictures in proper sequence; places figures on flannel board to tell story; recognizes when ideas are out of order	Rearranges jumbled story in proper sequence; locates cue words that give time sequence	Constructs a time line from research of events; reads a biographical story, then lists facts in order; places cause–and–effect pairs in proper order
Development of techniques of word recognition	Knows consonant and vowel sounds and blends; recognizes diphthong digraphs; attacks new words with confidence	Recognizes compound words; uses consonant blends easily; finds accented syllables; identifies other words with similar sounds; attcks more difficult words; uses glossary	Plays games based on word sounds; plays anagrams; stops to identify new words in silent reading; uses dictionary to aid in pronunciation; sounds out multisyllable words

Recognition of structure of words	Changes first or last letter to make new word; adds omitted first or last letter to make word; recognizes root words and simple compound words	Makes contractions; sees small words in large words; rearranges scrambled syllables; makes words from letters of large word; rearranges prefixes and suffixes	Identifies prefixes and suffixes; enjoys building words
Understanding punctuation marks and capital letters	Uses voice inflection in speaking and reading; recognizes that capitals and punctuation marks give meaning to stories	Adds capitals and punctuation marks to story; recognizes quotation marks and their purpose; recognizes italicized words	Distinguishes functions of semicolon, colon, dash
Ability to use the dictionary	Uses picture dictionary; plays alphabet games to strengthen letter sequence	Looks for multiple meanings of words; looks up pronunciations of simple words; plays games involving dictionary skill; arranges words in alphabetical order by first three letters	Learns about unabridged dictionary; uses special features in dictionary; selects meaning that best fits context; gains speed in using dictionary; refers to dictionary readily
Ability to read aloud pleasingly	Repeats words and phrases said by teacher; shares a poem or story in audience situations; reads aloud so group can hear	Reads conversation well; reads aloud to answer question or prove point; reads so that whole room can hear	Participates in choral reading; reads aloud to younger children; reads aloud to tape recorder for playback; can read a play with others
Recognition of contextual skills	Can suggest omitted words in story read aloud; supplies end words in simple rhymes; guesses meaning of words from context	Plays games matching words with phrases; guesses meanings before looking them up; suggests synonyms and antonyms	Recognizes words that change meaning when they change their accent; judges meaning from context; picks adjectives and adverbs that give clues to answers

Used with permission of: The Instructor, April 1967, F. A. Owen Publishing Company

By Carole Whiston, Margaret Morton, and Helen F. Bailey, from The Instructor, ©*F. A. Owen Publishing Company.*

13. Help children to live with greater satisfaction and more effectively with and through reading.

In Detroit, incidentally, a major study is underway involving 4,400 inner-city youngsters and six reading programs including both i.t.a. and UNIFON. Although final reports won't be in for some time on Detroit's Basic Reading Demonstration Project, Dr. Arthur M. Enzmann, the city's director of early childhood education, suspects that "it's entirely possible that we may prove what we already knew: that a well-trained and developed teacher can teach a child no matter what material she uses."[7]

Suggestions for Class Participation and Discussion

1. Bring into class as many of the materials as you can from each of the approaches outlined in this chapter (and any others). Take time to examine them.
2. What do you consider to be the strengths and limitations of each?
3. How would you feel about being asked to teach any one of these approaches in an experimental research program?
4. Read from current magazines any article pertaining to new approaches to the teaching of reading. Share your impressions in class.
5. Report on any very new and previously unreported approach to reading.
6. Consult magazine articles on recent reports from schools conducting experiments with the various approaches to reading.
7. Which approaches show great similarities and which ones are extremely different from the others?
8. Knowing what you do about children, about our language, and about how children learn, which approaches have the greatest appeal to you? Defend your position.
9. Which teaching materials do you think would be most appealing to children?
10. Respond to the quote at the end of the chapter.

Bibliography

BARBE, WALTER. *Educator's Guide to Personalized Reading Instruction.* Englewood Cliffs, N.J.: Prentice-Hall, 1961.

City of New York, Board of Education, *A Practical Guide to Individualized Reading,* 1960.

BROGAN, PEGGY, and FOX, LORENE. *Helping Children Read.* New York: Holt, Rinehart & Winston, 1961.

[7] "UNIFON: Pro or Con?" *The Reading Newsreport,* editorial, Jan., 1967.

DARROW, HELEN, and HOWES, VIRGIL. *Approaches to Individualized Reading.* New York: Appleton-Century-Crofts, 1960.

Exploring Independent Reading in the Primary Grades. Columbus: Ohio State University Press, 1960.

FITZSIMMONS. *Individualizing the Reading Program in the Elementary School.* Association for Supervision and Curriculum Development, Honolulu, 1964.

FRIES, CHARLES C. *Linguistics and Reading.* New York: Holt Rinehart & Winston, 1963.

GROFF, PATRICK. "Materials for Individualized Reading." *Elementary English,* Jan., 1962.

HARRISON, M. *The Story of the Initial Teaching Alphabet.* New York: i.t.a. Publications, Inc., 1966.

HAY, JULIE, HLETKO, MARY, and WINGO, CHARLES. *Reading with Phonics.* Philadelphia: Lippincott, 1960.

Hudson School District, *Individualized Reading,* La Puente, Calif., 1964.

JACOBS, LELAND, *et al. Individualizing Reading Practices.* Teachers College Bureau of Publications, New York, 1958.

LEE, DORIS, and ALLEN, R. V. *Learning to Read Through Experience.* New York: Appleton-Century-Crofts, 1963.

MIEL, ALICE. *Individualized Reading Practices.* Teachers College Bureau of Publications, New York, 1958.

OAK PARK ELEMENTARY SCHOOLS, *Reading: Grades 1–4 Individualized,* Oak Park, Ill., 1962.

REEVES, RUTH. *The Teaching of Reading in Our Schools.* New York: Macmillan, 1966.

SARTAIR, HARRY. *Individualized Reading, An Annotated Bibliography.* Newark, Del.: International Reading Association, 1964.

San Diego County Schools, *Teacher Inventory of Approaches to the Teaching of Reading,* San Diego, Calif., 1961.

Simi Valley, California Unified School District, *Language Experience and Individualized Reading,* 1966.

VEATCH, JEANNETTE. *Individualizing Your Reading Program.* New York: Putnam, 1959.

Whittier, California City Schools, *Self-Selection in Reading,* 1961.

Refer to the *Education Index* for many magazine articles on the various approaches to the teaching of reading.

The Skills and Attitudes of Reading— Silent and Oral

As one watches a child learning to read, he is involved in interpreting symbols. His primary goal is not the symbols, though they may be great fun in and of themselves. Their shape, their general configurations, their sounds may be pleasantly diverting. To be able to note likenesses and differences visually and orally may be pleasurable. But the child is conditioned early to know that these symbols are more than attractive, abstract designs of seeing and hearing. They are maps to meanings. They are vehicles to carry the reader into the mind of the writer. The child's real goals are to exploit the symbols for what they can help him to know, to be.[1]

—LELAND JACOBS

It is important to maintain focus on what reading has to offer the child and on what assistance we can give him in getting more from what he reads. All that we give him are the tools; we give him a wide selection of them and he takes his choice.

The more adept we become at anything, the more we enjoy doing it, and this is true of reading. A reasonable amount of drill, some word games, some exercises, some explanations, and some analysis

[1] Robinson, Helen (ed.). *Developing Permanent Interest in Reading.* Chicago: University of Chicago Press, 1956, p. 21.

need not be boring or frustrating to children if they are helped to see that the purpose is to facilitate their ability to read. As long as reading itself is pleasurable and profitable, and the means to the ends are not too uninteresting or too prolonged, children will take the hurdles in their stride.

Skills and Attitudes Developed in the Kindergarten

I. Getting ideas from pictures
   A. Telling about a picture
      1. Increasing language facility
      2. Recognizing objects and actions
      3. Making interpretations beyond what is seen
   B. Arranging pictures
      1. Awareness of sequence in action and in time
      2. Development of the left-to-right mechanics of reading
      3. Telling stories from picture sequences
II. Getting ideas from stories
   A. Awareness of characters, simple plot, and setting
   B. Differentiating between what is real and what is imaginary
   C. Retelling stories with sequence and detail
   D. Enjoying both prose and rhyme
   E. Observing that pictures relate to story content
III. Handling books
   A. Learning how to hold a book and turn the pages
   B. Awareness of left-to-right sequence and top-to-bottom page procedure
   C. Relating pictures to what is known about the story
   D. Respecting books and appreciating their beauty and diversity of content
IV. Auditory and Visual Perception
   A. Listening for and identifying common sounds
   B. Perceiving and locating sounds
   C. Listening for likenesses and differences in sound
   D. Singing many meaningful songs
   E. Noting likenesses and differences in children's names
   F. Seeing and feeling likenesses and differences in forms
V. Developing good speech
   A. Retelling stories with good expression
   B. Reciting rhymes with good expression and proper pacing

In individualized reading children work independently, with one another, or with the teacher—according to each child's interests and needs. (Photograph courtesy of the Seattle, Washington, Public Schools.)

  C. Recognizing the importance of appropriate volume, pleasantness, and choice of words in carrying on conversations and in telling things to the group

VI. Developing a wholesome attitude toward reading

  A. Anticipating learning to read because reading has been observed as a rewarding and pleasurable experience

B. Taking advantage of the "listening post" and other opportunities to hear stories and poems read

C. Experiencing dramatic play as a natural way of using language, enacting stories, and being himself or someone else (as he often is when he later reads stories)

Skills and Attitudes Developed in First Grade

Repeat many of the kindergarten experiences with children who need them.

Word Recognition Skills

I. Preparatory Experiences
A. Auditory Perception
1. Recognizing likeness in beginning word sounds
2. Developing ability to name many words when an initial sound is given
3. Developing ability to supply missing words when sentences are read and an initial sound for the missing word is given
B. Visual Perception
1. Noting likenesses and differences in letter forms
2. Noting likenesses in beginnings of words
3. Noting differences in lower case and upper case letters
4. Hearing that long words have many sounds and that *I* and *a* are single sounds and single letters
II. Vocabulary and thinking (All of this section is extremely important throughout the elementary grades; these skills and attitudes should be given careful thought and should be a part of many learning sessions.)
A. Continuous expansion of concepts (films, filmstrips, recordings, fieldtrips, discussions, demonstrations, sharing time, stories, reading of factual material by the teacher, collections)
B. Use of language in more complex ways
1. Conversations
2. Discussions in which many types of thinking develop:
a. Cause-and-effect relationships
b. Sequences in time, events, and steps in the solution of a problem

   c. Coordinate and subordinate relationships; the relationship of parts to the whole and the significance of wholeness

   d. Comparisons and contrasts (of people, situations, times, places, of any and all variables)

   e. Evaluations and appreciations

  3. Awareness of various sentence forms and punctuation

   a. Simple statements with capitals and periods

   b. Simple questions with capitals and question marks

   c. Complex sentences (awareness that phrases tell how, when, and where; helping children to read *in the, by a, under the, toward the,* etc.; almost automatically in their reading as part of our language pattern)

   d. Noting that commas and semicolons designate slight pauses, question marks require a raised intonation, periods require a lowered intonation

III. Phonics

 A. Initial consonants

 B. Digraphs (*sh, ch, th*) voiced and voiceless

 C. Initial consonant blends

 D. Working through words by using consonants and digraphs

 E. Using the sound of vowels in the initial position (*a, about, egg, eat, oh, us, you*)

IV. Structural analysis

 A. Awareness that some words are made up of parts they know (*hand*)

 B. Plural (*s* and *es*) and possessive (*'s*) forms

 C. Verb endings (*s, d, ed, ing*)

 V. Configuration

 A. Noting peculiarities in some words as to contour form and length

 B. Noting shapes of some letters that relate to meaning of the word

VI. Picture Clue

 A. Noting that pictures illustrate content

 B. Using pictures as an aid to understanding

Dramatizations are always fun, and they are excellent for improving the quality of good expression. (Photographs courtesy of the Detroit, Michigan, Public Schools.)

Comprehensive Skills

Observing purposes for reading
  Determining what happens in a story
  Finding out about the characters
  Reading for specific information
  Reading to answer questions
  Reading to raise questions
  Reading for enjoyment
  Reading to satisfy curiosity

Locating Information
  Getting information in pictures
  Referring to story titles
  Using the table of contents
  Using alphabetical arrangement (word card file)
  Using a picture dictionary (their own and others)

Evaluating Information
  Discussing what is relevant and irrelevant, what is factual and
    fanciful

Interpretation
  Free discussion (to determine what children actually get out of
    what they read)
  Discussing the main idea of a story
  Filling in subordinate details
  Interpreting the feelings, motives, values, and behavior of story
    characters
  Noting the *who, what, when, where,* and *why* in some stories
  Following through the plot development of stories

Creative and Critical Reading
  Making inferences about what has gone on before and what may
    happen next in a story that they read or a teacher reads
  Drawing logical conclusions; predicting outcomes
  Recognizing cause and effect relationships
  Anticipating plot development
  Making new endings for stories
  Making new generalizations about characters
  Stating opinions with regard to characters and what they did
  Verbalizing appreciation for a story they have enjoyed

Organizing what is read
  Following directions
  Classifying or relating pictures, words, phrases, sentences, related
    ideas, parts of the story, etc.

Extending experiences beyond the story
  Word study (talking about derivations, other meanings, etc.)
    homographs
    synonyms
  Related experiences (films, etc., to extend meanings)

Skills and Attitudes Developed in Second and Third Grades

Determine what help with skills of the previous grade some children may need.

Word Recognition Skills

  I. Phonetic Analysis
    A. Continued emphasis on initial consonants and digraphs
    B. Continued emphasis on working through a word with consonant and digraph clues along with the context clues
    C. Making generalizations of the vowel rules with cognizance of the many exceptions
    D. Introduction of such other phonetic clues as children can use (see Chapter 8 on phonics)
  II. Syllabication
    A. Help children to hear syllables in word and listen for natural breaks
    B. Divide words in syllables orally first
    C. Introduce generalizations from Chapter 7
    D. Use syllabication and detect those who need help
  III. Structural Analysis
    A. Compound words (combined and hyphenated)
    B. Contractions (one or more than one letter omitted)
    C. Plural forms (*f* to *v* and add *es*)
    D. Prefixes (*a, be, un*)
    E. Suffixes (*y, ly, er, est, less, ful, ed, s, ing, en*)
  IV. Context Clues
    A. Help children to use context in relation to syntax (known sentence parts and anticipated subsequent words)
  V. Dictionary Study (some children will need more help in Grades 4 to 6)
    A. Alphabetization to third letter
    B. Exploration of the dictionary, noting what information is in the front and back

    C. Significance of meaning (we can point to what we want, we can name what we want, we can tell how what we want is used, we can give a synonym for what we want, or we can make many related associations with a word; the dictionary gives us all the known meanings, but we must relate them to the context of our reading)

    D. Guide words

    E. Illustrations

    F. Diacritical marks (help children to use the key at the bottom of each dictionary page)

    G. Accent marks (note words such as *re'bel* and *reb'el*)

    H. Significance of "unabridged"

    I. Finding appropriate meaning for a given context

Comprehensive Skills

  I. Maintain awareness of purpose for reading

    A. Rate is influenced by purpose

    B. Thoroughness is influenced by purpose

    C. Greater depth for those skills taught previously

  II. Locating Information

    A. Referring to charts and graphs in the room

    B. Referring to something in a book or story to prove a point

    C. Skimming to find a name in a story or certain information

  III. Evaluating Information

    A. Challenge opinions and help children seek facts

    B. Help children to consider sources of information

    C. Help children to be conscious of conflicting opinions in the news

  IV. Interpreting What is Read

    A. Seek individual interpretations as much as possible to determine growth in interpretation

    B. Discuss reactions to stories and the news

  V. Organizing What is Read

    A. Outlining

      1. Getting the main idea from each part of a story

      2. Establishing subordinate ideas

      3. Summarizing and giving a report on what has been read

  VI. Critical and Appreciative Reading

    A. Challenging authors and reporters

    B. Reacting with conviction based on reason and proof

    C. Noting quality and worth in what is read

VII. Reference Reading
    A. Greater dependence on the dictionary
    B. Using the encyclopedia (some third-grade children may not
       be ready) (Since interest will be high when encyclopedias are
       introduced, plan to borrow an extra set so that each child
       can have a book. This is a good opportunity for children
       to seek out an interesting short article to prepare for oral

*A unit based on the intense interest of children affords a great variety
of reading experience. Reading is meaningful and significant when it
relates to what children want to know. (Photograph courtesy of the Cincinnati Public Schools.)*

reading. The audience situation will be good, and he will have incentive for reading well. Plan to spend several days in which the reading period is devoted to "living with" encyclopedias. A child might tell about the explorations within his volume.)

1. Exploration (giving children plenty of time to make discoveries)
2. Cross reference
3. Index volume
4. Types of information in an encyclopedia

C. Using the glossary (help children to be self-reliant)
D. World Almanac (children are fascinated by its contents)
E. Telephone book (discuss telephone courtesy as well as use of yellow pages, police and fire department dialing, long-distance dialing)
F. Maps (introduce the various kinds)
G. Globe (this is best for noting far-away places)
H. The library
   1. Library courtesy (politeness, quiet, consideration)
   2. Card file
      a. Alphabetical order
      b. Subjects
      c. Authors
      d. Cross references
      e. System for finding books
   3. Areas for browsing
   4. Newspapers and magazines
   5. Pamphlets
   6. Library responsibilities
      a. Returning books on time
      b. Keeping books clean
      c. Using care in turning pages
      d. Returning materials to the proper places when browsing

There is great variation among third- and fourth-grade classes and children. Some children may not be ready for some of the preceding experiences. Many such experiences will need to be introduced again in the fourth and fifth grades; frequently they need to be reviewed in the sixth. Many of the skills need refinement. More extensive use will be made of all reference materials in succeeding grades.

Additional Skills and Attitudes in Grades Four Through Six

Word Recognition Skills
  I. Reference to any phonic elements that any child may need
  II. Structural Analysis
    A. A study of the development of language
    B. Recognition of root words
    C. Introduction and review of inflectional forms (plurals, verb and adjective endings)
    D. Contractions (*can't, won't, don't, couldn't, let's, I've, I'll, it's, didn't, he'd, we've*)
    E. Meanings of prefixes (*dis, un, im, in, non, ant, con, com, fore, inter, trans, semi, tri, out, geo, mega, under, ex, re, de, tele*
    F. Meanings of suffixes (*less, ment, ful, ness, ly, tion, able, al, ical, age, ive, ish, ize, ic*)
    G. Review all syllabication (see Chapter 7)
  III. Dictionary and Glossary
    A. Establishing the dictionary habit
    B. Introducing primary and secondary accents
    C. Rapid use of the pronunciation key
  IV. Extending use of the context clue as greater understanding of sentence structure is developed and syntax becomes meaningful
  V. Extension of vocabulary through interest in words
Comprehension Skills (see Appendix N)
  I. Comprehending various types of materials
    A. Poetry
    B. Short stories
    C. Biography
    D. Newspapers
    E. Magazines
    F. Other areas of reading content
  II. Locating Information
    A. Proficiency in using the library
    B. Proficiency in knowing what kind of reference material to use for certain information
    C. Proficiency in using each type of reference material
    D. Using maps, diagrams, charts, schedules
      1. All types of maps should be familiar to students by the end of sixth grade

2. Skimming to locate needed information, favorite passages, etc.

III. Evaluation of Information
   A. Discriminating between cause and effect, fact and fiction, and recognizing the place of opinion in a democracy
   B. Discriminating between time and place relationships; understanding use authors make of such relationships
   C. Using evidence to make judgments and support opinions; establishing convictions based on sound reason
   D. Recognizing different styles and forms of writing

IV. Interpreting What Is Read
   A. Finding the main idea in paragraphs
   B. Finding the main ideas and subordinate ideas in an article
   C. Finding details to discover character traits
   D. Recognizing the sequence of ideas and events

V. Organizing What Is Read
   A. Making outlines
   B. Note-taking

Helping children become familiar with many of the sources of the library expands the horizons of interesting reading and enables them to become increasingly independent in gleaning information. (Photograph courtesy of the New York Public Schools.)

C. Reporting
D. Summarizing
VI. Appreciative and Critical Reading
    A. Appreciating imagery
    B. Appreciating beauty of words and expressions
    C. Expressing points of view and personal reactions.
    D. Analyzing an author's style
    E. Appreciating good organization
    F. Interpreting attitudes, emotions, motives
VII. Extending and enriching reading interests
    A. Wide explorations in reading
    B. Getting to know authors
    C. Establishing out-of-school reading interests

Reading Units

Since ninety-five per cent of our adult population reads newspapers, it behooves the schools to help children understand its contents, its place in the community and in American culture, and how to read it intelligently and critically. A unit on the newspaper in sixth grade would be interesting and valuable. One of the most succinct statements evaluating today's newspaper was made by Alvin Silverman:

The 1,760 daily newspapers of America are an important cornerstone of democracy. As long as the United States plays a major role in shaping the destiny of the free world, the press will play a major role in shaping the destiny of the United States.

Newspapers—huge collections of fact, opinion, and merchandise display, purchased each day of each week by nearly sixty million readers—can, at their worst, be self-servicing and unreasonable, shallow and prejudiced. To paraphrase a favorite nursery rhyme, when an American daily newspaper is good it is very, very good, and when it is bad it is horrid. Unfortunately, many of the very good ones are "horrid" on certain occasions, although seldom do the bad ones turn out to be very, very good.

If there is a single truth about the newspapers of the United States, it is that they are committed to the proposition that dictatorship and a free press do not and cannot exist simultaneously.

Aside from this, the American newspaper is almost too complex and contradictory for definition. To many of its readers it is the only complete record of events in the community, the state, the nation, the world, and, of late, in outer space. It forecasts everything from the weather to the scores of football games. It is the judge of what should be worn to a social function and how much should be paid for a piece of property. In 1,461 cities of the United States, the daily newspaper is both the conscience of the community and its daily chronicle of events.

A good newspaper tries, by stating its editorial opinions, to educate the populace and improve the quality of government. For the good of its readers, it seeks to better the community's economic and social condition. (Ironically, the same paper may also publish such material as horse-race entries and results, providing an impetus to illegal gambling that makes the poor man poorer and the dishonest man richer.) There is something for everyone in the newspaper. One reader may hasten to scan the stock market tabulations to see how his investments are faring, another the horoscope to see what luck awaits him. Still another reader may turn first to the top news stories of the day, and then go to the editorial page for an interpretation of these events which may challenge or bolster his own opinion. How good is a dramatic presentation, a television show, or an art exhibit? Many people must read the opinion of their favorite newspaper critic before they are prepared to say. On the same page that displays the time schedule of television and radio programs may be a biting criticism that could destroy many of these programs forever.

. . . . The editorial page usually features a regular political cartoon, satirizing prominent personalities or events of the day. Political analyses by nationally-known writers also appear on the editorial page, as well as the opinions of the paper's own columnists.

Throughout the paper is scattered local news and news of a general nature, from accidents to conventions, from weather reports to obituaries (articles about persons who have just died). Indeed, the "obits" are among the most widely-read of all the articles.

News items of special interest—sports, radio, television, movies, stamp collecting, bridge, gardening, books, musical performances, and art exhibits—usually are carried in sections of their own or in a regular place in a section.

Weddings, engagements, and other local society news items are also set off by themselves in a section that includes stories about parties and about the activities of women's civic, religious, and social organizations. Additionally, there often appear, in this "women's section" advice-to-the-lovelorn columns, household hints, and recipes.

Toward the back of the paper is the classified section, containing thousands of small advertisements put in the paper for an established fee by individuals having no connection with the paper, except perhaps as readers. The classified pages include official notices of public hearings; houses for rent or sale; lost and found notices; lists of articles for sale or items wanted, from baby rabbits and rare books to furnished apartments and used cars. The classified pages are probably most often used by people looking for employment and by business firms or private persons who have positions to be filled. These are called the "help-wanted columns."

By far the most popular and widely read section of the American newspaper is that national institution—the comics. The first well-known newspaper comic strip was printed in the *New York World* in 1894. It was Richard Outcalt's "Origin of a New Species." Since then, the "funnies," as they are also called, have passed through several stages of growth. At first they depicted the pranks of little children and were intended only to be funny. Then they looked in on universal family situations, some of which were as sentimental as they were amusing. Later, they introduced the crime fighters and the "wonder men" who could perform superhuman feats. Today, they are leaning toward sophisticated satires of American life, or of humanity in general.

Newspapers generally obtain their comic strips and cartoons from a national syndicate (United Press International or Associated Press) so that many comic characters have become celebrities by virtue of their exposure in papers all over the country. In fact, they often are more than celebrities; they are national heroes, who set patterns and customs for real people. When Joe Palooka, the good-natured prize fighter created by Ham Fisher, became the first comic character during World War II to put on a soldier's uniform, President Franklin D. Roosevelt personally thanked Fisher for helping to make the draft more palatable. Dick Tracy, the leading detective figure on American funny pages, has been a symbol of law and order since 1931. Al Capp's "Li'l Abner" strip is responsible for creating a holiday of sorts in "Sadie Hawkins Day," when American girls are supposedly allowed to pursue boys.

So many people in America read the comics that, during World War II, the strips were used to teach men and women in the armed forces. Favorite comic strip characters pointed out to soldiers who were learning other languages some of the difficult situations they could get into if they did not know the correct word.

Thus the newspaper, from banner headline to comics, offers its readers an enormously wide scope of material—to inform, to enlighten, to stimulate, and to entertain. Most of it is written by the newspaper's own staff of reporters, but no newspaper has a reporting corps large enough to give full coverage to the huge panorama of news. Help must be obtained from the wire services of the syndicates—Associated Press and United Press International.[2]

Reading the preceding account might be one way of introducing the class to a newspaper unit. Another way would be to bring several newspapers into the classroom and distribute a page to each child. After each child has had a chance to explore his page, a listing could be made of the contents of a newspaper. A general discussion of newspapers might lead to such questions as:

1. What are syndicates and how do they operate?
2. Who is on the *staff* of a newspaper?

2 Alvin Silverman, *The American Newspaper*. Washington, D.C.: Robert B. Luce, 1964.

3. What kind of a *production line* does a newspaper have?
4. What would a day in the life of a *reporter* be like?
5. How is a paper printed?
6. How is it put together?
7. Why do newspapers headline crime and accidents?
8. How do readers know what to believe?
9. Who are authorities of the news?
10. How is the truth distorted in writing and advertising?
11. What is meant by a *free press?*
12. How are pictures put in newspapers?
13. How do newspapers get distributed so quickly?
14. Who decides what is to be on a front page and how does he decide?
15. How are headlines chosen?

Children may raise these and other questions. Then they may volunteer to find answers, and plans can be made regarding how answers may be obtained, such as a trip to a newspaper establishment.

The following references may be helpful for class study of the newspaper:

Philip Ault, *News Around the Clock,* New York: Dodd, Mead, 1960; Frank Bond, *An Introduction to Journalism,* New York: Macmillan, 1954; Edgar Dale, *How to Read a Newspaper,* Chicago: Scott, Foresman, 1941; Alvin Silverman, *The American Newspaper,* Washington, D.C.: Robert B. Luce, 1964; Albert Sutton, *Design and Makeup of the Newspaper,* Englewood Cliffs, N.J.: Prentice-Hall, 1948: the *New York Times,* "News: The Story of How It Is Gathered and Printed," New York Times, Inc., 1949.

As a culmination of such a unit the class might report on answers to their questions at a program for their parents or a program for the P.T.A. so that adults, too, may become more informed about newspapers.

OTHER INTEREST UNITS

Periodically, children come to school with an intense interest in something they have heard on the news, seen on television or have become involved in in the community. Right now it could be the subject of outer space. When interest is high there exists the most important stimulant for learning, and the following steps can be taken to develop a reading unit on outer space:

DISCUSSION   Let children discuss all they have been hearing with regard to outer space. Notes can be made on the chalkboard with regard to the principal topics that seem to be foremost in their interests.

TOPICS   Topics such as these may come from the discussion:

Photographing the moon	Our astronauts
Preparation for man's habitation in space	Space capsules
Conditions on the moon	Weightlessness
Problems of landing on the moon	Russia's space efforts

QUESTIONS   In the course of discussion children will reach the limits of their fund of information, some arguments may arise, and some uncertainties will be evident. From these, need for research will evolve. Questions may be listed on the board.

RESPONSIBILITIES   Various individuals may volunteer to find answers to some of the questions, or the entire group may try to find answers to whatever questions they can.

RESOURCES   Newspaper clippings and magazine articles may be brought from home. The librarian may be informed at once that the class will be paying a visit to the library the next day to look for information on space, and she can be prepared to be helpful. An extra volume that includes the subject of "space" may be borrowed from another room's set of encyclopedias.

RESEARCH   The card file and indexes to magazine articles in the library should help children find material and may be brought out to the tables by those who locate it. Other children may browse through magazines and newspapers. The teacher and librarian must be at hand to help children select material that is in keeping with their ability to read. Markers may be put in places where there are good pictures to show.

PLANNING   Children's names may be listed on the board following the library visit and topics placed beside the name of whoever has found something he can eventually share. When topics are the same, two children may collaborate. Children who do not have topics may become interested in making or drawing things such as a launching pad, a space suit, interior of a space capsule, etc., with plans for an explanation. Little by little everyone will have some responsibility. A tentative time schedule for presentations may be made more definite each day. Plenty of time must be allowed for preparations.

A chalkboard space should be reserved for "Our Space Words and Phrases." Children are free to write whatever new words they come upon in their reading, being prepared to tell the meaning.

Children might be encouraged to write "flight-of-the-imagination" stories about space travel. Someone might make a chart showing distance from the earth to the moon, speeds of rocket ships, etc. Some children may be interested in writing poetry. Some reports may be written, and other children may plan to talk from an outline. Plans may include inviting children from another room to enjoy the final sharing period, or parents may be invited.

TEACHER'S RESPONSIBILITY   A teacher's interest and enthusiasm is a first essential. Then if she observes carefully, she will note how children may be helped in using the various study skills as they follow through on their responsibilities. She can bring in related films, read an interesting space story that children could not read themselves, bring in additional books from the public library, raise thought-provoking questions to stimulate thinking, and help children sense a satisfaction in what they are doing.

LEARNINGS   The vocabulary space on the chalkboard is likely to be filled. Games can be played in which the children challenge one another with the word meanings from the board, and the dictionary will get frequent use.

Outlines of reports will be prepared following careful reading of many types of references, and then rough drafts will be written until the child is satisfied that his work is ready for final presentation. Many children will have used a great many of the numerous study skills, and they will have served a purpose significant to them.

EVALUATION   The final presentation will show the results of all the efforts. A teacher will be conscious of which children need further help, and she will later look for opportunities to provide that help. All should feel a sense of accomplishment. The unit should not be suddenly dropped, but interest in reading and listening for further outer space developments should be keener and more rewarding because of their past study experiences.

Other unit topics that could be developed in much the same way are "Our Postal System," "Our Language," "Newspapers," "How Books Are Made." A teacher should help children to have different types of experiences in a later unit, especially the type that would provide for the kinds of help each child needs.

Lesson Plans

Careful planning assures a teacher of relaxed and rewarding sessions with children. Plans enable a substitute to take over effectively. Beginning teachers need to plan more carefully than those who are experienced and have many techniques in mind to meet the needs they can recognize so readily. The following are two suggested lesson plans.

PRIMARY-GRADE LESSON PLAN

A plan must be based on the story to be read or the activity to be carried out. (Because it would be difficult to choose a new story with which everyone is familiar, I am going to use *The Three Bears* as an example and assume that it is a new story that my class of first-graders has never heard or read before.)

School: ——————————————

Date: ——————————————

PREPARATION

Development of concepts. Talk about soup and let children tell about kinds of soup they like. Then explain that another word that means soup is *porridge*.

Discuss *woods*. (Some children will know what it means, but children in desert areas will not.)

Vocabulary development. Write *porridge* on the chalkboard. After just having talked about it most children are likely to know what it is. Use the initial sound clue, but the ending would be no help at all. Explain that it is the other word for *soup*.

Who's may be one of the first contractions that they have had in reading. Explain that the word means *who has* and that sometimes we shorten it and say *who's* so that when we write it we use the little mark that is called an apostrophe to indicate that we have left out some letters. Sometimes we may have such a word in which one letter is left out. *Who's* can mean *who is*. Challenge them to think of other words they know that are like *who's* (*it's, what's, where's*).

Motivation. "This story is about ———— [write "Three Bears" on the chalkboard as you say it]. Somebody gets a big surprise in this story. Read the story silently and then come up and whisper to me who you think had the biggest surprise." (While children are reading take notes of any troublesome words and later list them on the chalkboard to give individual help.)

Allow children to complete the story silently.

Follow-up discussion. Chuckle with the children about the big surprise that both the bears and Goldilocks had.

"How many groups of three's can you find in this story?" (This requires skimming to discover—*bears, bowls, chairs, beds.*) This story lends itself to dramatization, and those children needing help with good expression could be called upon to play the various roles. Ask others to join in the parts (Who's been ————?"—get variation in expression). "Wasn't that a 'fun' story?"

SIXTH-GRADE LESSON PLAN

Advance preparation. Make cards with the following notations:

Police telephone number
World Series winner of last year
Pronunciation of *Guatemala*
Depths of the ocean
Birthdate of A. A. Milne
Signers of the Declaration of Independence
Highest waterfall
Syllabication of *dynasty*
The past presidents of the United States
Information about Lyndon Johnson
Area code number
Information about Clare Booth Luce
Newspaper circulation
Life in Alaska
Biography of Robert Louis Stevenson
Information about the carp
The latitude of Los Angeles
The height of the Himalayas
How to call the fire department
Cost of a pleasure trip to Europe

Information about ants
The dates of Eisenhower's term of office as president
Information about the Spanish-American War
The difference between flora and fauna
Information on animals of Australia
How buttons are made
How much rainfall there is in Northern Africa
How many pitchers have pitched no-hit games in World Series
The country bordering Nigeria
Entertainment highlights in Europe
Life of James Whitcomb Riley

Purpose. To check acquaintance with reference sources.

Procedure. The following should be listed on the chalkboard:

Dictionary	Library card catalog
Encyclopedia	Telephone book
World Almanac	Atlas
Who's Who in America	Travel folders

Two members of the class choose teams. The above cards are turned face down and team members alternate taking turns drawing a card and telling where the information is to be obtained. In some cases there is more than one correct answer. A team gets a point for each correct answer. The other team may challenge. Whoever is wrong gets a point taken away. Students may go to the sources for verification.

Follow-through. The teacher makes a notation of those who have difficulties, and they form a group for further help with the reference materials and play the game again another time.

Encouraging Breadth of Reading

Many children can read almost at the adult level when they leave third grade. Others will still need help with clues and skills in the sixth grade, but teachers should help those who need help all along the way. When a child has acquired the skills, he should be given opportunities to use them. Topics such as careers, hobbies, and sports may be researched. The library has much to offer, and he is ready for stimulation. A "Wheel of Good Reading" in which he is challenged to sample the many varieties of books is good for the able reader. (See Chapter 14 and Appendix O.)

Book Reports Versus Sharing Good Books

In school children's rating of preference for various kinds of school experiences, book reports nearly always come at the bottom of the list (one rating showed "ug" written after "Book Reports") The reason is probably that they are teacher-imposed—they are tagged-on chores of drudgery after an otherwise delightful experience. The task seems formidable. It is not that children do not like to share their book experiences, but rather, in the words of the children themselves:

1. It's like the teacher didn't trust that you had read the book. Nothing ever comes of the report anyway.

The acquisition of reading skills should lead right into purposeful use of these skills. (Photograph courtesy of the Detroit, Michigan, Public Schools.)

2. There's too much writing to do to tell enough about the story.

3. Why take all the time to tell about a book other kids have read or that they'd rather read for themselves?

4. I never know how to do it. There's so much in a book.

5. It's about the dullest thing anyone could ever have to do.

And teachers have this to say:

1. I've never been able to develop a form that would fit all the books that children read.

2. Some books are truly difficult to summarize briefly. It would be a challenge to an adult.

3. Children would much rather have a story read to them than to hear a book report—no matter how good it is.

4. The simple written form doesn't really tell much about the child's actual interpretation of what he has read, and a long one wastes so much of a child's time when he would rather be reading another good book.

5. There isn't time for much oral reporting, and written reports have no very real purpose other than making sure the child has read the book. I know children don't like to do them.

(See Appendix M for a book report form that is adequate and not likely to stifle a child's interest in reading.)

Here are some alternative suggestions:

Children like to keep records of what books they have read. Suggest that they use a card for each book, writing title and author plus anything they would like to recall about the book during "Book Talk" time. Such items might be the following (there might be one or more than one to a book):

A certain character or characters
The plot
A certain incident
A beautiful passage
Something I would criticize
Something that set me to wondering
Something that inspired me
Something that gave me an idea
Something that reminded me of what I had done at one time
Something that almost made me cry
Something that I thought was extremely funny

Something that I don't believe
Something I think others would like to know
Something to cause others to want to read the book

Have a "Book-Talk Time" about every two weeks after children
are capable of reading books independently. A teacher might say,
"I reread *Charlotte's Web* the other day and I think I can understand why it is so popular. It seems to have everything a good story
should have. What do you think about it?" After conversation wanes
with regard to the many interests in *Charlotte's Web*, a lead question might be, "What other books do you think are likely to become
as popular?" Many times the discussion goes on from one book to
another with no further prompting from the teacher. Children look
upon this as a respectful approach to book-sharing. It is the kind of
sharing adults would do with regard to good reading. Other times
lead questions should take them into other of the above items, and
more children should be drawn into the discussion.

Children enjoy challenges. Sometimes prepare a guessing game of
authors and what books they wrote, characters in stories, plot
clues, etc.

Readability formulas can help to some extent in determining
reading levels of materials. This, combined with a teacher's or librarian's good judgment and a child's interest, serves in helping the
child to get the book that is best for him. The following formulas,
each of which must be studied carefully, are most commonly used:

"A Formula for Predicting Readability," by Jeanne S. Chall and Edgar
   Dale
"How to Test Readability," by Rudolf Flesch
"Gray-Leary Method for Predicting Readability"
"A New Readability Formula for Primary-Grade Reading Materials,"
   by George Spache
"Cloze Procedure: A New Tool for Measuring Readability," by W. L.
   Taylor

The teacher and librarian must help the child to find what reading material is suitable for his level.

There are more than forty different predictors that have been considered in an effort to measure readability. These include the number of
familiar words, the number of unfamiliar words, the length of sentences, number of sentences, type of sentences, number of pronouns,
number of abstract words and percentage of polysyllabic words.[3]

[3] Jeanne S. Chall, *Readability*. Columbus: Ohio State University Press, 1958.

The teacher and the librarian can do much to pass on a respect, a reverence, and a deep appreciation for books that will help nurture a child's reading tastes and help give him a lifetime interest. In the words of Holbrook Jackson,

Reading is an adventure: you go with the poets into the realms of fancy and imagination; you see life with the novelist; you go down to the sea in ships and unto the ends of the earth with the great explorers; the scientist takes you into his laboratory; in biography you are let into the mystery of men's lives; the historian reconstructs the past and gives you glimpses of the future; and the philosopher gives you a glimpse of his wisdom.[4]

Be careful to expose children to truly exciting books, good books that are well within the child's ability to read. Sometimes a child will "stretch out" a bit to read what suddenly appeals to him, but on the whole he is more comfortable with what can be read easily. Librarians come to know children, and it is amazing how quickly children appreciate such persons who will help them find many satisfying books. A child likes to nurture old interests but he also needs to seek new ones. He sometimes likes to browse, sample this book and investigate that one until finally the choice is his.

You may read a book throughout. You may *study* it, learning all the information it contains completely and systematically. You may *skim* a book, gaining merely a general idea of its contents without bothering about detail. You may *skip* through a book reading only those passages here and there which concern you. You may turn at once to just those chapters or sections which interest you. You may look at only the one paragraph or line that matters. According to what a book can give you, so must you treat it.

You will need experience, however, before you can use books properly in this way. If you don't know how to do it you might skim a book and miss everything that mattered; you might refer to it for one piece of information and not find it because you didn't know where to look.

It is impossible to lay down any rules to guide you, for each book and each reader is different.

The essential thing, however, is to appreciate exactly what you want. Say to yourself, "Why have I taken up this particular volume? What do I want to get out of it? What can it give me that is valuable to me?"— and you are not likely to go wrong.[5]

---

[4] Holbrook Jackson, "The Joy of Reading," in *The Wonderful World of Books*, ed. by Alfred Stefferud. New York: New American Library, 1953, p. 32.

[5] Lionel McColvin, "How to Use Books," in *The Wonderful World of Books*, ed. by Alfred Stefferud. New York: New American Library, 1953.

Kinds of Books

BIOGRAPHY

Although biography has long been important in upper grades, books of biography are now being written appropriate for second- and third-grade children, but the content would interest many fourth- to sixth-grade children (see Appendix, Easy Books). It is best to precede individualized reading of biography with such biographies as *Thomas Jefferson,* by Gene Lisitzky (published by Viking Press). A good time to read it would be when children are being launched on a study of American history. Through such oral reading a teacher can help children to enter into the thoughts and feelings of the biographical subject, to step into his shoes and feel the determination in his step, to sense the deep concern he had for his responsibilities, to feel the thrill of his accomplishment. Biography and history can make the past seem very near and real. Biography can help kindle fires of aspiration, appreciation of noble deeds, and a sense of the responsibility that each person has to contribute toward making the world a better place in which to live. We have come through a period of questioning and criticism in our reading of history. Now there is an apparent need for a sense of appreciation and responsibility. Books of biography can help in that accomplishment.

Through oral reading, teachers can assist children in getting much more from their individualized reading. Read biographies so that the child cannot help but identify with the character. Help children see the importance of establishing the time and place in their thinking as the story develops. Help them to know the circumstances with which the character must cope and to see how courage, conviction, and regard for humanity help him succeed. None of this should be done through preachment but rather through an oral interpretation so vivid that children can grasp and savor the story themselves. Many of the heroes of today and yesteryear rose up through tremendous difficulties and this is the type of encouragement that can mean much to our underprivileged children and others as well.

SHORT STORIES

The short story is a condensation in time, in events, and in scope. We never get all the details surrounding people and happenings in a short story that we get in a full-length novel. It is a good idea to help children see how an author of short stories must operate. The short-story writer must grasp the attention of the reader immediately and place him in a familiar setting with characters he feels he knows and with a plot that develops fast. Each detail must count for something important in the solution of a problem, the unfolding of a mystery, or the involvement of a personality. Events must happen fast, and there must be a satisfying conclusion with no wasted explanations. Children can be helped to see that in order to get the most from a short story they must allow themselves to be "taken in" at the very outset of their reading. They must be alert to each detail. Their thoughts must move along as rapidly as the fast pace of the story. Skipping a paragraph would be like losing an ingredient in a recipe—one could miss an extremely important clue or a highly significant fact. Short stories require careful, alert reading.

NOVELS

Novels, on the other hand, are more rambling. Descriptions, character analysis, little side plots, and many details are injected into the stream of the story. Read a good short story from a magazine and let children decide if any paragraph could have been omitted. Then read a book chapter by chapter and let children discuss the important and lesser significant elements. All this becomes an important part of the "how" and "what" of reading. It can lead to a better understanding and appreciation of literature.

POETRY

Poetry must first be *heard* to be enjoyed. Its effectiveness is based on feeling tone and beauty, euphony, and cadence of expression. For the very young child it is the rhythm, the rhyme, and the enchantment that can cause him to ask for more. Poetry is not easy to read because controlled vocabulary is almost impossible, and the "expected" type of sentence structure is often sacrificed for maintenance of rhythm. Thus the unusual words and unpredictable sentence structures cause reading problems with regard to poetry. Teachers should do the reading, even when poetry appears in the child's book. Until a child is well along the road to independent reading he should not be expected to read poetry without having had it read to him first. If he is permitted to enjoy it on many occasions before it appears in his books, and then if the way is paved for his success in reading it, there is much less likelihood that he will find it distasteful.

Providing well-read poetry on records or tape at the "listening post" is a means of helping children enjoy it. If you know of anyone in the community who recites poetry very well, invite that person into the school to share a half-hour of well-chosen poems with the children. Let children join you in some of the verse they particularly enjoy. Memorization should come naturally if and when children have enough appreciation of a poem to want to learn it. Some children may learn many poems and others may be content to merely listen. We can expect as much diversity in taste for poetry as we find in taste for stories.

If teachers have read poetry to children from kindergarten through the various grades, you will find children asking for books of poems. I cannot think of anything more enjoyable than a good book of poems on a rainy afternoon. Your appreciation of poetry (or any kind of literature) is contagious in the classroom.

What's a poet good for? To give us words for the music in ourselves. To give us words to live by; great, swinging words for our dreams to march to. For just as it takes a child to remind us of the joy in simple things, so it takes a poet to show us the wonder of what is before our eyes.[6]

Oral Reading

As one child said, "If writing is putting down talk, then reading is taking it back up again—only someone else does it usually." And, to some extent, so it is. A child's speech is an indication of how well we can expect him to read orally; it is also an indication of the way he thinks and responds to what he sees and says. That is why such a long chapter was devoted to language development. Language development must be continuous throughout life in order to keep abreast of changing times and to seek self improvement. Only as we give young children an opportunity to read aloud can we ascertain what and how they are reading silently. Furthermore, children are usually eager to read, if only they can find an interested

---

[6] Louis Redmond, "Boyhood: Made in America," in *The Wonderful World of Books,* ed. by Alfred Stefferud. New York: New American Library, 1953.

adult to listen. "Let me read it," "I can read it"—such statements are familiar to teachers of young children.

Reading a brief page from a preprimer is not as good a check on reading as reading from sentences on the board might be. Children often memorize the contents of the first pages of a preprimer. This is the way most of us began reading. When several sentences with words in various contexts are on the board and the teacher says, "Who can read the sentence that tells where Mother went?", the children are reading for thought, and when they read aloud they are actually transforming the printed symbols into language and using it in spoken form with all the inflection natural to their own way of speaking. Reading a sentence or two in such situations is adequate in the beginning stage to check on a child's oral reading and to let him know that it is meaning he is conveying to those who listen.

SETTING STANDARDS   Although children can never be expected to read equally well, there are certain qualities that all need to consider and strive to attain, such as:

1. Getting the thought, knowing all the words, and planning the phrasing before starting to read orally.
2. Reading loudly enough so all can hear.
3. Using inflection appropriate to content.
4. Changing pace in accordance with content.
5. Occasional eye contact with the audience.
6. Living the story.
7. Putting emphasis on significant facts or ideas.
8. Portraying the mood of the story.
9. Using a few gestures if they add to the effectiveness of the story (never anything that calls attention to yourself, but only gestures that enhance the meaning of the story).
10. Appear at ease, comfortable, and relaxed.

Helping children with oral reading is much like helping them with speaking. They must feel secure and relaxed to be free to put forth their best efforts. They must know what it is they are going to say before they can project it to an audience. Therefore, the material must be such that it can be read very easily silently. It must be within their range of interpretation and expression. Do not choose content that calls for dialect foreign to the experience of the child. To read before the group, a child should be well prepared with something new that will hold the interest of the group and thus he feels rewarded for his efforts.

Sometimes merely reading a sentence from the chalkboard is enough to assure the teacher that a child can read well. Such children may be the first to go back to their seats after a small group-reading session. Those whom the teacher feels need help are asked to find a sentence or two they would like to read, and while some are getting ready the teacher calls one at a time to come up beside her. With the very slow learner, the teacher may read the sentence first, then have the child read the chosen sentence with her and finally to her. The child feels much security in doing it this way until he is ready to do it all on his own. If individual words are causing difficulty the teacher puts them on word cards and the child goes to his seat to trace over them as he says them to himself. If expression is the problem, the teacher helps the child with diction, emphasis, and modulation.

After the period of initial reading instruction, children are ready to read sentences and paragraphs that answer questions, that they especially like, or that tell about someone or something. A teacher is mindful of the quality of the oral reading that goes into such experiences, and the end of the group session can still be devoted to those who need individual help. It is best not to have the poor readers struggle through a paragraph while those who are listening become uneasy and restless—this is not good for either the readers or for the listeners. Let the fluent readers do the oral reading first to the group and send them away to do other things, and let the others receive individual help from the teacher. As soon as a slow learner can achieve fluent reading status, suggest that he read what he has accomplished to the group and get the group to react appreciatively with you when the child finishes. Always avoid individual embarrassment, but be quick to praise success and get group approval for the child when he succeeds. Sometimes finding new material at a lower reading level will give the slow learners a "pick-up" in self-confidence and respect from the others. (See Appendix R for interesting books with easy content.)

PREPARATION FOR GOOD ORAL READING

THE TEACHER AS A MODEL   Reading to children with all the inflections, change of pace, and feelings of suspense that make stories come alive is an unforgettable lesson in oral reading. Children's upturned faces with expressions changing according to the mood of the story indicate that they are with you in living the action of the story. A good reader or teller of tales is capable of taking an audience away from the here-and-now and wafting them into the spell of an enchanting tale. One of the greatest joys of childhood should be the many great pieces of literature especially appropriate to the young listening audience. If oral reading serves no other purpose, it should help children to be ready for their turn at passing on the rich heritage of literature to their children and their children's children. The teacher who can make literature so appealing through reading and telling that the inspiration will be long lasting in each child is serving a lifelong purpose. (Appendix O lists books to be read aloud at each age level.)

DRAMATIZATION Mention was made earlier of how important dramatization can be in kindergarten to develop expressive speech. It paves the way for reading conversation in stories and for putting good expression into oral reading. Enacting stories at every grade level is a very natural and interesting means of developing flexible animated renditions of what others have written. In addition to the little plays that are found in readers, magazines, and holiday leaflets, there are books of plays for young children available. Fifth- and sixth-graders enjoy play production. Often, there is equal satisfaction and profit from enacting a well-liked story. (See Appendix K.)

After children achieve good oral reading status, it is time for them to select, with some help from the teacher, interesting stories and poems to read independently. If they find something that no one else in the class has read and they want to read it to the class, this would be a valuable oral reading experience for the child and for the class, too. With good reading ability children may take over the teacher's job of reading to the class from time to time. Not all children should be expected to become excellent oral readers any more than we would expect every child to become a poet or an artist. They should all have as much opportunity as possible, but no one should be pressured.

Frequently adults are called upon to read minutes of meetings, scriptures, reports of all kinds, correspondence, and data. While the percentage of silent reading we do far exceeds the amount of oral reading, there is still a definite need to be able to read well orally. When one can read well orally, he is likely to enjoy it, and there is much literature in which the beauty of language, the eloquence of speech, and the richness of our heritage of stories and poetry can be

shared with others. An evening spent with a reader who can take us with him to other lands, other ideologies, other aspirations, flights of imagination, and beyond the ordinary realm of today is long to be remembered and frequently sought after. The world needs more individuals with such capabilities, and the making of such readers begins with the inspirations and challenges of teachers in the elementary grades.

LEARNING TO READ

To learn to read, we climb and climb
A long high mountain trail.
The path is steep and sometimes rough;
Each child seems small and frail.
Sometimes we reach a broad flat ridge
And pause to look ahead;
Like reading in an easy book
With words that we have read.
The view grows broad as up we climb
But steeper grows the way;
Our steps seem surer and more safe
With skills we use each day.
We scale the cliffs and rise on high
To look down far below
And view the fund of knowledge
That books have helped us know.
We're challenged then to reach the top
And know that we have won
A glimpse of all the kingdoms
That lie beneath the sun.
From up on high we know we have
A vast expansive look
At all the mysteries, science, arts,
That come inside a book.

—Verna Dieckman Anderson

Suggestions for Class Participation and Discussion

1. What constitutes good silent reading?
2. Observe children in a classroom situation. How much lip movement and vocalization did you observe? What variety of silent reading experience did you observe?

Oral reading by the teacher inspires children to read effectively. Sixth-graders become capable of taking their classmates into the realms of adventure and excitement through books. (Photographs courtesy of the Detroit, Michigan, Public Schools.)

3. Explain the relationship of a child's ability to speak well and with ease to his ability to read well orally.
4. Explain how a child needs to be able to read well silently before he can be expected to read well orally.
5. What situations in your life have called for oral reading? Did you feel adequately prepared?
6. How significant is speed reading to you? When do you think an opportunity for speed reading should come? Are there dangers involved? Explain.
7. Were you ever caused to be embarrassed when you were learning to read? If so, how could it have been avoided?
8. What reading have you heard that "carried you away" as you sat and listened? Discuss.
9. Check into some of the material in Appendix O suggested for oral reading to children. What selections do you like and why?
10. Read a carefully selected story to a group of children and observe their reaction. Ask them what they liked about your reading.

Bibliography

BERKELEY, Unified School District, *Reading Guide,* Berkeley, Calif., 1963.

BETTS, EMMET A. *Foundations of Reading Instruction.* New York: American Book Co., 1957.

BLOOM, BENJAMIN, *et al. Compensatory Education for Cultural Deprivation.* New York: Holt, Rinehart & Winston, 1965.

BOND, GAY, and TINKER, MILES. *Reading Difficulties, Their Diagnosis and Correction.* New York: Appleton-Century-Crofts, 1957.

BOTEL, MORTON. *How to Teach Reading.* Chicago: Follett, 1962.

Burbank, Unified School District, *Teacher's Guide to Reading Instruction,* Burbank, California, 1959.

BURTON, WILLIAM H. *Reading in Child Development.* Indianapolis: Bobbs-Merrill, 1956.

CARTER, HOMER L., and McGINNIS, DOROTHY J. *Teaching Individuals to Read.* Boston: Heath, 1962.

City of New York Board of Education, *Reading and Literature in the Language Arts: Grades 1–6,* 1957.

———, *Sequential Levels of Reading Growth,* 1963.

DAWSON, MILDRED A., and BAMMAN, HENRY A. *Fundamentals of Basic Instruction.* New York: Longmans Green, 1959.

DeBOER, JOHN J., and DOLLMANN, MARTHA. *The Teaching of Reading.* New York: Holt, Rinehart & Winston, 1960.

Denver Public Schools, *Independent Learning Activities toward Creativity Through the Language Arts—Grades 3 and 4 Reading,* Denver, Colo., 1962.

DURRELL, DONALD. *Improving Reading Instruction.* New York: Harcourt, Brace & World, 1956.

GANS, ROMA. *Reading Instruction for Today's Children.* New York: Bobbs Merrill, 1963.

HERRICK, VIRGIL, and JACOBS, LELAND. *Children in the Language Arts.* Englewood Cliffs, N.J.: Prentice-Hall, 1955.

HESTER, KATHLEEN. *Teaching Every Child to Read.* New York: Harper, 1955.

HILDRETH, GERTRUDE. *Teaching Reading.* New York: Holt, 1958.

JUDSON, HORACE, and BALDRIDGE. *The Techniques of Reading.* New York: Harcourt, Brace, 1954.

Long Beach Unified School District, *Guide for Teaching Reading in the Primary Grades,* Long Beach, Calif., 1961.

Louisville Public Schools, *Curriculum Guides for Reading* (Kindergarten, Grades I, II, III and IV, V and VI), Louisville, Ky., 1900.

Mobile Public Schools, *Reading for Living and Learning in Today's Schools,* Mobile, Ala., 1960.

Nederland Public Schools, *A Guide for Achievement Levels Program Grades 1–6,* Nederland, Tex., 1900.

Palm Springs Public Schools, *Teacher's Guide for the Teaching of Reading in the Elementary Grades,* Palm Springs, Calif., 1961.

Phoenix Elementary Scools, District 1, Maricopa County, *Teachers' Guide for the Teaching of Reading,* Phoenix, Ariz., 1963.

San Diego County Schools, *An Inventory of Reading Attitudes,* San Diego, Calif., 1961.

SANFORD, BISHOP, GILLESPIE, and CROSBY. *Reading Comprehension* (Reading Spectrum). New York: Macmillan, 1964.

Scotch Plains–Fanwood Public Schools, *Creative Seatwork (Reinforcement and Enrichment Ideas),* Scotch Plains, N.J., 1964.

SHAW, PHILLIP B. *Effective Reading and Learning.* New York: Cromwell, 1955.

SMITH, NILA BANTON. *Reading Instruction for Today's Children.* Englewood Cliffs, N.J.: Prentice-Hall, 1963.

STRANG, RUTH, and BRACKEN, DOROTHY. *Making Better Readers.* Boston: D. C. Heath, 1957.

TINKER, MILES, and McCULLOUGH, C. M. *Teaching Elementary Reading* New York: Appleton-Century-Crofts, 1962.

WHEELER, ARVILLE. *The Teaching of Reading* (6 booklets). New London, Conn.: Croft, 1959.

Look up current magazine articles on related topics.

CHAPTER 12

Evaluation
in Reading

Give a man a taste for reading and the means of gratifying it, and you cannot fail to make him a happy, as well as a better man. You place him in contact with the best society and the best minds in every period in history, with the wisest and the wittiest, the tenderest and the bravest, those who have really adorned humanity. You make him a citizen of all nations and a contemporary of all ages.[1]

Webster's Dictionary defines evaluation as "assessing the value of; appraising." There is a positive quality to such meanings. In other words, we are to look at what is right about reading. Too often the negative aspect—what is wrong about what the student is doing and how he is doing it, or how many wrong answers he gave in a certain test—has been the predominant consideration in evaluation. Perhaps that is why there is often a feeling of pressure and frustration when tests are mentioned to older students.

[1] Staiger, Ralph, and Sohn, David (eds.), *New Directions in Reading*. New York: Bantam Books, 1967.

276

The Basis for Evaluation

It is important, first of all, to establish what it is we are evaluating. These are the objectives toward which we would want every child to strive:

1. Increased vocabulary—not mere decoding of words but meaningful word recognition.
2. Quick and easy grouping of words into thought units—phrases, clauses and sentences, which comprise the patterning of our language—with complete comprehension.
3. Comprehension of paragraphs and increasingly longer content units.
4. A growing delight in the ability to read and the uses to which reading may be put.
5. Ability to evaluate what is read in terms of facts, purposes, and interests.
6. Use of the higher thought processes incorporating the gleanings of reading.
7. An increased knowledge of the variety of materials available and how to read them efficiently.
8. A discriminative taste for what is good in reading content.
9. Ever-expanding use of reading in wholesome daily living.
10. Enjoyment and skill in oral reading.

Who Should Do the Evaluating?

The child is the one who should profit from the evaluative process. As part of the curriculum he should frequently ask, "How am I doing?" Because he works directly with the teacher, often they should both ask, "How are we doing?" How easy it has been for some teachers in the past to say, "He is a poor reader," and merely indicate that fact by giving him a poor grade on his report card or making a comment to that effect. The child may accept the dishonorable label, but it does not help him become a better reader. True assessment must be made with the child. A teacher and each child must ask, "Where are we and where do we go from here?" Each objective must have an accounting. If progress is not satisfactory, an analysis must be made in order to know what can be done

Interpreting test results to children so that difficulties may be analyzed, help given, and next goals planned cooperatively is making the best use of a testing program. (Photograph courtesy of the Seattle, Washington, Public Schools.)

about it. It is more important for the child to know what next steps he must take in his learning and how he can go about taking them than to merely know where he stands.

Parents are eager to know what progress the child is making, and he should be able to report almost daily what he is learning and why. He should have frequent opportunities to take a book or other reading material home so that he can show his parents his capabilities and be proud of them. The parent's role should be one of interest, encouragement, and assistance (when absences have made outside help necessary). If word cards help, or more practice in reading silently or orally is required, a teacher must make contact with the parent so that complete understanding exists as to how the help is to be given. "How are we doing" is sometimes a threefold assessment made by teacher, child, and parents. How much use of reading does the child make at home? Both the teacher and the parents must keep their expectations within the achievement range of the child. What mention does he make of outside of school reading? What comments do parents make about his attitude toward reading? Does he talk at home about what he has read there or in school? Does the family converse about what the various members read? Does he participate and how does he react to such conversations? What is his level of thinking with regard to what he reads? Does he analyze? Does he relate it to himself, to community welfare, or to national and international problems? Is he curious about many things? Does he appreciate the works of many good writers: reporters, fact finders, explorers, scientists, historians, and poets? These are the important considerations that should go along with the acquisition of reading proficiency. They will determine the breadth of use he will make of reading when he leaves school.

Many skillful teachers and administrators of our times have been aware of the limitations of our evaluative techniques.

Not all evaluation is objective. Much that is of value has not yet been reduced to scores and norms. For example, interest, ambition, enthusiasm, creativity, and initiative are not directly measurable in the same way that we measure skill in reading, factual knowledge in content areas, and performance in mathematics. The evaluation of these factors is still highly subjective.[2]

Although the broad aims of reading instruction have been recognized for many years, too little has been done to accomplish them. Much greater use of discussion of reading should take place in our classrooms—the kind of discussion in which children are respected as adults in the expression of their opinions about what they read. One sixth-grade boy remarked to his teacher, "I like to read newspapers and news magazines now because we get to talk about what we read and it makes more sense." Mere reporting is not enough. Such leading questions as: What effect do you think this war—or this strike—or this riot—or this invention—or this piece of legislation—or this election is having on our economy (prices, food supply and distribution, public welfare, taxes, foreign relations, etc.)? Children like to be challenged to think and they read avidly to participate. Such participation should be observed and encouraged but it is never tested. Discussions of good books is equally important. What makes a book "good?" Why do authors write books—do they have messages, axes to grind, proposals to make? What do books do for

2 Daisy M. Jones, "Providing Materials and Identifying Procedures To Develop Reading Efficiency in Content Areas," *Promoting Maximal Reading Growth Among Able Learners* (Helen Robinson (ed.). Chicago: University of Chicago Press, 1954, p. 174.

you? These are things that are not tested, but they help children to recognize that reading is a means to further ends. Notations can be made from time to time to be used as an addition to the student's file folder.

Tests may be used as part of the appraisal and they should be administered by the teacher. Children know her and respond to her directions more readily than to a stranger giving the test. A stranger in the room often causes some young children to respond abnormally.

When Do We Evaluate?

Evaluation should be a part of the curriculum. As teaching and learning take place there should be a continuous checking of its effectiveness. Anything that is done in the classroom should be worth doing well, and children should be helped to have pride in work well done. At the end of each activity a child might ask himself, "Have I done the best I can do?" This is all we have a right to expect of any child, and the quality and amount of the achievement will vary with each child's potentialities. When group instruction is concluded it is often easy and beneficial to check each child as he leaves the group. Such checking might involve finding a certain sentence on the board that tells _____ and reading it, reading certain word cards that had given trouble earlier in the session, whispering a word to you that starts like the beginning of a certain name (a sound that had previously been confusing to the child), or whispering a word that would rhyme with another, if that had been his difficulty. Thus you are making sure he knows (at least at that time) what you had attempted to teach. If he does not know, give him the necessary help that will enable him to achieve his goal (by tracing over a difficult word and taking the word card with him to be returned the next morning and be checked again; to remain with you until all the other children have gone to their seats so that you can give him more time and help; or to go off with another child to work on the problem together). Great is the thrill when accomplishment is made. However, it may be only temporary—sometimes a child may know a word today and have forgotten it by tomorrow, so evaluation must be continuous. Sometimes a new learning supports a previous one—for example, learning phonics clues supports the context clue and both used together makes word recognition easier. A child may not learn a word in one context today but he may learn it in another context tomorrow.

Although we evaluate every day there is also need to re-evaluate over longer periods of time. Many children forget easily. The sad and discouraging fact is that often it is the child who learns slowly who is the most likely to forget. Little check-ups of previously learned vocabulary, word recognition clues, and phonetic elements will determine the need to reteach (there are such tests in Appendix F). These check-ups are also good at the beginning of second grade to indicate the kinds of help each child may need. Some group instruction may be planned according to the needs of a number of children, and sometimes individual help may be required.

After a Christmas vacation it is often startling how much some children may have forgotten. It is much better to pick up the loose ends and start from where certain children need help, rather than try to force the entire class to move ahead to new learnings that invariably are based on what they should have learned very well previously. Individualized or small-group help pays dividends. If a child shows great hesitation in reading and makes many errors in comprehension exercises, you will know that it is time to check up on basic learnings such as those represented in the check-ups in Appendix F. Help that is given following recognition of need can soon put the child on the road to success again and thus maintain his interest in reading. (Suggestions appear in Appendix J.)

At the beginning of second and third grades, teachers should expect children to have forgotten much over the vacation period. Check carefully on children's needs and reteach the basic vocabulary word recognition clues, and elements of phonics. Start reading in books these children have never read but that are at an easy level. Thus the material will be new and interesting but will afford them a chance to relearn forgotten skills while getting satisfaction from reading and yet not have to struggle with new skills.

How Do We Evaluate?

Praising work that is well done is a positive evaluation and a stimulant to continuous effort. Short-sighted goals are best for young children so that attainment can be appraised frequently. Success is a great motivation. Each day should bring rewards in self-satisfaction in work completed on time, work done to one's best ability, and advancement over what one knew or could do the previous day. Expressing thrill over these achievements with children is a great stimulant. It is as important to let a child know that you are dissatisfied with poor work when you know he could have done better as it is to praise good work. For example, when he brings up a piece of work carelessly done, you may remark, "I wonder whose work this can be? It has Jimmy's name on it, but I know his best work wouldn't look like this. Let's throw this in the waste basket. We wouldn't want anyone to see work like this with Jimmy's name on it." He knows you are kidding and yet he senses your expectations. There is seldom time for a child to do work over, but the next time it is well to remind him that you are expecting his *best,* and you are likely to get it. Helping a child to recognize his own best efforts, to be proud of them and to want to produce them, is what is all important in his own independent life.

INDIVIDUAL RECORDS

Progress charts on which each member of the class is checked on packs of word cards, learning the alphabet, learning basic phonetic elements, or reading books independently can be good incentives for continuous effort, are ever-present records of achievement, and show at which level a child is in case of absence. With children who forget easily it may be necessary to go back and recheck some previous accomplishments. After absences, help from other members of the class, home members, or the teacher is important. When parents come to school these records can be a point of departure for discussion.

OBSERVATIONS

As a teacher observes children read silently and listens to them read orally she should jot down on a pad of paper any specific help each child may need. At the end of the day she should go through these jottings and plan how she might work on the individual needs the next day. These slips of paper with individual observations noted on them should be placed in each child's individual folder. Frequently the teacher should go through these folders to make sure some help has been given to each child in accordance with his needs. Also include such observations as a child's delight in reading, his wide use of reading, and his tastes in reading.

Worksheets and Workbooks

More will be said about materials in another chapter, but it is important here to note that the purpose of any worksheet or workbook exercise is to help establish some particular reading skill. To accomplish the purpose it must be checked with the child so that he knows what his mistakes are and can experience some teacher help in righting his wrongs and in reenforcing the correct learning. When many children make similar mistakes it is evident that additional teaching should be done on that particular skill followed by another similar exercise. In each case it must be pointed out to children what it is they are learning and to be conscious of it as they do each part of the exercise. For additional reenforcement of the learning it is a good idea to ask the next day, "What was it we learned from the worksheet or workbook page we did yesterday?" Call on a child who especially needs more reenforcement. In carefully prepared workbooks one skill builds on previously developed skills, and there is continuity, relatedness, and step-by-step progress. Even so, the alert teacher will be judicious in determining if additional help is needed in a particular skill or if certain pages could be omitted to save time and yet not lose any needed help.

Inventories

The teacher who is with each child from day to day is in a position to know the variations in his behavior, the severity of his frustrations, the consistency of his wholehearted efforts, and his attitudes and values—all of which cannot be assessed by testing and all of which are very important. The items that appear on most tests are important, too, and they should have a place on a total inventory. Again, it is the teacher who is in the best position to know how consistently children work diligently. She is in the favored position to evaluate each and every type of growth, development, and knowledge the child attains. Therefore, a carefully kept inventory of each child by the teacher is usually the best possible evidence of total development and readiness for next steps.

The check list previously mentioned under the heading "Toward Growing and Knowing" gives a good over-all view of each child's physical development, much of which could have taken place in the home, nursery school, and early kindergarten. The Kindergarten Inventory as shown in Appendix C is an excellent piece of material for every kindergarten teacher to duplicate and place in each child's file folder. It can offer guidance throughout the year as to her responsibilities for the child's development, and if she makes frequent checks on children's progress these inventories will be very useful in reporting to parents and in helping her to know each child's needs for help. They will be of great help to the first-grade teacher in determining individual needs and in grouping. All inventories should remain in the child's file folder and passed on to the next teacher as part of his record.

The "Primary Inventory" in Appendix F gives a check on various reading skills. It can be used toward the end of first grade to determine areas in which children need help, at the beginning of second grade to see what children have forgotten during the summer, when new children come to the class to determine their individual needs, toward the middle of second grade to see if the children are proficient in the basic skills; it can also be used toward the end of the year for any children about whom there is uncertainty as to what skills they possess. In third grade, too, newcomers might be checked on each of these reading skills. A record of his independent reading should be kept and discussed with him occasionally to broaden interests. Of course, the inventories do not check on his ability to read critically, or the actual use he makes of reading in daily living. Any notations that teachers might add to each child's file folder are valuable to the next teacher in determining his individual needs.

Occasionally we find an over-age child in fourth grade whose basic needs are revealed by the primary inventories. Until the basic help is given he cannot be expected to do well with more advanced reading. Getting worksheets or workbook pages from preceding grades after basic instruction is given may help to reenforce the learning so that he can fill in the gaps of what skills he lacks.

If children have received good instruction in the primary grades: if good attitudes are established, if concepts have been expanded and language facility has been developed, reading should serve many purposes to fourth-, fifth- and sixth-grade children. An inventory should reveal the extensive uses the child is making of reading as well as the additional skill he is acquiring. The acquiring of desirable reading tastes is very important at this age, and an inspiring teacher can do much to guide interests down desirable paths. Appendix P suggests a wide range of books at each reading level. There is so much good literature available that there should be no time for the trashy element to creep in. The alert teacher will make sure that undesirable literature does not come into the room, and she should challenge able readers to keep records of diversified areas of reading entitled, for example, "My Reading Design" (see Chapter 14). This record should go into the student's file folder.

Tests

A CHILD'S INTRODUCTION TO TESTING

Why do some college students have an emotional trauma when tests are given? There are many instances of students doing poorly on tests even though all semester they had done well in all class discussions, term projects, and reports. In the backgrounds of such students there must have been a mental fixation of fear and anxiety attached to testing. This is too bad. From the very beginning, the first test a child takes should be looked upon as a kind of game (aren't many games tests of skill of one type or another?). Tests are games to find out what we know and what we need to work on next. Many reading series have little tests to be given at certain intervals in the children's progression. Some are on vocabulary, sentence reading, story content, and various reading skills. Whatever the test, the teacher should be very familiar with how to give it. She should be relaxed and pleasant so that children feel no tension.

SUGGESTIONS FOR ADMINISTERING A TEST

1. Be sure every child has two sharpened pencils with erasers.
2. Appear calm, pleasant, and relaxed.
3. Be sure children are comfortably seated and as far apart as possible in a well-lighted, adequately ventilated room.
4. Explain that a test is a kind of game that shows what they know and what kind of help they need.
5. Explain that when they come to something they do not know they are to go on to the next item, and later if they have time they can go back and try the skipped item again.
6. Explain the test directions as simply as possible and have an example on the chalkboard.

7. Distribute the tests and ask all to leave the test face down on their desks until everyone has his and the teacher says, "Turn them over and begin." "Begin" means writing their names on the test and then proceeding.

The teacher should sit quietly where she can observe all the children. If they look up from their tests she should be ready with a reassuring smile. If the test is timed, she tells the children to stop when the time is up and collects the tests immediately. All tests should be analyzed carefully to see what mistakes are common. Plans for total group, small group and individual instruction can be made. The attitude of the teacher following a test should be expressed by saying, "Isn't it good we found out what we know and what we don't know? Now we can be helped in accordance with what we need." There should be no great emphasis on who received the highest score or how each ranked. Because learning takes place following a test, the teacher may remark, "Now we know many of the things we discovered we needed to know in that test we took. The next time we take a test it will be much easier for us and again we'll find out what we need to learn next." Teacher-made tests in which all can achieve well serve as summations of certain learnings and give children better feelings about tests than when they take standardized tests based on materials that may be very different from what they are accustomed to reading.

STANDARDIZED TESTS

Standardized tests are very carefully prepared by outstanding educators who are particularly interested in the specifics of comparison. The items within the test are carefully analyzed to be sure they are appropriate to the grade level in which they are finally placed. Trial runs are given to be sure the difficulty range is appropriate, and nationwide samplings are taken based on carefully selected communities representing cross sections of the population with all types of variations so that national norms may be established. These factors are also the basis for scoring, which comes as close as possible to a national average with all variables taken into account. Thus children taking the tests are being measured against a national average. These tests are not based on any particular reading approach or on the use of any particular reading materials. All phases of reading are included that can be measured by a written test. There are also a few oral reading tests on the market.

The best way to make a study of standardized tests is to make a collection of those most commonly used and make them available for the college class to examine over a period of time. Reading the manual and advertising folders will give valuable information about each test. The test should be a *reliable* one that gives a consistent or correct measurement of skill. It should be *valid* and measure the aptitude, ability, or skill that it claims to measure. It should be *objective* so that different scorers obtain the same score for a pupil. It should be *standardized* based on a large group of pupils so that adequate norms are provided. Most tests are prepared in three forms, each testing the same reading skills but using different words and sentences of the same difficulty.

When comparing the test scores of a class with national norms these questions should be asked:

1. How many of the children in this class are transient students?
2. At what age do children enter school in this district?
3. How many of the children in this class have below-average I.Q.'s and how many have above-average I.Q.'s?
4. How many children have language problems?
5. What social-economic advantages do these children have?
6. How much time is spent in the daily program in the teaching of reading as compared with time spent on it elsewhere?
7. How does the length of the school day and the school year compare with other schools?
8. How much absenteeism has there been?
9. How do teacher training requirements compare in this state with other states with regard to reading methods courses?
10. Have these children had a fully qualified teacher each year?
11. How do teacher salaries in this state compare with other states?
12. How do school budgets for various reading materials compare with budgets elsewhere?

Many times as a result of standardized test scores great pressures are placed on teachers and students by administrators and the community. According to the establishment of norms, half the schools must be below average and half above. Any of the above factors can cause scores to be in the lower half. Hard-working teachers and hard-working children may not always get fair recognition when a community looks at standardized test scores. Those in favored positions may get more honorable recognition than they deserve. It is easy for well-paid, highly trained teachers working in privileged communities of very stable population with children having high I.Q.'s and an abundance of opportunities, materials, and encouragement to come up with very high standardized test scores. For example, the outcome of a newly revised standardized test in one community made front-page news in the daily paper. For two years the teachers in that community had been pressured with the introduction of a new approach to the teaching of mathematics, and a considerable amount of time was devoted to it. Suddenly early in the year a standardized reading test was given unexpectedly before first-grade children had synthesized their various reading skills on unfamiliar reading materials. The resulting scores were slightly below national norms in first grade, and the community was quick to blame the schools. No consideration was given to the number of Mexican children with language problems who were in the schools or any of the other factors that influence test scores and averages. Sometimes the administration of standardized tests can be more harmful than helpful in a school system.

A positive result of such tests would be analysis of the strengths and weaknesses of the class as a whole and of each individual. It may give the teacher an indication of how children apply the word recognition techniques and other skills of reading to new and unfamiliar material. It would be best for a committee of teachers to select the tests they felt to be most valuable in their teaching situation, but this is not always the way tests are selected.

ELEMENTARY READING TESTS

Kindergarten Tests

American School Reading Readiness Test (Public Schools Publishing Co., 1955, 35¢ for specimen set)
Abilities measured:
Vocabulary
Visual Discrimination
Recognition of words
Following directions
Memory of geometric forms

Gates Reading Readiness Tests (Teachers College, Bureau of Publications, Columbia University, 1939, 30¢ for specimen set)
Abilities measured:
Picture directions
Word matching
Word-card matching

Rhyming
Letters and numbers

Elementary Reading Tests (prices quoted are subject to change)

Harrison-Stroud Reading Readiness Profiles (Houghton Mifflin, 1956, 80¢ for specimen set)
Abilities measured:
Visual discrimination
Using context clues
Auditory discrimination
Using context and auditory clues
Using symbols
Giving the names of letters

Lee-Clark Reading Readiness Test (California Test Bureau, 1951, 25¢ for specimen set)
Abilities measured:
Visual discrimination in letters
Conceptual maturity
Vocabulary-word forms
Following instructions

Metropolitan Readiness Test (World Book Co., 1950, 35¢ for specimen set)
Abilities measured:
Reading readiness
Number readiness
Drawing a man

Monroe Reading Aptitude Tests (Houghton Mifflin, 1939, 40¢ for specimen set)
Abilities measured:
Visual and auditory discrimination
Motor control
Speed and articulation in speech
Language development

Murphy-Durrell Diagnostic Reading Readiness Test (World Book Co., 1949, 35¢ for specimen set)
Abilities measured:
Auditory discrimination
Visual discrimination
Learning rate

Van Wagenen Reading Readiness Scales (Psycho-Ed, Research Lab., 1954, 50¢ for specimen set)
Abilities measured:
Listening vocabulary
Range of information
Perception of relations
Memory span for ideas
Word discrimination

What Do Diagnostic Reading Tests Diagnose?
SKILLS INCLUDED IN SIX ANALYTICAL READING MEASURES

	Botel Reading Inventory	Developmental Reading Tests — Silent Reading Diagnostic Tests	Durrell Analysis of Reading Difficulty	Gilmore Oral Reading Test	Diagnostic Reading Scale	Gates-McKillop Reading Diagnostic Tests
Silent Reading Comprehension			X		X	
Oral Reading Comprehension			X	X	X	X
Oral Reading Accuracy			X	X	X	
Oral Reading Rate			X	X	X	
Listening Comprehension						
Word Recognition (oral)	X		X		X	X
Word Recognition (silent)		X				
Word recognition in context (silent)		X				
Phrase Reading (oral)						X
Recognition of phonetic word elements (oral)	X				X	X
Recognition of phonetic word parts (silent & listening)		X	X			
Root Words (silent)		X				
Rhyming Words (listening or silent)	X	X				
Word Opposites (listening and/or silent)	X					

Skill						
Reversible Words (silent)	X					
Visual memory of words (silent)						
Word Blending (silent)	X	X				
Word Blending (oral)		X		X		X
Saying Syllables		X		X		X
Number and accent syllables (listening)			X			
Syllabication (silent)	X	X				
Identifying Letter Sounds (listening)	X	X				
Identifying Beginning Word Sounds (listening)	X	X		X		X
Identifying Word Endings (listening)	X	X		X		X
Saying Letter Sounds		X			X	X
Identifying consonant blends and digraphs (listening)	X		X			
Saying consonant blends and/or digraphs		X			X	X
Identifying long and short vowels (oral)		X			X	X
Identifying long and short vowels (listening)	X		X			X
Naming capital and lower case letters (oral)	X	X				X
Spelling (listening)		X				X
Spelling (oral)		X				X

SOURCE: Thaddeus M. Trela, "Skills Included in Six Analytical Reading Measures." *Elementary English* (April, 1966), p. 371. Reprinted with the permission of the National Council of Teachers of English and Thaddeus M. Trela.

Oral—oral response required of one being tested.
Listening—said by tester, testee marks answer in test booklet.
Silent—from directions in the test booklet testee responds in booklet.

In selecting a test it is important that the pictures a child is to see and understand be large and precise enough so that he can look for details without eye strain. Some tests require as much as ninety minutes' time, and it is best to give children breaks between parts of the test so they do not become too tired. Study test manuals carefully.

Elementary Grade Reading Tests

(Prices quoted are subject to change.)

American School Achievement Tests, Grades 2–3; Grades 4–6 (Public School Publishing Co., 1958, 35¢ per specimen set)

California Reading Test, Grades 1–2; Grades 3–4; Grades 4–6 (California Test Bureau, 1957, 50¢ per specimen set)

Durrell-Sullivan Reading Capacity and Achievement, Grades 2.5–4.5 (35¢ per set); Grades 3–6 (50¢ per set) (World Book Co., 1945)

Developmental Reading Tests, Grades 4–6 (Lyons & Carnahan, 1956, 50¢ per specimen set)

Gates Primary Reading Test, Grade 1–2.5; Advanced Primary Grade 2.5–3; Gates Basic Reading Tests, Grades 3–8 (Bureau of Publications, Teacher's College, Columbia University, 1958, 40¢ per specimen set)

Iowa Test of Basic Skills, Grades 3–5; Grades 5–9 (Houghton Mifflin Co., 1956, $3.00 per specimen set)

Iowa Silent Reading Test (World Book Co., 1943, 35¢ per specimen set)

Lee-Clark Reading Test, Primer, Grade 1; First Reader, Grades 1–2 (California Test Bureau, 1958, 25¢ per specimen set)

Metropolitan Reading Tests, Grades 1, 2 (25¢ per set); Grades 3–4 and Grades 5–7.5 (35¢ per set) (World Book Co., 1950)

SRA Achievement Series, Grades 2–4; 4–6 (Science Research Associates; 1957, 35¢ per specimen set)

Stanford Achievement Test, Grades 1 through 6 (World Book Co., 1966, 35¢ per specimen set)

Sequential Tests of Educational Progress (Reading, Educational Testing Service, 1957, $1.25 per specimen set)

These tests check on various aspects of vocabulary development, comprehension, and study skills in different ways and each has certain strengths unique to that particular test. It is a good idea to make careful comparisons and decide which test is most complete and best suited to your needs.

A Student Profile

Test results, reading records, oral reading inventory, silent reading inventories, and teacher's observations of a child's attitude toward reading, his uses of reading, his ability to be selective, his critiques and his breadth of interests in reading are all factors that go into the total picture of a child and his progress in reading. Through this information next steps can be planned, and reading can continue to be interesting, challenging and purposeful. All such information should go into the child's permanent record file so that the next teacher can profit from it.

When United States norms were established for the revised Stanford Achievement Tests it was proven that children over the United States are reading better now than they were fifteen years ago. At the fifth grade level children are one half year advanced in reading over what they were fifteen years ago, and at the eighth grade level they are advanced by a full year.[2]

Suggestions for Class Participation and Discussion

1. How do you feel about taking tests and being evaluated by testing?
2. How would you go about determining a child's progress?
3. It is best to wait until toward the end of the year to give first-grade children a standardized test. Why?
4. Examine various readiness tests. Which one do you prefer? Why?
5. Defend your reasons for selecting a particular test for first grade.
6. Select a test for the grade you intend to teach and defend it.
7. How might a teacher come to know how much use a child makes of reading in daily life?
8. What records would you want to keep to be sure you had a complete profile of a child's progress in all the objectives of reading?
9. How could you enhance a child's delight in reading?
10. React to the quotation at the end of this chapter.

Bibliography

Austin, Mary C., Bush, Clifford L., and Huebner, Mildred H. *Reading Evaluation*. New York: The Ronald Press, 1961.

Austin, Mary C., and Morrison, Mildred B. *The First R*. New York: Macmillan, 1963.

Blair, Glenn. *Diagnostic and Remedial Reading*. New York: Macmillan, 1956.

Bond, Guy, and Tinker, Miles. *Reading Difficulties: Their Diagnosis and Correction*. New York: Appleton-Century-Crofts, 1957.

Bradfield, Luther. *Teaching in Modern Elementary Schools*. Columbus, Ohio: Merrill, 1964 (listing of publishers of tests and addresses).

[2] Richard Madden, in a report at a Reading Workshop in San Diego, Calif., June, 1966.

CHAUNCEY, HENRY, and DUBLIN, JOHN. *Testing: Its Place in Education Today*. New York: Harper & Row, 1963.

deHIRSCH, KATRINA. *Predicting Reading Failure*. New York: Harper & Row, 1966.

DOLCH, E. W. *A Manual for Remedial Reading*. Champaign, Ill.: Garrard, 1945.

DURRELL, DONALD. *Improving Reading Instruction*. Tarrytown-on-Hudson, N.Y.: World Book, 1956.

ERICKSON, MARION J. *The Mentally Retarded Child in the Classroom*. New York: Macmillan, 1965.

FERNALD, GRACE M. *Remedial Techniques in Basic School Subjects*. New York: McGraw-Hill, 1943.

HEILMAN, ARTHUR. *Principles and Practices of Teaching Reading*. Columbus, Ohio: Merrill, 1961.

National Education Association, Department of Elementary School Principals. *Reading for Today's Children*, 34th Yearbook, 1955.

REEVES, RUTH. *The Teaching of Reading in Our Schools*. New York: Macmillan, 1966.

ROBINSON, HELEN. *Corrective Reading in Classroom and Clinic*. Chicago: University of Chicago Press, 1953.

————. *Why Pupils Fail in Reading*. Chicago: University of Chicago Press, 1946.

SLEISENGER, LENORE. *Guidebook for the Volunteer Reading Teacher*. Teacher's College Bureau of Publications, New York, 1965.

STRANG, RUTH M., and BRACKEN, DOROTHY. *Making Better Readers*. Boston: Heath, 1957.

TORRANCE, E. PAUL. *Gifted Children in the Classroom*. New York: Macmillan, 1965.

WOOLF, MAURICE D., and WOOLF, JEANNE A. *Remedial Reading Teaching and Treatment*. New York: McGraw-Hill, 1957.

ZINTZ, MILES. *Corrective Reading*. Dubuque, Iowa: William C. Brown, 1966.

Refer to the *Education Index* for many current articles on evaluation.

CHAPTER 13

Common Problems in Learning to Read

By the time they are five years old, disadvantaged children of almost every kind are typically one or two years retarded in language development. This is supported by virtually any index of language development one cares to look at.[1]

Retardation

Children are generally considered to be *retarded* in the test program aspects of reading if their test scores indicate that they test one and a half to two years or more below the test norm of their grade. In a sense disadvantaged children coming into first grade are retarded before they ever start the formal aspects of learning to read. This is especially true when we consider the result of research carried out by Gertrude Whipple in the Detroit Public Schools.

[1] Carl Bereiter, *Language Programs for the Disadvantaged* (Richard Corbin and Muriel Crosby, ed.), Champaign, Ill., National Council for Teachers of English, 1965, p. 196.

When the words used by the children living in low socio-economic urban areas were checked against the vocabulary contained in three leading series of first-grade readers, it was found that the subjects used approximately 50 percent of the words in the readers. Furthermore, the subjects failed to use 20–50 percent of five word lists (Dolch, Gates, International Kindergarten Union, Rinsland and Thorndike) recommended for primary grades. Therefore, the vocabulary of the subjects of the study differs substantially from both first-grade readers and standard primary-grade word lists.[2]

To have meaning to the child and to be important to him, reading must be based on his language and the experiences it represents. Commercial reading materials are prepared with vocabulary and content based on what is considered the language and experience level of the grade for which it is intended. So are the tests. There is often a gap between the children and the materials before some children actually begin first grade.

This does not mean that all children in a class should be delayed in starting to read from basic materials nor does it mean that the disadvantaged children cannot be started to read. It does mean that much time must be devoted to the expansion of concepts and development of language with those who need it in addition to the normal expansion one would expect to work on with all children. Chapter 5 gives many suggestions for the development of language. Many of the activities suggested in Chapter 6 can be used. In addition much use should be made of films followed by discussion in which children do the talking. These children need to do and talk about many things. Identifying pictures in many kinds of catalogs, workbooks, magazines, and picture dictionaries with freedom to talk about colors, uses, classifications, and the "hows," "whens," "wheres," and "whys" of picture content can be beneficial to these children. Privileged children should often visit with underprivileged as they look at pictures, have free play, or work on little projects.

Speech problems are often a part of the language problem and it is well to review parts of Chapter 5. It is especially important for adult speech improvement classes to be made available to parents of children who use especially poor English. It can be a major contribution to the child's future opportunities.

Too often, little thought is given to elements of slow learning

2 Dominic Thomas, "Oral Language of Culturally Disadvantaged Kindergarten Children," in *New Directions in Reading* (Ralph Staiger and David Sohn, eds.), New York, Bantam Books, 1967.

until the children reach third or fourth grade. Here retardation of a year and a half is not only recognizable from tests but from the handicaps the children experience in their reading deficiency in other areas of the curriculum. They can not read arithmetic problems, they have difficulty with social science and science books. By this time they are aware of their weaknesses and their attitude toward reading is negative. Each year that children's problems are allowed to go unheeded and unresolved the greater will be the retardation and the more negative will become the children's behavior. They do not like what they cannot do well and their frustrations are often expressed through disregard, mischief, or truancy.

CAUSES OF RETARDATION

In addition to language deficiency there are many other contributary causes of retardation. Usually more than one cause is involved. Many causes are interrelated—that is, a physical handicap causing retarded learning can also cause emotional instability and faulty attitudes. Reading progress may be blocked or arrested at any stage so it behooves all teachers to be alert to any indication of a child's progress not measuring up to what his potentialities might be. The sooner causes can be determined the sooner progress can be reinstated and other effects avoided. Chapters 4 and 5 emphasized the importance of detecting symptoms of physical imperfections and weaknesses. It is a tremendous advantage to a child if these can be corrected before the first grade.

Reading and learning clinics should have on call an ophthalmologist, an otologist, a neurologist, a pediatrician, a psychiatrist, a psychologist, and a reading specialist. With this kind of interdisciplinary approach to learning problems, a child has every chance to have his learning problems analyzed and diagnosed. A poor physical check-up is worse than none at all because parents and teachers after such examinations are likely to rule out all possibility of physical factors that may continue to interfere with progress.

In referring a child to a clinic it is important to submit reports of any observations that might be useful to the examiners. These should include parents observations as well as those made at school.

On the basis of everyday patterns, a discerning teacher may detect evidences, more or less predictive, of potential reading disabilities—

specific weaknesses in drawing and in form perception; ill defined handedness; reduced acuity; atypical directionalities in movement patterns, and so on. When the norms of visual behavior are more widely known by teachers and parents, it will be possible to use naturalistic observations of spontaneous behavior for the benefit of children who need early guidance in solving their visual problems. Such observations should both precede and supplement formal visual skill tests. They become doubly important, under professional guidance, for appraising the responses of the child to lens assistance and to special visual training procedures. Naturalistic observations of the spontaneous child is at times more valuable than technical observation, because it brings into view the total child and his unitary action system.[3]

A complete diagnosis takes the following factors into account:

PHYSICAL DEFECTS   *Sight.* The Executive Committee of the Section on Ophthalmology of the American Medical Association has issued a good definition of visual efficiency:

Visual efficiency is defined as that degree of percentage of the competence of the eyes to accomplish their physiologic functions, including (1) corrected visual acuity, for distance and near, (2) visual fields, (3) ocular motility with absence of diplopia, and (4) binocular vision. Although these factors do not possess an equal degree of importance, vision is imperfect without the coordinated action of all. Other functions, although secondary and dependent, are recognized as important, such as color perception, adaptation to light or dark, and accommodation.[4]

Beginning teachers of reading are not expected to understand all that is implied in the above paragraph. Its purpose is to make it clear that merely testing a child's vision with a Snellen chart is not enough. Ophthalmologists and educators working together can help children with vision problems to correct what is possible to correct and to adjust to what adaptations need to be made. It is the expert clinician whose services must be sought. Marion Frostig of California has developed visual perception tests for reading clinic use and is devoting much time in further study of children with reading problems due to faulty vision. Others are coming into the field and children will benefit from the results of such research as teachers are advised by clinics as to what adjustments need to be made in the classroom for those children.

Defects of Hearing. The following summary gives us insight into

3 Arnold Gesell, Frances Ilg, and Glenna Bullis, *Vision, Its Development in Infant and Child,* New York, Harper & Row, 1949, p. 284.

4 Delwyn G. Schubert, *The Doctor Eyes the Poor Reader,* Springfield, Ill., Charles C Thomas, 1957, pp. 14–15.

the relationship of hearing loss in its broadest sense to aspects of reading:

Hearing losses commonly fall into two categories—perceptive (nerve) loss and conduction type loss. Conduction loss is a loss in loudness due to the fact that the sound is blocked in its transmission to the inner ear. Examples of the causes of such loss are wax in the ear, otitis media damage, and otosclerosis. Nerve loss is due to actual deterioration or lesions within the inner ear structure—especially the organ of Corti. Neural pathways leading to the brain also may be involved. Usually the child with a nerve loss hears vowel sounds but cannot hear many or all the voiceless consonants. These include p, t, h, f, th, s, sh and ch. Difficulties with voiced consonants also are likely. These involve the following: b, d, v, th, z, zh, j and w. Some typical confusions growing out of the inability to hear voiced consonants are d for g, b for d, v for z, etc. Lastly, the nerve-deaf child tends to confuse nasal sounds such as m, n, and ng.[5]

Again the purpose of the paragraph is not to burden the beginning student of reading with clinical detail but to show that a watch test in diagnosing hearing loss is not sufficient and that hearing loss is a decided handicap in learning and in teaching phonics and reading. The teacher's role is to detect hearing difficulty and to see that a referral is made to a competent clinician.

Inconsistent Dominance. One of the controversial issues of our time in the field of reading is the significance of lateral dominance. By this we mean that there is disagreement as to whether a strong preference for use of the right hand and right eye is advantageous in reading. There are those who feel that because the natural use of body muscles is from the center of the body outward on either side it would be advantageous in reading from left to right for the right eye to be dominant. There is further argument with regard to dominance in the following statement:

The most widely discussed theory of dominance is that of Dr. Samuel T. Orton, a neurologist. Orton started with the generally accepted fact that the right hemisphere (side) of the brain controls the left side of the body. He assumed that the right-sided person develops memory traces for printed words in a part of the left hemisphere, and also develops memory traces in the right hemisphere which are mirror images of those on the dominant side. When the clearly right-sided person reads, only the memory traces on the dominant side are aroused. In the consistently left-sided person, the right hemisphere is similarly dominant. If, however, the individual fails to develop a consistent dominance of one side over

5 Delwyn G. Schubert, *ibid.*, pp. 14–15.

the other, difficulties arise. In that case, according to Orton, there will be confusion and conflict in learning to read and spell and the reversal errors will be prevalent. Orton suggested the term strephosymbolia (meaning twisted symbols) to describe what he calls "the reading disability" and seemed to assume that poor reading which can be explained on other grounds is of little importance.

The present status of the Orton theory is still that of an unproved hypothesis. While it has met with fairly wide acceptance among neurologists, its basic neurological assumptions have been challenged by studies of the effects of brain operations.[6]

A very recent discussion of the topic has this statement:

The research evidence on laterality has neither conclusively supported nor refuted either position. However, it is interesting to note that diagnostic techniques and teaching methods to counteract the effects that are supposed to accrue from a lack of laterality have already been devised and are presently used by some public and private institutions. Probably the most widely publicized program is that of Delacato. He has set up a program for developing dominance based on appropriate sequence in body positions while sleeping, coordination of the body while crawling or walking, and visual training for the sighting eye (such as one would use when looking into a microscope). Leavell developed a method for using a stereoscope to train the nondominant eye to coordinate with the dominant hand. Barger reported a program to train children who make reversal errors to read mirror writing and then switch to normal print. All these programs claim to achieve outstanding results.[7]

It will be interesting to watch current magazines for further research on dominance.

In some cases parents and teachers may observe no symptoms of physical causes of retardation. Yet specialists may find thyroid or endocrine gland malfunction to be contributing causes of slow learning. A child deserves a physical examination before he, parents, and teachers get discouraged with extremely slow progress.

INTELLECTUAL DEFECTS An intelligence test is usually administered by a psychologist who has had training and experience in administering that kind of test. The score yields the child's mental age or what is known as M.A. This mental age is divided by the child's

[6] Albert J. Harris, *How to Increase Reading Ability*, New York, David McKay, 1961, pp. 251–52.

[7] Karen Tinker, "The Role of Lateral Dominance in Reading," from *New Directions in Reading* (Ralph Staiger and David Sohn, eds.), New York, Bantam Books, 1967, p. 180.

chronological age or what is known as C.A. and the result is multiplied by 100 to do away with the decimal. The result is the child's intelligence quotient or I.Q. I.Q. levels are classified as follows:[8]

Idiot	0–25
Imbecile	25–50
Moron	50–70
Borderline	70–80
Low Normal	80–90
Normal	90–110
Superior	110–120
Very Superior	120–130
Near Genius	140 and over

Children with I.Q.'s under 70 are usually in special classes and seldom can read much above fourth-grade level. It is understandable that children with I.Q.'s of 80 can not be expected to read as well as children with I.Q.'s of 120 or more. Neither is it satisfactory for children with I.Q.'s of 120 or more to be reading at or below grade norms. They should be stimulated to do much better.

Until recently it was felt that intelligence tests were very reliable and that a child's I.Q. remained stable, except for the very young child. With the advent of the Head-Start programs and with an emphasis on language development it is evident that extent of experience and language facility can have great bearing on intelligence test scores. Such conclusions are very reasonable because testing is dependent on these two factors. The same holds true for success in reading. It is a challenge to all educators of young children to give them every opportunity to have rich and varied experiences, to talk freely about what they see and do, and to think beyond mere fact. An able teacher must help children to be curious, to get at the how and why relationships of what they encounter, to be inquiring, to consider cause and effect, and both to question and appreciate. Children with I.Q.'s over 120 should be afforded opportunities for advanced thinking, creativity, and self-selection of materials. One can never be sure of the potentialities of an underachiever and no child should be ignored because of a low I.Q.

EMOTIONAL DEFECTS Children with emotional problems have difficulty settling down to the confinement of reading. A pediatrician may advise against having such children start reading until they have been helped in other ways. On the other hand, failure in reading can cause tensions and emotional trauma. Children are sensitive.

8 Delwyn G. Schubert, *op. cit.*, p. 28.

When other children are reading and doing other things they cannot do, they feel neglected. A poor report card with displeasure at home could cause a dislike for school. Many would rather stay home than face tasks that are too difficult or be with children they consider superior. Attitudes become additional deterrents to progress and a child's rebellious ways may cause some teachers to give up in their unsuccessful attempts to help.

A child's image of himself is extremely important in his relationships with his teacher and everyone else. If he feels inferior, incompetent, and neglected, he is likely to withdraw or exhibit antagonistic behavior.

Although competition frequently creates a situation that appears highly stimulating, its effects on those who are cast in inferior roles are likely to be destructive. A fifth grade teacher once reminded the group that no physically disabled youngster would be expected to participate in a running race; yet frequently children with learning disabilities are placed in competitive settings that are equally inappropriate.[9]

That is why much emphasis is placed on challenging children to compete with their own previous records or achievement. Sometimes there is stimulation in children competing with those with whom they are evenly matched.

Reading is not an entirely relaxed activity. If there is interest and enthusiasm behind the child's efforts, there is and should be a reasonable amount of anxiety. However, expectations beyond his ability to achieve can cause too much anxiety.

Neville, Pfost, and Dobbs report in the June, 1967, issue of *The Reading Newsreport:*

A group of 54 boys from seven through fourteen years of age were enrolled in a special six weeks summer reading course. They were tested with the Test Anxiety Scale for Children (TASC) by Sarason. On the basis of the TASC the group was labeled LA (low-anxiety), MA (middle-anxiety) and HA (high-anxiety). Those labeled MA made gains in comprehension significantly greater than those labeled LA or HA. There was no significant difference in vocabulary learning between the groups.

The hypothesis suggested by the authors is that vocabulary learning is less complex a task than development of comprehension skills and that too little or too much anxiety has a greater effect upon the more complex task.

[9] George Manolakes, *The Elementary School We Need.* Washington, D.C., Association for Supervision and Curriculum Development, 1965, p. 35.

Sex Differences

Questions have been raised for some time with regard to the higher incidence of retardation in reading among boys than among girls. Recent pertinent statements include the following:

It is interesting to note that large school systems report that boys make up 75% to 80% of all reading disability at the upper elementary level. Several past research studies overwhelmingly supported the fact that girls maintain a significant superiority over boys in beginning reading. Arthur Gates, who reported a study involving over 6,000 boys and 6,000 girls in grades 2 through 8, analyzed the reading test scores of these students. Again, the scores of the girls were significantly higher than those of the boys at all grade levels. Gates suggested that the differences might be due to environmental rather than hereditary causes. Perhaps girls experienced life situations involving greater opportunities, incentives and respect for reading. Different role conceptions in our culture may cause the act of reading to lack importance for boys in general.[10]

International Reading Association reading research (explained earlier in this book) has this to say with regard to sex differences in reading:

Another general finding was that girls tended to have a greater degree of readiness for reading at the beginning of first grade and tended to read at a higher level of reading at the end of the first grade. In most cases differences in reading achievement which favored girls at the end of the year disappeared when criterion scores were adjusted for differences in prereading ability. A related finding in this investigation was that none of the treatments had a unique effect on the achievement of boys and girls. That is, no significant treatment by sex interactions were found to exist. On the average, girls tended to read better in all programs.[11]

Helen Robinson has conducted research in this area and has reported similar findings.

Jo Stanchfield wondered if separating girls and boys into classes of their own sex would make a difference in reading achievement. She reports the following:

10 Jo M. Stanchfield, "Do Girls Learn to Read Better Than Boys in the Primary Grades," in *New Directions in Reading*, Ralph Staiger and David Sohn, eds., New York, Bantam Books, 1967, p. 59.

11 Guy Bond and Robert Dykstra, "The National First Grade Study—Report on the Findings," *The Reading Newsreport*, Wethersfield, Conn., Vol. 1, No. 7 (June 1967), p. 38.

Using 550 children in the first grades of the Los Angeles City Schools, reading was taught in sex segregated groups. Care was taken to provide a wide range of socioeconomic levels. Two reading periods were offered, one in the morning and one in the afternoon. The outcome of this study was that, after statistical analyses of reading achievement and reading growth, boys taught in the absence of girls did not show more significant gains in achievement or in growth than boys taught in mixed sex groupings. Again, the girls as a group achieved more significantly than boys and showed greater reading growth.[12]

In the Stanchfield study teachers reported that boys were so extremely active compared with girls that they lacked the verbal facility of girls; they were less adequate in articulation, enunciation, pronunciation, and auditory discrimination; they listened less intently; they had a shorter attention span; their interest was more difficult to arouse and sustain; they were less motivated to please the teacher and to assume responsibility; and they had less self-direction for the act of reading than girls.

With these findings in mind perhaps we should ask ourselves, "Should we expect equal achievement in reading of boys and girls?" "What difference does it make if girls scores are a little higher?" We do know that boys learn to read, and more appealing materials are being produced for them. Let's not lose sight of the fact that boys need muscular activity and that long periods of confinement in forcing them toward greater achievement in reading can cause disinterest and resentment. Short periods of instruction with immediate goals, stimulating content related to boys' interests and recognition of accomplishment will help to keep boys interested and achieving.

Types of Reading Difficulties

REVERSALS

Some children are inclined to say "was" for "saw" and vice versa; "no" and "on" are often confusing and "now" and "won" may sometimes cause trouble. A vision irregularity may be the cause and an ophthalmologist should check a child's eyes when other

---

[12] Jo M. Stanchfield, "Do Girls Learn to Read Better Than Boys in the Primary Grades?" *New Directions in Reading*, (Ralph Staiger and David Sohn, eds.), New York, Bantam Books, 1967, p. 60.

corrective techniques are not effective. Maturity seems to be one element to be considered.

Professor Edfeldt of the University of Stockholm made a study of reversals and made this concluding statement, "The reversal tendency occurs commonly during the kindergarten age, during which it gradually disappears," and "reversal tendency normally seems to have vanished by the ages of eight and one-half to nine years.[13]

From this study it would seem that children with the reversal problem may have been pushed into reading at too early an age. It is another strong argument to delay book reading until children's eyes are ready for it.

In teaching beginning reading much emphasis should be placed on the first letter of words and on viewing the word from left to right. Thus, no mention was made of final blends, word endings, or appearances of rhyming words in the first experiences that children have with printed words. There is a danger in directing children's attention to the ending of words until reading from left to right is very well established. When the reversal tendency is observed, take one of the words and teach it well, completely disregarding the other for a time. In the case of "was" and "saw," the word "was" is more common and should be used for teaching purposes. Write it on the board and ask the child to trace over the first letter and have him say the word as he gets the feel of that letter. Place great emphasis on observing the first letter of each and every word. The word may be printed on a card and the first letter may be cut from sandpaper and pasted on so the child has the additional feel of roughness as he rubs his finger over it in forming a mental image of that first letter. Throughout the day and for several days make frequent reference to that word and its first letter. By getting this one word thoroughly established in the child's mind, he can no longer get it confused with any other, unless there is vision irregularity.

When words that look much alike such as: *went, want, were, where, this,* and *these* are confusing to children, again it is a good idea to teach one very thoroughly and then move on to another so that a child cannot possibly confuse the one he knows so well. It is somewhat like meeting two people at the same time and noting that they look much alike. If we can get to know one of them very well, we are no longer confused but if we always have a contact with them together we are likely to continue to be confused.

13 Delwyn G. Schubert, *op. cit.,* p. 25.

LIP MOVEMENT

Unless silent reading is introduced along with the first recognition of printed words, many children are likely to use lip movement and some are even likely to vocalize or move throat muscles in their attempts at silent reading. It must be explained that we can know what a word is by looking at it with our eyes and not using our lips, tongue or throat at all. The early establishment of this quality of silent reading can prevent lip movement and it facilitates speed of silent reading considerably. If a child is discovered to use lip movement, give him the simple explanation of how silent reading can be done by using only our eyes. Then ask him to place a finger on his lips to keep himself from using them. Children usually overcome this habit quite easily.

WORD-BY-WORD READING

When too much emphasis in beginning reading is placed on individual words or when a strong alphabetic, phonemic, or phonetic approach is used, children may become so conscious of each letter within words that the fluent quality of meaningful reading is lost. In such cases a teacher must do much work with phrases and short sentences. List such word groupings or clusters on the chalkboard as:

on the table	the dog
over the wall	a little ball
behind the door	a big book
under the chair	a pretty vine

Then challenge the children to find:

A phrase that tells where a vase of flowers might be. (If they read it word by word, ask them to tell you the answer first and then read it the way they told it.)
A phrase that tells where a broom might be kept.
A phrase that tells where a boy might like to climb.
A phrase that tells where a ball of yarn might roll.
Challenge them to read the other groupings of words that fluently.

Developing some experience stories in which the content is well known may help such children to read more fluently. They need to become more conscious of grouping words for meanings and of the natural patterning in our language. Verse speaking, story telling, and dramatizations help if the child's manner of speaking is at fault as well as his manner of reading. (See Appendix K for more suggestions for improving oral language.)

POOR COMPREHENSION AND INTERPRETATION

The comprehension part of a reading test is probably the best indication of what a child is capable of doing with the reading skills he has. If too much emphasis is placed on the decoding process, comprehension is likely to be low in relation to the other part scores. This is why so much emphasis was placed on word games and early reading experiences in which meaning is foremost in the child's mind. The symbols can be looked upon as direct clues to meanings and the child is then ready to use the meanings in his thinking—to make assessments, associations, or projection of thought.

If children come into the class without this kind of background, help must be given to establish a reading-for-meaning attitude. Experiences such as those in Chapters 6, 7, 8, and 11 and those in Appendixes D, I, and J are helpful. The experiences should use words at the maturity level of the child. They could be words pertaining to sports or whatever other interest the child might have. When he is given simple materials to read, he should be encouraged to ask himself frequently, "What am I reading about?" "What does this tell me?" Thought questions should become progressively more complex. At first simple recall may be an immediate goal. *How, when, where,* and *who* questions are of this type. Then cause and effect relationships should be a goal. Of course, much depends on the type of material that is being read and whether it lends itself to this development. Thus, flexibility in wide use of materials and techniques is important. Critical analysis of material, selection of facts relating to an important problem, and appreciation of an author's style, his selection of words, his phrasing, and the feeling he leaves with his reader are all important aspects of comprehension and interpretation. Oral reading done well by the teacher followed by general class discussion can often be good introduction to individual endeavors in the more complex thought processes.

SLOW RATE

There has been much controversy over speed reading at the adult level. It has been making its way into the elementary grades as well. In colleges where fast reading is important there are special courses in speed reading. College students read from 250 to 300 words a minute and speed courses have brought many students up to about 700 words. Many reading experts claim that beyond that level the participant is only skimming and cannot possibly comprehend the total content at greater speeds. However, Evelyn Wood and Frederick Babbel, insisting that speeds up to 2,200 words a minute can be achieved, have instituted schools to teach adults to read that fast. Their theory is that the eye must focus down the center of the page and that peripheral vision grasps the content of the entire page. The important considerations are comprehension and emotional stability. Speed at what price must always be our concern. It is more natural for some people to move any type of muscle faster than certain other people. We should expect some people to read faster than others.

The normal beginning reader makes an average of two fixations per word or, in other words, sees or recognizes less than one whole word at each fixation. This statistic was determined by photographing the reading of over a thousand first graders by *The Reading Eye*, a camera made especially for this purpose. In this country-wide testing, each child read a selection of approximately one hundred words. During the reading the average child made 224 fixations, about two fixations per word or an eye span of 0.45 of a word. This average span of recognition increases very slowly to 1.11 or slightly more than one word per fixation, for normal college students reading at an average speed of 280 words per minute. The average number of words seen at each fixation does not reach one whole word until the eleventh grade.[14]

In the case of young children, security in word recognition, facility in grouping words in accordance with our natural language patterns, adequate backgrounds of experience to make the content meaningful, and well-written manuscript are all conducive to fluent and rapid reading. If a child's interest is intent enough, he will hasten of his own accord to accomplish the purpose reading helps to serve. Much reading material is not intended to be read fast. The purpose for reading must somewhat govern the rate.

[14] George D. Spache, *Reading in the Elementary School*, Boston, Allyn & Bacon, 1964, p. 9.

A child needs to pause frequently in his reading and ask himself:

What have I been reading about?
Why is this important to me?
Is this a principle or fact worth remembering?
Is this character or these characters people I should like to know?
 What mental image do I have of them? Are they acting wisely?
What is the author trying to do in this story? What is his theme?
Have I had comparable experiences?
Is there any pleasing quality in the way words are used?

Thus children can savor what they are reading and speed is of minor importance. Children must be helped to know what material needs very careful scrutiny in accordance with the purpose it serves. Some children need more time to grasp ideas and to do it without emotional stress. Our aim should be to help each child to have the facilities that will enable him to read at his own optimum rate in accordance with the purpose and materials he chooses to use.

HESITATION, REPETITION, AND WORD DIFFICULTIES

The child who is not sure of each next word is likely to use some device to attempt to cover up his inadequacies. Repetition or going back to the beginning of a sentence for a fresh start is one such technique. Some children will hesitate or vocalize with "uh," "uh," or stammer over the initial sound of the word. Much of this in a child's reading indicates that the child is attempting to read material that is too difficult. The child may be given help with the difficult vocabulary before he proceeds, he may be given assistance with phonics or word analysis clues, or he may be discouraged from reading further in the material that he has chosen to read and be helped to find other material within his reading range.

Sir Fred Schonell of England was the first to develop a quick assessment test based on words used in basic reading materials commonly used in England. Lists of ten words at each reading level were taken from the materials. They were representative of the difficulty of the particular level from which they were taken. A child was asked to read from these lists of words beginning with the first level. Whenever the child missed more than two words, he was started with materials at that level. Many clinics in the United States have developed similar listings of words representative of commonly used materials in this country for use in selecting books to fit the child's level of reading ability. The following quick assessment inventory was developed at the clinic at San Diego State College, San Diego, California.

San Diego State College—Quick Assessment[15]

The following is an oral screening device for use in classrooms and clinics. A skilled clinician can in a matter of 3 minutes ascertain a reading level and can gain some knowledge of the student's word attack skills.

Each list of 10 words should be typed on an index card so that the

PP	Primer	1
see	you	road
play	come	live
me	not	thank
at	with	when
run	jump	bigger
go	help	how
and	is	always
look	work	night
can	are	spring
here	this	today

2	3	4
our	city	decided
please	middle	served
myself	moment	amazed
town	frightened	silent
early	exclaimed	wrecked
send	several	improved
wide	lonely	certainly
believe	drew	entered
quietly	since	realized
carefully	straight	interrupted

5	6
scanty	bridge
business	commercial
develop	abolish
considered	trucker
discussed	apparatus
behaved	elementary
splendid	comment
acquainted	necessity
escaped	gallery
grim	relativity

[15] Courtesy of Margaret LaPray, Supervisor, Learning Difficulties, and Professor at San Diego State College, San Diego, California.

child doesn't ever see more than 10 words at a time. Write in the words that the child substitutes.

When a child's level of reading ability is ascertained, a wide variety of materials may be made available for him to make his own personal selection for individualized reading. If an inventory such as the one in Appendix F is used, a teacher will know what kind of individual or group instruction the child needs. He may be included with whatever other individuals or in whatever small groups need the same kind of assistance. Giving him an opportunity to select his own book for independent reading may open a door of interest that he may never before have experienced. H. L. Mencken refers to his discovery of Huckleberry Finn in this way, "It was probably the most stupendous day of my whole life."[16] Many children and adults have attested to the fact that a certain book made the process of reading suddenly become important—important enough that they were ready for any kind of help the teacher had to offer. Thus, it is important for every classroom to have an array of captivating books to magnetize young readers.

Dyslexia

Dyslexia is most succinctly defined as failure to read. Such a definition is devastating and fatal—devastating and fatal in that it is completely negative. No child who has been exposed to the reading process long enough to be evaluated is a 100 per cent failure unless he has an extreme physical, neurological, or emotional problem in which case the child is not ready for an assessment in reading. To assess reading in all fairness to a child one must determine his place in the developmental sequences of reading development. If he is an underprivileged child, he may have such a limited experience background and language facility that he has only a narrow range of concepts for making print meaningful, in which case we must start where he is and move as fast but as carefully as we can to develop reading as a part of his life.

There is no such thing as an exact reading level for any child. Each child actually has many reading levels, depending upon a variety of factors. Even these various reading levels fluctuate from time to time.

Teachers have too long felt that reading level can be measured exactly. They have perhaps been motivated to react in this way by the demands of parents and school administrators who insist that the reading level

16 Henry L. Mencken, *Happy Days,* New York, Alfred A. Knopf, 1940.

of the child be recorded on some kind of a permanent record. Unfortunately reading is not a single skill, but is a combination of many factors. Arriving at some medium grade level of each of these various skills is an approximation of a reading level. Any belief that more than a mere approximation of reading level exists is false.[17]

First Considerations

SELF-CONFIDENCE AND RAPPORT

A child who feels that he is a reading failure needs both a platform of self-confidence and rapport with a teacher so that he can start with assurance and trust.

If a child has been exposed to reading at all, there is something he can read: his name and at least a few common words. If a teacher starts by finding out what the child does know, she can establish that platform of confidence.

An eight-year-old boy who had failed second grade at another school came into a new school situation at midyear. His report card indicated almost no progress or interest in reading. At the end of his first day in the new school he enthusiastically told his mother, "I know one tenth of reading all ready. I know: *is, a, the, I, and, to,* and *you.* These are the most important words 'cause they're used so much. I've got a book I can read too. It's mostly pictures but I know all the words." The mother explained later that it was the first time the child had ever expressed any interest in reading but from that day on he made slow but steady progress.

The most commonly used words are a good beginning for a platform of self-confidence. Those few words comprise about a tenth of children's reading and such knowledge gives encouragement. A child needs to work with someone who is interested in *what he does know,* who helps him to know a little bit more without pushing and who seems happy doing it. He looks with favor and trust upon such a person and rapport is established. This kind of working relationship gives him encouragement, support, and incentive.

NEW APPROACHES AND MATERIAL

When a child has experienced failure or developed a negative attitude toward reading in any situation, he needs a different ap-

---

[17] Walter B. Barbe, *Educator's Guide to Personalized Reading Instruction.* Englewood Cliffs, N.J.: Prentice-Hall, 1961, p. 70.

proach with new materials. A language experience approach is often good at the beginning of a new contact with a child who has just moved into your room situation. Giving him a chance to tell about his pets, what he likes to do, his family, or the games he likes to play may afford a few simple sentences for recording and reading. From them some of the most commonly used words may be drawn and put on word cards. As soon as several words have been learned with the same first sound, help the child to hear and know that initial consonant. Help him to use each of the clues of word recognition as was explained in earlier chapters. Beginning phonics can relate to any words the child knows. Older children may start with many more advanced words than first graders would use. Their stories of self-experience would relate to more advanced interests.

Fortunately there are now many very easy-to-read books at the interest level of any child. As soon as enough basic vocabulary has been established the child should explore these books and find the ones he would like to read.

As the somewhat reluctant reader begins to develop a sight word vocabulary, gains control of the word recognition skills, and begins to read both experience type sentences and easy book material, a teacher should generate interest in what books have to offer. Very easy reading books have these experiences to offer:

Enjoyment of pets
Going places and doing things
Sports of all kinds
Being carefree and gay
Living with adventure
Helping to resolve a mystery
Seasonal, holiday, and family fare

Giving a child a chance to browse as you stand by to add a little enthusiasm often sets the stage for getting him started on independent reading.

Challenging and Inspiring the Able Readers

It is not enough to provide interesting materials for children to read and to be sure they have the mechanics and skills of reading. It is also important to help them put the substance of reading to good use and to develop broad interests and appreciations. This should be happening along with the acquisition of skills. As early as when children listen to teachers read various kinds of material they can discuss the characters, plot, mood, and theme of a story and the incidents that lead up to the solution of a problem or mystery. Such discussions can help children to challenge the authenticity of what is read, to recognize reliable sources of information, and to appreciate quality in writing. Throughout the elementary grades frequent reading by the teacher of many different kinds of materials should be followed by discussions to give children such insights.

The contest is not between heart and head, but between more perfect and less perfect understanding. Whatever tells us what a passage may mean would also, if we let it, tell us whether and how to believe, disbelieve, or keep an open mind. The arch problem of Truth is never solved once for all; though the more we know about it, the better our local decisions should be. It is a "huge hill," indeed, on which Truth stands, and we will be fortunate if we never suppose we have ascended it.[18]

Suggestions for Class Participation and Discussion

1. Did you have any reading problems as a child? Discuss them.
2. What is your opinion about speed reading?
3. Has any one in the class taken a course in speed reading? Discuss the techniques that were used.
4. Select any one reading problem and read what other authors have to say about it. Discuss in class.
5. Read a current article on some piece of research relative to one of the topics in this chapter. Discuss it in class.
6. Visit a reading clinic if it is possible and discuss your observations.
7. Appendix R lists books of high interest but easy reading level. Look for some of these books in the library and become familiar with them. Bring some that you especially like to class.
8. Discuss ways of expanding concepts and developing language facility at the grade level you intend to teach.
9. Check the word lists mentioned in the second quotation in this chapter and discover the twenty-five most frequently used words. Why are these good to know? How can you use them in your teaching?
10. Discuss the quotation at the end of the chapter.

[18] I. A. Richards, *How to Read a Page,* Boston, Beacon Press, 1942, p. 241.

Bibliography

BOND, GUY, and TINKER, MILES A. *Reading Difficulties: Their Diagnosis and Correction.* New York: Appleton-Century-Crofts, 1957.

CLELEAND, DONALD, and BENSON, JOSEPHINE. *Corrective and Remedial Reading.* Pittsburgh: University of Pittsburgh Press, 1960.

DALE, EDGAR, and SEELS, BARBARA. *Readability and Reading: An Annotated Bibliography.* Newark, Delaware: International Reading Association, 1966.

DOLCH, E. W. *A Manual for Remedial Reading.* Champaign, Ill.: Garrard Press, 1945.

DURKIN, DOLORES. *Reading and the Kindergarten, An Annotated Bibliography.* Newark, Delaware: International Reading Association, 1966.

FAY, LEO. *Reading in the Content Areas: An Annotated Bibliography.* Newark, Delaware: International Reading Association, 1966.

HARRIS, ALBERT. *How to Increase Reading Ability.* New York: David McKay, 1961.

KOTTMEYER, W. *Handbook of Remedial Reading.* St. Louis: Webster Publishing Company, 1959.

KRESS, ROY, and JOHNSON, MARJORIE. *Providing Clinical Services in Reading. An Annotated Bibliography.* Newark, Delaware: International Reading Association, 1966.

LORETAN, JOSEPH, and UMANS, SHELLEY. *Teaching the Disadvantaged.* New York: Teachers College Press, 1966.

RASSMUSSEN, MARGARET. *Feelings and Learning.* Washington, D.C.: Association for Childhood Education International, 1965.

ROBINSON, HELEN M. *Corrective Reading in Classroom and Clinic.* Chicago: University of Chicago Press, 1953.

——. *Why Children Fail in Reading.* Chicago: University of Chicago Press, 1946.

——. *The Under Achiever in Reading.* Chicago: University of Chicago Press, 1962.

ROSWELL, FLORENCE, and NATCHEZ, GLADYS. *Reading Disability, Diagnosis and Treatment.* New York: Basic Books, Inc., 1964.

SCHUBERT, DELWYN, and TORGERSON, THEODORE. *Improving Reading in the Elementary School.* Dubuque, Iowa: Wm. C. Brown, 1963.

STRANG, RUTH. *Diagnostic Teaching of Reading.* New York: McGraw-Hill, 1964.

WOOLF, M., and WOOLF, J. *Remedial Reading.* New York: McGraw-Hill, 1957.

Your Reading Problems (Practical Helps from Experienced Teachers). Darien, Conn.: The Educational Publishing Company, 1947.

ZINTZ, MILES. *Corrective Reading.* Dubuque, Iowa: Wm. C. Brown, 1966.

CHAPTER 14

Materials
and Organization
in Teaching Reading

Technology and Classroom Machines

Middlebury schoolmen Joseph Cashman and Kenneth Bilodeau wrote their proposal into a Title I project, and hired Oscar Yohai, Reading Consultant for the Wethersfield, Connecticut Public Schools, to spend the summer developing the pattern of operation for the new program.

Both Cashman and Bilodeau encouraged Yohai to feel free to disregard "tradition" in building the program. Their idea was to build a technologically-aided curriculum which, no matter how unorthodox, would produce results.

Yohai's budget was $13,000. And the program he devised with it is a marvel of eclectic practicality.

Although the program borrows equipment and materials from almost every possible source, it adheres faithfully to a single criterion-for-selection, namely, "How well will it work with children?"

After a summer of effort, Yohai was ready to equip Middlebury with a complete Learning Studio to house his ideas.

Children from the primary grades in two elementary schools are scheduled so that they may use the center for at least a half hour each day, as well as after school and on Saturdays.

And Yohai's hybrid—and creative—uses of technology are enough to lure them there in droves.

316

Here's a sample of some of the most-used learning Studio features:

One section of the room is equipped with an Audio Notebook hookup (manufactured by Electronic Futures, Inc., Dodge Avenue, North Haven, Connecticut). This hookup allows children to tune into any one of three instructional channels using wireless headsets. Teachers can program the channels with any type of audio materials available, including their own teacher-constructed tapes. This provides the possibility for individualized, self-instructing materials for pupils at every level.

Filmstrip projectors, film cartridges, and tape recorders are also available throughout the Studio. And each has a rich variety of accompanying software, including the "Listen and Do" program of Houghton Mifflin, complete sets of Eye-Gate reading film-strips, and the full Weston Woods literature program, a series of quality children's books reproduced on film with sound narration, (Weston Woods, Weston, Connecticut).

The EDL "Look and Write" transparencies are also used at the Studio. But they're used with a technological twist. The teacher still works orally with the transparencies, but she speaks into a microphone, and the children with whom she is working wear headphones. In this way, the only children who can hear her are those she intends to instruct. The rest of the group is not disturbed.

In his search for useful equipment and software, Yohai also discovered a new newly-invented machine called an Elco Mastermatic. (In fact, he bought one of the first models produced.)

The Mastermatic is a filmstrip projector with an attached cartridge tape player. It's easy for a child to operate, and it allows for the use of an unlimited number of different tapes with the same filmstrip. Thus, teachers can use a basic film-strip supplied by a manufacturer and still make their own tapes to suit individual needs.

The teachers in Yohai's Studio have also gone into the film-producing business. Using Studio equipment, they are able to make their own photographs and produce instructional and supplementary filmstrips. Children's experience stories are illustrated with actual shots made in the classroom and school, and filmed phonics drills and vocabulary exercises are "made-to-order."[1]

This report reminds one of traveling around the world with all the electric gadgets that are sometimes given as bon voyage gifts— electric travel iron, electric toothbrush, electric shaver, and compact tiny electric coffee kit. They all seem so practical, but at some stops the current is very different and you have to use various adapters and even then the iron won't heat very much. In some places the wall socket is very different, and when you use a little pressure to "make things work" you get a ruined gadget or a short circuit that sends the manager to your room.

[1] "The Technology Gap," *The Reading Newsreport*, editorial, Nov.–Dec. 1966.

So it is with gadgets and children—they do not all fit into the same situations. The teacher must be the multipurpose adapter. She must guard against electrocution, short circuits, ruined equipment, hurt children, and against "things not happening that should be happening."

This does not mean that there is no place for modern technology in our schools. Far from it. Most of us wish we were twenty years younger to experiment with each new thing that comes along. But it is important to know your equipment thoroughly—what it will and will not do—whether it is economical in terms of expenditure and what time it saves or what it does that less expensive equipment could not do, and to become very adept with it before bringing it into the classroom.

"THE TALKING TYPEWRITER"

The New York "Talking Typewriter" project is an attempt to teach prekindergarten children to type "by machine." Each fingernail tip of a child's hand is colored differently to match a section of the keyboard. In this way he learns correct fingering. First he learns to find a letter he sees above the typewriter. Later, a voice tells him what letter to type. If he touches the wrong letter nothing happens. If he touches the correct letter that letter appears on the paper. Thus, it is a trial and error process until he learns the letter positions and they become increasingly automatic. Next, he "types" stories that appear on cards for him to type. Still later he writes from dictation. Finally he writes his own compositions. This project is a million-dollar experimentation financed by the Office of Economic Opportunity under contract with the New York City Schools. The machine is estimated to cost $30,000. Its worth has yet to be determined.

These are questions that should be asked with regard to any new device:

1. What purposes will this equipment serve?

2. How flexible is it? Does the whole room have to be put in darkness so everyone must be watching the same thing at the same time? Can it be used with children who read slowly; who may need to listen a second or third time before they know what to do; who forget what it was they started to do five or ten minutes later; who become more interested in the gadget than in what it is doing?

3. Does it break down frequently and need repair services from a factory a few hundred miles away or can it be repaired locally?

4. What is the cost with regard to the school's total budget for all equipment and materials? What is its relative worth?

5. What do eye specialists and psychologists think of it?

6. Do the teachers themselves want it and feel that it will serve their needs?

Too often school boards are eager to be the first to have what is new, and teachers are not even consulted with regard to the teaching potentialities of what salesmen sometimes pressure them into buying.

Fortunately, there is money for research, and new materials, new machines, and new methods are being tried and results are soon broadcast so that some guidance can come of it. Even so, what may work well in one situation may not be what is needed in another.

SPEED-READING DEVICES

Reading Boards, Tachistoscopes, Controlled Readers, Reading Rate Controllers, Reading Accelerators, Rate Readers, Flashmeters, the Tach-X, and training films are some of the devices on the market today designed to increase speed in reading. Many are intended for adult use, but they are making their way into the high schools and some are being sold as aids for elementary children. More will be coming.

Miles A Tinker has done a considerable amount of research into the use of various speed devices with elementary school children. He finds that "The improvement obtained by eye-movement training, with or without elaborate apparatus, is no greater than that resulting from motivated reading alone." He also states,

The use of pacing devices too often becomes a ritual tending toward an over-emphasis upon the mechanics of reading to the sacrifice of adequate attention to the more important processes of perception, apprehension, and assimilation. This mechanical training may result in a decrease in the flexibility and adaptation of reading habits that characterize good readers.[2]

With young children it is a great mistake to exert pressure for speed. Speed comes with security in knowing the reading process

---

[2] Miles A. Tinker, "Devices to Improve Speed of Reading." *The Reading Teacher*, April, 1967, p. 608.

and in being interested in the material to be read. It is more important to know how to read the various kinds of materials in accordance with the degree of carefulness they demand than to make children feel that everything must be read quickly.

Reading or Learning Clinics

Some of the best developments in recent years are the reading and learning clinics. They are costly and many schools should share the cost of one good clinic. The very best available ophthalmologist, medical doctor, psychologist, psychiatrist, pediatrician, and nutritionist should be on call in the reading clinic, along with the services of well-qualified reading specialists to diagnose reading problems and make recommendations. There is no doubt that reading problems in our schools would be greatly reduced if such services were available and teachers were encouraged to make referrals to them.

Excellent clinical analysis is basic to resolving many of the reading problems teachers face.

Teaching Aids

READING SPECIALISTS

Reading specialists can do much to help children make rapid progress once a truly professional multidisciplinary diagnosis has been made. They demonstrate the techniques that the busy classroom teacher may not know or have time to use. They also give expert advice to teachers and parents. In some cases they work with retarded children for a period of time each day.

TELELECTURE

During the summer of 1967 an innovation by the telephone company has enabled Head-Start teachers in five Appalachian states to have weekly in-service meetings without leaving their classrooms. A spokesman telephone connection enables everyone in a small room to hear a voice coming over a telephone wire and to respond to that voice. Once a week a telephone operator ties all seventeen telephones to a central in-service center in Charleston, West Virginia.[3] Consider the long-range possibilities of such a development for round-table discussions by foremost educators, statesmen, and scientists. Consider also the potentialities for workshops, demonstrations, and instruction when this is tied up with television.

LIBRARIES OF TOMORROW

Wonderful developments in libraries are taking place and each year will bring dramatic changes.

Libraries of the future will be amazingly efficient. Microfilm, computer analysis, central storage banks, dial access, and on-demand printing will revolutionize research and note-taking. Reading and creating of tomorrow will be enhanced greatly by technology.

RECORDINGS AND TAPES

More and more classrooms are being equipped with "listening posts" where children may listen to good literature, good music, and recorded or taped programmed instruction. All children can be helped to appreciate well-read literature and thus to aspire to read it effectively. An appreciation of good music may lead to wide reading pertaining to composers and their works. For some children programmed instruction may be a type of individual challenge they need. It need not comprise all of instruction, but it might be a small worthwhile part of it.

Another use of tapes is taping children's oral reading so that they can hear themselves and set new goals of self-improvement. Rerunning a tape made a month ago and comparing it with one made recently may give a child much encouragement through recognition of his own progress.

OVERHEAD PROJECTION

The overhead projector affords teaching facility that films and film strips lack. The page of a book is projected so a whole class may see certain details of a picture or graph the teacher is using to clarify their thinking. She can use a pencil to point as she explains. A great many transparencies are now available for use as teaching aids in any area of the curriculum. In reading they offer expansion and clarification of concepts, substance for teaching, and stimulation.

3 *The Reading Newsreport*, June, 1967.

SLIDES AND FILMS

Both slides and films may be used at any level to help expand concepts. Care should be taken in their selection so that whatever is shown is true to life—true to natural coloring, true to habitat, and not lost in too much detail.

There are many good story-telling films, some with marionette characters and some with real-life characters. The stories are well told, and if a teacher does not feel capable of telling or reading stories well the films will serve a very good purpose of allowing children to hear excellent oral expression. However, if a teacher tells stories well, the children would have the advantage of observing facial expression and gestures that can add to the effectiveness of oral expressions. On the other hand, films can show action and background that words alone cannot. There is need for both.

Catalogs from some city school audio-visual departments are as large as telephone books—the selection is tremendous. Films provide an excellent point of departure for good class discussion leading to depth of thinking and extensive oral communication. Concepts through seeing and hearing are often established through films before reading takes place. The Head-Start child is afforded many opportunities for learning through films, and at each age level there are needs for films that books cannot serve. Life in far-away places, life in ages past, art, space, invention can all be made more real through motion pictures and sound than through the words of books. And books are more meaningful after such experiences.

TELEVISION

Television is in its infancy as far as education potentialities are concerned. For teachers it has all the possibilities mentioned with regard to telelecture plus many it is impossible to foresee. For children it can bring any part of the world or outer space into full view. The quality and rewards to our children will depend on the demands and ingenuity of educators.

COMPUTERS

Some day soon cards may be punched with a child's recognized needs and the computer will "suggest" the materials, approach, or diagnosis. The potential is great but the *followthrough* must be humanized.

Teaching Materials

TRADE SETS OF MATERIALS

Many companies are now developing complete sets of materials for language development that include incentives for oral language, written language, literature to be read to children, and material for children to read. Some of these sets are very expensive, and if school budgets are limited such a purchase might deprive teachers and

Helping children become familiar with many of the resources of the library expands their horizons and enables them to become increasingly independent in gleaning information. (Photograph courtesy of the New York City Schools.)

children from having other worthwhile materials. All buying must be considered carefully to be sure good materials of various kinds are included within a budget.

NEWSPAPERS AND MAGAZINES

Because the reading of newspapers and magazines is such common practice in American homes today (newspapers are read in eighty-six per cent of the households in America, and magazine circulation has increased one hundred and ten per cent since 1940),[4] it is only natural that they should come into the classroom. Children seek out parts of the newspapers and magazines of the adult world and also enjoy many magazines designed especially for children.

George E. Norvell sent questionnaires to approximately 3,280 boys and girls to determine their magazine interests. He made an extensive study of periodical reading and came to the conclusions outlined in Tables 12–2 and 12–3.

SUMMARY   Careful studies of periodical reading by many investigators justify the following:

1. Reading magazines and newspapers is popular at all age levels, beginning with the primary grades.

2. For every adult reader of books, there are two readers of magazines.

3. Two out of three adults read magazines, ninety-five per cent read newspapers, and fewer than half read books.

4. Adult readers with an eighth-grade education spend more than four-fold as much time on periodicals as on books.

5. Of the thousands of magazines published, children and adults alike are largely uninformed as to which could serve them best.

6. Aside from radio and television, periodicals are for the vast majority the principal sources of information about the world, from the local community to the Congo.

7. Following school days, periodicals provide the most important means of lifetime education for American citizens.

8. There are important values in periodicals of which the majority of readers are unaware.

9. Classroom instruction can improve taste and promote independent judgment regarding periodicals.

10. Very few adults have developed plans for the efficient reading of newspapers.

[4] International Paper Co., *The Reading Explosion*, New York, 1962.

11. Certain quality magazines published for adults are as well liked by children eight to ten years old as are the most popular children's magazines.

12. Too often the magazines recommended by professional educators are not read willingly by children.

13. Schools generally have made little effort to guide the newspaper reading of girls and boys.

There is need for a good children's newspaper, designed for sharing in a classroom the way a newspaper is shared in the home. *My Weekly Reader* has excellent content but it is designed so that every child must have a copy to use as a worksheet, which makes it very expensive, and it is not really a newspaper to be shared by all children. (See Appendix S for a listing of school magazines.)

PAPERBACK BOOKS

The International Paper Company reports that every day a million paperback books are sold. Statistics cannot keep pace with the titles. They vary as greatly in subject matter as they do in quality. Because they are so much a part of adult reading today, it is important that children have an opportunity to get acquainted with some of the best paperback books and are helped with evaluative standards.

Although many of the paperbacks are most appropriate for junior and senior high schools, more are now coming on the market at the elementary grade level. Scholastic Publisher includes some at first-grade level. Lists of titles can be obtained from:

Pocket Books, Inc.
630 Fifth Avenue
New York, N.Y.

Institutional Book Service
1224 W. Van Buren Street
Chicago, Ill.

Scholastic Services
902 Sylvan Avenue
Englewood Cliffs, New Jersey

Ludington News Company
1600 E. Grand Blvd.
Detroit, Mich.

Reader's Choice
904 Sylvan Avenue
Englewood Cliffs, N.J.

Paperbound Book Guide
For Elementary Schools
R. R. Bowker Company
1180 Avenue of the Americas
New York, N.Y.

Many times when children are asked to name favorite books they include books they own at home. There is pride in ownership and those books are read again and again. In homes with limited budgets

Table 12-2. The Interests of Boys and Girls, Grades 4 to 6, in 31 Magazines Listed in the Order of Popularity (1962)*

Magazine	Boys No.	Score	Magazine	Girls No.	Score	Magazine	Boys and Girls No.	Score
Boys' Life	1263	89.3	National Geographic	760	86.5	National Geographic	1655	87.9
National Geographic	895	89.2	American Girl	706	86.0	Boys' Life	1519	80.1
Popular Science	591	86.7	Calling All Girls	834	84.2	Junior Scholastic	1043	79.7
Popular Mechanics	640	85.9	Seventeen	433	84.1	Junior Natural History	320	79.3
Hot Rod	669	85.4	Junior Scholastic	518	80.2	Scouting	570	78.4
Junior Natural History	208	81.7	Modern Screen	98	79.1	Explorer	475	75.7
Scouting	453	81.6	Junior Natural History	112	76.8	Saturday Evening Post	1421	74.2
Model Airplane News	227	80.1	McCall's	1062	75.9	Life	2731	73.6
Explorer	319	79.9	Scouting	117	75.2	Hot Rod	773	73.5
Junior Scholastic	525	79.1	Saturday Evening Post	649	74.8	Popular Science	735	73.2
Saturday Evening Post	772	73.6	Life	1354	74.4	Modern Screen	174	72.5
Life	1377	72.8	Children's Digest	1029	72.7	Reader's Digest	2107	71.5
Reader's Digest	1049	70.9	Reader's Digest	1058	72.1	Current Events	338	70.0
Newsweek	472	69.0	Photoplay	111	71.6	Children's Digest	1934	69.9
Current Events	201	68.4	Current Events	137	71.5	Look	2339	68.9
Children's Digest	905	67.0	Explorer	156	71.5	Popular Mechanics	788	68.8
Look	1172	66.9	Junior Red Cross News	221	71.0	Newsweek	801	68.2
My Weekly Reader	1336	66.5	Boys' Life	256	70.9	American Girl	756	67.0
Modern Screen	76	65.8	Look	1167	70.9	My Weekly Reader	2666	67.0
Time	739	65.7	Children's Activities	169	69.8	Junior Red Cross News	414	66.9
Junior Red Cross News	193	62.7	My Weekly Reader	1330	67.5	Seventeen	560	66.9
Children's Activities	122	61.7	Newsweek	329	67.3	Calling All Girls	902	66.0
Child Life	211	60.4	True Confessions	100	67.0	Photoplay	199	65.9
Photoplay	88	60.2	Child Life	264	66.7	Children's Activities	291	65.8
True Confessions	102	52.9	Better Homes & Gardens	650	62.6	Model Airplane News	251	65.1

Magazine	No.	Score	Magazine	No.	Score	Magazine	No.	Score
Seventeen	127	49.6	Good Housekeeping	595	61.6	Child Life	475	63.6
American Girl	50	48.0	Hot Rod	104	61.5	Time	1398	62.9
Calling All Girls	68	47.8	Time	659	60.0	McCall's	1662	61.8
McCall's	600	47.6	Popular Science	144	59.7	True Confessions	202	60.0
Better Homes & Gardens	411	44.0	Popular Mechanics	148	51.7	Better Homes & Gardens	1061	53.3
Good Housekeeping	355	39.4	Model Airplane News	24	50.0	Good Housekeeping	950	50.5

Source: George W. Norvell, "The Challenge of Periodicals in Education." *Elementary English* (April, 1966), p. 403. Reprinted with the permission of the National Council of Teachers of English and George Norvell.

* The questionnaire was submitted to approximately 3,280 children (half boys and half girls).

Table 12–3. The Interests of Boys and of Girls in Grade 3 in 12 Magazines Listed in the Order of Popularity (1962)*

	Boys			Girls			Boys and Girls	
Magazine	No.	Score	Magazine	No.	Score	Magazine	No.	Score
Popular Science	185	88.1	My Weekly Reader	970	85.3	National Geographic	501	85.5
National Geographic	275	86.0	National Geographic	226	85.0	My Weekly Reader	2015	83.9
Popular Mechanics	148	84.1	Jack and Jill	908	82.8	Popular Science	256	81.8
Children's Activities	134	82.5	Children's Digest	439	79.0	Junior Natural History	179	79.6
My Weekly Reader	1045	82.4	Humpty Dumpty	834	77.5	Children's Activities	257	79.5
Junior Natural History	110	82.3	Junior Natural History	69	76.8	Children's Digest	841	77.7
Children's Digest	402	76.4	Children's Activities	123	76.4	Jack and Jill	1657	76.0
Child Life	195	76.2	Popular Science	71	75.4	Popular Mechanics	191	75.8
Humpty Dumpty	715	73.2	Child Life	221	73.5	Humpty Dumpty	1549	75.4
Jack and Jill	749	69.1	Look	401	67.5	Child Life	416	74.9
Life	591	69.1	Popular Mechanics	43	67.4	Life	1131	66.3
Look	494	63.0	Life	540	63.5	Look	895	65.3

Source: George W. Norvell, "The Challenge of Periodicals in Education." *Elementary English* (April, 1966), p. 403. Reprinted with the permission of the National Council of Teachers of English and George Norvell.

* The questionnaire was submitted to approximately 2,720 children (half boys and half girls).

for book buying it might be a service to parents before Christmas to send home a list of books, both paperback and hard-bound, that are at the children's reading level and that would be good for a child's home library. The hard-bound books are much more durable, the paper is of better quality, and the illustrations are better reproductions, but no child should be deprived of owning a few good books because of exorbitant costs.

ABC BOOKS AND PICTURE DICTIONARIES

Both ABC books and picture dictionaries are useful in expanding concepts through word-and-picture associations and in helping to familiarize children with use of the large and small letters of the alphabet. Children should have many opportunities to explore both types of books freely. Some good picture dictionaries are:

CLEMENS, ELIZABETH, *Pixie Dictionary* (Holt, 1960)
  Short definitions, colored illustrations; teacher's manual available (kindergarten–3)
McINTIRE, ALTA, *Beginning to Read* (Follett, 1959)
  Picture dictionary; upper and lower case manuscript; daily life pictures (preschool–1)
MACBEAN, DILLA, *Picture Book Dictionary* (Children's Press, 1962)
  Large type; full-color illustrations (1–2)
MOORE, LILIAN, *Golden Picture Dictionary* (Golden Press, 1954)
  A beginning dictionary; fewer pictures, more definitions (2–4)
OFTEDAL, LAURA, *My First Dictionary* (Grosset, 1948)
  Some full-page pictures of related nouns; single object illustrations in color (preschool–2)
REED, MARY, *My First Golden Dictionary* (Golden Press, 1957)
  Simple colored illustrations, large guide letters (kindergarten–3)
SCARRY, RICHARD, *Story Book Dictionary* (Golden Press, 1966)
  New and different; good for parent to enjoy with child (kindergarten–3)
SCOTT, ALICE H., *Giant Picture Dictionary for Boys and Girls* (Garden City, 1949)
  Advanced (3–6)
WALPOLE, ELLEN, *Golden Dictionary* (Golden Press, 1944)
  Small colored illustrations; good picture groupings (1–3)
WRIGHT, WENDELL, *Rainbow Dictionary* (World, 1959)
  Upper and lower case guide letters; many colored pictures (1–3)

Third-graders who have made satisfactory progress are ready by mid-year for dictionary study followed by general use of a good school dictionary. Some schools wait until fourth grade.

Several publishers of school dictionaries publish good charts and teaching aids for giving dictionary instruction.

Children appreciate the opportunity to explore a dictionary and an encyclopedia before being helped to use them efficiently. (Photograph courtesy of the Boston Public Schools.)

Instruction in use of the dictionary was given earlier in this book, but mention might be made here of the available enlargement of a dictionary page published and distributed free of charge by Scott, Foresman Company, publishers. This large dictionary page is excellent for posting on the chalkboard and giving children a chance to explore the various contents of a dictionary page (alphabetical listing, guide words, definitions, spelling, syllabication, accent, diacritical marking key, word forms, pictures). The following dictionaries are especially good:

Webster's New World Dictionary, elementary edition (Macmillan, 1962)
　　Has good teacher's manual
Thorndike-Barnhart Beginning Dictionary (Scott, Foresman, 1959)
　　Easy-to-understand definitions; over eighty pages of suggestions for teaching

Webster's Elementary Dictionary (Merriam-Webster, American Book Co., 1959)
   Pronunciation is shown by phonetic spelling of word; definitions of words are given from oldest to newest
Thorndike-Barnhart Junior Dictionary (Scott, Foresman, 1959)
   Scott, Foresman dictionaries use the schwa
Webster's Elementary Dictionary for Boys and Girls (Merriam-Webster, American Book Co., 1957)
   Has addenda of new and scientific words
Winston Dictionary for Schools (John C. Winston Co., 1959)
   Has the largest number of entries of the books listed; an annual edition is published

ENCYCLOPEDIAS

By mid-fourth grade many children are ready to use the encyclopedia. *The World Book, Junior Britannica,* and *Compton's* are all good for elementary classroom use. *The World Book* provides some excellent teaching aids to use in introducing children to use of the encyclopedia.

ATLASES, MAPS, AND GLOBES

Reference is often made in stories to the country or other geographical location of the setting of the story. A large pull-down map, an atlas, and a globe may give the children a relative idea of where the action of the story takes place.

The following are some evaluative criteria for selecting maps, globes, and atlases for elementary classroom use:

1. They must be up-to-date and of recent publication to show the many changes that have taken place in various parts of the world.
2. The maps should not attempt to show too much. Either political or physical features on any one map is enough for children at 4- to 6-grade levels. Boundaries of countries should be clearly shown, and the mark indicating location of a city should be properly located.
3. Names should be clearly printed and symbols should be easy to understand and use.
4. A globe should be easy to handle, and lines of latitude and longitude should be easy to follow.
5. All details should be authentic, and the maps, globes, and atlases should be durable.

Interpreting the Reading Program to the Public

Educators have been sitting back and listening while critics have accused the schools of not teaching reading, of failing to recognize easy panaceas and quick "cure-alls." It is time the public was made aware of the true causes of reading problems. Explanations of our language and of individual differences must be made clearly and frequently. This book is full of explanations and quotations that teachers may use in giving explanations to P.T.A. groups and to newspapers and in talks to the public.

Demonstrations in regular classroom situations, television broadcasts of good teaching, and pictures along with commentary will help the public to understand. Cite research studies where many experimental programs show that highly advertised panaceas are not superior to sound practices. Cite the fact that the newly standardized Stanford reading test shows that children today are reading better than children did fifteen years ago. State facts and invite the public to see the fine work going on in the schools.

Parents and the Reading Program

Parents have seven major responsibilities in the teaching of reading:

1. Provide adequate nutrition, rest, respect, and love for the child.
2. Provide opportunities for rich and varied experiences so that children will have many concepts with which to make reading meaningful.
3. Show interest in what children can read.
4. Be enthusiastic and appreciative of their progress.
5. Provide good reading material in the home.
6. Assure the public that your child is learning to read.
7. Cooperate with the teacher if your child needs clinical analysis and special assistance.

Classroom Organization

Just as there have been innovations in materials, so too have there been attempts at new types of classroom organization that show promise.

Ungraded classrooms vary among schools, but they are all designed to remove the rigidity of grade placement, failure, repetition, and the "holding back" that some bright children have experienced in graded systems. Much better use of individualized instruction, flexible grouping, and congenial teacher-pupil relationships can be achieved in ungraded classrooms.

Some schools have regular graded classrooms in which children are homogeneous in ability to read, and other children are placed in an ungraded room according to where they fit best and can be helped to do better or helped to accelerate, as the case may be.

Other schools have what is known as a primary block and a middle-grade block. Others have an extremely flexible grouping throughout the elementary grades. The important guidepost in determining any classroom program should be: Make sure each child is with the teacher and in the situation where he can work to his optimum ability with interest and enthusiasm.

Flexibility in Grouping and Individual Instruction

1. As children's needs change they may be moved from one group to another where they can work to greatest advantage.

2. Occasionally very different groups may be formed to work on projects such as oral reading or a dramatization.

3. Occasionally some children should not come to the group at all when it is felt that the instruction to be given is not needed by these children and they can use their time to greater advantage doing other things.

4. Occasionally a group may be brought together with a common interest such as rocks, shells, cars, baseball, etc. to discuss books on the specific interest, work on common vocabulary, and have an opportunity to share information and thus become more enthusiastic about exploring the interest through reading.

5. Sometimes a child or several children may be invited to visit another group for certain purposes. Maybe that group is reading a story about something in which he is interested; maybe they are getting help on something with which he, too, needs help; maybe it is a "try-out" to see if he might eventually fit into that group.

6. When group activity gets underway and a teacher finds that some of the children catch on to the instruction easily and have no need for further explanations or exercises, those children may be

invited to do other things and leave the group. This gives the teacher a chance to work more closely with the ones who are left, and time is not wasted by those who learn easily. Before leaving the group those who seem to know may be challenged to read quickly what is on the board or give some evidence of knowing what has been presented.

7. Have a "catch-up" period in the daily schedule. Many children need to complete work they have started.

8. Increase the amount of self-selection and individualized reading activity as reading skills and proficiency are acquired. Let reading serve children's purposes more and more. However, young children need guidance to develop wide interests and a teacher should help in two ways: she should provide a wide range of good material at various reading levels from which selection may be made; she should help children to be sure they are selecting books within their reading range. Sometimes it is good for a child to "stretch" his capabilities a bit with a difficult book if his desire to read it is great enough. As adults, we sometimes start a book and then decide it is not for us. Children should have the same privilege.

9. Group reading records. Place a "Wheel of Good Reading" chart on a bulletin board with categories such as biography, animal stories, sports stories, hero stories, mystery, science stories, stories about other countries, adventure stories, poetry, nature stories, holiday stories, stories about how people earn a living, stories about our government, folk tales. Such a wheel could be simplified for third grade. Children could be challenged to read books from each category and put their initials in the category when the book has been completed.

10. Individual reading records. "My Reading Design" is a leaflet (available from The Hubbard Company, P.O. Box 100, Defiance, Ohio, at a small cost) that has a very good listing of categories and subtopics with an individual wheel, or design, and a page on which a child is to list the books he reads and then place the number corresponding to the book in the design. This is a good way to stimulate breadth of reading.

Care must be taken so children do not remain on a plateau in their reading ability. It is fine for them to use their skills and to enjoy reading in this way, but teachers have a responsibility for helping children to grow continuously. There is frequent need for instruction and guidance to enable children to reach higher levels of reading achievement.

11. Advanced instruction may meet certain individual needs. If there is a child in the class who does not fit into any group as far as instructional needs are concerned, he might find individual advanced instruction challenging if he can be given material that is the most appropriate to his level of accomplishment. Sometimes he may be invited to various group sessions—for experiences in oral reading in one group, for sharing of interesting reading content in another, for certain instruction in another—and he can work by himself on certain interests. Programmed reading used flexibly may serve certain individuals well.

CLASSROOM MANAGEMENT IN READING INSTRUCTION

1. A child must be helped to know that there is a significant purpose in what he is doing. Whether he is in a reading group or working independently, each child should be aware that there is a reason for his doing what he is doing and that it is important to him. A teacher should explain these reasons and make them important. Because they are important the child has the responsibility of staying with the task and of behaving in accordance with what is appropriate to the completion of the task and with respect for what other children are doing.

2. Children must be engaged in activities that are within their achievement range. Children cannot be expected to work well independently if the task is too difficult. That is why a teacher must exert special care to be sure every child knows what he is to do and how to do it within a reasonable range of effort on his part.

3. Children must be aware of available resources for help and how to use them. In the primary grades, if a word puzzles a child and he has tried his own techniques to no avail, he should be free to go to another child, point to the word, and expect the child to whisper it to him. In grades four through six the children should have dictionaries, encyclopedias, globes, and an atlas available. When all self-assistance fails, they should feel free to call on the services of another child if they do it without disturbing others.

4. Children should be aware of what behavior is necessary for everyone in the room to be able to complete their work. This means that they have the responsibility of not bothering anyone except in cases of great need, and then consulting others quietly. It means, too, that they should be responsible for helping someone else when called upon, quietly and with the least possible talking.

5. Children come to know what routines are established in the classroom and why. They also know the need for flexibility when it is explained and they are expected to cooperate.

6. Children must be helped to regard mistakes with respect. Correction must be looked upon as a part of teaching and learning. A mistake is only a sign of need for help. To laugh or to criticize when a mistake is made is to hinder teaching and learning and it is to be discouraged.

7. Children must be helped to respect those who have special problems. Ask your group of children, "What can we do to help children who wear glasses? children who have other disabilities?" This places responsibility on the children themselves. With such an approach great care is given needy children on the playground and in various classroom situations.

8. A child must be helped to be responsible for knowing what to do with spare moments—those times when he finishes his work before it is time for a next activity, those times when he does not need to do the work others are doing. He should always have an interesting book available and he should always ask himself if he has any unfinished work of any kind. Creative interests should be so well stimulated that he looks eagerly to opportunities to have time to write or draw. Appreciative interests should be stimulated to the extent that he is eager to listen to good music or literature at the listening post or enjoy books of famous paintings, sculpture, glass, ceramics, or architecture. Reading should enrich these experiences, and these experiences should nurture interest in more reading.

TIME ALLOTMENT FOR READING INSTRUCTION

FIRST GRADE When children have first experiences with reading, instruction periods must be kept brief. Interest span of the group can be your guide, but generally ten to fifteen minutes will be the most profitable. Brief periods several times a day are better than one long period. Too long a period can tire children so that they lose interest and are not enthusiastic about another chance to read. Each week the time may be prolonged until by the end of the first semester you may spend about thirty minutes in group session with a variety of experiences within that time. As children gain independence in reading, more and more time can be spent in independent work so that a total of possibly an hour might be attributed to reading experiences throughout the day, plus incidental reading in other subject areas.

SECOND AND THIRD GRADES   Much depends on the classroom organization for reading in determining how time shall be allotted. Much depends also on the needs of the students. For example, if many test below grade level, or if an inventory shows that many neither like to read nor can read well, a very different approach must be made than if many are avid readers and read very well.

Word and sentence games interspersed frequently for short durations during the day may meet with interest and enthusiastic response by those who need help with basic vocabulary and fluent reading of sentences. Much independent reading based, for example, on a report for social studies, finding out the answers to questions raised in science, or the enjoyment of a piece of good literature would comprise reading experiences for the very able reader. After second- and third-grade teachers have been with the children long enough to discover their specific needs, groups may be formed in which basic instruction is given so that the children get the help they need. These groups would change frequently with flexible use of materials. Time allotment would vary; on some days as much as an hour might be given to reading while other days may require that a larger block of time be devoted to something else in the curriculum. Flexible scheduling pays off if attention span, interest, and purposes are taken into account.

FOURTH TO SIXTH GRADE   If children are lacking in basic skills it is well to spend much time helping to establish them. The subject matter can be social studies, science, arithmetic, or anything else, but the help must be in reading. Vocabulary, word recognition, comprehension are all essential to reading in any subject area. Start with material children can read, and apply what you know from preceding chapters. Good diagnostic tests can put you on the track of what help individuals need.

Reading Materials

Spend some time in the curriculum library of any teacher training institution. Note the abundance and variety of delightfully illustrated readers, the detailed and appealingly colorful kits for language experiences, phonics, and vocabulary development, and the shelves of gay, inviting books that in our own childhoods would have seemed like treasures indeed. There should be no problem with inviting children to read. (See Appendix J.) Visit the children's library frequently to keep up with new books.

BASIC READING SERIES

There has always been variety among basic or basal reading series in differences in choice and number of words, differences in story content, and differences in guidebooks, wordbooks, and other teaching accessories. Now the differences are more extreme. Because new series are published so frequently it is impossible to include a current listing. A listing of many leading publishers of basic and supplementary books appears in Appendix Q.

With i.t.a. and UNIFON we have books with unfamiliar symbols. With "Words in Color" we have another innovation in children's readers. Certain linguistic approaches put emphases on the decoding process apart from meaning and we have rhyming words, phrases, and some nonsense combinations of letters that rhyme with the others. Other linguistic approaches use meaningful sentences, but the content is different from a diversified word recognition approach. A few writers have gone so far as to remove pictures from beginning books lest children depend on pictures as clues rather than use the clues they are "supposed to use."

There are so many extremely well-written, well-illustrated, and well-planned series that it is difficult to make a selection. Here are criteria that might be used in selecting a good basic reading series:

1. Read the teacher's manual to see if the basic teaching philosophy meets with your approval.

2. Is the print in the preprimers clear and bold?

3. Is the content meaningful and interesting?

4. Are the illustrations meaningfully related to the content without too much extraneous detail? Are the colors true to what is illustrated? Are the illustrations realistic?

5. Are there books for various reading levels within each grade?

6. Does the teacher's guide give interesting ways of presenting the various skills?

7. Is there fine literary quality in the books for Grades 4 through 6?

8. Is there complete coverage of the different types of literature and factual materials with instructional aids to help children read each type efficiently?

SUPPLEMENTARY READERS

Supplementary readers are often used to reenforce skill development, to improve the quality of oral reading, and to give slow learners new material from which to learn the skills they failed to achieve before. Rather than benefiting by rereading basic readers, slow learners are stimulated by new materials that may accomplish the same skill building. Such books, in variety, are used in an individual approach.

In selecting supplementary readers these criteria may be considered:

1. Through inspection of the teacher's manual, does the series serve the needs you recognize?

2. Does the content lend itself to fluent reading?

3. Is it attractive and will the stories appeal to the children who will be reading them?

4. Are there new and interesting approaches to the various skills that will enable slow learners to grasp them easily?

AUXILIARY BOOKS

Many basic series are providing auxiliary books that use similar vocabulary for independent reading. Especially at the preprimer and primer levels such material is excellent in giving children self-confidence. After children are well along in primers it is a challenge to them to have a chart on which are listed the various auxiliary books. They may write their initials after the book title on the chart after they have read it. This is the beginning of completely independent reading. Usually by the time children have read all the auxiliary preprimers, they will have finished the basic primer and prehaps a supplementary one and will be ready for auxiliary primers. With careful development of the word recognition clues and basic skills it is surprising how widely children can read at this level. It is important that books with bold type, fluent content, and appealing pictures be available when children are ready for them. Auxiliary books differ from ordinary library books in that the vocabulary is somewhat controlled, the sentence structure is simpler, and the print is larger. Many libraries, however, are beginning to include such books on their shelves and librarians are directing young readers to these books.

Library Books or Trade Books

A good classroom library in which children can avail themselves of its facilities at all times has many advantages. Appendixes O, P, and R provide listings of books of various interests and ability levels. Teachers at all grade levels should devote some time to reading to children. This reading should exemplify the best qualities of oral reading. The selections should be the finest literature available for children at their grade level. The experience should help children to be more enthusiastic about wanting to read and to be able to read well. As soon as children acquire the word recognition techniques and have gained enough independence in reading, they should be encouraged to check out books from the library if someone is available to give them some guidance. Lists of good books for children can be obtained from the following sources (prices and addresses subject to change):

1. Superintendent of Documents, Government Printing Office, Washington, D.C.
   Children's Books, 1964; Children's Books, 1966
   Annotated lists of some 200 titles; 20¢ each
2. American Library Association, 50 East Huron St., Chicago, Ill.
   "Best Books for Children"
   Issued annually in March; $3
3. National Council of Teachers of English, 508 South Sixth St., Champaign, Ill.
   "Adventuring with Books" (yearly publication including lists for kindergarten through sixth grade with annotations, publishers, and prices; 75¢)
   "Books for Beginning Readers" (a good list for children with immature reading skills; $1)
4. McGinniss, Dorothy. *Guide to the Selection of Books for your Elementary School Library.* Somerville, N.J.: Baker and Taylor Co., 1967.
5. *The Horn Book,* Association for Childhood Education, International.

Association for Supervision and Curriculum Development, various state reading circle programs, many county and city libraries, and various college children's literature instructors prepare carefully selected lists of good children's books each year.

Workbooks

For many years some educators have condemned workbooks and other educators have helped to prepare them, and teachers all over the country have put them to use. Numerous articles have been written and a little research has been done pertaining to use and abuse of workbooks. The crux of the problem seems to relate to the quality of the workbook and the way in which it is used.

What are the qualities of a good workbook?

1. It should be prepared by someone with successful experience in teaching reading at the grade level for which it is intended.

2. The print and illustrations should be large enough so that it is appropriate for the age level for which it is prepared.

3. There should be a carefully planned sequence of reading readiness skills and word recognition techniques including the common elements of phonics and the various skills of comprehension and uses to which reading may be put. Two or three pages should be provided for each type of such development.

4. There should be interesting variety in the types of exercises so that skills are developed within different types of context.

5. Workbooks with perforated pages are best for flexibility.

6. A workbook may parallel a basic series of readers but it should not be dependent on the reader. A teacher should be able to use it with or without the reader.

7. There should be pages occasionally that check on interrelated use of many previously taught skills.

How can a workbook be used flexibly?

1. Available workbooks should be those that develop and reenforce the various skills required by children of their particular grade level and the preceding grades.

2. After a skill has been introduced by the teacher through explanation and chalkboard work, each child may do a page as proof for himself, for the teacher, and for his parents as evidence that he knows how to use that skill effectively.

3. If he makes a mistake, the page serves as a diagnosis of his misconception or improper use of the skill. It is a clue for the teacher to give help. After further explanation and help are given, another page using the same skill in other context is tried. If he errs again, further help is needed and a third page is tried.

4. Many children will need only the first page on which a particular skill is used. If it is done correctly he may tear the page from the book and take it home, or it may be kept in a large envelope to be bound with other pages to be taken home later.

5. While children who need extra help are doing second and third pages, children who have mastered the skill are free to do independent reading.

6. The review pages help to see how well children remember what has been learned and they point up the specific needs of the child in accordance with the errors he makes. Careful re-teaching and use of previous workbook pages or teacher-prepared worksheets may help to ascertain relearning and use of the skill.

7. There may be days when no workbook page needs to be done by anyone because no new skill has been presented that day or because everyone has caught on quickly and easily. There may be days when two or more pages (they may not be in sequence) may be done because several techniques or skills have been taught. There may be days when a teacher-prepared worksheet may serve a particular purpose that the workbook does not include. There should be days when a child is free to choose a book and read independently to prove to himself that the skills he has acquired really work and can bring him enjoyment and satisfaction.

What purposes can workbooks serve?

1. Carefully selected pages can reenforce a skill immediately after it is taught.

2. Workbook pages checked with the child can show him, the teacher, and the parents what he knows and what further help he needs.

3. Workbook pages can be diagnostic in that a teacher can study the type of mistakes the child is making and thus determine the cause of his difficulties.

4. Review pages give evidence of how well a child remembers and can relate various skills to a challenging situation.

5. Workbooks can save a teacher's time spent in preparing various worksheets to accomplish the same purposes.

6. Individual needs can be met quickly and easily. Extra pages from workbooks should be filed by skills and used as various children show the need for reenforcement of a particular skill.

7. They may assist in the establishment of good work habits. If properly presented each page may be a challenge for the child to do his best, to be neat, and to be aware of the purpose the activity is to serve. A check mark should be placed on the corner of each page that shows evidence of the child's best work. If it is worth doing at all it is worth doing well, and children feel that their efforts are

appreciated when they are given some indication that it has been observed.

What limitations do workbooks have?

1. Unless each page is checked carefully and the child made aware of his mistakes, unless reteaching is done, unless the child knows the purpose of his completing the page, and unless he is motivated to do it to the best of his ability, the time spent on workbooks is wasted.

2. It takes a considerable amount of time for the teacher to check each workbook and follow through with the help each child may need. After one child's workbook has been found to be correct, that child may help to check others. Children making the same mistakes may be helped at the same time.

3. Workbook exercises can become frustrating and boring unless presented with inspiration, challenge, and careful instruction.

What workbooks are especially useful?

If a basal series of readers is selected carefully so that you know the material has been prepared by well-qualified people, then the workbooks that accompany the series may also be best since they are planned to support and reenforce the skills in accordance with suggestions in the teacher's manual.

If children coming from another school are found to be extremely lacking in basic skills, instead of starting them back in the early books of the series you are using, it is often more interesting for the child, and his progress is likely to be faster, if *New Reading Skilltext* (published by Charles E. Merrill, 1300 Alum Creek Drive, Columbus, Ohio 43218) is used. After the child's needs are determined through a reading inventory check list, the correct level *Skilltext* may be selected. Often a child will move rapidly through stories such as *Bibs, Nicky,* and then *Uncle Funny Bunny,* and, if instruction is carefully given along the way, the child who may have entered fourth grade with a first-grade reading score may in a few months be able to join his classmates in reading at their level. If a new child is found to have no phonics background when he moves into a third or fourth grade, a phonics program along with inspirational and challenging teaching can help the child to use phonics in a meaningful way.

The thing we must learn as teachers is that there is no perfect contribution or perfect material; there is only a perfect teacher; and that per-

fect teacher is the one who evaluates each contribution to see what it can be and mean in an entire program which consists of much more than any one contribution.[5]

Suggestions for Class Participation and Discussion

1. Visit a classroom and observe how the class is organized for reading. Were children grouped? How much individual instruction took place?
2. Visit a classroom and observe classroom management. Which of the principles of good management did you observe? Which were lacking?
3. How do the materials available in schools today compare with what you used when you learned to read?
4. Go to the curriculum library and examine the basic readers for the grade level you intend to teach. Be sure to examine the teacher's manual. What three series do you prefer and why?
5. Examine workbooks for the grade level you intend to teach. Which ones do you prefer and why?
6. Listen to recordings and make a list you would like to have for a "listening post" at the grade level you intend to teach.
7. Preview some films and film strips and make a selection for the grade level you intend to teach.
8. Examine children's magazines. Discuss features that you like in three of them.
9. Examine pocketbooks and make a list of the ones you would like to use at the grade level you intend to teach.
10. React to the quotation at the end of the chapter.

Bibliography

ANDERSON, ROBERT. *Ungraded Primary School.* New York: Harcourt Brace, 1963.

BROWN and BROWN. "New Horizons in Materials," *The Instructor.* Mar., 1967, pp. 109–110.

CLEMENTS, FIELDER, and TABACHNICK. *Social Study: Inquiry in Elementary Classrooms.* Indianapolis: Bobbs-Merrill, 1966.

DALE, EDGAR. *Audio-Visual Methods in Teaching.* New York: Holt, 1950.

DAVIS, D. C. *Patterns of Primary Education.* New York: Harper & Row, 1963.

ERICKSON, CARLTON. *Fundamentals of Teaching with Audio-Visual Technology.* New York: Macmillan, 1965.

---

5 Constance M. McCullough, from the Fifth Edith P. Merritt Memorial Lecture presented at San Francisco State College, June, 1966.

GOODLAD, JOHN, and ANDERSON, J. *The Nongraded Elementary School.* New York: Harcourt, Brace, 1954.

GOODLAD, JOHN (ed.). *The 65th Yearbook of the National Society for the Study of Education.* Chicago: University of Chicago Press, 1966.

KINDER, J. S. *Audio-Visual Materials and Techniques in Education.* New York: American Book, 1959.

LADLEY, WINIFRED. *Sources of Good Books and Magazines for Children: An Annotated Bibliography.* Newark, Del.: International Reading Association, 1965.

————. *Using Audio-Visual Materials in Education.* New York: American Book, 1965.

KNELLER, GEORGE (ed.). *Foundations of Education.* New York: Wiley, 1967, Ch. 17.

LUMSDAINE, A. A., and GLASER (eds.). *Teaching Machines and Programmed Learning: A Source Book.* Department of Audio-Visual Instruction, National Education Association, 1960.

MILLER, RICHARD I. *The Nongraded School.* New York: Harper & Row, 1967.

MURRAY, THOMAS R., and SWARTOUT, SHERWIN G. *Integrated Teaching Materials.* New York: David McKay, 1963.

SHORES, LEWIS. *Instructional Materials: An Introduction for Teachers.* New York: The Ronald Press, 1960.

Southern Humboldt Unified School District, *Ungraded Primary Curriculum Guide, Book I Reading,* Miranda, Calif., 1964.

SPACHE, GEORGE. *Classroom Organization for Reading Instruction, An Annotated Bibliography.* Newark, Del.: International Reading Association, 1965.

SPACHE, GEORGE. *Sources of Good Books for Poor Readers: An Annotated Bibliography.* Newark, Del.: International Reading Association, 1966.

STEFFERUD, ALFRED (ed.). *The Wonderful World of Books.* New York: New American Library, 1963.

TARBET, DONALD. *Television and Our Schools.* New York: Ronald Press, 1961.

WITTICH, WALTER A., and SCHULLER, CHARLES F. *Audio-Visual Materials.* New York: Harper, 1957.

Refer to the *Education Index* for current articles on materials, techniques, and classroom organization.

CHAPTER 15

Research in Reading
and a Look
to the Future

With more ideas coming from more fields of endeavor, more typewriters clicking off more pages, more plans for more approaches, more promotion conferences for more sales, more gadgetry, more advertising, and more money for buying, the busy teacher is saying, "How do I know what is good, what is worth trying, what is best for children?" No one can say with any degree of accuracy, "This is best for all schools," or "This is best for all teachers," or "This is best for all children." But there are a few guidelines that may help in formulating judgments:

1. Be sure that the person or persons behind the idea, the approach, the books, the materials, or the machine has had teacher training education and has had successful teaching experience with children.

2. Be sure the books or other products come from a reputable company.

3. Check with some of the leading educational organizations and see what they have to say. The organizations most closely associated with the teaching of reading and young children would be:

a. International Reading Association, Newark, Delaware
b. National Council of Teachers of English, Champaign, Illinois
c. Association for Childhood Education, International, Washington, D.C.
d. Association for Supervision and Curriculum Development, Washington, D.C.
4. Consult with education professors at your local college.
5. Consult reports of research studies. Do not rely on reports made by a promoter of an approach, material, or gadget but check on studies made by the organizations mentioned previously.

Reports of Research in Reading

For teachers who have never had a course pertaining to educational research, books such as *Introduction to Educational Research,* by Travers, or *Understanding Educational Research,* by Van Dalen, might provide good background information. Either of these books should be available at any college library or book store.

The American Educational Research Association, which is a department of the National Education Association, publishes an *Encyclopedia of Educational Research* through The Macmillan Company, and this is probably the most complete summation of research studies compiled in any one volume; it is available in most college and university libraries. The periodical, *Review of Educational Research,* published also by the American Education Research Association, gives critical summaries of research in the various fields; it, too, should be available at colleges and education libraries.

The Educational Records Bureau (21 Audubon Avenue, New York City) publishes *Research in Reading during Another Four Years,* giving very good summaries and an excellent bibliography of research studies. The U.S. Government Printing Office (Washington, D. C.) provides the following publications: *Research in Reading at the Primary Level* (an annotated bibliography, Doris Gunderson, ed.), 1963; *Research in Reading for the Middle Grades* (an annotated bibliography, Warren G. Cutts, ed.), 1963. Watch for new compilations from this and other sources.

The University of Chicago; the University of Syracuse, New York; University of Pittsburgh; National Reading Conference; and Claremont College, California, have large reading conferences each year and publish a bulletin after the conference that includes papers by outstanding educators as well as some material on research. Most education libraries have current as well as previous conference reports. The International Reading Association, Newark, Delaware, publishes a yearbook after each annual meeting that has a large section on research.

The following periodicals contain research reports as well as other interesting articles for classroom teachers:

Journal of Educational Research
Journal of Educational Psychology
Elementary English
Elementary School Journal
Education
Journal of Social Research
Educational Records Bulletins
The Reading Teacher
Reading Research Quarterly
Clearing House

Educational Administration and
  Supervision
Journal of Experimental Education
Phi Delta Kappan
The Reading Teacher's Mailbox
School Review
National Education Association
  Journal
The Reading Newsreport
Educational Leadership

The N.E.A. (National Education Association, Washington, D.C.) has published a series of bulletins on "What Research Says to the Teacher." These are usually on file in a curriculum materials library and are especially interesting to classroom teachers.

The Educational Research Information Center has published a complete index to 1,740 documents relative to the culturally disadvantaged, including research reports, descriptions of projects, and limited evaluation of materials. This index (No. FS. 5.337:37001) is available from the U.S. Government Printing Office (Washington, D.C., at 65¢ per copy; price subject to change). All the reports date from 1960. (They may also be obtained in microfilm.)

The Scope of Research Studies

Many studies relate indirectly to the teaching of reading even though they are not catalogued as such. For example, various aspects of physical development, the age at which children enter school, the size of classes, and organization of the school curriculum all affect the teaching of reading. Of course, there are also a great many studies based directly on all phases of reading development, such as the age at which various aspects of reading may be introduced.

The quantity of research projects far exceeds the quality. Helen Robinson of the University of Chicago, in her article, "The Status of Reading Research Today,"[1] alludes to the fact that "research is voluminous but of rather poor quality." Much of the research is done by doctoral students who must complete a bite-size piece in a short time and seldom do more than the one piece. These pieces are seldom referred to except by other doctoral students and the bits of findings are seldom put to practical use.

In the past there had been little communication among those interested in research and consequently there was much duplication of effort. Russell G. Stauffer writes:

> If our mutual concern and long-range objective is to build excellence in education, then how wonderful it would be—would it not?—if we could create a science, research, teaching complex in education that would institute and test innovations on a solidly-established venture of cooperative effort. Then, by 1976, CFA (Computer Forecast Art) might bring about a declaration of education that could go a long way toward developing every student's potential to its fullest and make the entire universe safe for democracy.[2]

Colleges and professors are vying with one another over certain funds available as research grants, and there is much scurrying just before deadline dates to get proposals into writing.

If we are really striving to improve the quality of reading instruction, it is time for groups of educators to do some serious planning over a period of time so that there is not so much duplication of effort and so many faulty projects with inconsequential results.

Perhaps more doctoral projects should be of the type where data is analyzed and studies of materials made as, for example, was reported in the April, 1966 issue of *The Reading Teacher*. In this study, words were listed from the five commonly used basal reading series for Grades one, two and three. These words were analyzed for a sound-symbol frequency count. Such information is valuable as a guide for teaching phonics.

Promising Projects and Procedures

Millions of dollars are now available for research that had never been heard of before. Large foundations, the federal government, and special endowments make large-scale research possible.

The United States Office of Education reported that over 100 mil-

[1] Helen M. Robinson, "The Status of Reading Research Today," in *Reading and Inquiry*, International Reading Association, Newark, Del., 1965.
[2] Russell G. Stauffer, "CFA 1976." *The Reading Teacher*, Dec. 1966, p. 202.

lion dollars was available for research and related activities for the fiscal year 1966.[3]

The following projects and procedures show promise:

ERIC CENTER

The Education Research Information Center, created by the United States Office of Education, has general headquarters in Washington, D.C. It was established for the purpose of collecting, disseminating, and exchanging ideas relative to education. At last there seems to be a general depository where information can be dispersed quickly and easily. It should be a beginning toward the next needed step. Let's take a long hard look at what has been done, what we have learned from what has been done, and then decide what can be done with what we know, and decide further what we need to find out next.

ERIC/READING

ERIC/Reading has been established at the University of Indiana at Bloomington and is operated jointly by the university and the International Reading Association. It is an attempt to do for reading what the ERIC Center in Washington, D.C. is doing for the entire curriculum. Abstracts, microfiche cards, summaries, and many types of data related to reading are available through this Center. Such a service is tremendously valuable for professors, students, and classroom teachers. It should be a means of making worthwhile procedures, techniques, and materials generally known as soon as they have been proven by qualified researchers in classroom situations.

IDEA

IDEA (Institute for the Development of Educational Activities) is a project sponsored by the Charles F. Kettering Foundation to test new ideas for the improvement of education in the schools. Many interesting reports should be forthcoming.

MULTIDISCIPLINARY APPROACH

For a long time educators have recognized the need for expert advice from those skilled in pediatrics, psychology, genetics, anthro-

[3] Glenn C. Boerrigter, "The USOE's Support of Extramural Research." *Phi Delta Kappan,* June, 1966, p. 555.

pology, social work, and other fields relating to child growth and development. Some colleges and universities have been attempting to combine resources of these fields in developing courses in child growth and development. Some are utilizing talent from these areas in their clinics. So, too, must educational research seek, respect, and combine outside forces to determine what is best for children.

Many very limited studies have been made with regard to children learning to read at three and four years of age. In some cases it was concluded that these children did as well or better than other children when they reached third grade. Psychologists and ophthalmologists might quickly ask, "But at what expense? What effect might such early concentration on print have on a child's eyes?" And the psychiatrist might ask, "How frustrated does the child become when he is being taught at this age?" He knows what such frustrations can do to the child's emotional development. The pediatrician knows what types of muscular experiences the three- and four-year-old should be having and how he may be deprived of them if too much time is spent teaching him to read. He might ask, "Why teach him to read so early? Wouldn't it be more economical of time to wait and teach him later when reading can serve more purposes in his life?" Who knows what breadth and depth of concepts, what stimulation of interests, what joys of childhood he could be experiencing during the time reading is being thrust upon him at the ages of three and four?

I could not agree with you more in your statement regarding the importance of pre-reading experiences. I can have a full blown emotional outburst over the imposition of reading on pre-school children. These children are neither physiologically ready nor experientially ready for such symbolic emphasis. The dangers involved, in "too early reading" are far greater than the benefits. There is much evidence to indicate that if pre-reading experience, readiness development, and all other communicative skills are developed, even through second grade, the child will teach himself to read almost as a normal process of development. This evidence also indicates that such children are better readers than those who have been thrust into it too early.[4]

The various disciplines, too, would help us evaluate children's progress on a much broader base. Academic achievement would be considered along with the total growth and development of the child

4 Gerald N. Getman, Section Chairman of the Optometric Extension Program (International), a nonprofit foundation for education and research in vision, in a summary statement, March, 1967.

to be sure that a child whose teacher proudly announces that he has read over a hundred books and scored highest in certain reading tests has not been deprived of other equally significant growth opportunities. Experts in the various fields will help to keep reading in a proper perspective in relation to a child's total welfare.

First-Grade Reading Studies

NATIONWIDE PROJECTS   Perhaps one of the most extensive research studies was instigated by Professor Donald Durrell of Boston University, sponsored by the U.S. Office of Education and coordinated by Professor Guy Bond at the University of Minnesota. It involved twenty-seven first grades in various parts of the country. There was good geographic distribution, but the groups were not equally matched to the extent that it would be fair to contrast results among groups. Various approaches to the teaching of reading were used, and tests were administered at the beginning and toward the end of the 1964 to 1965 school year. It was found that the classroom teacher is the greatest determining factor in the success of any program. No one method could be declared clearly superior to another because all classes taught phonics to some extent, all used some writing experiences, all taught the alphabet, and all provided a variety of reading materials. Although many problems prevented very definite conclusions, the total project stimulated much interest in the improvement of reading instruction. All those engaged in the study feel that they benefited from it. Fourteen of the participating schools are continuing with their studies into a second year. There was no significant difference in the final achievement of i.t.a., linguistic, language arts, or basal reader approaches. (Summaries of all twenty-seven studies appear in the May and October, 1966, and May, 1967, issues of *The Reading Teacher*.) Such studies help to subdue publicized claims of superiority made by drastically new and different approaches to the teaching of reading. More of these studies are likely to be made with improvement in accounting and evaluation.

Head-Start Programs

Also on a nationwide basis the federal government is providing assistance to underprivileged children through the implementation of Head-Start programs in school districts qualifying and seeking aid in the education of the preschool age group. College classes have been set up for the teachers working with these children and many studies are under way evaluating such programs. In many instances expectations have been too high. Even if children from Head-Start programs do not measure up to other children in certain readiness tests, who can say how much lower their scores may have been if they had not had the Head-Start experiences. Those working with Head-Start children are becoming so aware of the many areas of extreme deprivation in the lives of these children that they are recommending boarding schools for children coming from homes of hopeless, extreme depravity. Not only do these children experience deprivation in their homes, but the negative influences on their development are serious handicaps that a Head-Start program alone cannot overcome. Follow-Through is the next step in this venture.

ACTION RESEARCH

"Action research" is experimentation that teachers can do in their own classrooms. You are not bound by contracts or formalities. You may pick and choose techniques or materials you feel worthy of a trial with your children in your situation. If indications are that it isn't "clicking," drop it and use your own best judgment in working with those techniques, those materials, and that philosophy that gives children the best possible opportunities.

Into the Future

Another question that comes from beginning teachers after they leave college is, "How do I keep up with new trends and with what is happening in education after I leave college?" Certainly becoming interested in research studies and trying out what seems plausible in your situation is one way of keeping abreast with the times. Other ways would include the following:

1. Join local and national education organizations such as: *Association of Childhood Education, International.* This organization concerns itself with topics pertaining to the development and education of children at the primary level. There are local, state, and national meetings, and the publication, *Childhood Education,* has interesting professional articles each month. Become active in such an organization.

Association for Supervision and Curriculum Development. This organization at local, state, and national levels provides stimulating meetings and its publication, *Educational Leadership,* presents articles by leading educators on timely topics in the field of curriculum.

International Reading Association. Local, state, and national meetings focus attention on problems related to the teaching of reading. *The Reading Teacher,* issued each month of the school year, brings up-to-the-minute reports on reading research, problems, and trends in the field of reading.

2. Make a practice of reading some professional books each month. Students never have time to read all the books listed in the various bibliographies that are provided in their courses, but keeping these bibliographies and continuing to read from them is a stimulating experience. Also looking for new books at an education library can bring many new ideas to you.

3. Spend time browsing in a curriculum library (county, city schools, or college) and check out courses of study, curriculum guides, bulletins, etc. that may enrich your teaching.

4. Visit the display booths at education conventions and note the new materials. Pick up free bulletins, book lists, etc. so that you can do some evaluating when you go back home.

5. Subscribe to professional magazines such as some of those listed previously in this chapter.

6. Share your problems, ideas, and talents with other teachers. It is good for your morale and theirs to be interested in other teachers and to know they are interested in you. Take the initiative in being friendly and strive for mutual respect and cooperation—it can be very rewarding.

7. Develop broad interest. Travel, if you can, in the summer; have a hobby or two and be vitally interested in the cultures of the world. You will be a more interesting person and you will find other people more interesting if you can appreciate many things. Your outside interests will add flavor to your teaching as well as zest to your life.

A Final Challenge

Those of you who are just finishing your college education and are on the threshold of becoming teachers have golden opportunities before you. You have sparkle, the vigor, and the personal charm of youth. With a background of conscientious study, guided student teaching experience, and enthusiasm for your chosen profession, you have an integrity and a freshness that is envied by those who have lived and served the major part of their careers. You have nothing to fear but the discouragements that come to all who allow themselves to be discouraged. You have the promise of great satisfactions and long-lasting gratifications if you strive to make each day worthy of your own scrutiny. You are the key figures who influence what children are likely to become. They will remember you for what you say, what you do and what you are—but more especially for how you accept them as they are and inspire them to become what they will. Your function in society is more important than that of a banker, a lawyer, or even a doctor—you have more lasting influence than any of them. You have a self-imposed obligation to children and you alone can evaluate most effectively the total development that takes place in the children you teach. You have tremendous resources at your disposal, but you must remember, always, that the greatest determining factor in any classroom situation is you, the teacher.

Along with an obligation to children, teachers have an obligation to their profession. Share what talents you have in whatever ways you can. Show more appreciation and less criticism in working relationships with others. Dare to try the new, and when it proves successful write an article, speak at a professional meeting, or give a demonstration about it. You are challenged to be a leader of the great tomorrow in education.

Learning to read and reading to learn never stops—it goes on each day of the year, each year of our lives; so, too, must teaching to read and reading to teach—the challenge is not to criticize but to find better ways.
—Verna Dieckman Anderson

Suggestions for Class Participation and Discussion

1. Report on some interesting research study from any of the sources mentioned in this chapter.
2. Why is it so difficult to carry on research from year to year in our schools?
3. What would be some of the hardships involved in carrying on a research project?
4. Explain how something that has proved successful in one classroom situation might not be successful in another.
5. How might a teacher get help if she had a classroom problem?

6. Check three books in the bibliography you hope to read when you find time after graduation.
7. Find out more about the various teacher organizations. Discuss them in class.
8. Browse through the various teacher magazines in the library. Which ones do you feel would be of greatest value to you as a teacher? Why?
9. Investigate to see if any educational conferences will be held in or near your community during the coming months. Could you arrange to attend? (Many education organizations do not charge college students a registration fee.) Examine some of the yearbooks of the education organizations.
10. Discuss the quotation at the end of the chapter.

Bibliography

American Association of School Administrators, *Educational Research Service Circulars* (issued 8 to 12 times a year; on file in most libraries).

ARTLEY, A. STERL. *Your Child Learns to Read*. Chicago: Scott, Foresman, 1953.

CHASE, MARY ELLEN. *Recipe for a Magic Childhood*. New York: Macmillan.

Education Index. Bronx, N.Y.: H. W. Wilson Co. (This index to magazine articles is published every month at a cost of $18 per year. Most libraries have bound volumes and current copies giving students an excellent access to articles on any topic in education.)

Encyclopedia of Educational Research. New York: Macmillan (see latest edition).

GAGE, N. L. (ed.) . *Handbook of Research on Teaching*. Chicago: Rand McNally, 1963.

GANS, ROMA. *Common Sense in Teaching Reading*. Indianapolis: Bobbs-Merrill, 1963.

Good Reading for Parents. National Congress of Parents and Teachers (700 N. Rush Ave., Chicago, Ill., 15¢). An excellent list of books and pamphlets to recommend to parents.

GRANT, EVA (ed.). *P.T.A. Guide to What's Happening in Education*. New York: Scholastic Book Services, 1965.

GRUENBERG, SYDONIE. *The Parent's Guide to Everyday Problems of Boys and Girls*. New York: Random House, 1958.

HILLSON, MAURIE (ed.). *Current Issues and Research in Education: Elementary Education*. New York: Free Press, 1967.

HUNNICUTT, C. W., and IVERSON, W. J. *Research in the Three R's*. New York: Harper, 1958.

HYMES, JAMES. *Before the Child Reads*. New York: Harper, 1958.

———. *A Pound of Prevention*. New York State Committee on Mental Hygiene, 1947.

———. *Understanding Your Child*. Englewood Cliffs, N.J.: Prentice-Hall 1952.

JENKINS, GLADYS. *These are Your Children*. Chicago: Scott, Foresman, 1953.

LARRICK, NANCY. *A Parent's Guide to Children's Education*. New York: Pocket Books, 1963.

————. *A Parent's Guide to Children's Reading*. New York: Pocket Books, 1958.

MACINTOSH, HELEN. *How Children Learn to Read*. Supt. of Documents, U.S. Government Printing Office, 1952.

McKEE, PAUL. *A Primer for Parents: How Your Child Learns to Read*. Boston: Houghton-Mifflin, 1957.

PLESSAS, GUS. *Sources of Reading Research, An Annotated Bibliography*, International Reading Association, 1965.

Research in Reading of the Middle Grades. U.S. Department of Health, Education & Welfare (latest edition).

SEIPT, IRENE. *Your Child's Happiness: A Guide for Parents*. New York: Collier, 1955.

SHANE, HAROLD, et al. *Improving Language Arts Instruction Through Research*. Washington, D.C.: Association for Supervision and Curriculum Development, 1962.

STRANG, RUTH. *Helping Your Child Improve His Reading*. New York: Dutton, 1960.

TOOZE, RUTH. *Your Children Want to Read*. Englewood Cliffs: Prentice-Hall, 1957.

WITTY, PAUL. *Helping Children Read Better*. Science Research Associates, 1950.

Your Child from One to Six and *Your Child from 6 to 12*. Supt. of Documents, U.S. Government Printing Office (20¢).

Sources of Pamphlets for Parents

American Society for Family Living, 32 W. Randolph, Chicago, Ill.
Child Study Association of America, 9 E. 89th St., New York 28, N.Y.
Parent's Magazine, Bergenfield, N.J.
Public Affairs Pamphlets, Inc., 22 E. 38th St., New York 16, N. Y.
Science Research Associates, 259 E. Erie St., Chicago 11, Ill.
Supt. of Documents, U.S. Government Printing Office, Washington, D.C. (current listings are published).

APPENDIX A

Child Development Activities

Activities for Developing Bilateral Coordination

(Muscular development so that both sides of the body relate properly and synchronize in activities)

1. Tracking. Circles are made from cardboard and stuck to the floor with rubber cement with spacing just right for children to use left-right hand-knee coordination. If these tracks are spaced around the outer extremities of the room the children can track each other around the room. They should be encouraged to look from left to right and proceed with regular left-right movement. As soon as they catch on to how it is done, they can do it to music.

2. Animal dramatization. Children pretend they are certain four-footed animals. Tag, Follow-the-Leader, and Guess What Animal I Am can be played, giving plenty of time for performance.

3. The tops and bottoms can be removed from large barrels or cardboard drums. (Make sure they are clean and have contained no harmful chemicals.) A maze may be set up with arrows for children to follow on their hands and knees.

4. A jungle gym and other types of bars can develop good left-right coordination if children are encouraged to climb hand over hand and foot over foot as they go upward, shifting weight as they go (instead of taking a step and pulling the other foot up to the same rung and then proceeding in this way to the next).

5. A strong suspended rope or pole can challenge children to move hand over hand supporting their weight with their feet as they climb.

6. A low trampoline or a bedspring with a mattress or thick matting is wonderful for children to learn to balance themselves as they attempt to walk left-right-left-right across and back again.

7. It can be a challenge to children to walk between two chalk lines drawn across the floor or playground. These lines can be drawn closer and closer together as children become more proficient in walking between them, left-right-left-right, without stepping outside the lines. Outstretched arms help to maintain balance.

8. Hopping (two hops on one foot and then two hops on the other). Relays can be run this way after a while.

9. Skipping is a next step after a child has learned to hop, and this can be done to music. Movement of the arms helps to maintain balance. Demonstration is the best way to teach skipping.

10. Marching, running, and galloping can be demonstrated and then done to music.

11. Children may pretend they are skating (gliding with one foot and then the other). Actual skating is excellent for left-right coordination. Skates are a good gift to recommend to parents for their children.

12. Climbing stairs is good experience for young children if they climb left over right, right over left, etc., with corresponding shift in body weight.

13. A line may be drawn and children may be challenged to see how far they can jump from that line, each day trying to improve their own records.

14. A tricycle is a valuable piece of equipment for home, Headstart and Follow-Through programs, nursery school, or kindergarten outdoor play. A large, double circle would provide a good course. Counting the number of circuits in taking turns affords good counting experience, too. Propelling a wagon and steering it around the course is also a good activity.

15. A skate board on a very slight incline is excellent for body balance. A very young child might lie on it and steer it by twisting his body slightly. Then he can try sitting on it and guiding it with his hands. Discourage standing on it until you are reasonably sure the child can do it without getting hurt.

16. Walking a beam. At first young children may be challenged to walk along the flat side of a six-inch plank. Then the plank may be supported on the narrow side and the child challenged to walk left over right over left, etc., without stepping off. Outstretched arms are required for balancing.

17. A heavy plywood board may be suspended between two large wooden blocks and bolted securely. There should be enough spring in the board so that it affords a challenge to the child to maintain his balance as he attempts to jump up and down.

18. A wheelbarrow that children may use to haul things from one place to another is very good for developing body balance.

19. Standing straight with feet together and arms outstretched, challenge children to touch the left foot with the right hand and

then the right foot with the left hand. Also, with arms extended over head, challenge them to stoop and touch their toes without bending their knees.

20. Exercises to be done on resting rugs or mats:

a. As they lie on their stomachs with their hands clasped together on their backs, challenge them to lift both legs and turn their heads from side to side without touching their chins on the mat.
b. Have them pretend they are windmills, lying on their backs and moving both arms and legs out and down to music.
c. As they lie on their backs, have children raise the right leg, extend the left arm, and turn their heads to the right on one count; raise the left leg, extend the right arm, and turn the head to the left on the next count.
d. While they sit with legs together and arms extended, have them reach down and touch their toes to music.
e. While they lie on their backs with hands on hips, have them raise both legs to music, then raise them alternately; then with legs down flat, try to sit up and then lie down to music.

21. For older children, bicycling, swimming, dancing, and skating afford good opportunities for developing good body coordination.

Activities for Developing Eye-Hand Coordination

1. *Block Play*. Various sizes and types of blocks serve many purposes. All of them involve eye-hand coordination, but many additional learning experiences are involved simultaneously. Large or small body, hand, and finger muscles come into play according to the size of blocks and their weight. Boards and corner pieces with grooves and metal pipes or bars that prevent such building from falling apart are excellent for the development of buildings. Consider the possibilities for planning, group cooperation in building, language development, and countless concepts as activities take place within the completed structures.

Blockcraft Blocks (made by the Blockcraft Co., Cedar Springs, Michigan) are especially recommended for eye-hand coordination. Other additional learning possibilities they afford are matching shapes, getting the feel of various shapes, and observing, identifying and sorting colors.

Large 12″ × 6″ × 4″ hollow blocks with openings for the hands at either end afford many building possibilities.

Nested blocks afford another challenge for eye-hand coordination. A type of nested blocks known as 'Percolator' provides for additional experiences such as recognizing shapes, textures, sizes, curves and planes, top and bottom, inside and outside, filled and empty, etc.

Blocks are usually expensive items of equipment, and certain kinds might be made by a woodworking class or at a lumber yard or mill.

2. *Balls and Bean Bags.* A large beach ball is probably the easiest type of ball for the very young child to manipulate. He can use the large muscles of his arms for grasping it, and he can give it a shove to send it away. It gives him the feeling of roundness, and he comes to know how to cope with movement of objects about him.

For first throwing and catching experiences, bean bags are better than balls. They are easier to hang on to and they will not roll far beyond the area of play as balls sometimes do. A child's first attempts to throw and catch are random. Tossing underhand is easier than overhand for first attempts. After tossing and catching can be done easily, a bean bag board with large holes in it may be introduced for the additional challenge of getting the bag into one of the holes while standing behind a goal line. Still later, certain amounts of credit may be ascribed to each hole and a game evolves. Such a game may be used when children are learning to count: first by one's, then two's, five's, ten's, etc.

Large balloons blown up, tied to each child's wrist, and tossed around on the playground give very young children a chance to use many muscles in trying to catch them and set them in motion again. The slow motion of the balloons and their very light weight give little children a much better chance to achieve control over them than if heavier balls are used. A lawn is the best place for this activity.

Soft balls that are not made of rubber and are a size that would fit nicely into the hands of young children are best for their throwing and catching experiences because they will not bounce far out of the play area.

Large rubber balls are best used within circles of children for rolling, pushing, catching, and bouncing experiences. If the children are sitting or standing close enough the ball is not likely to get outside the circle.

"Hotball" is a good game for the very young. The children are seated close together in a circle. The large ball is given to one child.

He puts it on the floor and rolls it around under his hands getting it "hot." Then he shoves it across the floor to the other side of the circle. The child to whom it comes takes the ball and rolls it around under his hands getting it "hot" again and then pushes it across the floor, and so the game proceeds.

"Dodge ball" is more difficult. The children stand in a circle and one child is "It." He stands in the circle and tries to dodge as the ball is thrown across the circle. If "It" is touched by the ball, the child who had thrown the ball becomes "It." Be careful not to use a heavy ball that would knock children off their feet.

In a game called "Teacher" one child stands about five feet in front of a line of children. He tosses a large ball to each child in turn, down the line. If a child fails to catch the ball he must go to the end of the line. When the "teacher" has tossed the ball on down the line and reaches the end, the first child in line becomes the new "teacher" and the old one goes to the end of the line. If several large balls are available, it is good to have several games going at the same time so that children do not have to wait so long to have a turn. For variation the "teacher" might bounce the ball to each child and the child returns it with a bounce.

Children need freedom to talk about the feel of roundness, about throwing, catching, missing, bouncing, and all the other terminology and properties of balls and ball play. A child comes to know that certain balls bounce when dropped and that when a certain amount of pressure is exerted in the downward thrust, the ball will bounce high enough for him to catch. The correct spatial relationship and coordination enables him to bounce and then to catch the ball. With more and more opportunities to see, feel, use, and talk about different balls, he comes to recognize a golf ball, a ping pong ball, a tennis ball, a football, a baseball, a volley ball, a soft ball, and he knows their identifying qualities. Later, when he reads, he has meaning association to bring to printed material about such experiences.

3. *Form Boards.* A board into which such forms as a circle, a square, a triangle, and various other shapes will fit is excellent for the development of eye-hand coordination. Other boards with shapes of various simple objects are equally good. Little knobs on each of the figures make it easier for the very young child to manipulate them. An equally important part of the experience is for the children to be encouraged to talk about things that are square, round, etc., so that these shapes take on expanded meanings.

4. *Puzzles.* When children have become adept at using form

boards they are ready to enjoy picture puzzles. "Judy Puzzles" (available from most educational supply houses) are sturdy, colorful, and related to the interests of young children. They vary in degree of difficulty but would not challenge many children above first grade. In fact, many pre-school and kindergarten children become very adept at putting them together. Jigsaw puzzles are a good rainy day recess time activity for older children. They afford a good challenge for noting details and regarding spatial relationship.

5. *Manipulative Toys*. A wooden frame through which the child pounds wooden pegs and into which he can place wooden screws (a hammer and screwdriver come with such a set) is a good manipulative toy.

Shoe-lacing devices are very good for the young child.

Sturdy dump trucks for use in an outdoor sand or grain box afford young children incentives for much dramatic play as well as developing coordination.

A sand-elevating device is good for use in an indoor sand or grain box.

Snap beads and other put-together and take-apart toys are good for the improvement of finger dexterity.

Trains and tracks (sturdy ones) that can be assembled are challenging, too.

6. *Modeling Material*. Play dough, plasticene, and clay afford good manipulative materials for eye-hand coordination and the development of creative powers. The advantage of clay is that it can be dried, fired, and preserved; the other materials are for temporary use. Talking about what they are doing should be part of the children's work.

7. *Sorting Experiences*. Sorting blocks, beads, buttons, bolts, screws, etc. by size, shape, and colors, and aligning them or stringing them, is good experience in noting likenesses and differences as well as for developing good eye-hand coordination. (When beads are used for sorting there is the problem of their rolling away. A strip of cellophane tape with the sticky side up fastened to the table at either end with other small strips of tape overcomes the problem. The child places the beads along on the sticky tape.) Talking about the objects they are sorting and discussing how they will be used adds to the meaningfulness of the experience.

8. *Peg-Board Activity*. At first, large pegs to be put in large holes may be a challenge to the beginner. As dexterity develops the children may be challenged to create designs using smaller pegs. Discus-

sions of colors, shapes, designs, etc., should be part of the experience.

9. *Chalkboard Activity.* Sticks of chalk may be molded into balls of clay that will fit easily into a young child's hand. This is easier for him to hold than a stick of chalk. With these, children may be challenged to draw circles, squares, triangles, and other forms in large size on the chalkboard. Straight lines, curved lines, broken lines and dots and dashes may be made and discussed. Challenging children to follow directions such as *up, down, over, straight line, curved line,* etc. at the chalkboard is good for ear, eye, hand coordination. Having chalk in both hands and following such directions as *make a circle, make two straight lines or two curved lines* is good for bilaterality. There are many occasions in life when both hands must be used, and the muscles of each need to be strengthened through use. Respect is given for a child's preferred hand, as in writing, but both hands are needed in typing.

10. *Use of Templates.* Templates are forms (usually of plastic or hard rubber composition) that have both inner and outer edges and give children the feel of shapes. Large-sized ones of circles, squares, triangles, rectangles, and diamonds can be used on the chalkboard. Medium-sized ones can be used on large sheets of paper at tables or desks. A child should be encouraged to hold the form, feel all around it with both hands, and to talk about how it feels and what is observed (for example, a triangle has three straight sides that are the same length and three corners that feel sharp, while a square has four equal sides and four corners, etc.). In each case, these templates are helping children to form a clearer and more lasting mental image as eyes and hands coordinate. Templates of the letters of the alphabet are good three dimensional forms that some children need when they are ready for recognition of letters. Templates are good to develop greater sensitivity to form.

11. Using a stick and writing in sand is a good intermediary step between chalkboard writing and use of a pencil.

12. Using pipe cleaners to make various forms may follow template use. It is one way of checking to see how well children are retaining visual images and how well they can create forms.

13. Sandpaper, Pellon, or felt figures manipulated on a flannel board is a good eye-hand coordinating activity besides providing language experiences.

14. Measuring and pouring sand from a measuring cup into various containers requires good coordination and can be a part of playing store or house.

15. Sculpturing in sand (making roadways, buildings, etc.) has many learning facets. With damp sand children can mold many shapes and then discuss them.

16. First attempts at using scissors might be cutting random bits of colored paper to paste on a black background for color effect. Then children might be challenged to cut along an oval line drawn around a picture. As children gain more control of hand and finger muscles, more intricate cutting can be achieved. Eye-hand coordination is important in all such activity.

17. Experimental painting with large brushes and heavy water color paint is another coordinating experience. Help should be given regarding how to hold the brush, wiping superfluous paint against the side of the jar, and making strokes on the paper. Beyond that, the child is free to get the feel of painting, to experiment with color, or to create his own forms.

18. A pan or pail of water and a medium-sized paint brush may be used on an outside wall.

Activities for Strengthening Eye Muscles

1. Have a ball or other weight suspended at the eye level of the child. Start it swinging to the left and right and ask the child to keep his head stationary but follow the ball with his eyes only.

2. Have the child lie flat on a mat and follow the movement of a swinging object with eye movement only.

3. Slides and films are available for eye muscle development.

4. A sequence of pictures illustrating a story with which the children are familiar may be mounted on a bulletin board or along a chalk tray at the child's eye level. He is encouraged to follow the sequence from left to right. Anything that is used on the bulletin board or chalkboard should always guide a child's vision from left to right to facilitate the mechanics of reading.

5. Helping children to be conscious of light intensity, color intensity, and speed of movement aids in visual development.

6. Have children make fists of both hands but hold up both thumbs. With arms fully extended move them as far left as possible and then as far right as possible, asking the children to follow the movements with their eyes without moving their heads or bodies.

7. Ask the children to fold their hands, with their thumbs standing straight, side by side about six inches from their eyes. Then

direct them to look at their thumbs; then at some object the teacher mentions that is some distance away in the room; then back at the thumbs; again at a distant object in another part of the room and back to the thumbs, etc.

8. Ask a child to tell you, without moving his head, what he sees as far to his left as he can see and then as far to his right as he can see.

Suggestions for Developing the Percepts of Touch

1. Provide opportunities for feeling, observing, and comparing.

a. Roundness, as of balls, circles, apples, grapes, oranges, pumpkins, grapefruit, and any other round objects in the environment.
b. Flatness, as of a table top, the floor, a book, chair seat, etc.
c. Curvature, as of a chair back, a vase, a pitcher, etc.
d. Roughness, as of sandpaper, propelling a tricycle or wagon on gravel, texture of nylon net and carpeting.
e. Smoothness, as of glass, a varnished surface, a pencil, metals.
f. Variations of softness, hardness, temperature, etc. Let the children feel a piece of foam rubber and compare it with a piece of plywood and a piece of glass (do not use broken glass); let them feel a windowpane when it is in the shade and again when the sun shines on it.
g. Height and depth; the up and down of climbing stairs; sliding down a slippery slide; feeling ice and feeling water at various temperatures.
h. Feeling and talking about the qualities of plasticene, sand, clay, felt, paper, paste, cotton, wool, water, glass.

2. Instead of frequently telling children not to touch, guide them into careful handling of fragile articles.

3. Help children to know how to handle baby chicks, puppies, kittens, butterflies, etc. with respect and loving care.

4. Help children to be aware of things it is best not to touch—things that are on a stove that might be very hot, frosted window-panes (a child might freeze his tongue by putting it on the frost and even more dangerous would be putting it on a metal in near-zero temperatures), things that might be poisonous, blades that are very sharp, guns, etc.

5. Play "Blindman's Buff." The blindfolded child must identify

the first child he comes upon by feeling his face, his clothing, and the size and shape of his body. He has one guess and if it is wrong he goes on to another child. Hair style is often a good clue. When he guesses correctly that child becomes "It." A variation is to have a class divided into two teams, and give three points for a correct guess at the first attempt, two points for a right guess at a second attempt, and one point for a third try.

Suggestions for Developing the Sense of Smell

1. Discuss smells that many children are likely to have experienced: flowers, perfumes, skunk, onion, spices, etc.

2. Raise the question, "How can being able to recognize various smells help us?" (to identify smoke, gas fumes, flowers, etc.).

3. Bring in as many different flowers with scents as possible. Let the children identify them.

4. Ask children to think about the smells of home: Mother's kitchen when she bakes bread, cake or cookies; bonfires; clean clothes.)

5. Explore the environment for other smells and encourage children to become more aware of environmental smells: the strong smell of gasoline when Father gets his gas tank filled; the smell of bleach, soap, or ammonia when Mother washes; mothballs; the smell of tar when flat roofs are repaired; gum and candy.

6. Talk about the more subtle smells: the air after a rain; lilacs in the rain; autumn bonfires; perfumes that ladies wear; foods cooking; a florist shop or greenhouse; a tree in blossom.

7. Talk about smells and what you expect to see that goes with the smell.

8. Discuss what small children might do if they smelled smoke or gas (leave the house and seek an adult immediately).

9. Discuss pleasant smells and develop an attitude of appreciation for flowers, good home smells, etc.

Suggestions for Improving Listening and Auding

1. Speak at a rate that is easy to comprehend.

2. Speak clearly and directly in words and phrases that can be easily understood by those expected to listen.

I'm richer than pirates who plunder the sea
For I have a mother who reads stories to me.
(Photograph courtesy of the International Paper Company.)

3. Be sure any child with hearing deficiency symptoms is referred to a reliable clinic.

4. Seat children with hearing problems near you.

5. Give directions very explicitly and only once except in exceptional cases.

6. Do not repeat what children say.

7. Help children to want to be good listeners.

8. Use the child's own name and direct pleasantries to him:

"Jim, you have a very nice smile."

"Joan, I like the way you tidied the book shelves."

"Bobby, I see you know how to tie your shoes all by yourself."

"Mary, would you please bring the book from my desk?"

"It's wonderful, the way everyone followed those directions after I gave them only once."

"I wonder if Frank will listen so well this time that he can follow the directions without any more questions."

"Sally, your hands look soft and clean. You did a nice job of washing them."

"See how neatly Edna and Marie have hung up their wraps."

"George, you were a very good helper all day."

9. Establish minds that are set for listening by saying, "I'm going
to ask you to raise your hand if you remember what you are to do
when I get through giving you the directions."

10. Prevent interruptions by making sure every child knows what
he is expected to do before he leaves the circle, saying "If you know
exactly what to do, you may leave the circle and get started. If you
have questions, stay and get them answered before I start working
with another group."

11. Challenge children to listen to all sounds on their way to
school. Discuss which were lovely, which irritating, which loud, etc.
Help children to appreciate the sense of hearing.

12. Challenge children to listen for beautiful sounds in the home.
Discuss the beauty of voices, sounds of breezes in the trees, babbling
brook, music, singing, etc. Help to establish an appreciation of
beauty in sound.

13. The following game is very appealing to children and it is
amazing how it contributes to the development of acuity in listening.
One child goes outside the room and closes the door. Another child
tiptoes to the door and knocks. The first child says, "Who is it?" The
second child says, "It is I." The first child tries to guess who it is. He
gets two chances. The game may proceed as a relay with the class
divided into two teams. A player who can guess on his first chance
gets three points, two points for a second chance, and one point for
a third chance. It is always surprising how proficient even very
young children become in identifying voice quality although the
children try to change their voices.

14. Before the children leave school to go home ask them to remember all the things they "listen to" at home that night. Discuss
these the next day with emphasis on "Did you have to be told more
than once?" and "Wasn't that a pleasant experience?" and "Isn't it
surprising how many things we hear when we 'tune in' on them?"

15. Ask children to close their eyes and listen for any and all
sounds. After three to five minutes discuss what was heard.

16. Discuss the problem of having to "tune out" what other groups
are discussing or any other noises when there is work that needs
concentration.

17. Use a "listening post" (a phonograph or tape arrangement with individual earphones) where children can hear stories and poems during spare time. Check to be sure the child can hear with each side of the earphone. Check the volume to be sure it does not blast in his ears. Provide good listening materials.

18. Give children an opportunity to talk about listening experiences they have had to determine the quality of listening. The recall of listening and the exactness of detail are important aspects of listening. Children can become more conscious of what constitutes good listening and aspire toward it.

19. Play such "follow-the-directions" games as;

a. "Simon Says." "It" gives quick changes in direction such as "Simon says, 'Touch your nose' "; "Simon says, 'Touch your knees.' " If "It" gives a direction without prefacing it with "Simon says," those players doing the act have not listened carefully and are out of the game. It is a challenge to see how long the players can remain in the game.

b. "I Stoop, I Stand." "It" quickly changes the directions as players stoop or stand in accordance with what is said. Those who make an incorrect response are eliminated.

c. "Fruit Basket." Each child is given the name of a fruit. "It" calls out two fruits and they must exchange seats. "It" tries to capture one of the seats as the exchange is made and the child without a seat becomes "It." "It" may call, "Fruit basket upset," and all players must exchange chairs.

20. Challenging children to repeat after you a series of digits, lines of a poem, words of a song, etc. are good listening and memory-span experiences.

APPENDIX B

Speech-Sound Check

Ask the child to say each word after you, and check the ones he says incorrectly. If he does not respond to help, refer him to a clinic. (Check a speech-age expectancy chart.)

Initial	Medial	Final
at	catnip	baa
bug	rabbit	rub
candy	act	picnic
dog	adding	bad
egg	bed	
fun	after	calf
go	agree	rug
hot	behind	
in	winter	fun
jump	engine	edge
keep	turkey	pick
lunch	yellow	ball
money	camera	arm
nut	into	can
on	not	
pin	apple	nap
quick	squeak	antique
run	farm	car
sing	fasten	grass
toy	better	get
up	supper	
vase	ever	have
wind	blowing	below
you		
zoo	magazine	prize

Digraphs	Diphthongs	Blends	
ch (chicken)	au aw (crawl)	bl (blue)	pr (prize)
sh (shoe)	oi oy (boil)	br (brown)	sl (slide)
th (throw)	ou ow (house)	cl (clown)	sm (smile)
th (this)	eau ew (few, beautiful)	cr (crumb)	sp (spin)
ng (sing)		dr (drink)	spl (splash)
ph (telephone)		fl (fiower)	st (stick)
wh (what)		fr (friend)	str (street)
		gl (glass)	sw (swim)
		gr (green)	tr (train)
		pl (please)	

Unusual Patterns

—Baby talk	—Nasal	—Accent	—Monotone	—Gutteral
—Lisp	—Racial	—Breathy	—Indistinct	—Other

APPENDIX C

Kindergarten Inventory

Duplicate an inventory for each child, place his name on it, and put it in his folder. Check each question whenever the child measures up to expectations by placing a red "x" after the question. You can easily see from time to time those areas in which he still needs help.

Listening

Is he eager to hear stories told and read to him?

Is his span of listening attention consistently good?

Does he voluntarily go to the "listening post" to enjoy music and
   stories?

Does his face show animation as he listens?

Does he follow directions after listening to them once?

Can he perform three or more performance tasks, such as opening
   the door, closing the window, and bringing the book from the
   table?

Can he repeat five digits after you say them (6, 8, 2, 4, 1)?

Can he repeat a sentence of about fifteen syllables. (The boy ran to
   his mother and gave her a big, big bear hug)?

Does he listen well when other children are talking?

Can he retell a story without omitting significant details?

Can he recite short poems and jingles after hearing them a few
   times?

Observation

Is he alert to what is new in the classroom when he arrives?

Does he enjoy looking at pictures and picture books?

Does he note details in a picture so that he can tell about them
   when he looks away from the picture?

Does he attempt to tell a story from the pictures he sees in a book?

Is he alert to likenesses and differences in pictured forms?

Can he recognize his own name when it is listed with other names?

Can he recognize the various colors?

Does he identify a penny, a nickel, a dime and a quarter?

Can he count the fingers on both hands?

Can he observe things that are big and things that are little; light
   and heavy; soft and hard; tall and short?

Is he curious about what is on the bulletin board?

Can he identify various common animals, foods, flowers, birds, etc. in pictures?

Manipulation

Can he tie his shoes?

Can he put on his wraps by himself?

Can he button his coat or sweater?

Does he put details into his drawings and paintings?

Can he manuscript his name?

Can he skip?

Can he open and close a door easily?

Can he draw a person with many details?

Can he put puzzles together quickly and easily?

Can he draw a circle, a square, a triangle, a straight line, a cross?

Can he manipulate blocks and build satisfactorily with them?

Socialization

Does he make friends easily?

Does he enjoy group activities?

Does he assume a leadership role in some situations?

Is he a good group member in allowing others to have turns?

Thinking and Comprehension

Does he know his full name and address?

Does he know his telephone number?

Can he count to twenty?

Can he respond to such phrases as *under the table, on the chair, beside the cupboard, above the door, in the desk?*

Can he help to compose little stories?

Can he classify by buildings, people, fruits, dishes, furniture, toys, clothing?

Can he explain *yesterday, today,* and *tomorrow?*

Can he use terms such as *most, less than, more than, the same as, a half of, both, as much as,* and *different than?*

Does he understand what is meant by opposites such as big-little; high-low; fast-slow; in-out?

Can he answer when, why, what, where, and how questions?

Does he understand simple incidents of cause and effect?

Can he help to resolve simple classroom problems?

Does he know *left* and *right?*

Can he differentiate between what is real and what is make believe?

Communication

Does he make all of the speech sounds correctly (with possible exceptions of *g, th, z,* and *j*)?

Does he use proper inflection for declarative and interrogative sentences?

Does he express his thoughts well?

Does he enjoy the give and take of conversation?

Can he retell stories with ease and facility?

Does he use a wide variety of words in his communications?

Can he express himself adequately when sent on an errand (to the principal, librarian, or school nurse)?

Interests and Attitudes

Does he like school?

Is he helpful to classmates?

Is he responsible for completing tasks?

Does he do his share of cleaning up after activities?

Does he handle books and materials carefully?

Is he enthusiastic about on-going activities?

Is he curious about things?

Does he remain reasonably calm when things go wrong?

Does he accept suggestions graciously?

Does he respond well to challenge and inspiration?

Is he interested in wanting to learn to read?

Is he concerned about the welfare of others?

PERSONAL CHARACTERISTICS CHECKLIST

Flits about	Sometimes settles down	Works well alone and with others
Very easily frustrated	Moderate frustration level	Calm and patient
Extremely shy	Personable	Very outgoing
Placid	Generally interested	Enthusiastic
Very inattentive	Usually attentive	Applies self diligently
Feels inadequate	Usually tries	Self-confident
Sullen	Usually happy	Very pleasant and friendly to all
Extremely nervous	Usually restrained	Very well-adjusted
Impulsive	Usually adapts	Very adaptable
Constantly in need of help	Usually capable	Very self-reliant
Clumsy	Average coordination	Very well-coordinated
Poor eye-hand coordination	Average coordination	Excellent eye-hand coordination
Mental retardation	Average reasoning	Very good reasoning and problem solving
Forgets easily	Average memory span	Excellent memory
Unimaginative	Average imagination in creativity	Very creative

HOME SITUATION CHECKLIST

One or no parent Unemployment Foster home Grandparent care Both parents work all day	Average home solidarity	Both parents Child's needs recognized and nurtured
Quarrelsome environment Smothering affection	Average give-and-take	Mutual affection
Extremely poor English (foreign language used)	Average	Excellent language communication
Deprived of good learning experience "Don't-touch-it" environment	Average opportunities	Rich environment
Family moves frequently	Average mobility	Stable home
Poor parental attitude toward school	Average interest shown	Interest and cooperation shown
No reading in the home	Some reading	Parents read to children Abundance of good reading materials
Child participates in family planning and in conversations	Occasional participation	Little or no opportunity for family conversation
Child has a good image of himself and maintains respect for the self image of other family members	Average opportunities for developing "self" and "other" relationships	Little or no opportunity for self enhancement and development of good feelings toward others

APPENDIX D

Developing Readiness for the Context Clues

The following sentences should be read aloud by the teacher, with a pause for each missing word:

Mother ———— cookies sometimes. (*Sometimes* challenges children to think of as many words as possible that would make good sense, such as *makes, bakes, frosts, ices, hides, sends.*)

We send Christmas ———— to friends. (Such exercises are good vocabulary stretchers and they also pave the way for use of context clues.)

I have a ———— and a ————. (This affords many possibilities, but the words must sound right with *a*.)

I like to go to ————. (Help children to note that you did not say *a* before you stopped and that certain words would require the *a* sound. *Shows* would sound right but *show* would not. *School* and *church* would sound right but *ball game* would not. This is a peculiarity of our language and children must become conscious of it from the start.)

A ———— is our friend.

Cars have ———— on their wheels.

Green ———— might make us ill.

The people living next door are called our ————.

We drink ———— to help us grow.

We pick up ———— from the floor.

Playing ———— is lots of fun.

Smoke goes up the ————.

There are ———— and ———— in a house.

People read ———— to get the news.

Doors have ————.

Plants need ———— and ———— to help them grow.

We ———— with a needle and thread.

To pound nails we need a ————.

Sometimes houses are made of ————.

Mother picked a ———— of pretty flowers.

Our ———— is red, white, and blue.

———— make good pets.

Birds ———— and ————.

Carrots are a ————.

We can ———— and ———— with our feet.

Holidays we like are ———— and ————.

After Friday is ————.

The sky is ———— and the grass is ————.

The farmer ———— seeds in the ground.

A box has ———— sides. (The teacher may need to have one handy to verify the answer.)

Candy has ———— in it.

We play outside to get fresh ————.

We blow our noses in ————.

After school we go ————.

A dog is a ————.

Pillows are made of ————.

Rocks can ————.

We can ———— and ———— at a table.

APPENDIX E

Tension-Releasing Exercises[1]

With arms outstretched I turn and twist
Both my arms and both my wrists;
Then with three hops and a little bound
I turn myself halfway around.
Then with a hand upon each hip
I stand on tiptoe and dip, dip, dip.
Then with three hops and a little bound
I turn myself right back around.
(*Repeat twice.*)

AIRPLANES

From down on the ground it zooms up high (*children squat with palms
and fingers flat together and zoom upward*);
Way up and around in the blue, blue sky (*palms together move back
and forth high over head*).
Here comes another plane down, down, down (*hands and bodies start
the decline*);
Bringing some people to visit our town (*wiggle fingers to indicate
people*).

With hands on my hips and feet together tight
I jump to the left and I jump to the right;
I jump forward and I jump back
Then I jump up and down like a jumping jack.
Then with hands up high I look all around
And with knees very stiff I touch the ground.
(*Repeat.*)

I reach up high to pick apples (*both arms reaching*);
I stoop down low to pick grapes (*bend at the waist and let arms hang*);
I climb a ladder for some big red cherries (*arms and legs climbing*)
But I squat down low to pick ripe strawberries (*squat and put hands on
the floor*).

With arms outstretched and fingers spread
I raise my arms high over my head.
I turn my hands in and I turn my hands out
Then my whole body I turn round about.
With hands on my hips on one foot I hop
Till I've turned all around and then I stop.
Then on the other foot I hop once more
Until I stand where I stood before.

[1] By Verna Dieckman Anderson.

Prancing like ponies with head held up high
Waving my arms like birds in the sky
I'm getting my exercise so I keep fit;
And now I am ready to quietly sit.

(To be used before story telling)

Here are Grandma's glasses. (Make a circle with fingers around each eye.)

And here is Grandma's cap. (Make a pointed cap with both hands above the head.)

This is the way she folds her hands and puts them in her lap. (Now children are ready for a story so proceed immediately.)

APPENDIX F

Primary Reading Inventory

This inventory is designed to assist the teacher in knowing what kinds of help a child needs. It is especially useful when a new child comes into the school with nothing but a report card.

I. SILENT READING CHECK

Manuscript the following selection on a piece of tagboard. Observe the child as he reads it silently. Make a notation of eye movements, lip movements, vocalization, difficulties, attitude, persistence. Then ask him to read it aloud (use the oral reading checklist that follows on the next page).

Jim's grandmother and grandfather were getting old. They wanted Jim's father to have the farm. So Jim and his mother and father left the city and moved to the farm.

Jim liked living on the farm. His father gave him a pony. Jim rode all over the farm. Soon Grandfather's dog became his dog. The dog liked to run beside the pony. He liked to play with Jim.

Jim went to school on a bus. He made new friends, but he missed his old friends. He wrote letters to them.

Ask the following questions:

1. Why did Jim go to the farm to live?
2. What helped him to like the farm?
3. Why do you suppose Grandfather's dog became Jim's dog?
4. What did Jim seem to miss most?
5. What did he do about it?
6. How would you feel about moving to a farm?

II. CHECK ON USE OF THE INITIAL CONSONANT, VOWEL, AND DIGRAPH CLUES

Manuscript the twenty-one sentences for the child to read and ask him to supply the missing words from the clues. The child is to supply the words orally.

1. I like to eat b———. (*Accept any word that makes sense.*)
2. I can w———.
3. What sh——— I do today?

4. We take pictures with a c_____.
5. It is fun to s_____.
6. I like ch_____.
7. A baby cat is a k_____.
8. J_____ and J_____ went up a hill.
9. G_____ is green.
10. Mother will not let us play with m_____.
11. A little dog is called a p_____.
12. We send l_____ to friends far away.
13. Girls like to play with d_____.
14. We watch t_____ at home.
15. One day of the week is Th_____.
16. Birds have f_____.
17. We get v_____ so we won't get small pox.
18. They were r_____ down the street.
19. We see h_____ on the farm.
20. Do not go a_____.
21. At n_____ we go to sleep.

III. ORAL READING

List each word that caused hesitation and use the following code
to note the word problem and how the child coped with it.

cc—used context clue; repeated the word (˘)
ph—used phonetic clues; used a reversal (∿)
o—omitted the word; added a word after this word (ˆ)
pw—paused and waited to be helped
p—paused but knew the word
t—was told the word
s—spelled the word and knew it
wr—used word root and prefixes and/or suffixes
m—mispronounced the word

POSTURE (rate + and —)

At ease
Kept both feet on the floor
Held book steadily
Turned pages easily
Kept book at appropriate distance from eyes

FLUENT INTERPRETATION (rate + and —)

Proper intonation and cadence
Correct phrasing
Correct treatment of punctuation
Conversational expression for direct quotations
Good voice modulation
Reflects appreciation for what is being read
Reveals comprehension and interpretation
Appropriate rate

ADDITIONAL COMMENTS

Name _____

Circle the words with a long vowel.

came	trip	boat	let	use
bring	eat	home	call	in
pie	me	come	street	on
girl	gave	coat	we	see

Name _____

Circle the words with a short vowel.

ran	rain	name	go	get
blue	not	have	sit	gave
do	can	cup	me	to
big	I	hop	read	find
see	jump	red	no	man
in	rock	late	show	day

Name _____

Put the words below where they belong.

Food	Colors	Names	Pets
_____	_____	_____	_____
_____	_____	_____	_____
_____	_____	_____	_____
_____	_____	_____	_____

cat	blue	Don	monkey
red	Carol	apple	Jim
Bobby	cake	yellow	bread
pie	dog	rabbit	green

Check on reversal tendency. Ask the child
to read the following words:

was	star	trap	no	won
on	meat	saw	now	team
part	rats	pin	nip	

Letter recognition and reproduction. Ask the
child to name the letters in all the words of
the following sentence. Then give him a
sheet of paper and a pencil and ask him to
write the letters as you spell each word to him.

The lazy boy jumped very quickly from

behind the box where he was hiding.

Name _____

Write 3 words that rhyme.

say _____ _____ _____

we _____ _____ _____

at _____ _____ _____

ring _____ _____ _____

nest _____ _____ _____

pan _____ _____ _____

Write endings for each word.

play _____ _____ _____

run _____ _____ _____

do _____ _____ _____

Name _____

Write a letter in each blank to make a good word.

t_ _l	r_n	g_ _d	b_ _
_ish	_end	w_ _	h_t
n_t	p_ _	_o	m_
f_ _d	i_	_an	_ _y

Name _____

Make words with the letters:

mjpu _____   hifs _____

nfu _____   odgo _____

byo _____   ni _____

ese _____   hmtore _____

lpya _____   nma _____

Name _____

Write the second letter of a word that means
what you do to a ball with a bat.

_____

Write the first letter of a word that means an
animal that says, "Me-ow."

_____

Write the second letter of a word that means
to look.

_____

Write the third letter of the alphabet.

_____

Write the first letter of a word that tells
the color of a fire engine.

_____

Write the fifth letter of the alphabet.

_____

Write the last letter of the alphabet.

_____

Write the last letter of a word that means
something to chew.

_____

What do the letters spell?

__ __ __   __ __ __ __ __

APPENDIX G

Understanding Our Children[1] (Summary)

THE KINDERGARTNER

1. He is active in a strenuous way. He runs, jumps, hops, climbs. He is energetic rather than fidgety.

2. He lives in a here-and-now day and world. He pretty well takes life as it comes because he is the center of his universe and whatever happens to him is interesting.

3. He takes pride in his own possessions and has a definite sense of ownership. "My" is his favorite word.

4. He worries a bit about his own ability to accomplish, and he demands adult help when he feels his own limitations. He is eager to know how to do things which lie within his capacity.

5. He can take part peaceably in small group activities without too much supervision. These are usually play or spontaneous dramatization activities. He can work also on a cooperative project, but he is working as an individual, not as a group member. He may make a radio for the playhouse if he is on "the furniture committee," but it is *his* radio and he is the one to decide where it shall be placed.

6. He is positive about things, inclined to be a bit dogmatic. He is quite sure that there is one way to do a thing, one answer to a question. He likes to argue about it—"worry" it like a little dog with a bone.

7. He is a great talker. He piles up details as he talks; he says the same thing over and over, but his vocabulary increases at a great rate so that his eagerness to talk bears fruit.

8. He loves to hear stories and poems and to be read to. He asks for his favorites over and over again.

9. He loves to work with materials. These help him to explore new abilities within himself.

10. He is becoming interested in numbers and words. He asks, "How many?" "How big?" "What does it say?" "What is this letter?"

11. He enjoys routine and reacts best to a program which calls for

[1] A bulletin published by the Denver Public Schools, Denver, Colorado, 1965. Used with permission.

varied activity and exercise, but within a fairly definite sequence and time schedule.

12. He is good—not because he distinguishes right from wrong (right is what mother and teacher tell him to do), nor because he is naturally an upright character, but because he wants to please, to oblige the grown-ups who seem to know how they want things done in this world where he still does not feel too much at home. When he was younger the world was all his. He is learning now that he must find his place in it and that many other people must be considered.

THE FIRST-GRADER

1. He is active, almost constantly in motion, whether sitting or standing.

2. He goes to extremes, finding it hard to modulate or to compromise.

3. It is difficult for him to make decisions. He wants both alternatives, finding it hard to give up rival possibilities. Blue or violet? Come in or stay out? Paint or clay? He wants to do and to have everything.

4. He wants to be first, to win always, and to be loved best. He finds it hard to adjust his behavior in terms of what he wants to do and what he should do.

5. He identifies himself with everything, projecting his feelings and actions into all situations. He is the center of everything; he behaves, thinks, feels from the standpoint of himself and his own experiences. He is dramatic in this association of himself with all situations.

6. He clarifies meanings and relationships through personal participation and creative activities.

7. He is very sociable and likes to be with other children, with himself as planner, leader, and social arbiter.

8. He is keen to start individual or group projects, but is unconcerned about finishing them. His six-year-old world is so full of a number of things, he does not have time or energy to do justice to each one. He has an exploratory attitude; he must find out something about everything.

9. He turns to his teacher to give him confidence in this new world of school, where his needs for recognition and security are

somewhat threatened. He craves praise and commendation and reacts badly to criticism.

10. He is a paradox. He reaches out for new things and scurries back for the old. He loves surprises, but he also likes stability. He demands a variety of experiences, but he also clings to the ritual and conventions of daily living.

11. He likes to do things on a game basis.

12. He tends to have emotional explosions. These are brought on by the little things of life more often than by basic demands, which he can take in his stride.

13. He takes inordinate pleasure in gifts, both in receiving and giving them.

14. He loves holidays, entering wholeheartedly into all phases of their celebration.

THE SECOND-GRADER

1. He is becoming more reflective, taking time to think. He can be reasoned with.

2. His personal relationships with his teacher and with other adults are very important to him. He is reaching out to them, and he needs assurance that he is liked and considered.

3. He is variable in his behavior and attitudes, assertive one day, amenable the next.

4. He is self-critical. He apologizes for his work and thinks that he can do better. Seven is the "eraser age."

5. He is a slow starter but cannot stop once he gets going. He does the thing he wants to do, or has learned to do, over and over without variation. This is because he lacks confidence in tackling something new.

6. He is serious about himself and about responsibility that may be given to him.

7. He responds enthusiastically to praise and is crushed by criticism.

8. He has lost his six-year-old freshness. He is even polite and sympathetic most of the time and is capable of genuine affection.

THE THIRD-GRADER

1. He is extremely active, both mentally and physically.

2. He is hungry for new experiences, reaching out for everything

he can get. At the same time he is held back by worry over whether he can cope with these new experiences.

3. He hides his great eagerness for approval behind an apologetic attitude toward his own work. "This paper doesn't look so good today, does it?" he says, even though he has struggled to make it perfect.

4. He needs an adult to rely upon, even though he is struggling for independence.

5. He is aggressive in his social relationships. He struggles to be as good as his peers. He battles for position. This is why the third-grade play area is always the noisiest.

6. He wants to be in on everything—plans, discussions, activities. He loves to be asked for suggestions.

7. He likes to work hard—he will tackle anything—and then evaluate his accomplishment critically.

8. He seeks a wide variety of interests and is beginning to lean toward science. He wants to investigate anything new in his life, from water guns to jet planes. He has so many interests to explore that he will pursue several at the same time.

9. He reaches out mentally in time and space, struggling to free himself from his immediate world. He is ready for new ideas but often interprets them in the light of his own experience.

10. He is at a money-conscious stage. He wants to earn money, to have it, to spend it.

11. He can work with fair independence in a group, provided there is a clear-cut purpose that calls for working together in the area of construction or expression.

THE FOURTH-GRADER

1. He is a developing personality, with marked abilities and interests of his own.

2. He is becoming self-motivated. He will carry on projects of his own devising, devoting much time and effort to them. His attention span is of gratifying length when he is doing the things a fourth-grader likes to do.

3. He is open to instruction—especially if it deals with facts and is presented in a forthright way. He collects facts as he does bottle tops. He loves to make inventories and lists, and dotes upon codes and emblems.

4. He is something of a perfectionist, like the seven-year-old, but

has greater ability to improve skills and techniques on his own initiative. He is willing to do the same thing over and over again to fortify his security. He works definitely to develop skills in physical and creative activities, as well as in subject areas.

5. He has a broad range of reading interests, although reading abilities vary at this age level. The average nine-year-old is trying to widen his world and, if he reads well, he is able to do this through books and stories about other people and other places. He likes to trace "from then to now" developments: the way people did it then —the way we do it now; how language, inventions, and ideas have developed. He is interested, too, in other parts of our country and of the world.

6. He is whole-heartedly entering the gang stage. What he says, does, eats, wears, plays is determined by what the other kids do.

7. He is a conformist—it is tragic to be different. His membership in a club or gang may be of short duration, but there is always another one to join—or, preferably, to organize.

8. He is developing a strong sense of right and wrong and is beginning to be reasonable. He can be guided best by a reason for desirable behavior. The reason, however, must relate to his own experience and interest. It must be clear-cut and within his ability to grasp. He is trying to develop a few basic standards, and likes stories of people whose deeds give him something to steer by. He loves to talk things over.

THE FIFTH-GRADER

1. That he is active, almost constantly in motion, is as true of the ten-year-old as of the six-year-old. He has an organic need for physical activity because of his rapidly growing and developing body. His activity is on the strenuous order whenever he can get away with it. He roughhouses, teases, and laughs without apparent reason.

2. He is wholeheartedly a peer among peers who set the pattern for each other in standards of speech, clothes, and manners. The ten-year-old turns to parents and teachers, however, to supply the values and standards that he is beginning to seek. These often lie in the fields of racial relationships, religion, and morals.

3. He is a learner, not only eager for factual information and able to memorize easily, but he also shows desirable growth in aesthetic areas. He is an interesting combination of realism and imagination.

4. He devours books of adventure, explanations of how and why

things work, and lives of scientists and adventurers. The ten-year-old who is not reading as rapidly as other members of his class may become increasingly discouraged.

5. He is ready for an introduction to history, for he has increasing ability to fit past events into proper sequence—not only acquiring facts, but putting them together as well. He is mainly interested in the adventure that has gone into the building of our country, not in the political and industrial phases of its development.

6. He still needs learning experiences that involve participation and doing.

7. He likes discussion of social problems. He can now see different sides of a question and is developing definite ideas of property rights, fairness, honesty, and reliability. Dr. Gesell speaks of "the social intelligence of the ten-year-old."

THE SIXTH-GRADER

1. He is a lazybones or a dynamo, because of wide variation in physical growth at this age. Some eleven-year-olds are approaching puberty and they may frequently seem lazy. They are so busy growing that they have little energy for anything else. Those who are not nearing puberty are super-energetic. There is wide variation, too, between girls and boys, with girls usually maturing more rapidly than boys.

2. He is somewhat variable in his moods and behavior.

3. He is still influenced widely by the peer group but is reaching out toward adults and wanting to share their world.

4. He is a bit over-critical of adults, even when reaching out toward their world, but he welcomes their leadership for the needed security it gives him. He is also getting to the "crush" stage.

5. He is able to work with a group on extended projects that call for cooperation and pooled thinking. He works best with a congenial group organized on the basis of friendship and interests.

6. He wants recognition and approval, but these must be based upon real achievement.

7. He is growing in his ability to generalize, to see relationships, and to foresee probable results.

8. He is interested in people, communities, and the world. He is becoming interested in and concerned about other people's ideas and beliefs. He wants to take part in drives and other community activities.

APPENDIX H

Vocabulary Development

To help children identify many items, describe them, and know the various uses to which they may be put:

1. Mount pictures from catalogues, phonics and readiness workbooks, and any other source of good clear pictures of single items. Place each picture on a separate small card leaving enough room at the bottom so words may be written in manuscript writing later. The children may be challenged to identfy the items telling all they know about a particular item. These items may then be grouped into such classifications as: foods, toys, furniture, transportation, communication, clothing, people, household items, etc. Later some of these classifications may be broken down into fruit, vegetables, meat, breads, desserts, salads, foods for breakfast, foods for lunch, foods for dinner, foods for baby, and so on. Whenever there seems to be misconception, bring the real item into the classroom for examination, handling, and use. Much discussion should include sizes, shapes, colors, kinds and utility.

A discussion of the use of *a* and *an* through listening experiences will help them to become familiar with that pattern of our language. When words are printed under the pictures, make a card with *a* and one with *an* and challenge children to combine each of these cards with appropriate other words. *The* may be added as another part of our language pattern. After these words come very fluently in oral identification of pictures and after the printed form of a few common items have been introduced, supply cards with *the ball, a car, an apple, a chair.* Play a game in which children are challenged to find the correct card in response to such questions as, "Can you find two words that tell what you would use to play?" (*A ball* or *the ball; a toy* or *the toy,* etc.) "What two words would you use to tell what you would like to eat?" (*An apple* or *the apple.*) Then introduce *this* and *is* and challenge children to make sentences for other children to read.

With older children who come to your classroom unable to read, a sporting goods catalog provides the kind of pictures that would appeal, and the procedure could be much the same. Kinds of automobiles and types of airplanes are stimulating for the fourth- to sixth-grade child needing an introduction to reading. The phonics clues can be presented from this more mature listing of words through helping children to hear likeness in beginning sounds and proceeding as presented in Chapter 8.

2. Three children can easily share a catalog, magazine, phonics or readiness workbook, picture book, or picture post cards and discuss what they see: identification of items, colors, uses, what might have happened before or after, and relate some of their own experience to what they see in the picture.

With older children various kinds of catalogs, picture dictionaries, and picture books on a great variety of subjects might be shared and discussed. Sometimes having an able, experienced child look at a book with two who need expansion of ideas and vocabulary is very helpful.

3. Bring in a tray with about three small objects each day for examination, demonstration, discussion, and use (if possible). The following are a few of the many possibilities.

a postage stamp   a flashlight   a marshmallow

Let children tell all they know before the teacher fills in with supplementary interesting information. A flash light might be taken apart to show how the batteries cause the light and how the switch causes contact and breaks contact. A bag of marshmallows in reserve so each child can have one adds to the lasting impression of taste as well as the observations of softness, whiteness, size, shape, and uses to which mothers may have put them.

a light bulb   a blotter   straw

Through the use of an extension cord the children may see how a light bulb will light up when it is screwed all the way into the socket—if the switch is on. It might be compared with the flashlight and discussion follow as long as their is interest and language growth. A teacher may have to explain where straw comes from and that animals sleep on it. It will be observed that there is a hole or passageway through it just like the "straws" through which they drink milk. The discussion may lead into some children telling of experiences on the farm such as sliding down a straw stack and children will observe how smooth and slippery straw would be.

They could continue by talking about other things that are slippery or that are straw colored. Discussion can go in various directions but if there is interest many new words will come into understanding and use.

a feather   a cork   a paper weight   a piece of styrofoam

A discussion would lead into comparison of weight and size including things that are very heavy and very light: big things that may be light and little things that may be heavy. Children could be shown how feathers shed water, and how they protect a bird from both cold and rain. Again the discussion could lead in many directions.

a magnet	a nail	a piece of string
a magnifying glass	a moth	a flower
a leaf	an orange	an egg
a set of spoon measures	a measuring cup	a ruler
a knife	a tack	a needle
a box of crayons	a box of paints	a box of payons
a penny	a nickel	a dime
a handkerchief	a paper towel	a tissue
a stone	a shell	some sand
a cone	a berry	a bean
a peanut	a walnut	a pecan
a compass	a mirror	a mask
a bottle	a jar	a can
a paper bag	a small box	a plastic bag
a turnip	a carrot	a potato
a top	a set of dominoes	a yo yo
a button	a zipper	a safety pin
a raisin	a prune	a fig or dried apricot
a brush	a sponge	a whisk broom
a bowl	a glass	a fork
a chain	a leather belt	a paper fan
a balloon	a candle	an electric fan
an apple	a gourd	a pumpkin

There are many other items that lead to good discussion, expanding vocabulary, developing concepts, and stimulating language development.

4. Challenge children to think of things made of wood, glass, paper, metal, cloth, or combinations of these materials.

5. Challenge children to make such associations as:

as light as a feather   as white as a marshmallow, etc.

6. Challenge children to explain what they would mean by:

a happy time	something funny	something delightful
something frightening	something lovely	something dangerous
something ordinary	something imaginary	something huge
something tiny	something unbelievable	something sharp
something unusual	something friendly	something courteous
something cautious	something careless	something helpful
something bright	something beautiful	

7. Challenge children to think of opposites, such as: hot-cold; large-small; tall-short; Older children may be challenged with much more difficult words.

8. Challenge children to think of synonyms: big (large, huge, etc.), little, strange, etc.

9. Challenge children to think of all the ways such things as the following could be done: send a message; go from one place to another; get home if you were lost; go to and from school; get the news; get food you eat; have a good time.

10. What things would we need to: bake a cake; take a trip; build a house; go camping; set the table; wash clothes; go shopping; go to school on a rainy day; go on a picnic.

11. What are all the things that we could say about a jar of tiny pickles? A teacher might have a jar of tiny pickles so that every child may have one before the discussion begins.

12. Challenge children to give more than one meaning for these words: run, pipe, can, shell, ice, bark, sheet, park, slip, call, date, yarn, strike, spring, roll, light, fall, cut, check, charge, change.

in	bear	cell	shoot	doe
inn	bare	sell	chute	dough

write	so	berry	seen	no	do
right	sew	bury	scene	know	dew

Challenge children to think of other homonyms, or to find them in the dictionary.

14. There are words that are spelled alike but have different meanings and are pronounced differently depending on usage as:

I saw a *tear* in her eye. There was a *tear* in her dress.
You may *read* this book. I have *read* it.
His ancestors were Polish. I must *polish* the furniture.

Challenge children to find others.

15. Challenge children to prepare interesting endings to make

good sentences with the following beginnings. Have them read in class.

The old windmill ———	From the hilltop ———
Sleighbells ———	At the top of the attic stairs ———
Suddenly the storm ———	As he entered the dark cold basement ———

16. Challenge children to make interesting beginnings for these endings:

——— slipped down the icy slope.	——— whistled in the wind.
——— could never forget his fright.	——— huddled in the cave.
——— struggled wildly.	——— called for help.

17. Challenge children to think of all the words that would describe people.

18. Challenge children to think of all the words that would answer the question "How"?

19. Leaves is the plural of leaf but leave has a very different meaning. Challenge children to find other peculiarities of our language.

VOCABULARY DEVICES

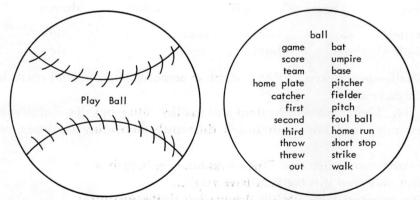

This is an example of a device that children may use individually or as a team. It may be made on colorful tagboard. In a similar fashion a house with household words; a barn with farm words; a store with store words; a fruit or vegetable basket with appropriate words, etc. may be used to establish various vocabularies for independent reading.

Arithmetic
Words

add   plus   together
subtract   minus   more   less than
divide   part-taking   long   short
equals   same-as
how   much   many
sum   difference

one	eleven	thirty
two	twelve	forty
three	thirteen	fifty
four	fourteen	sixty
five	fifteen	seventy
six	sixteen	eighty
seven	seventeen	ninety
eight	eighteen	hundred
nine	nineteen	thousand
ten	twenty	million

This may be reproduced on colorful tagboard and a similar one made for Social Studies and whatever other subjects the children are ready to use. (Each teacher should select words from the arithmetic book used at her grade level).

APPENDIX I

Games and Exercises for Word Recognition

1. To teach action words (*run, jump, skip, walk, write, look, cut, read*) ask the children to stand behind their chairs facing toward the back of the room while you place a word card on each chair. The children pick up their cards and do what the card tells them to do. The child with *look* goes to the window to tell what he *sees;* the child with *read* is to read the words on the chalkboard; the child with *cut* is to get a pair of scissors, etc.

2. Children enjoy challenge. The group may be divided into two evenly matched teams. Start with the child least likely to know the word, and then ask a member of the other team. Words such as the following may be used: *mother, father, work, play, book, pretty, color, birthday.* (Give children an opportunity to give meaning clues after they catch on to how it is done.) Use the following clues:

Find a word that means something father must do.
Find a word that means someone who gets dinner for us.
Find a word that means something we do with crayons.
Find a word that means something we do at recess time.
Find a word that means something we have when we are a year older.
Find a word that tells how something looks.

3. Team or individual competition may be used in this exercise. Put these phrases on the chalkboard:

The teacher asks:	*All About Peter*
Where did Peter go?	in the morning
Why did he go?	to the store
When did he go?	for some thread
How did he go?	on his bicycle
For whom did he go?	for his grandmother
What is the title?	
Can you make a story using these phrases?	

4. After children have been helped with new words on the chalkboard the following game might be played for general review. Choose a child who needs extra help to leave the room while the

remainder of the group chooses a word on the list. The first child returns and guesses by pointing to various words saying, "Is it _____?" to which the group responds, "No, it is not _____" until he selects the correct word. If he misscalls a word the teacher would have that word card for him after he completes the game and he can trace over it, saying it to himself.

5. Divide the group into two sections, giving each section a card pack of troublesome words (not more than ten). Challenge them to teach each other, and at the end of ten or fifteen minutes each child is checked and a point scored for each correct response to see which section comes out ahead.

6. Words are placed along the chalkboard. Children close their eyes while the teacher moves the words to new positions and takes one away. The children are challenged to determine which word is gone.

7. Following a lesson, difficult words are listed on the chalkboard. After going through them several times the children are challenged to say them individually, starting with those children most likely to know them. Each child starts at the top of the list and moves down. If he misses a word the teacher gives him a word card for that word and he remains in his chair to say and trace the word until it is his turn again; then he starts with the word he missed and goes on down the list. Any child who knows all the words goes on to other work.

8. Write all the words on the chalkboard that have caused difficulty in a particular story. Challenge children to use each word in a sentence as you write the sentence around the word. Then challenge the children to read all the sentences. As children go back to their seats, ask each child to read a sentence as he leaves.

9. The children in the group stand behind their chairs. A card pack of words on which the class has been working is used. Each child has a turn identifying a word. If he does it correctly he sits on his chair. If he misses the word he remains standing for another turn. When a word is missed, a child who is seated is challenged. Thus each seated child must remain alert. The object of the game is to see how long each child can remain seated. Because those who know the words are seated the others get more turns for the practice they need.

10. Following a reading lesson give each child a word card of a word he missed during the lesson. Have him say the word and trace over it with his index finger. Then collect the word cards and as the class says them ask each child to raise his hand when the word

he had held appears. Give that child a chance to say the word first.

11. Children stand behind their chairs. A word card is placed on each chair. The child who is least likely to know the words is chosen to go along the chairs and identify the words. When he comes to one he does not know, the child behind the chair may give him clues. The clues may be the initial sound, an initial blend, an initial digraph, or a word meaning. When he reaches the last chair he is given all the words he did not know, and a child who knew them all goes with him to a far corner to help him with his little pack of words.

12. Each child is given a word card. The teacher calls out an initial sound (single consonant, blend, or digraph), and all children having a word with that beginning is to put it on the chalk tray. Then all the children say the words that have been put there. They look for any that are incorrect, and help is given to the child who made the mistake. Then another initial sound is called and the game goes on.

13. Words are written beside each child's name who had trouble during the reading period. These are his words for the day. He may trace over them at any time and ask for help but is to be checked before going home.

14. Children in a group are divided into two teams. Words are shown alternately to the teams. A child gets one point for identifying the word, two points if he can give a definition for the word, and three points if he can also use it in a sentence.

15. At the end of three or four weeks a list of the most difficult words might be put on the chalkboard. After a careful review each child is challenged individually, starting with those who are most likely to know the words. The initials of each child are placed beside any word the child misses. If he can identify them all he leaves the group to do other things. Word cards are given to each child according to those words with which he needs further help.

16. Each child is given a word card. A sentence is written on the chalkboard and the children arrange themselves in front of the group to form the sentence. The other children read it.

17. Each child is given three word cards. The teacher pronounces a word and every child having a word that rhymes with the given word places it on the chalk tray. These words are read and checked to be sure there are no incorrect ones.

18. Each child is given five words for general review. A place is designated for name or object words, another for action words, and

still another place for words that are neither name nor action. The children distribute their words, and then each collection of words is read and checked by the group.

19. A wallpaper sample book may be used. A picture is pasted on each page to represent a word that is being learned, such as *apple, car, house, barn, store, ball, girl, boy, picture, chair, table, truck.* The group is divided into two teams. A member of one team takes the word cards and places each in the page corresponding with the appropriate picture. Then a member of the opposite team checks to see if they are correct as the teacher watches. A point is scored for each one that is correct. Then another member of the second team does the card placing and is checked by a member of the first team. Thus words are associated with their meanings and many children have the experience in a very interesting game situation.

20. Later this same wallpaper book may be used in a more advanced manner. Several objects may be on a page, or there may be a picture with action so that cards reading *a boy and his dog; a child with books, a car in a garage,* etc. may be used.

21. Two sets of sentence parts may be put on the chalkboard. A member of two opposing teams goes to each set and at the signal draws lines to the correct ending of each sentence.

A little dog	fell off the truck
Two red birds	began to bark
A funny noise	had two kittens
Six big boxes	sat on a wire
A mother cat	was heard

APPENDIX J

Purposeful Classroom Reading Experiences

FOOD RECIPES

Every classroom should be equipped with an electric hot plate. The following are easy to prepare:

Instant pudding	Rice cereal candy
Gelatin dessert	No-bake cereal cookies
Vegetable soup	Chili
Iced graham crackers	Popcorn

A recipe may be written on the chalkboard and the challenge made that when every child can read it plans will be made for a "Pudding Party" or "Cookie Party." Children may be checked at any convenient time and their initials placed beside the recipe. Children help each other and interest runs high. Be sure enough is made so that every child gets a taste and every child has a little part in the "doing." Paper towel place mats may be decorated while children wait for turns in participating.

LETTERS

After Christmas is a good time to bring in a short well-written letter on a large sheet of tagboard. Explain each part and read it to and with the children. Then mount it on a bulletin board with a table below it on which writing materials will be available for children to come and write at their convenience. Beside the salutation place word cards with *Uncle, Aunt,* and *Cousin.* Beside the closing place word cards reading *Love, Fondly,* and *Sincerely.* All along the side place word cards with such words as children mention with regard to the gifts they received and for which they will need to write thank-you notes. Thus the stage is set for an invitational kind of writing that does not pressure a child to start it before he is ready nor to complete it within a short writing period. Children may read their letters to the group if they care to or they may be kept "personal" and taken home to be mailed.

404

MESSAGES

A corner of the chalkboard may be used as a "Help Wanted" section. Such items would appear as:

James, will you please feed the goldfish today?

It is Sally's turn to water the plants.

Two strong boys are needed to carry books to the principal's office. Please volunteer.

Please don't forget your milk money tomorrow.

I need someone to go to the library.

A child who needs individual help with word cards might write an item and erase it when some one volunteers. These items should be changed every day so that interest is maintained.

Following a recipe gives children an opportunity to recognize the need to read carefully and to follow through with what was comprehended from reading. (Courtesy of the Cedar Rapids, Iowa, Schools.)

IMAGERY

Write a word such as *snow* on the blackboard and challenge children to add a word or phrase that would make a better mental image than *snow* alone. They may use a dictionary or their imaginations. Just before going home challenge the class to read all that appears. This is an example:

Snow—on the roof sparkles and gleams.
Crunchy snow under our feet.
Light fluffy snow that blows about.
Hard-packed snow we can walk on.

WORD CHALLENGES

When you are waiting for children to finish cleaning up or putting work away or getting wraps on, challenge the ones who are ready by asking them to think of all the words that tell where something could be: *in, on, among, between, under, over,* etc. The teacher should record them on the chalkboard as they are mentioned. By the time all the children are ready the list is complete for group reading. Another time the challenge may be to think of words that tell "when" and could be: *yesterday, today, tomorrow, afternoon, forenoon, tonight,* etc. Another time the challenge could be "how": *slowly, fast, swiftly, neatly, poorly, safely,* etc. Other times phrases instead of words might be recorded. These words and phrases are key elements in skimming and this kind of help is very useful.

WORD CHANGES

Challenge children to change a given word, such as *help,* in as many ways as they can. The list might include *help, helper, helpless, helping, helped, helpers, helper's.* Some words would include prefixes as well as many types of endings.

PHRASE CHALLENGE

Divide the group into two teams. Write on the board phrases such as:

in the house
under the table
by the door
through the window
over the wall
beside the bench
after the war
about the story
toward the end
into a garden

A child is challenged to read all the phrases and scores a point for each one read correctly. Then the teacher changes the final word of each phrase and a member of the opposite team reads them and is scored. Thus more fluent reading of phrases comes about and the key words become almost automatic.

UNPHONETIC WORDS

Challenge children to think of words to which phonics does not apply. Two children from opposite teams go to the chalkboard and write as many as they can think of. They get a point for each one that is not phonetic. Then members of the other team get points for being able to read the words.

COMPLETIONS

Write sentences on the chalkboard such as:

John went to the hobby shop to get some —————.

Challenge children to think of all the plausible words. Then change it to read:

John went to the bakery to get a —————.
Mary ————— to the shop on the corner.

APPENDIX K

Teaching Aids for Developing Better Oral Expression

CHILDREN'S PARTICIPATION IN STORY-TELLING

Encourage children to join in the refrain part of stories they know well—"No, no, by the hair of my chinny-chin-chin," "Who's been sleeping in my bed?", and "Oh, Grandmother, what big eyes you have!" Then let various children be certain characters as you tell the story. Let children manipulate the flannel-board characters and speak for them as you or some child tells the story.

DRAMATIC PLAY

Every kindergarten and first grade should have an assortment of adult clothing such as dresses, hats, purses, gloves, top coats, shoes, and a walking stick. Such accessories put children in the mood for role playing, and better expression is a likely outcome.

DRAMATIZATIONS

Some stories lend themselves to dramatization much better than others. The following are especially good:

Kindergarten
The Three Bears
The Three Billy Goats Gruff
The Little Red Hen
The Three Little Pigs
Three Little Kittens
The Brementown Musicians
Ask Mr. Bear
Caps for Sale
Little Red Riding Hood
Little Duck Learns to Talk
  First Grade
The Little Rabbit Who Wanted Red Wings
Rumplestiltskin
Chicken Little
The Turnip

The Pancake
Paddy's Christmas
The Bojabi Tree
   Second Grade
Stone Soup
Many Moons
The Five Chinese Brothers
Paddy's Christmas

Stories in various readers lend themselves to dramatization. At third-grade level and above children enjoy play production. Following are some sources:

Thirty Plays for Classroom Reading, Durrell, Donald (Plays, Inc.)
Bag of Fire, The Straw Ox, The Four Winds, Kissen, Fan (Houghton, Mifflin, 1964)
Radio Plays for Young People to Act, Schneiderman, Rose (Dutton, 1961)
Stories to Dramatize, Ward, Winifred (Anchorage, Ken. Children's Theater Press, 1952)

PUPPETRY

Stick puppets, hand puppets, and peep-through puppets all help children to overcome self-consciousness by "being someone else." Very little time should be spent in making such accessories unless it is an art project. It is the role-playing that is most important.

CHORAL SPEAKING AND FINGER PLAYS

The objective in elementary grades should be better oral expression and not a polished well-balanced performance. The fun of participating may help certain children overcome monotonous intonation and lead to the development of expressive and dynamic speech. Choral speaking may be initiated in the kindergarten through the use of nursery rhymes with five groups, as follows (or it may be done with only two groups):

GROUP I: Baa, baa, Black Sheep,
               Have you any wool?

GROUP II: Yes, sir! Yes, sir!
          Three bags full!
GROUP III: One for my master—
GROUP IV: One for the dame—
GROUP V: And one for the little boy who lives down the lane.

Two children may pantomime the following while the other children say the verse:

> Two little blackbirds sitting on a hill
> One named Jack and one named Jill;
> Fly away, Jack!
> Fly away, Jill!
> Come back, Jack!
> Come back, Jill!
> Two little blackbirds sitting on a hill
> One named Jack and one named Jill.

Five children may take part while the group recites:

> Five little pumpkins sitting on a gate.
> The first one said, "My, it's getting late!"
> The second one said, "There are witches in the air."
> The third one said, "But we don't care."
> The fourth one said, "I think we'd better run!"
> The fifth one said, "Isn't Halloween fun?"
> "Whoo-oo-oo," went the wind, and out went the lights.
> And the pumpkins ran home on Halloween night.

All children may participate in this one:

> Two tall telephone poles
>   (*pointer fingers erect*)
> Between them a wire is strung
>   (*two middle fingers touching*);
> Two birds hopped on
>   (*press thumbs against middle fingers*);
> And swung, swung, swung.
>   (*sway arms back and forth from body*).

In second grade "read-together" poems can be fun and are conducive to better expression. Starting in third grade children may become interested in taking high, low, and medium voice parts. The groups are not likely to be balanced, but the value lies in better intonation. Following are sources of good materials for choral speaking:

Choral Speaking Is Fun, Raubichek, Letitia (Noble, 1965)

Let's Read Together Poems, Brown, Helen, and Heltman, Harry (Harper, 1949)

Choral Reading for Fun and Relaxation, Brown, Helen (Westminster, 1953)

Better Speech and Better Reading, Schoefield, Lucille (Boston: Expression Co., 1937)

Speech Ways, Scott, Louise, and Thompson, J. J. (Webster, 1955)

APPENDIX L

Suggestions for Teaching the Alphabet and for Alphabetizing

1. When first-graders are ready to use the alphabet, it is usually early enough in the fall of the year that they are still very much interested in having turns on playground swings and teeter-totters. After the alphabet has been learned as a rote verse or song and has been said as a series of individual letters, it might be suggested that children take turns on swings and teeter-totters according to the length of time it takes those waiting for a turn to say half the alphabet. When they get to *M* it is time for the next person to have a turn and the group starts with *N* and proceeds through the alphabet. They say *A* when the swing is as far as it will go in one direction and *B* when it is as far as it will go in the opposite direction. The same is done with the teeter-totter—when one side is up the children say *A* and wait for the other side to be up before they say *B*. Thus they begin to be aware of the middle of the alphabet and approximate location of the letters as they say them orally.

2. Put all the children's first names on one side of the chalkboard. Challenge them to find which should come first for an alphabetical arrangement, which next, etc., as you write them on the opposite side of the chalk board. If children need to line up for any reason, suggest that it be done in the alphabetical sequence on the board. Thus they get the feel for where certain letters are in sequence. A week or two later use last names so they get the feel for other letter locations.

3. After using many four-line verses with the children, make cards available with the verses in manuscript so that the children may copy their favorites. File the verses by title or by author and keep them in a little file box. Ask the children to arrange their pages in alphabetical order before the pages are stapled and made into a booklet.

4. Help children to make individual picture dictionaries. A letter is printed on each page and a picture is found to go with each letter. *X, Y,* and *Z* may be put on the last page and a yo-yo or a zebra may be the picture. Use old readiness books and magazines for pictures.

5. Keep a file of word cards. Challenge various children to put the new ones in the proper places as they are introduced.

6. After the dictionary has been introduced challenge two children to see which one can find the approximate location of a given word most quickly.

7. Challenge children to tell you whether a given letter is toward the beginning, middle, or end of the alphabet. A contest may be held by challenging two teams and keeping score.

8. Help children to alphabetize songs they know or stories that have been read, in keeping a class record. Use alphabetization in as many ways as will be useful in the classroom and give children the responsibility for doing it.

9. Suggest that children make their own telephone directories. Have them alphabetize their friends' and relatives' names and include the fire department, the police, the family doctor, the family dentist, and any other numbers the child is likely to use. This familiarizes children with the large telephone book as well as provides a worthwhile experience with alphabetizing.

10. Have children make an alphabetized list of their favorite television programs with the station and time. They may do a little exploring, using T.V. guides and consulting newspaper schedules. Class discussions can help them to evaluate programs and to become aware of certain good programs with which some children may not be familiar.

APPENDIX M

My Reading Report

My name _____

Date I started to read the book _____

Date completed _____

Title of the book _____

Author _____

Kind of book _____

   (factual, fantasy, fiction, other lands, biography, poetry, short
   stories, other)

What I would like to say about it?

APPENDIX N

Reading Activities for Fourth, Fifth, and Sixth Grades

1. Write a descriptive sentence about each character in the story.
2. Copy the sentences that tell where the story takes place.
3. Write a paragraph telling why you would or would not like to be the principal character in the story.
4. Write five "Who said _____?" questions to challenge classmates.
5. Write a brief version of the story with a different ending.
6. Select five words from the story that could have other meanings according to the dictionary. Which of your words has the most meanings?
7. How much information is there in the first paragraph of the story about the "who," "when," and "where" of the story? How far do you have to read before all three questions are answered?
8. Select a story that other class members have not read. Check with the teacher and then prepare to read it orally to the class.
9. State the plot of the story in five brief statements.
10. Prepare an outline for one of the stories we have read and challenge a classmate to fill in the details in class.
11. Write a letter of advice to one of the characters in the story.

12. How many digraphs and diphthongs can you find on the first page of the story? List them.
13. Find difficult words in any of the stories we have read. Bring them to class and challenge classmates with pronunciations and meanings.
14. Find a sentence in one of the stories for each of the following: description, humor, question, exclamation, sarcasm, conversation.
15. Choose a favorite character from any story you have read and explain in a paragraph why that character appeals to you.
16. Write five completion sentences pertaining to any of the stories we have read.
17. Find five words in the story that describe; five that answer the questions how? when? where?
18. Find a poem you especially like to read aloud. Prepare it carefully.
19. What is there in some of the stories we have read that could apply to our daily lives?
20. What is the problem in this story? How was it solved?
21. Would you have done the same thing that the principal character did? Why or why not?
22. Find a story that lends itself to dramatization. Check with your teacher. Select your characters and practice during spare moments.
23. Write a story with the same characters but another plot.
24. Why do you think the story turned out the way it did?
25. What sentences answer the following questions? (Here list some questions to be answered by sentences from the story.)
26. How do you feel about the characters in this story? What is likely to become of each one?
27. What did you find out from this reading that you did not know before?
28. Select five words from the story and find other words that may be substituted for them. Bring these synonyms to class.
29. What would be another good title for the preceding five stories?
30. Find a sentence in which one word might be changed to make the meaning the opposite of what it is now.
31. What story has a title that does not reveal at all what it is about?
32. Is there a general theme for the stories you have been reading? Explain.

APPENDIX O

Books to Read to Children

(See Appendix Q for addresses of publishers)

Infancy without Mother Goose?
  How comfortless!
Early childhood without Fairy Tales?
  How unimaginative!
Later childhood without Hero Stories?
  How ventureless!
Adolescence without mysteries and inspiring biography?
  How disconcerting!
Life without reading?
  How lacking!
                              —VERNA DIECKMAN ANDERSON

PRE-SCHOOL AND NURSERY SCHOOL

Abingdon Press:
  Becker, *900 Buckets of Paint*
  Petersham, *The Rooster Crows* (rhymes)
Coward, McCann:
  Gag, *ABC Bunny*
Crowell:
  Aliki, *My Five Senses*
  Showers, *Let's Find Out About Touching, The Listening Walk*
Doubleday:
  Bright, *Georgie*
  Flack, *The New Pet*
  Haley, *One, Two, Buckle My Shoe*
  Showalter, *Around the Corner*
Dutton:
  Banister, *A Child's Grace*
Harcourt, Brace & World:
  Anglund, *In a Pumpkin Shell*
  Eichenberg, *Ape in a Cape*
  Rand, *I Know a Lot of Things*
Harper & Row:
  Bonsall, *It's Mine*
  Brown, *The Duck, The Country Noisy Book, Goodnight, Moon, The
    Important Book*
  Knight, *Where's Wallace?*
  Krauss, *The Growing Story*

Minarik, *Little Bear*
Rojankowsky, *The Tall Book of Nursery Tales*
Ulrey, *A Tree Is Nice*
Houghton Mifflin:
Wartburg, *Curl Up Small*
Alfred Knopf:
Duvoisin, *Petunia*
Miles, *A Day in Winter*
Lothrop, Lee & Shepard:
Buckley, *Grandfather and I, Grandmother and I*
Foster, *A Pocketful of Seasons, Tell Me, Mr. Owl*
Tresselt, *Wake Up, City*
Tuft, *The Rabbit Garden*
Zolotow, *Sleepy Book*
Macmillan:
Flack, *Ask Mr. Bear*
McGraw-Hill:
Blough, *Who Lives in This Meadow?*
MacGregor, *Theodore Turtle*
Platt & Munk:
Austin, *The Very Young Mother Goose*
Putnam:
Gramatky, *Little Toot, Loopy*
Rand McNally:
Wright, *The Real Mother Goose*
Random House:
Captain Kangaroo, *Captain Kangaroo's Story Book*
Frank (ed.), *Poems to Read to the Very Young*
Garten, *The Alphabet Tale*
Kramer, *Read-Aloud Nursery Tales*
Scott:
Brown, *A Child's Goodnight Book, Nibble, Nibble*
Green, *Everybody Has a House*
Joslyn, *What Do You Say, Dear*
Sneider, *While Suzie Sleeps*
Wright, *Saturday Walk*
Scribners:
Francoise, *The Thank-You Book*
Viking Press:
Ets, *In the Forest, Just Me, Play with Me*
McCloskey, *Make Way for Ducklings, One Morning in Maine, The Snowy Day*

KINDERGARTEN AND FIRST GRADE

Abingdon Press:
Guy, *A Baby For Betsy*
Schlein, *How Do You Travel?*

Coward-McCann:
  Gag, *Millions of Cats*
Crowell:
  Brown, *The Little Fir Tree*
  Everds, *The Lazy Lion*
Doubleday:
  Bright, *Georgie's Halloween*
  Brown, *Red Light, Green Light*
  Flack, *Angus and the Ducks* (and other Angus stories), *The New Pet*
  Ipcar, *Brown Cow Farm*
  Kessler, *Big Red Bus*
  Rickert, *The Bojabi Tree*
  Sauer, *Mike's House*
Follett:
  Bruna, *The Circus*
  Champion, *Mother Goose Rhymes*
  Dikeman, *Henry's Wagon*
  Field, *Wynken, Blynken and Nod*
  Lowe, *The Little Bear Who Wanted Friends*
Harcourt, Brace & World:
  Anglund, *A Friend Is Someone Who Likes You, Love Is a Special Way
    of Feeling*
  Barry, *A Is for Anything*
  Joslyn, *Baby Elephand and the Three Wishes*
  Langstaff, *Over in the Meadow*
  Munari, *Who's There, Open the Door, The Birthday Present*
Harper & Row:
  Brown, *Three Little Animals*
  Chalmers, *The Cat Who Liked To Pretend, A Christmas Story, Mr.
    Cat's Wonderful Surprise*
  Heilbroner, *The Happy Birthday Present*
  Hoban, *A Baby Sitter for Frances, Bread and Jam for Frances*
  Hurd, *No Funny Business*
  Krauss, *A Hole Is to Dig, The Happy Day, The Littlest Rabbit*
  Kundhardt, *Gas Station Gus*
  Lobel, *A Zoo for Mr. Muster*
  Rukeyser, *I Go Out*
  Zion, *All Falling Down*
Holt, Rinehart & Winston:
  Caudill, *Did You Carry the Flag Today, Charlie?*
  Hogrogian, *Always Room for One More*
Houghton Mifflin:
  Allen, *Everyday Insects*
  Anderson, *Billy and Blaze*
  Bannon, *Red Mittens, The Scary Thing*
  Burton, *Katy and the Big Snow, Little House, Mike Mulligan and His
    Steam Shovel*
  Payne, *Katy No-Pocket*

Rey, *Curious George* and other *Curious George* stories
Ward, *The Biggest Bear*
Knopf:
  DuVoisin, *Petunia's Christmas, Two Lonely Ducks*
  Ipcar, *I Like Animals*
  McNulty, *When A Boy Wakes Up in the Morning*
  Monsell, *Paddy's Christmas*
  Steiner, *My Slippers Are Red*
  Watson, *Whose Birthday Is It?*
Lippincott:
  Bennett, *Little Witch*
  McGinley, *Lucy McLockett*
Lothrop, Lee & Shepard:
  Adams, *Mr. Picklepaw's Popcorn*
  Buckley, *My Sister and I, The Little Boy and the Birthdays*
  Friedrich, *The April Umbrella*
  Holl, *The Rain Puddle*
  Janice, *Little Bear's Christmas*
  Rice, *The March Wind*
  Tresselt, *Autumn Harvest, Follow the Wind, Hide and Seek, Hi, Mr.*
    Robin, Rain Drop Splash
Macmillan:
  Association for Childhood Education International, *The Umbrella*
    Books
  Charles, *How to Get From Here to There*
  Slobodkin, *Trick or Treat*
McGraw-Hill:
  Fatio, *The Happy Lion*
Morrow:
  Beim, *The Smallest Boy in the Class*
  Brim, *Andy and the School Bus*
  Cleary, *Two Dog Biscuits*
  Haywood, *Here Comes the Bus*
  Zim, *Things Around the House*
Putnam:
  Buchheimer, *Night Outdoors*
  Craig, *Spring Is Like the Morning*
  Rosner, *Let's Go for a Nature Walk*
Rand, McNally:
  Barrows, *Read-Aloud Poems Every Child Should Know*
Random House:
  de Brunoff, *The Story of Babar*
  Eastman, *Are You My Mother?*
  Larrick, *Piper, Pipe that Song Again*
  Seuss, *If I Ran the Zoo*
Scott, Foresman:
  Arbuthnot, *Time for Poetry*

Scott:
  Anderson, *Red Fox and the Hungry Tiger*
  Collier, *I Know a Farm*
  Slobodkin, *Caps for Sale*
Scribners:
  Dalgleish, *The Thanksgiving Story*
  Snyder, *One Day at the Zoo*
Vanguard Press:
  Geisel, *And To Think that It Happened on Mulberry Street*
  Slobodkin, *The Friendly Animals*
Viking Press:
  Angelo, *The Acorn Tree*
  Bemelmans, *Hansi, Madeline*
  Buff, *Dash and Dart*
  Clark, *Tia Maria's Garden*
  Daugherty, *Andy and the Lion*
  Gay, *What's Your Name?*
  Graham, *Timothy Turtle*
  Keats, *Whistle for Willie, The Snowy Day*
  Yashima, *Umbrella*
Watts:
  Stevenson, *A Child's Garden of Verses*
Whitman:
  Beattie, *Poof, Poof*
  Justus, *Little Red Rooster Learns to Crow*
  Randall, *Fun for Chris*

SECOND AND THIRD GRADES

Atheneum Press:
  Raskin, *Nothing Ever Happens on My Block*
  Snyder, *Black and Blue Magic, The Velvet Room*
  Weik, *The Jazz Man*
Children's Press:
  Radlauer, *Fathers at Work*
Crowell:
  Child Study Assn., *Holiday Story Book*
  McEwen, *Away We Go* (Poetry)
Doubleday:
  Kipling, *New Illustrated Just So Stories*
  O'Neill, *Hailstones and Halibut Bones* (Poetry)
Harcourt, Brace & World:
  Beim, *Two Is a Team*
  Estes, *The Hundred Dresses, The Moffats*
  Haywood, *"B" Is For Betsy*
  Joslyn, *There Is a Dragon in My Bed*

Severson, *Miracles on Maple Hill*
Travers, *Mary Poppins*
Harper & Row:
  Brelis, *The Mummy Market*
  Carlson, *The Empty Schoolhouse*
  Enright, *Thimble Summer*
  Jackson, *Call Me Charlie*
  White, *Charlotte's Web*
Holiday House:
  Black, *Busy Water*
  Rounds, *The Blind Colt*
Holt, Rinehart & Winston:
  Enright, *The Saturdays*
  Ness, *Sam, Bangs and Moonshine*
  Withers, *Tale of a Black Cat*
Knopf:
  Fenner, *Time to Laugh*
Little, Brown:
  Little, *Mine for Keeps*
Lothrop, Lee & Shepard:
  Holl, *Mrs. McGarrity's Peppermint Sweater*
Macmillan:
  Association for Childhood Education, International, *Silver Umbrella,*
    Told Under the Christmas Tree
  Collodi, *The Adventures of Pinocchio*
  Hader, *Lost in the Zoo*
  Lewis, *When I Go to the Moon*
  Spyri, *Heidi*
McKay:
  Van Gelder, *Monkeys Have Tails*
Parnasus Press:
  Ritchie, *Ramon Makes a Trade*
Scott, Foresman:
  Arbuthnot, *Time for Fairy Tales, Old and New*
Scribners:
  Brown, *Stone Soup*
  Goudy, *The Day We Saw the Sun Come Up*
  Kahl, *The Duchess Bakes a Cake*
  Ness, *Tom Tit Tot*
  Politti, *Rosa*
Viking Press:
  Gates, *Sensible Kate*
  McCloskey, *Homer Price*
  Tudor, *Becky's Christmas*
Watts:
  York, *Miss Know-It-All*

FOURTH, FIFTH, AND SIXTH GRADES

Doubleday:
  de Angeli, *The Door in the Wall*
Follett:
  Hunt, *Up a Road Slowly*
  Taylor, *All of a Kind Family*
Harcourt, Brace & World:
  Behm, *The Golden Hive: Poems and Pictures*
  Isbert, *The Ark, Rowan Farm*
  MacPherson, *The Rough Road*
  Ottley, *Boy Alone*
  Steele, *The Far Frontier*
Harper & Row:
  Calhoun, *Katie John*
  DeJong, *Along Came a Dog, The House of Sixty Fathers, The Wheel
    on the School*
  Gipson, *Old Yeller*
  Johnson, *The Bearcat*
  Stolz, *A Dog on Barkham Street*
  Wilder, *Little House in the Big Woods*
Houghton Mifflin:
  Forbes, *Johnny Tremain*
  North, *Mark Twain and the River*
  O'Dell, *The King's Fifth*
Little, Brown:
  Atwater, *Mr. Popper's Penguins*
  Bowman, *Mike Fink*
  Cameron, *The Wonderful Flight to the Mushroom Planet*
  Jackson, *The Taste of Spruce Gum*
  Lawson, *Ben and Me*
  Sawyer, *Joy to the World: Christmas Legends*
  Sharp, *The Rescuers*
Macmillan:
  Anderson, *Afraid to Ride*
  Brink, *Caddie Woodlawn*
  Carroll, *Alice's Adventures in Wonderland*
  Sperry, *Call It Courage*
  Vroman, *East of the Sun and West of the Moon and Other Tales*
Viking:
  duBois, *The Twenty-One Balloons*
  Gates, *Blue Willow*
  Gray, *The Cheerful Heart*
  McCloskey, *Homer Price*
  Rankin, *Daughter of the Mountains*
  Seredy, *The Good Master*

A P P E N D I X P

Books for Independent Reading

American Book Co.:
Constantine, *The Little Red Hen, The Gingerbread Boy*
Georeou, *The Elephant's Funny Ways*
Hitte, *The Other Side of the Fence*
Langhans, *Pets and Places*
Leavell, *Open Windows*
Stone, *Tommy Goes Shopping, Nancy Cooks Breakfast*
Beckley:
Battle, *Jerry, Jerry Goes Riding*
Chandler, *Kala's Pet, Taka and His Dog*
Cordts, *Tommy O'Toole and Larry*
Gustafson, *Shad and the Circle-C Ranch, Tim and the Tall Grain Farm*
Benefic Press:
Chandler, *Tall Boy and the Coyote*
Derman, *Monkey Island, Poker Dog*
Children's Press:
Elkin, *Lucky and the Giant*
Greene, I-Want-To-Be Books as follows:

Airplane Hostess	*Fireman*	*Road Builder*
Animal Doctor	*Fisherman*	*Scientist*
Baker	*Librarian*	*Ship Captain*
Ballet Dancer	*Homemaker*	*Space Captain*
Baseball Player	*Musician*	*Storekeeper*
Bus Driver	*News Reporter*	*Telephone Operator*
Carpenter	*Orange Grower*	*Teacher*
Coal Miner	*Pilot*	*Train Engineer*
Cowboy	*Policeman*	*Truck Driver*
Dairy Farmer	*Postman*	*Zoo Keeper*
Dentist	*Restaurant Owner*	
Doctor	*Farmer*	

Konkle, *Once There Was a Kitten*
MacBean, *Picture Book Dictionary*
Ray, *We Live in the City*
Stuart, *The Airplane at the Airport*
True, *Number Men*
Warner, *Hurray for Hats*
Weil, *Animal Families*
Coward, McCann:
Von Hippel, *The Story of the Snails Who Traded Houses*

Doubleday:
  Bright, *Georgie*
  Flack, *Angus and the Ducks*
  Parsons, *Rain*
  Kesslet, *Do Baby Bears Sit in Chairs?*
Dutton:
  Hogan, *Cubby Bear and the Book*
Educational Publishers:
  Craig, *Puss-in-Boots*
Follett:
  Dupree, *Too Many Dogs*
  Erickson, *Just Follow Me*
  Georgiady, *Gertie, the Duck*
  Guilfoile, *Have You Seen My Brother?*, *Nobody Listens to Andrew*
  Hastings, *Big New School*, *Pearl Goes to School*
  Kaune, *My Own Little House*
  King, *Mabel, The Whale*
  Meeks, *The Curious Cow*, *The Hill That Grew*, *Something New at the Zoo*
  Olds, *Miss Hattie and the Monkey*
  Seyton, *The Hole in the Hill*
  Vreeken, *Henry, The Boy Who Would Not Say His Name*
  Woods, *Little Quack*
Garrard:
  Dolch:
Big, Bigger, Biggest
I Like Cats
In the Woods
Monkey Friends
Once There Was a Bear
Once There Was a Cat
Once There Was a Dog
Once There Was an Elephant
Once There Was a Monkey
Once There Was a Rabbit
Tommy's Pets
Some Are Small
Zoo Is Home
D. C. Heath:
  Brumbauth, *Donald Duck and His Nephews*
Houghton Mifflin:
  Rey, *Curious George Flies a Kite*, *Curious George Learns the Alphabet*, *Feed the Animals and See the Circus*
Lippincott:
  Leary, *Bucky's Friends*, *Happy Ranch*, *Making Friends*
Lyons & Carnahan:
  Bond, *Fun with Us*, *Ride with Us*, *Play with Us*, *Many Surprises*, *Three of Us*
Macmillan:
  Gates, *Hundreds of Turkeys*, *My Dog Laddie*, *Peanuts*, *The Pony Polly*, *The Kid*, *Sing, Canary, Sing*, *Tip*, *Three Elephants*, *Rusty Wants a Dog*
  Lopshire, *Put Me in the Zoo*

Random House:
  Eastman, *Go, Dog, Go*
  Seuss, *Green Eggs and Ham*
  Sieg, *Ten Apples Up on Top*
Rand McNally:
  Brod, *How Would You Act?*
Steck-Vaugn:
  Ashley, *The Biggest House, Some Do and Some Don't*
  Atkinson, *The Horney Toad Kite*
  Bishop, *Prissy Misses*
  Bradbury, *Happy Acres*
  Carter, *Happy Long Legs, Willie Wade*
  Davis, *Pinkie, Rickie*
  DeVault, *The Jack Rabbit*
  Gary and Smith, *Metzi*
  Guy, *The Book of Tongues, A Book of Trails*
  Hubka, *Bernie, Octavius*
  Lorella, *The Little Shell Hunter*
  Munch, *The Armadillo, Horned Lizzards, The Road Runner*
  Nelson, *All The Sounds We Hear*
  O'Leary, *Biffy, Polk-Along*
  O'Brien, *Animal Tots*
  Pearson, *Buttons and His Sunday Coat*
  Pierce, *The Smile That Traveled Around the World*
  Sharp, *Downy Duck Grows Up, Secret Places, Watch Me, Daffy, Straight Up*
  Smith, *Up a Tree, The Sleepy Squirrel*
  Walker, *To the Circus*
  Young, *Every Day a Surprise*
Viking:
  Garrett, *Angelo the Naughty One*
  Gay, *Look, Small One*

SECOND AND THIRD GRADES

Abelard, Schuman:
  Watts, *Weeks and Weeks*
American:
  Coatsworth, *Seven Sleepers*
  Ely, *Who Is It?*
  Georgeou, *The Monkey and the Alligator, Who Was the Strongest?*
  Sondergaard, *The Horse with the Flying Mane*
  Stone, *One Pet Too Many, The Animal Surprise*
Beckley:
  Battle, *Jerry Goes on a Picnic*
  Bialk, *Tizz Is a Cowpony, Tizz and Company, Tizz on a Packtrip, Tizz Plays Santa Claus, Tizz Takes a Trip*

Chandler, *Buffalo Boy, Little Cedar's Tooth*
Meeker, *How Hospitals Help Us*
Walker, *Shining Star, The Indian Boy*
Children's Press:
Allee, *The Vegetables on Your Plate*
Ballard, *Reptiles*
Bauer, *At Home*
Boreman, *Bantie and Her Chicks*
Broekel, *Tropical Fishes*
Brown, *Look and See*
Carona, *Chemistry*
Carter, *Houses, Oceans, Ships and Seaports*
Clark, *Dinosaurs*
Colonius, *At the Bakery, At the Library, At the Zoo, At the Post Office*
Copeland, *Little Eskimos*
Courtright, *Jolly Blue Boat*
DeWitt, *The Littlest Reindeer*
Eggleston, *Things that Grow*
Elkin, *Schools*
Erickson, *Animals of Small Pond*
Foster, *Seeds Are Wonderful, Your Kitten*
Frahm, *Bacteria*
Friskey, *Birds We Know, Johnny and the Monarch, Mystery of the Farmer's Three Fives, Perky Little Engine*
Gates, *Conversation*
Gee, *How Can I Find Out?*
Gibson, *Garden Dwellers, Our Weather*
Green, *Apples from Orchard to Market*
Harmer, *Circus, Pioneers*
Harvey, *Cotton Growing*
Hastings, *All Kinds of Days, At the Dairy, Playground Fun*
Haynes, *Health, The Biggest Pig*
Hengesbaugh, *I Live in So Many Places*
Hinshaw, *Your Body and You*
Hoffman, *Family Helpers*
Israel, *Sheep on the Ranch, The Tractor on the Farm*
Johnson, *Truck Farming*
Konkle, *The Christmas Kitten*
Kramer, *Big Beasts*
Krum, *Read with Me*
Leavitt, *Tools for Building*
Lewellen, *Farm Animals, Moon, Sun and Stars, Toys at Work*
Lund, *Attic of the Wind*
Marks, *Fish on the Tide*
Martini, *Cowboys*
McGrath, *Clouds*
Miner, *Our Post Office and Its Helpers*

Moore, *The Magic Spectacles*
Nighbert, *Cloth*
Nordie, *A Dog for Suzie*
Podendorf, *Animal Babies, Animals of the Sea and Shore, Energy, Indians, Magnets and Electricity Pebbles and Shells, Pets, Plant Experiments, Rocks and Minerals, Science Experiments, More Science Experiments, Seasons, Space, Spiders, Sounds We Hear, Time, Trees, Weeds and Wild Flowers, Weather Experiments*
Posell, *Dogs, Deserts, Horses, Whales, Transportation*
Reck, *At the Railroad Station, Some Days to Remember*
Rees, *At the Bank, Our Flag*
Rockwell, *Sally's Caterpillar*
Russell, *Fruit*
Sevrey, *Communication*
Stever, *At the Freight Yard, At the Wholesale Market*
Ziner, *Time, Wonderful Wheels*
Doubleday:
Adam, *The Big, Big Box*
Dutton:
Schwartz, *The Night Workers*
Follett:
Berg, *The O'Learys and Friends*
Brouillette, *Butterflies*
Carlton, *Benny and the Bear*
Dillon, *Salmon*
Field, *The Gingham Dog and the Calico Cat, The Dinkey Bird, Wynken, Blynken and Nod*
Hastings, *Pearl Goes to School*
Hoff, *The Four Friends*
John, *Hummingbirds*
Leonard, *Buried Gold*
Moore, *The Night Before Christmas*
Olds, *Miss Hattie and the Monkey*
Neal, *Sound*
Page, *Rocks and Minerals*
Schoenknecht, *Ants, Frogs and Toads*
Victor, *Machines, Magnets, Friction*
Wood, *Beavers*
Four Winds Press:
McGovern, *If You Lived in Colonial Times*
Garrard:
Dolch, *Animal Stories, Bear Stories, Circus Stories, Dog Stories, More Dog Stories, Elephant Stories, Horse Stories, Lion and Tiger Stories, Wigwam Stories, Tepee Stories, "Why" Stories, Zoo Is Home, On the Farm, Friendly Birds, Dog Pals, Golden Girl, Jan and the Reindeer*
Hale, E. M. & Co.: Many special editions of good books

Harper & Row:
  Averill, *The Fire Cat*
  Baker, *Little Runner of the Longhouse*
  Greene, *What Do They Do? Policemen and Firemen*
  Hoff, *Albert the Albatross, Chester, Danny and the Dinosaur, Grizzwold, Julius, Last One Home Is a Green Pig, Little Chief*
  Heilbroner, *The Happy-Birthday Present*
  Hurd, *Come and Have Fun, Hurry Hurry, Johnny Lion's Book*
  Löbel, *Lucille*
  McClintock, *David and the Giant, What Have I Got?*
  Minarik, *Cat and Dog, No Fighting, No Biting, Little Bear, Little Bear's Friend, Father Bear Comes Home, Little Bear's Visit*
  Selman, *How to Become a Nature Detective*
  Stolz, *Emmet's Pig*
  Wiseman, *Morris Is a Cowboy*
  Zion, *Harry and the Lady Next Door*
Holiday:
  Funk, *I Read Signs*
  Thompson, *Camp in the Yard*
Holt, Rinehart & Winston:
  Sebastian, *Rivers*
Houghton Mifflin:
  Bannon, *The Best House in the World*
  Ciardi, *I Met a Man*
  Rey, *Curious George Goes to the Hospital*
  Stringer, *Penny*
Knopf:
  Olds, *What Will I Wear?*
Laidlaw:
  Abney, *Stories We Like*
Lippincott:
  Palmer, *A Ride on High*
Little, Brown:
  Christopher, *The Reluctant Pitcher*
  Emberley, *The Parade Book*
McGraw-Hill:
  Blough, *Discovering Plants*
  Schwartz, *Go on Wheels*
Macmillan:
  Gates, *Pueblo Indian Stories, The Princess with the Dirty Face*
Putnam:
  Kumin, *Follow the Fall*
  Thompson, *The Horse that Liked Sandwishes*
Steck-Vaugn:
  Garry and Smith, *Creepy Caterpillar, Flagon the Dragon*
  O'Leary, *Cappy Cardinal, The Goat Who Ate Flowers*
  Sharp and Young, *Little Lost Bo-Bo, Rainbow in the Sky*

Smith, *Poncho and the Pink Horse*
Winkler, *The Boy Who Saw an Alligator in His Bathtub*
Viking:
  Buff, *Dash and Dart, Elf Owl, Forest Folk*
  Clark, *Tia Maria's Garden*
  Freeman, *Fly High, Fly Low*
  Hall, *The World in a City Block*
  Jones, *This Is the Way*
  Lindgren, *Christmas in Noisey Village*
  Keats, *Whistle for Willie*
  Leaf, *The Story of Ferdinand*
  McCloskey, *Time of Wonder, One Morning in Maine, Blueberries for Sal*
  Sayers, *Tag-Along Tooloo*
  Schreiber, *Bambino the Clown*
  Watson, *My Garden Grows*
Watts: A large group of *First Books* by various authors. *Let's Find Out Books*—more than thirty titles
Webster:
  Ware, *The Goat that Learned to Count, Kathy and the Doll Buggy, Jimmy Potter Buys a Lollipop, Journey to the End of the Earth, The Little Woman Who Forgot Everything, The Lost and Found Ball, Mr. Hazelnut, Peter Johnson and His Guitar, The Town that Forgot It Was Christmas*
Whitman:
  Bishop, *Riddle Raddle, Fiddle Faddle*
  Chapin, *Squad Car Fifty-Five*
  Udrey, *What Mary Jo Shared*

Fourth, Fifth, and Sixth Grades

Abelard:
  Beatty, *Davey's Adventure with the Clyde Beatty Circus*
Abingdon:
  Carruth, *She Wanted to Read*
Atheneum:
  Wojciechowska, *The Shadow of a Bull*
Atlantic:
  Burnford, *The Incredible Journey*
Bobbs-Merrill:
  Mullen & Kamm, *The Junior Illustrated Encyclopedia of Sports*
Children's Press:
  Carpenter, "Enchantment of America" Series (a book about each state), *Far Flung America*
  Hillyer, *The Young People's Story of Our Heritage* (a fifteen-volume set of excellent material)
  Ozone & Hawkinson, *Birds in the Sky*

Criterion:
  Edmonds, *Our Heroes' Heroes*
Crowell:
  Galt, *Peter Zenger, Fighter for Freedom*
  Krungold, *And Now Miguel*
Day:
  Winders, *Horace Greeley: Newspaperman*
Dodd, Mead:
  Coggins, *Hydrospace*
  Cosgrove, *Eggs*
  Lieberg, *Wonders of Heat and Light*
  Robinson, *The Hole in the Mountain*
Dutton:
  Vance, *Windows for Rosemary*
Doubleday:
  Benery-Isbert, *The Ark, Rowan Farm*
  deAngeli, *The Door in the Wall, Copper Toed Boots, Thee, Hanna*
  Sterling, *Forever Free, Secret of the Old Post Box*
Follett:
  Hunt, *Up a Road Slowly*
  Taylor, *All-of-a-Kind Family*
Four Winds Press:
  Davidson, *Helen Keller's Teacher*
  Rood, *Bees, Bugs and Beetles*
Garrard:
  Parlin, *Amelia Earhart*
Golden Press:
  Lehr, *Storms*
Hale, E. M. Co.:
  Many special editions of good books
Harper & Row:
  Carson, *The Sense of Wonder*
  White, *Charlotte's Web*
  Wilder, *The Little House* books (excellent example of good writing)
  Wyler and Baird, *Science Teasers*
Harcourt, Brace & World:
  Estes, *The Hundred Dresses*
  Hutchinson, *The Dollar Horse*
  Norton, *The Borrowers*
  Shephard, *Paul Bunyan*
  Travers, *Mary Poppins, Mary Poppins Comes Back*
Hastings:
  Adrian, *The Indian Horse Mystery*
Hawthorn:
  Honour, *The Man Who Could Read Stones* and other Honour books
Holiday:
  Kjelgaard, *Big Red*

Houghton Mifflin:
 Forbes, *Johnny Tremain*
 Holling, *Paddle to the Sea* and other Holling books
 Malcolmson, *Yankee Doodle's Cousins*
 Nolan, *John Hancock* and other Nolan books
 O'Dell, *Island of the Blue Dolphin*
 Tolkien, *The Hobbit*
Holt, Rinehart & Winston:
 Belting, *The Stars Are Silver Reindeer* (poetry)
 Corbett, *Pippa Passes*
Lippincott:
 Brown, *Coins Have Tales to Tell*
 McDonald, *Mrs. Piggle Wiggle*
Little, Brown:
 Fleishman, *Mr. Mysterious & Co.*
Macmillan:
 The Macmillan Classics (40 titles). *Frontier West* books (11 titles)
 Baum, *Antarctica*
 Sperry, *Call It Courage*
McGraw-Hill:
 Bush, *Mary Anning's Treasures*
 Ronan, *The Stars*
McKay:
 Funk, *Cecelia's Locket*
Melmont:
 Blaine, *Flower Box Mystery*
Messner:
 Noble, *Nellie Bly, First Woman Reporter*
Morrow:
 Buehr, *The Magic of Paper*
 Earle, *Strange Companions in Nature*
 Zim, *Sharks* and other nature and science titles
Norton:
 Gray, *Horsepower*
Prentice-Hall:
 Feravolo, *Easy Physics Projects*
 Sullivan, *Animal Timekeepers*
Rand:
 Cavanah, *Adventure in Courage: The Story of Theodore Roosevelt*
 Henry, *Brighty of the Grand Canyon* and other Henry books
Random House:
 Farley, *The Black Stallion*
 Fleming, *Chitty-Chatty Bong-Bong*
Roy:
 Pringle, *The Young Einstein*
Scott:
 Anderson, *The Boy and the Blind Storyteller, Yong Kee of Korea*
 Feagiles, *A Stranger in the Spanish Village*

Viking:
   Angelo, *The Bells of Bleeker Street*
   Bailey, *Children of the Handcrafts*
   Buff, *Big Tree*
   Billings, *Bridges*
   Clark, *Santiago, Secret of the Andes*
   Daugherty, *Marcus and Narcissica Whitman*
   Disraeli, *New Worlds Through the Microscope*
   DuBois, *Twenty-One Balloons*
   Gates, *Blue Willow*
   Gray, *The Cheerful Heart*
   Jewett, *Which Was Witch?*
   Lawson, *They Were Strong and Good*
   Leach, *How the People Sang the Mountain Up*
   Liers, *A Black Bear's Story* and other fine animal stories
   Ravielle, *Wonders of the Human Body*
   Sauer, *The Light at Tern Rock*
   Schreiber, *Bambino, The Clown*
   Seredy, *The Good Master, The Singing Tree*
   Stoutenburg, *Animal Tall Tales*
Walck:
   Hornby, *Gypsies*
   Wilkins,*Wizards and Witches*
Warne:
   Williams and Ellis, *Round the World Fairy Tales*
Westminster:
   Whitney, *Secret of the Emerald Star*
Whitman:
   Hawkinson, *Our Wonderful Wayside*
World:
   Cole, *Poems of Magic and Spells*
   Hagon, *Cruising to Danger*

APPENDIX Q

Directory of Publishers of Children's Books[1]

Abelard-Schuman, Ltd.
6 W. 57th St.
New York, N. Y.

Abingdon Press
55 E. 55th St.
New York, N. Y.

Atheneum Publishers
162 E. 38th St.
New York, N. Y.

Bantam Books, Inc.
271 Madison Ave.
New York, N. Y.

Benefic Press
10300 W. Roosevelt Rd.
Westchester, Ill.

Bobbs-Merrill Co., Inc.
4300 W. 62nd St.
Indianapolis, Ind.

Children's Press, Inc.
Jackson Blvd. at Ravine
Chicago, Ill.

Coward-McCann, Inc.
200 Madison Ave.
New York, N. Y.

Thomas Y. Crowell Co.
432 Park Ave. S.
New York, N. Y.

Doubleday & Co., Inc.
Garden City, N. Y.

E. P. Dutton & Co., Inc.
201 Park Ave. S.
New York, N. Y.

Follett Pub. Co.
1010 W. Washington Blvd.
Chicago, Ill.

Golden Press, Inc.
850 Third Ave.
New York, N. Y.

Grossett & Dunlap, Inc.
1107 Broadway
New York, N. Y.

Harcourt, Brace & World, Inc.
750 Third Ave.
New York, N. Y.

Harper & Row, Publishers
49 E. 33rd St.
New York, N. Y.

Holiday House
8 W. 13th St.
New York, N. Y.

Houghton Mifflin Co.
2 Park St.
Boston, Mass.

Alfred A. Knopf, Inc.
501 Madison Ave.
New York, N. Y.

J. B. Lippincott Co.
E. Washington Square
Philadelphia, Pa.

Little, Brown & Co.
34 Beacon St.
Boston, Mass.

Lothrop, Lee & Shepard Co.
419 Park Ave. S.
New York, N. Y.

McGraw-Hill, Inc.
330 W. 42nd St.
New York, N. Y.

1 Addresses are subject to change.

David McKay Co., Inc.
119 W. 40 St.
New York, N. Y.

The Macmillan Co.
866 Third Ave.
New York, N. Y.

William Morrow & Co., Inc.
425 Park Ave.
New York, N. Y.

Thomas Nelson & Sons
18 E. 41st St.
New York, N. Y.

Oxford University Press
101 Fifth Ave.
New York, N. Y.

Pantheon Books, Inc.
22 E. 51st St.
New York, N. Y.

Parnassus Press
33 Parnassus Rd.
Berkeley, Calif.

The Platt & Munk Co., Inc.
200 Fifth Ave.
New York, N. Y.

Pocket Books, Inc.
1 W. 39th St.
New York, N. Y.

G. P. Putnam's Sons
200 Madison Ave.
New York, N. Y.

Rand McNally & Co.
8255 Central Park Ave.
Skokie, Ill.

Random House, Inc.
457 Madison Ave.
New York, N. Y.

Wm. R. Scott, Inc.
8 W. 13th St.
New York, N. Y.

Scott, Foresman & Co.
1900 E. Lake Ave.
Glenview, Ill.

Charles Scribner's Sons
597 Fifth Ave.
New York, N. Y.

Simon & Schuster, Inc.
630 Fifth Ave.
New York, N. Y.

Vanguard Press
424 Madison Ave.
New York, N. Y.

The Viking Press, Inc.
625 Madison Ave.
New York, N. Y.

Henry Z. Walck, Inc.
101 Fifth Ave.
New York, N. Y.

Frederick Warne & Co.
101 Fifth Ave.
New York, N. Y.

Franklin Watts, Inc.
575 Lexington Ave.
New York, N. Y.

The Westminster Press
Witherspoon Bldg.
Philadelphia, Pa.

Albert Whitman & Co.
560 W. Lake St.
Chicago, Ill.

Whittlesly Press
330 W. 42nd. St.
New York, N. Y.

Wilcox-Follett Co.
1010 W. Washington Blvd.
Chicago, Ill.

The World Publishing Co.
2231 W. 110 St.
Cleveland, Ohio

Publishers of Readers, Workbooks, and Other Skill-Building Materials

Allyn & Bacon, Inc.
695 Miami Circle, N.E.
Atlanta, Ga.

American Book Co.
55 Fifth Ave.
New York, N. Y.

Benefic Press & Beckley-Cardy Co.
10300 W. Roosevelt Rd.
Westchester, Ill.

Bobbs-Merrill Co., Inc.
4300 W. 62nd St.
Indianapolis, Ind.

Educational Publishing Corp.
Darien, Conn.

Four Winds Press
Scholastic Magazines, Inc.
50 West 44th St.
New York, N. Y.

Garrard Publishing Co.
862 Scarsdale Ave.
Scarsdale, N. Y.

Ginn & Co.
Back Bay
P.O. Box 191
Boston, Mass.

E. M. Hale & Co.
Eau Claire, Wis.

Harper & Row
49 E. 33rd St.
New York, N. Y.

Holt, Rinehart & Winston
383 Madison Ave.
New York, N. Y.

D. C. Heath & Co.
285 Columbus Ave.
Boston, Mass.

Houghton Mifflin Co.
2 Park St.
Boston, Mass.

Laidlaw Bros.
Thatcher and Madison Sts.
River Forest, Ill.

J. B. Lippincott Co.
E. Washington Square
Philadelphia, Pa.

Lyons & Carnahan
407 E. 25th St.
Chicago, Ill.

The Macmillan Co.
866 Third Ave.
New York, N. Y.

Melmont Publishers, Inc.
1224 W. Van Buren St.
Chicago, Ill.

Scholastic Services
902 Sylvan Ave.
Englewood Cliffs, N. J.

Science Research Associates
259 E. Erie St.
Chicago, Ill.

Scott, Foresman & Co.
1900 E. Lake Ave.
Glenview, Ill.

Silver Burdett Co.
Box 362
Morristown, N. J.

L. W. Singer Co.
Syracuse, N. Y.

Steck-Vaugn Co.
Box 2028
Austin, Tex.

The World Publishing Co.
2231 W. 110th St.
Cleveland, Ohio

Webster Publishing Co.
1154 Reco Ave.
St. Louis, Mo.

APPENDIX R

Easy Books with High Interest Level for Elementary Grades[1]

Benefic Press (Beckley Cardy Co.)

Air Space-Age books (First two in the series have second-grade and last three third-grade reading difficulty, with up to sixth-grade interest.)

American Indian Series (First four have first reader difficulty; next two have second reader, and the last has third reader difficulty; interest third to sixth grades.)

Button Books (From preprimer to third-grade reading difficulty, with wide range of interest. They are about family life and appeal to most children.)

Cowboy Sam Books (Range from preprimer through third-grade reading difficulty. These Western theme books appeal to most children, and the content makes for fluent reading.)

Dan Frontier Series (From preprimer through third-grade difficulty. Interest range up to sixth grade for the last several books of the series.)

Easy To Read Series (6 very easy books.)

Jerry series (Preprimer through third grade. Four books of small-boy adventures of interest through fourth grade.)

Pioneer Series (Fourth-grade reading difficulty, but of interest through sixth grade.)

Sailor Jack Series (Preprimer through third-grade reading difficulty. The humor and action make them appealing to most children from primary to sixth grade.)

Tommy O'Toole Books (First- to third-grade reading difficulty. These stories about a young Irish railroad man would appeal to most children through fourth or fifth grades.)

What Is It Series (First- to fourth-grade difficulty with interest level several grades higher.)

Big Top, Monkey Island, Poker Dog, Pony Ring, Pretty Bird, and *Surprise Egg* are other books published by this company at first-grade reading difficulty level but of interest to children through third grade.)

Bobbs-Merrill Co., Inc.

Childhood of Famous Americans Series (Third- through fourth-grade reading difficulty, but these simple biographies appeal to children through sixth grade. Many titles.)

Raggedy Ann stories (Primary level.)

Children's Press, Inc.

True Book Series (First- to third-grade reading difficulty with interest

[1] See Appendix Q for addresses.

436

through sixth grade. Easy, colorful, and appealing. Very good for concept development (space, spiders, reptiles, etc.).

Crowell Co.

The Clyde Bulla books (12 titles) (Third-grade reading level.)

Doubleday & Co. (Garden City, New York)

The Signal books (10 titles) (Fourth-grade reading level.)

Garrard Publishing Co.

Basic Vocabulary Series (Second-grade reading level, but of interest from first through sixth grades.)

Discovery Books (Third-grade reading level, but of interest through sixth grade.)

First Reading Books (First-grade reading level, but of interest several grades above first.)

Folklore of the World (Third-grade reading level; interest through sixth.)

Follett Publishing Co.

Just Beginning to Read Series (Many very easy books.)

Read to Know Books (Informational in easy-to-read format and primary vocabulary.)

Farm Life Series (Fourth-grade reading level.)

What Is It? Series (Fourth- to sixth-grade reading level.)

Big City Books (Fourth- to sixth-grade reading level.)

Indian Folklore Books (Second-grade difficulty, through sixth-grade interest.)

Pleasure Reading Books (Third-grade difficulty, through sixth-grade interest.)

Harper & Row

Wonder-Story Books (Fourth- and fifth-grade difficulty would interest sixth-graders.)

I Can Read Books (Primary level.)

Harr Wagner Publishing Co.

Deep-Sea Adventure Series (Second- through fifth-grade difficulty, interest through sixth grade.)

Jim Forest Readers (First- through third-grade difficulty, interest through sixth grade. Good conservation content; ten good titles.)

Morgan Bay Mystery Series (2.3 to 4.1 reading difficulty, interest through sixth grade. Very appealing.)

Reading Motivated Series (4.5 to 5.3 difficulty, interest through sixth grade. Factual; abundant aids to phonics, comprehension, and research skills.)

Wildlife Adventure Series (2.6 to 4.4 difficulty, interest through sixth grade. Authentic and interesting.)

Americans All (4.4 reading difficulty level, interest through sixth grade. Historical and contemporary.)

D. C. Heath & Co.

Our Animal Story Books

Holt, Rinehart & Winston
  Books to Begin On Series (Very easy but of interest to age 9.)
  Pogo Series (Easy with wide range of interest.)
Houghton Mifflin Co.
  Read by Yourself Books (Primary level.)
  Franklin Series (Fourth- to sixth-grade level.)
  Piper Series (Fourth- to sixth-grade level.)
  North Star Series (Nation's heritage theme; fourth- to sixth-grade reading level.)
Macmillan Co.
  *Aviation Reader*s (First-grade difficulty, interest through sixth grade. *Straight Up* and *Straight Down* are about a helicopter.)
  Core-Vocabulary Readers (Primer through third-reader difficulty. High interest level; easy-to-read print.)
G. P. Putnam's Sons
  Beginning-to-Read Biographies (Second- to third-grade difficulty, interest through sixth grade. Lincoln, Kennedy, Columbus, and Hale biographies in easy-to-read vocabulary and style.)
Random House, Inc.
  Beginner Books (First- and second-grade difficulty. High interest; riddles, etc. Many titles.)
  Landmark Books (About a hundred titles for grade levels 4–6.
Reader's Digest
  Reader's Digest Skill Builders (Parts I and II for grades 2 to 6.)
Science Research Associates
  Pilot Library IIa (Fourth-grade reading level.)
  Pilot Library IIb (Fifth-grade reading level.)
  Pilot Library IIc (Sixth-grade reading level.)
Scribner's
  Three Boys Series (Reading difficulty about third- and fourth-grade levels, interest through sixth grade.)
Scott, Foresman
  New Reading for Independence Series (First- to third-grade difficulty; First- to fifth-grade interest.) Also simplified classics. (Fourth-grade level.)
Southwest Regional Laboratory for Educational Research and Development (Inglewood, Calif.)
  Instant Reading Series (*Sam,* the first book, has only three words in 28 pages. Other books are to follow.)
U.S. Bureau of Indian Affairs (Supt. of Documents, Washington, D.C. 20402)
  Concepts Series, Health Series (Interest level for all ages; first- and second-grade reading level.)
Wheeler Publishing Co. (161 East Grand Ave., Chicago 11)
  American Adventure Series (Second- through sixth-grade reading difficulty. Each book is lettered to show difficulty: e.g., "A" is second grade, "B" is third, etc. These tales are interesting at two to three grades above reading level.)

Webster Pub. Co. (1154 Reco Ave., St. Louis)

Junior Everyreaders (Versions of popular books at about third-grade
reading difficulty but of interest to older children; especially good
for retarded sixth-grade children.)

Steck-Vaugn, Children's Press, and the King Co. have many single titles
that are written at about second-grade difficulty but with wide appeal.

APPENDIX S

Magazines for Elementary School Children[1]

American Girl, The (Girl Scouts of America, 830 Third Ave., New York; monthly; $3). Activities and hobbies for girls; idealistic stories for upper elementary and junior high school.

American Junior Red Cross News (American National Red Cross, National Headquarters, Washington, D.C.; published eight times a year; $1.20). Includes a variety of activities and fine stories.

Boys' Life (Boy Scouts of America, New Brunswick, N.J.; $3). Activities and hobbies for boys; good stories for upper elementary and junior high school boys.

Calling All Girls (Better Reading Foundation, Inc., Bergenfield, N.J.: $5). Appeals especially to pre-teenage girls.

Child Life (Child Life, Inc., 3516 N. College Ave., Indianapolis, Ind.; monthly except July and August; $5). Activities and hobbies for elementary age children; stories and poems.

Children's Digest (Better Reading Foundation, Inc., Bergenfield, N.J.; monthly except July and August; $5). Stories; excerpts from books; puzzles and comics; ages 6–12.

Children's Playmate (Mueller Printing & Lithograph Co., 6529 Union Ave., Cleveland, Ohio; monthly except August and January; $3.50). Activities and hobbies for children 6–12; stories and verse.

Elizabethan (Periodical Publications, Ltd., 2 Breams Bldg., London, E.C. 4; monthly; $4). British; fine quality; upper elementary.

Field and Stream (Holt, Rinehart & Winston, Inc., 383 Madison Ave., New York; monthly; $4). Hunting, fishing, and camping, with emphasis on conservation.

Geographic School Bulletin and *National Geographic Magazine* (National Geographic Society, 17th & M St., Washington, D.C.; the bulletin is published weekly during the school year at $2; the magazine is published monthly at $8 per year). Interesting geographic material for schools, but children enjoy the adult publication, too.

Golden Magazine (Golden Press, Inc., 1220 Mound Ave., Racine, Wis.; $4). Good stories, puzzles, games, and other activities, as well as informational material.

Highlights for Children (2300 W. Fifth Ave., Columbus, Ohio; monthly except July and August; $4 to schools and libraries, otherwise $6). A fine variety of activities, stories, verse, factual material.

Jack and Jill (Curtis Publishing Co., Independence Square, Philadelphia, Pa.; monthly; $3.95). Stories, poems, and activities; grades 3–6.

Know Your World (American Educational Publications, 55 High St., Middletown, Conn.). Weekly newspaper—high interest level with read-

[1] Prices and addresses are subject to change.

ing level ranging from second- to third-grade during the year. Strong emphasis on basic skills.

Model Airplane News (Air Age Inc., 551 5th Ave., New York; monthly; $4). Appeals to model airplane enthusiasts.

Natural History (American Museum of Natural History, Central Park West at 79th St., New York; monthly Oct.–May; bimonthly June–Sept.; $5.50). Interesting nature articles; outdoor living for all ages.

Nature and Science (The Natural History Press, Garden City, N.Y.; 18 issues $2.70). For upper elementary children; fine content.

News Explorer (Scholastic Magazines, 902 Sylvan Ave., Englewood Cliffs, N.J.; weekly during school year; $2; also *Junior Scholastic*). Timely news at children's level.

Plays (Plays, Inc., 8 Arlington St., Boston; Oct.–May; $6). Non-royalty plays for primary grades through high school. Simple staging; easy-to-read print. Fluent content for development of better expression.

Popular Science (355 Lexington Ave., New York; monthly; $4). Interesting content: industrial arts, handcrafts, hobbies, and experiments.

Ranger Rick's Nature Magazine (381 W. Center St., Marion, Ohio, 44302; 10 months, $6). Excellent nature material and charming pictures; appeals to children of all ages.

Seventeen (Radnor, Pa.; monthly; $5). Fashions, beauty hints, short stories; very popular with teenage girls.

Sports (McFadden Publications, 205 E. 42nd St., New York; monthly; $3). Articles on sports and sports personalities.

Stamps (H. L. Lindquist Publications, 153 Waverly Place, New York; weekly; $3). Interesting to all stamp collectors.

Wee Wisdom (Lee's, Summit, Mo., monthly; $2). Stories, games, puzzles for primary grade children.

Zoonooz (Zoological Society of San Diego, Box 551, San Diego, Calif. 92112; monthly; $4). Charming animal pictures and interesting factual material about animals; enlarged pictures are available at nominal cost.

APPENDIX T

Sources of Teaching Aids[1]

Audio-Visual Materials Handbook, Indiana University, Bloomington, Ind. (latest revision)

BLOOMER, *Skill Games to Teach Reading,* Dansville, N.Y., F. A. Owen Pub. Co.

BROWN et al. *Audio-Visual Instructional Materials Manual.* San Jose State College, San Jose, Calif., 1957.

Children's Catalog (annual supplement). New York, H. W. Wilson Co.

Children's Reading Service, *Audio-Visual Catalog,* Brooklyn, N.Y.

CUNDIFF, RUBY. *101 Magazines for Schools, Grades 1–12.* Nashville: Tennessee Book Co., 1959.

Dade County Schools, *Manual of Classroom Games,* Miami, Florida, 1954.

DE BERNARDIS, AMO. *Use of Instructional Materials.* New York: Appleton-Century-Crofts (latest revision)

Dolch Materials (request catalog). Champaign, Ill.: Garrard Press.

Educational Film Guide (annual supplement). H. W. Wilson Co., New York.

Enlargements of Animal Pictures, Zoological Society, Box 551, San Diego, Calif., 92112. (Ask for available listing of pictures and prices.)

FARGO, LUCILLE. *Activity Book for School Libraries;* also Activity Book No. 2. Chicago American Library Assn.

Filmstrip Guide (annual supplement). New York: H. W. Wilson Co.

Free and Inexpensive Learning Materials (1966–67 ed., $2). Div. of Surveys & Field Services, George Peabody College for Teachers, Nashville, Tenn. 37203.

GATES, ARTHUR, et al. *Practice Exercises in Reading.* New York: Teachers College Bureau of Publications.

Iowa Reading Circle Books. Des Moines, Iowa (published each year). (Colorado and Wisconsin have reading circle catalogs, too.)

Iowa State Education Assn., *Instructional Games,* Des Moines, Iowa.

KINGSLY, BERNARD. *Reading Skills, Games, Devices and Aids to Improve Reading.* San Francisco: Fearon, 1959.

Landmark Enrichment Records and Filmstrips, New York, Enrichment Teaching Materials Co. (ask for current catalog).

LEESMA, ROBERT. *Audio-Visual Materials for Teaching Reading.* Ann Arbor, Michigan, 1954.

Let's Play Games. Boston: Ginn.

Living and Learning in the Primary School, Alameda, Calif., County Schools, Oakland 7, Calif.

MILLER, BRUCE. *Sources of Free Pictures; Sources of Free Teaching Aids; So You Want to Start A Picture File* (Box 319, Riverside, Calif., 50¢ each).

---

[1] Prices and addresses are subject to change.

MOTT, CAROLYN, and BAISDEN, LEO. *The Children's Book on How to Use Books and Libraries.* Chicago: Scribner, 1955.

MURRAY, DON, *et al. Integrated Teaching Materials: How to Choose, Create, and Use Them.* New York: Longmans, Green, 1961.

Non-Oral Primary Seatwork. Chicago: Primary Education Service.

Reader's Digest Reading Skill Builders. Pleasantville, N.Y.: Reader's Digest Services, Inc.

RESS, ETTA S. *The Use of Pictures to Enrich School Resources.* Mankato, Minn.: Creative Education Society, Inc., 1953.

ROBERTS, INA. *Slogans that Circulate Books* (946 Magnolia Ave., Los Angeles, Calif.).

RUFSVOLD, MARGARET, *et al. Guides to Newer Educational Media: Films, Filmstrips, Phono-Records, Radio, Slides, Television.* Chicago: American Library Association.

RUSSELL, DAVID, and KARP, ETTA. *Reading Aids Through the Grades.* New York: Teachers College Bureau of Publications, 1951.

SALISBURY, GORDON, and SHERIDAN, ROBERT. *Catalog of Free Teaching Aids* (P.O. Box 942, Riverside, Calif., $1.50), 1958.

SANTA, BOANOL, and HARDY, LOIS. *How to Use the Library.* Palo Alto, Calif.: Pacific Books, 1955.

SCHRAMM, LEWIS (ed.). *New Teaching Aids for the American Classroom.* Stanford, Calif.: Stanford University Press, 1960.

Selected Bibliography (disadvantaged). Institute for Developmental Studies, School of Education, New York University, 1966.

SPACHE, GEORGE. *Resources in Teaching Reading.* Gainesville: University of Florida Press, 1960.

STARR, JOHN W. *Selected Reading Games and Devices for the Primary Grades* (also one for intermediate grades). Eugene: University of Oregon Press, 1958.

SVE Film and Filmstrip Catalogs. Chicago: Society of Visual Education (published each year).

The Tape Recorder in the Elementary Classroom. Minnesota Mining & Mfg. Co., St. Paul, Minn., 1955 (25¢).

Teacher's Manual for Webster's New World Dictionary. New York: Macmillan (elementary edition).

Textbooks in Print. New York: R. R. Bowker (published each year).

Uncommonly Good Materials for Remedial Reading. Claremont Graduate School, Box 8, Claremont, Calif.

WAGNER, GUY, and HOSIER, MAX. *Reading Games.* Darien, Conn.: Educational Publishing Corp., 1960.

WILLIAMS, CATHERINE. *Sources of Teaching Materials.* Bureau of Educational Research, Ohio State University, Columbus, Ohio, 1960.

WITTICH, WALTER, *et al. Guides to Free Curriculum Materials, Free Films, Free Film-Strips, Free Tapes, Free Scripts, and Free Transcriptions* (four guides). Randolph, Wis.: Educator's Progress Service.

Index